Children with learning difficulties

A Collaborative approach to their education and management

Edited by

Margaret Fawcus MSc FRCSLT

Visiting Professor in Clinical Communication Studies
City University, London

Whurr Publishers Ltd

© 1997 Whurr Publishers Ltd

First published 1997
by Whurr Publishers Ltd
19b Compton Terrace,
London N1 2UN,
England

Reprinted 1998 and 2000

British Library Cataloguing in Publication Data
A catalogue record for this book is available from the
British Library.

ISBN: 1-86156 018 4

Printed and bound in the UK by Athenaeum Press Ltd,
Gateshead, Tyne & Wear

Children with learning difficulties

This book is dedicated to Anne and Alan Clarke who have done so much to bring about positive changes for people with learning difficulties.

Contents

List of contributors

Mike Blamires MSc, BSc, PGCE – Special Educational Needs Research and Development Centre, Canterbury Christ Church College, Kent.

Dermot M Bowler PhD MSc BA – Department of Psychology, City University, London.

Karen Bunning PhD, MRCSLT – Department of Clinical Communication Studies, City University, London.

Margaret Fawcus MSc, FRCSLT – Department of Clinical Communication Studies, City University, London.

Janet Gompertz MSc, LRCSLT – Department of Clinical Communication Studies, City University, London.

Chia Swee Hong MA, Cert Ed, SROT, Dip COT – School of Occupational Therapy and Physiotherapy, University of East Anglia, Norwich.

Dorothy Jeffree M Ed – Formerly Senior Research Fellow, Hester Adrian Research Centre, University of Manchester.

Alex Kelly BSc (Hons), MRCSLT – Mental Health and Learning Disability Service, Southampton Community Health Services.

Myra Kersner MSc, MRCSLT, Dip DVTH – Department of Human Communication Science, University College, London.

Sarah Lister Brook PhD, BSc, MAPPSci, AFBPsS – Department of Psychology, University of Surrey.

Chris Robertson MA, BA – Special Educational Needs Research and Development Centre, Canterbury Christ Church College, Kent.

Janet Tod MPhil, BSc – Special Needs Research and Development Centre, Canterbury Christ Church College, Kent.

Helen Tyler MPhil, BA, LRAM, Dip MT(N–R) – The Nordoff–Robbins Music Therapy Centre, London.

Preface

This book is intended for all those professionals whose work brings them in contact with children with learning difficulties, but who do not always have the opportunity to share their expertise with others. Whilst the contributors were asked to give the theoretical rationale for the approaches they are using, it was considered that the book would be both more useful and interesting if it included examples of the activities and techniques used. The book has therefore attempted the somewhat ambitious task of covering both the theoretical underpinning and the practical application of the work of a varied group of professionals.

Both the terms *learning difficulties* and *learning disabilities* are used interchangeably, as both are in current use.

In editing a multi-disciplinary book of this kind, with a broad base of learning difficulty or disability, arbitrary decisions have to made in determining what should be included. It was decided to extend the boundaries of the book to include autism and Asperger syndrome. The problem of dyslexia has also been included, since it contributes so pervasively to learning difficulties at school. Under-achievement at school may be a complex combination of cognitive impairment as well as specific reading and writing problems.

The authors also cover a wide developmental lifespan, working with young babies up to adolescents, and the whole spectrum of mental handicap, from mild learning difficulties to children with severe learning difficulties and profound and multiple handicaps.

Margaret Fawcus

Introduction

MARGARET FAWCUS

It now seems inconceivable that, less than fifty years ago, the terms 'feeble-minded, imbecile and idiot' were the accepted terminology of the day. This book bears testimony to the profound changes that have taken place in the care and management of a minority population that was generally regarded as ineducable and in need of custodial care. As Tizard (1992) said, custodial care was considered 'the correct solution, on both humane and scientific grounds, to the social and genetic problems of mental deficiency'.

Methods of assessment were crude and inappropriate and most of the large institutions built in the nineteenth century were the permanent home of both the so-called morally and mentally defective. Many of them also housed the epileptic, the cerebral palsied, the deaf and the mentally ill. They also included the group of cognitive and behaviourally disorded people who would now be labelled autistic.

In the absence of expert psychometric evaluation, many of those compulsorily detained under Mental Deficiency Act of 1913 were within the accepted limits of 'normal' intelligence. Many of them came from socially disadvantaged backgrounds and had been the victims of cruelty and abuse (Tizard, 1992).

The poignant story of Joey Deacon (1974), which received considerable publicity at the time, highlighted the inappropriateness of many of these placements. Joey was committed to St. Lawrence's Hospital, Caterham, a large and forbidding Victorian subnormality hospital, when he was seven years old. Joey had cerebral palsy, his speech was virtually unintelligible and he was totally dependent on others for his care. The story is a remarkable one and bears testimony to Joey's intelligence and determination.

Joey was transferred from the children's wards to a male ward in 1936, when he was sixteen years old. Ernie, who was to become a friend of Joey, was admitted to the same ward in 1944. Ernie, unlike others, had the ability to understand Joey and they became close friends. In 1946, they were joined by Michael, who was admitted to St. Lawrence's when he was sixteen years old. Michael was not physically handicapped, and moreover, he could write.

It was not until 1970, however, that Joey decided to write the story of his life, dictated to Ernie, who 'translated' it for Michael, who then laboriously wrote the story down. A fourth friend, Tom, bought a second-hand typewriter and taught himself to type, using one finger of each hand. Fourteen months later the autobiography was complete.

On the final page, Joey writes, 'Ernie has taken the words out of my mouth, and with the help of Tom and Michael and some of the staff put them on paper.' Joey spent half of his years in silence, unable to give voice to his needs, his opinions or his feelings. Fortunately, the development of increasingly sophisticated and custom built communication aids are enabling those with severe physical handicap to communicate. Access to assessment and provision of aids is still not always easy, and many children, adolescents and adults are still locked within their bodies unable to communicate.

In a book entitled *Elsie -- a person of no importance?* Wilkins (1989) gives an account of woman who was fortunate to be discharged into the care of a retired missionary family after spending fifty-two years of her life in institutions. Elsie had been in care since the age of two years. Her parents were apparently still living, but the reason for her being taken into care was not known. Elsie was employed as a parlourmaid and gradually responded to an environment which allowed her to develop emotionally and intellectually after years of institutionalisation.

The present author was employed as a speech therapist at the Manor Hospital in Epsom, Surrey, and worked with a number of profoundly deaf adolescents and adults who were obviously of normal intelligence. They had been committed because of behavioural problems, such as persistently absconding from home or residential care. A single incident illustrates the intellectual capacity of one of these deaf adolescents. Having a somewhat unorthodox approach to therapy, I was amusing John by blowing cigarette smoke down my nose (unthinkable in the present climate)! He responded immediately by finger-spelling the word 'dragon'!

Yet another case illustrates the apparent lack of care in the examination and committal of these so-called patients, despite the medical model which then prevailed. Edward was referred for speech therapy as a result of the concern of his workshop instructor, who was impressed by his good work habits and ability to learn. He reported on Edward's communication difficulties and extreme shyness. The medical officer in charge of the male side at that time was an enlightened and humane man, who decided that Edward had developmental aphasia – a very progressive concept in those days. Careful observation of his rather fragmentary speech output revealed a consistent pattern of omission of high frequency speech sounds. It also became clear that he was having considerable difficulty in processing speech. As a result of these observations, Edward was referred for an assessment of his hearing. The audiogram revealed a classic high-frequency bilateral hearing loss which was sufficient to account for his difficulties, including a failure to achieve at school. Bearing in mind his speech and language difficulties, the failure to make a routine audiological assessment before he was committed was a serious case of professional neglect.

Unlike many others, this story had a happy ending because Edward was discharged and returned to his family and we managed to secure him a job as an office boy which he held down successfully. In the time between his referral for speech therapy and ultimate discharge from the institution, Edward demonstrated his ability to acquire numeracy and literacy skills in a one-to-one situation.

Whilst these accounts are anecdotal, they do reveal that the custodial care system, whilst probably set up with the best intentions, was essentially flawed. It is disturbing to contemplate the number of so-called 'mentally deficient' children and adults who were inappropriately committed and thus deprived of the specialist help and social support from which they might have benefited. In addition, the sheer size of the hospitals and the medical model of care meant that any other problems they had tended to be confounded by the inevitable effects of institutionalisation.

Despite the inappropriateness of this model of care for many of the residents, there were institutions which had schools (the Manor was one of these) and one began to see the employment of psychologists who brought with them a totally different approach to assessment and management. This marked the first step towards what Tizard (1992) decried as the 'demedicalisation of mental deficiency' and the stage was set for the profound changes which were to take place.

Anne and Alan Clarke, amongst other eminent psychologists, were at the forefront of this movement for change. With the publication of an historic paper in *The Lancet* (1953) they challenged the concept that the IQ was a constant factor throughout a person's life. They demonstrated significant IQ increments in many people when they were exposed to more favourable environmental conditions. This idea was quite contrary to the received wisdom of the day, but began to have a profound effect on people's thinking.

The year 1958 saw the publication of their jointly edited book, *Mental Deficiency – The Changing Outlook*, which one reviewer described as a contemporary classic in mental retardation. This became a standard textbook on the subject (Clarke & Clarke, 1958).

The Mental Health Act of 1959 reflected the influence of the Clarkes and other eminent psychologists. It had already become clear that custodial care was not appropriate on economic or humanitarian grounds for those who would now be described as having mild learning difficulties.

The Act emphasised the need for voluntary rather than compulsory admission, and recommended a shift from custodial to community care. Local authorities were therefore empowered to build training centres and hostels to receive those who had previously been inmates as the large subnormality hospitals were gradually closed down.

It has been this shift to community care which has marked one of the most profound changes in the provision and care for those with learning difficulties. Changes in terminology followed, in line with a more enlightened approach to education and management. Educationally, children were classified as educationally subnormal, mild, moderate or profound, and the emotive words feeble-minded, imbecile and idiot began to disappear from all but the public vocabulary.

Inevitably, provision did not always keep pace with demand for training and hostel places, and some local authorities were more dedicated and more affluent than others in making provision for a growing population of people with learning difficulties within the community. Provision was patchy and remains so. Far too many people, sometimes quite elderly and/or institutionalised, were discharged into the community with little or no support, prey to untrained landladies in guest houses.

They filled the places vacated by summer visitors in seaside resorts, with no provision for either training or leisure pursuits. Other authorities made valiant efforts to provide support for those either living in custom-built hostels or for those considered capable of caring for themselves. Respite care was made available, so that families could have a break from the demands of caring for a mentally handicapped relative.

With the emphasis on community care came the concept of normalisation. This has been defined by Clarke, Clarke and Berg (1985) as 'enhancing the development of processes to the highest possible level in the individual' and 'promoting a life context which is as ordinary and normal as possible'. Whilst most people would subscribe to this process of normalisation, lack of resources, living in even a small institution, and other practical problems such as challenging behaviours, may make implementation of the principles difficult.

These principles were embodied in the *Declaration of the Rights of Mentally Retarded Persons* (General Assembly of the United Nations, 1971) which, among other things, stated that the mentally retarded person has a right to education, training, rehabilitation and guidance as will enable him to develop his ability and maximum potential. In addition, wherever possible, the mentally retarded person should live with his own family, or with foster parents, and participate in different forms of community life. The declaration went on to say that if institutional care is necessary it should be provided in surroundings and other circumstances as close as possible to those of normal life.

A number of voluntary organisations, such a Parents for Children and

Be My Parent, acted as pressure groups in persuading social services and other adoption and fostering agencies that there were parents prepared to take on the challenge of providing a normal home environment for children with learning difficulties, including those with both mental and physical handicap. Many of these parents were given very little practical support and often had to fight for the specialist educational facilities their children needed. Given greater professional support to the natural parents, many of these children would probably not be put up for adoption and fostering in the first place.

An important aspect of the movement towards normalisation is the increasing number children with learning difficulties who are now being educated in ordinary schools, both at pre-school and primary levels. As Mittler (1992) has said, the education of children with learning difficulties has changed out of all recognition over the past twenty years. However, total integration makes considerable demands on often limited resources, and Mittler and Farrell (1987) have suggested a provisional model of integration in which all children with severe learning difficulties are educated in special classes with special resources. Mittler commented that integration is less likely to happen as the severely impaired child grows older and relatively few of these children attend ordinary secondary schools.

Regarding the future for integration in the light of recent changes in education, Mittler poses a number of questions: Will schools, now that they are required to publish their results and compete with one another for both pupils and resources, still wish to take children with special educational needs, particularly at the severe end of the spectrum? Will such children be able to cope with the demands of the National Curriculum in ordinary schools? Are the financial resources available to provide the necessary support staff on which successful integration depends?

While considerable research has been and is being carried out in the field of mental handicap, there is still an urgent need for methodologically sound research into the relative efficacy of different approaches to education and care.

This book reflects the changes that have taken place and illustrates the diversity of techniques and approaches now available in working with children with learning difficulties. Sensory stimulation and integration are being widely used with severely subnormal children (Chapters 5, 7 and 8). Social skills training has become an accepted part of the work of both teachers and therapists (Chapters 6 and 7). Creativity and communication are being encouraged through developmental play, drama and music therapy (Chapters 3, 8 and 9). The use of alternative methods of communication, such as signing, has become widespread in encouraging both the development of speech and in facilitating communication in children with little or no spoken language (Chapter 4). It is possible that difficulties in communicating feelings and needs lead to many of the challenging behaviours that develop in children with severe communication problems.

The introduction of the National Curriculum and the Education Reform Act of 1988 have posed considerable challenges and problems, particularly in the education of children with severe learning difficulties. These new developments and other aspects of educational philosophy and practice are elaborated and discussed in Chapters 10, 11 and 12.

A number of Colleges of Further Education and Adult Education Centres now run classes for older adolescents, so that continuing education can occur in a normal community setting. Such developments are in line with the principle of normalisation.

Psychologists have provided much of the theoretical underpinning and research in the field of mental retardation. They have been responsible, more than any other professional group, for bringing about the shift from custodial to community care and from the medical model of care to a multi-disciplinary approach. Chapters 1 and 2 provide a theoretical background to our understanding of learning difficulties and describe the role of the psychologist in both assessment and management.

References

Clarke ADB, Clarke AM (1953) How constant is the IQ? Lancet (ii) 877–80.

Clarke ADB, Clarke AM (1958) Mental Deficiency: The changing outlook. London: Methuen.

Clarke ADB, Clarke AM, Berg JM (1985) Mental Deficiency: The changing outlook. 5th edn. London: Methuen.

Deacon JJ (1974) Tongue-Tied: Fifty years of friendship in a subnormality hospital. London: National Society for Mentally Handicapped Children.

Mittler P (1992) Education of children with severe learning difficulties: challenging vulnerability. In Tizard B (Ed) Vulnerability and Resilience in Human Development. London: Jessica Kingsley.

Mittler P, Farrell P (1987) Can children with severe learning difficulties be educated in ordinary schools? European Journal of Special Needs Education 2: 221–36

Tizard B (1992) Vulnerability and Resilience in Human Development. London: Jessica Kingsley.

Wilkins J (1989) Elsie: A Person of No Importance? Published privately.

Chapter 1

From General Impairment to Behavioural Phenotypes: Psychological Approaches to Learning Difficulties

DERMOT M BOWLER AND SARAH LISTER BROOK

Introduction

Throughout the history of humankind, some individuals have been recognised as different from others in ways that would now be called behavioural or psychological. Explanations of why such individuals were different depended heavily on the prevailing cultural climate, an example of which is the old Irish reference to people who would now be referred to as either psychotic or as having learning difficulties as a *duine le Dia* or 'person-with-God'. The advent of the Enlightenment in Europe in the 17th century demanded more rational and less metaphysical explanations of such phenomena, exemplified by Itard's famous description of Victor, the so-called 'wild boy' of Aveyron in France (see Lane, 1977). Victor was discovered at the age of 12 years in the forests of south western France. He had no speech, had no sensitivity to extremes of heat and cold, showed great skill in climbing trees and preferred a diet of wild, uncooked food. In short, although able to survive, he showed none of those behaviours by which most people adapt to their social world.

Although Itard was a physician and although he enlisted the help of Pinel, another medical doctor, his approach to Victor's difficulties was essentially an educational one. He viewed Victor's plight as being principally the result of a poor environment and that environmental manipulations could put matters right. As we shall see, Itard's approach was a presage of many current conceptions of how people with behaviour similar to that of Victor's should be treated. Any historical account of learning difficulties is fraught with terminological problems with labels

1

that are initially introduced to replace earlier, more abusive ones becoming assimilated into the general vocabulary of pejorative labels. Here, although we will use the term 'learning difficulties' to describe the broad class of individuals whose global intellectual development lags behind that of their fellows, we will also refer to terms that might now be considered offensive but which were appropriate to the historical period under discussion (for a scholarly review of classification and terminology see Clarke & Clarke, 1985).

Over the two centuries that separate us from Itard and the Wild Boy, society's treatment of people with learning difficulties has varied from treating them as freak-show exhibits, to locking them away in institutions for the protection of the wider society and viewing their plight as an incurable medical condition. By the turn of the 20th century, people with learning difficulties in Western societies were locked up in asylums for the 'mentally deficient' and along with people who were then called lunatics, they were seen as a threat to the social order necessitating their segregation from society at large. Sometimes assessments of their capabilities were carried out in order to determine which of them might be suitable to help with the running of the asylum, but rehabilitation or preparation for a return to the community was not seen as an option. It was in this climate that the new science of psychology began to be applied to people with learning difficulties. The birth of psychology as an experimental science dealing with behaviour and mental life is generally attributed to Wilhelm Wundt who founded his psychological laboratory in Leipzig in 1876 (Farr, 1987). Prior to Wundt, psychological enquiry consisted mainly of philosophical analysis, or speculation based on introspection. Following on from Wundt, the new science of psychology developed a number of strands of activity, many of which were of relevance to, or became applied to, the study of learning difficulties. It was in the area of assessment and in the classification of severity of intellectual impairment that psychology first became applied to learning difficulties.

Measuring intelligence: the psychometric approach

The branch of psychological science concerned with the measurement of abilities and psychological attributes such as intelligence and personality is known as psychometrics. Psychometricians are principally concerned with how an individual's level of performance on a particular test compares with the performance of the general population (see Rust & Golombok, 1989 for a review of psychometric theory). The beginnings of the psychometric approach can be traced to the English scientist Francis Galton who, in the 1880s, tried unsuccessfully to demonstrate that high intelligence was correlated with other measures such as head circumference or reaction time. It was, however, the work of Binet in Paris that provided the foundations of modern intelligence testing. His task was to develop tests that would identify children in the French school system who were in need of additional educational input, since in France at that time, all children, regardless of ability, had to attend school. Binet argued that, rather than testing the physical or motor abilities that were thought to underlie intelligence, children should be given problems to solve, and that their performance on a range of problems should be measured against the average performance of children of the same age, a procedure known as *norm referencing*. The test developed by Binet is still used today in a revised form known as the *Stanford-Binet Intelligence Scale*, a detailed description of which can be found in Anastasi (1986).

Although there is great debate about the precise nature of 'intelligence', or whether there are one or many intelligences, for most individuals, scores on the different sub-scales of the Stanford-Binet test are highly inter-correlated and are very good predictors both of school achievement and of performance on other intelligence tests. Tests are said to be inter-correlated when a child's good performance on one reliably predicts good performance on another and *vice versa*. However, high inter-correlations are not always found in individuals with learning difficulties, with some individuals showing very uneven profiles of performance across tests. (Further discussions of the nature and measurement of intelligence can be found in Rowe, 1991.)

As we have just seen, the rationale behind norm-referenced tests such as the Stanford-Binet is that a child's performance can be compared with that which is typical of children of different chronological ages. If a child aged eight years performs at a level that is the average for five-year-old children, then this child is said to have a *mental age* of five years. Similarly, an eight-year-old whose performance is at the average for ten-year-olds is said to have a mental age of ten years. Binet refined his quantification of children's intellectual development through his concept of *Intelligence Quotient* or IQ, which he defined as:

$$IQ = \frac{Mental\ age}{Chronological\ age} \times 100$$

So, the child just mentioned, who has a mental age of 10 and a chronological age of 8 will have an IQ of 125, and a typical or 'average' child, whose mental and chronological ages are the same, will have an IQ of 100. We can then speak of an average or 'normal' IQ as being 100. The term 'normal' here is a statistical term referring to what is typically found in the general population, and not to some morally or socially defined correct or desirable behaviour.

If we test a large number of children on tests such as the Stanford-Binet or other similar tests, we find that most children's mental ages are within a few months of their chronological ages. In other words, most children's IQs are around about 100. As we move away from the 100 point, we find progressively fewer children. This phenomenon is illustrated in Figure 1.1, where the lowest horizontal axis represents IQ and the vertical axis represents number of people observed as having a given IQ. The particular pattern of observations shown in Figure 1.1 is referred to as the *Normal Distribution* and is symmetrical about its *mean* or average value of 100. You will notice that the horizontal axis is marked off in units of 15 IQ points on either side of the mean. These represent Standard Deviation Units (designated 'σ' in the diagram), which are a measure of the variability that is found in normal distributions. The advantage of standard deviation units is that they allow us to determine what proportion of the population has an IQ at or below a given value. Inspection of Figure 1.1 shows that approximately 68% of people have IQs between 85 and 115 and that about 95% lie between 70 and 130. This means that roughly 5% are either above 130 or below 70 so, since the distribution is symmetrical, 2.5%, or 1 person in 40 has an IQ of less than 70. It is this property of the normal distribution curve that has formed the basis of numerous classification systems that have been used with people with learning difficulties.

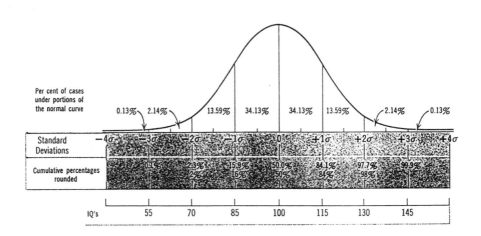

Figure 1.1: The normal distribution and its application to IQ scores. (Adapted with permission from the Psychological Corporation.)

This use of intelligence testing as a tool for classifying people with learning difficulties represents one of the first involvements of psychologists in the care and management of these individuals. The role of the psychologist was to devise, standardise and administer tests, and to determine into which category the individual should be put. It is worth noting in this context that Binet's original idea that children whose mental ages lagged behind their chronological ages were 'retarded' is implicit in this approach to describing people with learning difficulties. The notion of retardation suggests that the developmental processes in such individuals take place in the same manner but at a slower pace than in the majority of children, and that catching up is at least a theoretical possibility. An alternative view is that the development of individuals with learning difficulties is 'different' in crucial respects from normal development. On this view, adverse early experiences, whether physical or psychosocial, affect the cognitive system in such a manner that subsequent development does not follow those pathways that are found in the majority of children. This 'development v difference' debate in learning difficulties has waxed and waned over the decades (see Zigler & Hodapp, 1986, for a review) and the two positions still have their strong advocates.

A moment's reflection will show that the choice of which point on the normal distribution curve to choose as a cut-off point for mental retardation/deficiency/subnormality is a somewhat arbitrary matter and depends to some extent on the socio-cultural context in which it is made. In predominantly agrarian societies where most work consists of simple repetitive, manual tasks, many individuals with IQs of 50 or less would be economically productive. Increasing technological complexity, however, makes more and more demands on individuals' problem-solving skills and potentially renders increasing numbers of people as 'learning disabled' in some way. We make this point only to show that there are no absolute levels of intellectual impairment; consideration must always be given to the overall context in which the individual operates.

Nevertheless, despite these caveats, most of the IQ- or MA-based classification systems have taken an IQ of below 70 as the starting point of learning disability or mental subnormality. The English Mental Deficiency Acts of 1913 and 1927 divided the 'mentally deficient' into 'idiots', 'imbeciles' and 'feeble minded', roughly corresponding to IQ ranges of 0–20, 21–50 and 51–70 respectively. It was not until the Mental Health Act of 1959 that these terms were replaced by severe subnormality (IQ 0–50) and subnormality (IQ 51–70). In the same year, the English Handicapped Pupils and Special Schools Regulations deemed severely subnormal persons to be ineducable and subnormal persons to be Educationally Subnormal (ESN). Corresponding American terminology deemed severely subnormal people to be the 'trainable mentally retarded', and subnormal people the 'educable mentally retarded'.

An important point to note here is the start of a recognition that education was a possibility at least for some people who were considered at the time to be subnormal, and that some special educational provision appropriate to their needs should be provided.

This shift in emphasis was due in large part to a series of scientific investigations by psychologists working within the traditions of learning theory. Throughout the post-war decades, a growing body of literature demonstrated that it was possible to promote learning in people who had previously been deemed to be ineducable, resulting in the change in public policy embodied in the Education (Handicapped Children) Act 1970, which re-labelled formerly ESN children as ESN (mild) or ESN(M) and formally ineducable children as ESN (severe) or ESN(S). Subsequently, the Warnock Report of 1978 reflected the growing emphasis on the learning difficulties experienced by 'the educationally subnormal' by re-labelling ESN(S) children as 'children with severe learning difficulties' (SLD), and ESN(M) children as 'children with moderate learning difficulties' (MLD).

Measuring intelligence – Adaptive behaviour

So far, we have concentrated on intelligence test scores as criteria for classification of people with learning difficulties. In general, the tests commonly used to measure intelligence, such as the Stanford-Binet and the Wechsler scales etc. (see Anastasi, 1986 for reviews) generally measure an individual's ability to solve verbal or non-verbal problems, ranging from answering questions of general knowledge, through defining words, through assembling jigsaw puzzles of varying complexity to matching geometric designs. However, capacity for problem-solving is not perfectly correlated with ability to make one's way in the world. Those of us who know some people with learning difficulties can think of individuals whose measured IQ is often quite low but who can nevertheless live reasonably independent lives. Similarly, there are examples of people who are highly intelligent but who find everyday living difficult.

To assess the competences not usually tapped by conventional IQ tests, numerous researchers have developed measures of *adaptive behaviour* to overcome the limitations of conventional IQ tests. The shift in policy from one of 'care and containment' to 'education and training', and the increasing body of experimental literature showing that even severely retarded individuals could learn given the right circumstances, gave rise to questions concerning what people should be taught and how we might measure the usefulness to the individual of what is taught. Assessments relating to these kinds of interventions were less concerned with how an individual performed in relation to the general population and more concerned with whether or not they could perform a given skill at a given level. Unlike the norm-referenced tests described earlier, these tests are often called *criterion-referenced tests*.

As Clarke and Clarke (1985) point out, social incompetence has often been used as a criterion for the definition of mental retardation and although there is no one-to-one correspondence between having social difficulties and having low intelligence, the probability of social difficulties increases with diminishing IQ. In order to provide some standardised measures of social adaptation, scales such as the *Vineland Social Maturity Scales* (Sparrow & Cicchetti, 1989) and the *Adaptive Behaviour Scales* (ABS) (Nihira, Foster, Shellhaus & Leland, 1974) have been developed. More detail on the content and use of these tests is given in the next chapter.

Although, as we shall see, the role of the psychologist in learning difficulties has gone beyond issues of measurement and classification, psychology has made an important contribution to the field through its development of measurements that are reliable and valid. Reliable measures are those that give similar results when used repeatedly on the same person on different occasions or when administered by different testers. A ruler, for example, would be of little use if the measurements it gave of someone's height varied markedly depending on the day of the week on which the measurement was taken or on who was doing the measuring. Valid measures are those that measure what they are supposed to measure. A thermometer, for example, is not a valid measure of height. Readers interested in how psychological tests are constructed (the science of *psychometrics*) should consult a text such as Rust and Golombok (1989).

As far as classification is concerned, learning difficulties are now conceptualised as centring around psychological and social adaptation to the world. Attempts to classify individuals have moved from small numbers of categories based on ill-defined criteria to multi-dimensional assessments taking intellectual and social adaptation as well as organic causes into account. The role of the psychologist has changed from someone who measures psychological attributes and assigns labels to someone who tries to conceptualise difficulties in psychological terms with a view to devising strategies to help the individual better adapt to everyday life. This shift from categorisation and labelling marks a shift in attention to psychological processes, and it is to a consideration of the different psychological processes that we now turn.

Learning theory

At the start of the present century, psychologists became dissatisfied with existing approaches to their discipline which tended to focus heavily on introspection, or looking inside oneself, in order to understand the workings of the human mind. Instead, scientists such as JB Watson argued that only publicly-observable events should count as data in psychology and that the task of the psychologist was to identify if and how environmental events and changes in behaviour were related. Watson's main contribution to this area was based on the work of the Russian physiologist Pavlov and has become known as *Classical Conditioning*. Pavlov's most famous experiment was to take a dog and present it with food. The dog's reaction to the smell of the food is to start salivating, which is the natural outcome of the way dogs are made. Pavlov called the food the 'unconditioned stimulus' (US) and the salivation the 'unconditioned response' (UR). Pavlov then rang a bell every time the dog was presented with food, having previously shown that the bell on its own did not produce salivation in the dog. After a number of bell-food pairings he then presented the bell alone and found that it now produced salivation in the dog. So the bell had gone from being a 'neutral stimulus' to a 'conditioned stimulus' and the salivation in response to the bell was now a 'conditioned response'.

Two additional and related strands of behavioural research that have achieved wide application in the area of learning difficulties relate to the 'operant psychology' of BF Skinner and the work of W Bandura (see Lieberman, 1993 for a review of these two approaches, and Kiernan, 1974; Carr & Yule, 1987 and Cipani, 1989, for reviews of their application to learning difficulties). On the basis of his work with rats and pigeons, Skinner argued that all organisms emitted behaviour (or *operants*) and that the survival or extinction of any particular behaviour was determined by the consequences of that behaviour for the organism. If an operant has positive consequences (eg. if a hungry rat presses a lever and this is followed by food), then it is likely to happen again. If it is followed by unpleasant consequences (eg. an electric shock following the lever press), then it is not likely to happen again. These two types of consequence, food and shock, we call 'positive reinforcement' and 'positive punishment' respectively. If, on the other hand, we have a situation where the rat is given an electric shock and must press a lever in order to stop it, then every time the rat is given a shock, it will be likely to press the lever. This procedure is called 'negative reinforcement'; negative because it involves taking something (the shock) away, and reinforcement because it increases the chances of a lever press occurring. Similarly, negative punishment would involve removing something pleasant as a consequence of a given behaviour.

In addition to the concepts of positive and negative reinforcement and punishment, Skinner also introduced the concept of 'stimulus control'. If a rat is rewarded for pressing a lever when a red light is shining but not when a green light is on, then it will learn to lever press only at the red light. In other words, its behaviour has come under the control of the light.

The work of Bandura (1977) has extended behaviour theory to the human context by demonstrating that people do not always have to be directly reinforced for their behaviour in order for it to re-occur. Humans can experience 'vicarious reinforcement and punishment', whereby their own behaviour can be influenced by what they see happening to other people who engage in that behaviour. So, in a classic study, Bandura (1965) showed that children who saw an adult punished for 'beating up' an inflatable doll were less likely to behave aggressively towards the doll in free play than were children who had not seen an adult, or had seen an adult who was rewarded for playing 'beating up the doll'.

Classical and operant conditioning and social learning theory have all formed the basis for a wide range of effective educational and management strategies for people with learning difficulties. Examples of such applications are given in Chapter 2.

Cognitive psychology – The information-processing perspective

In addition to being interested in how to change the behaviour of people with learning difficulties for the better, psychologists have also been interested in the 'how' and the 'why' of difficulties in learning. What factors underlie a failure to learn? Such questions have made use of other approaches to the study of psychology, the most important of which is *cognitive psychology*.

From the 1950's onwards there was a growing dissatisfaction with behaviourism as a complete account of how organisms – and in particular, people – relate to their environments (see Gardner, 1985, for a review). At that time, digital computers had arrived on the scene and people became very interested in systems that took in information from outside (or had information put into them), operated on this information and then generated some sort of output. Engineers began to find ways of comparing input-output relations in order to work out what was happening inside the system without actually having to open the system up. Psychologists rapidly became interested in this approach and after years of languishing on the sidelines, the study of the internal workings of the mind became once again respectable in psychology.

A good example of an information-processing account in psychology is the study of memory. As an exercise, try taking your telephone directory into a different room, looking up a number at random and then remembering it while you walk back to the telephone. Observe what you do in order to help you to remember the number. Now repeat the experiment, but this time, think of the number 100 and count backwards in sevens. In the first case, you probably found yourself repeating the number over and over again (a process termed 'rehearsal') in order to remember it. In the second case, unless you have an abnormally good memory, you will have completely forgotten the number. Observations such as these have led scientists to posit a *short-term memory system*, also sometimes called *working memory*, which has limited capacity and is temporary. New information is either held in short term memory until discarded or lost or it is transferred to *long-term memory* from which it can be retrieved (or not, as is often the case).

A great deal of scientific research has gone into elucidating the mechanisms underlying how the different components of the memory system operate and some of this research has proved useful in helping us to understand learning difficulties. For example, it is now well documented that the rehearsal processes that we all automatically use to hold information in our short-term memories are not usually spontaneously used by people with learning difficulties. However, if such people are trained in the use of rehearsal, then their memory performance can be improved considerably, with knock-on effects for their general problem-solving ability.

Another short-term memory strategy that most people use spontaneously is 'clustering'. Imagine you have a long list of items to remember – say the telephone number 003536633125. This is more easily remembered if you know that it is the number for an international call from the UK. In this case you can split it up into the components of International Access Code, Country Code, Area Code and Number, or 00 353 66 33125. Similarly, if you are given a long list of words to learn which contains the names of items of furniture, fruit and modes of transport, even though the members of the different classes of items might be jumbled up in the list, the way people tend to present the items at recall shows that they remember items of the same category in groups. This 'category clustering' of items helps us to remember more items, but is something that people with learning difficulties need to be taught how to do. Comprehensive reviews of work on memory strategy training with people with learning difficulties can be found in Kail and Hagen (1977) and Dockrell and McShane (1993).

The conclusions that we can draw from the kind of work just described is that the so-called deficiencies that are seen in people with learning difficulties are not always related to their having a smaller *capacity* to handle information. Instead, they appear to deploy inefficient *strategies* when processing data. Such observations had important implications for applied psychologists working with clients, prompting a shift from pure behavioural methods to a combination of behavioural and cognitive techniques commonly referred to as the 'cognitive-behavioural approach', applications of which can be found in Chapter 2.

Despite the considerable theoretical and technical advances brought about by the application of behavioural and cognitive/information-processing psychology to the question of learning difficulties, some problems still remained. Initially, the two approaches tended to see learning difficulties, retardation or whatever in relatively pure psychological terms. The general line of reasoning was that if the relevant missing or inefficient psychological processes (such as learning or short-term memory strategies) could be identified, then programmes could be initiated to circumvent these difficulties and thereby improve the adaptive behaviour of the individual. However, not all individuals responded to interventions in the same way, and the degree of improvement seemed to vary in relation to the initial level of impairment of the individual. Whilst successes were often quite striking with individuals with mild or moderate difficulties, less spectacular results were found with more severely impaired individuals. Moreover, some improvements wrought by, for example, memory strategy training, seemed in many cases to be limited to tasks that were similar to those on which the client was trained; improved performance often did not generalise to related situations. Observations such as these led to a re-consideration of the question that first brought psychologists into the field of mental deficiency, namely that of *individual differences*, or why different individuals perform differently in different situations.

Behavioural phenotypes

As we have seen, the care and management of 'mental deficiency' used to be seen largely as a medical problem, since many 'mental defectives' were seen as having obvious biological damage. Those who showed no overt evidence of biological involvement were assumed to have some, as yet unmeasurable, impairments to their brains. The historical developments in pure and applied psychology just outlined marked a shift away from biological considerations towards issues of identifying mechanisms underlying behaviour, using an understanding of these mechanisms to promote more adaptive and intelligent behaviour. However, although the milder forms of learning difficulties are often associated with poor physical and social conditions of upbringing and with lack of psychological stimulation, more severe forms are often, if not invariably, associated with some kind of biological damage or dysfunction.

In many cases, biological factors leading to mental retardation are of a 'one-off' nature, such as trauma in pregnancy, maternal alcohol use or smoking, lack of oxygen at birth or certain viral infections early in childhood. Very often it is impossible to be certain of exactly what has caused a particular child to have severe learning difficulties, but in cases where there is obvious brain damage some biological cause is presumed. Readers who are interested in the different factors that can cause brain damage leading to mental retardation should read Rosenblith (1992).

An additional biological cause of mental retardation stems from genetic abnormalities that are inherited by children from their parents. The best known of these is Down syndrome after Langdon Down, who first identified it in 1866. People with Down syndrome have a characteristic facial appearance that gave the syndrome its early name of mongolism. The degree of learning difficulty shown by people with Down syndrome can vary from non-existent to very severe. In 1959, people with Down syndrome were found to have an abnormality of their genetic material. The usual set of genes for a human being consists of 23 pairs of chromosomes which carry the genes that are the blueprint for our physical structure. In most people with Down syndrome, the 21st chromosome exists as a triplet rather than a pair, hence the term 'trisomy-21' sometimes used to describe these individuals. This condition results from a fault in the mother's egg-production mechanism, a fault which becomes more likely to happen as a woman gets older. Trisomy-21 is the commonest form of Down syndrome, although there are other forms, some of which are not related to the age of the mother. Although there is a common stereotype that people with Down syndrome are happy, outgoing, sociable and possibly clumsy, systematic studies have not always borne this out. Research has shown that they usually have severe learning difficulties, are less likely to show autistic-like behaviours and are at an increased risk of early development of Alzheimer's disease.

In the last paragraph it was mentioned that the normal human genetic endowment consisted of 23 pairs of chromosomes which form the blueprint for the physical structure of that individual. This genetic endowment is referred to as the person's 'genotype'. In fact, not all genes in an individual's genotype get translated into an actual bodily structure. Some genes are *dominant* and others are *recessive*. For example, we all carry two genes for eye colour. In the genetics of eye colour, the gene for brown eyes is dominant and that for blue eyes is recessive, so if we have two brown eye genes, we will have brown eyes, and if we have two blue eye genes, we will have blue eyes, but if we have a blue and a brown eye gene, then we will have brown eyes. So a brown eyed person can carry a blue eye gene but this will not be detectable by looking at that person's eyes. It may, however, result in that individual's having blue-eyed children. In this case, the individual's genotype is blue + brown but his or her eye colour or 'phenotype' is brown. So, the phenotype is the 'expression' of the genotype and depends on the balance of dominant and recessive genes.

But dominance and recessiveness is not the whole story. As we have seen, the human genotype consists of 23 pairs of chromosomes, but one of these pairs consists of the *sex chromosomes* – XX in a woman and XY in a man. The remaining 22 pairs are called *autosomes*. If we imagine superimposing the letter Y on the letter X, we can see that there is an arm of the letter X that is not covered by the Y. If there is a recessive gene on this arm, and if the child is female, that gene will have a corresponding gene on the other X chromosome. However, if the child is male, then there is no corresponding location on the Y chromosome. This means that sometimes recessive genes become expressed in boys more often than in girls. The best example of this is red-green colour-blindness, which is the result of an X-linked recessive gene. Women who carry the gene are usually not colour blind because they have a compensating dominant gene on the other X chromosome. However, men who inherit the gene from their mothers will always be colour blind because they have no possibility of having a compensating gene. This kind of disorder is what we call a sex-linked disorder.

So far, our discussion has centred on physical characteristics. However, the identification of a genetic basis for Down syndrome led many researchers to explore the possibility that there might be behavioural phenotypes in addition to physical phenotypes that result from specific genetic abnormalities.

In a useful review article on behavioural phenotypes, Turk and Sales (1996) divide up three groups. The first of these they term *autosomal chromosome anomalies*. This group includes Down syndrome, which we have already dealt with. Other autosomal anomalies include tuberous sclerosis which can produce severe learning difficulties with hyperactivity and autistic features, Williams syndrome, Angelman's syndrome, Prader-Willi syndrome and phenylketonuria. Possession of the gene for tuberous sclerosis does not always result in psychological disorders, which illustrates that often the relationship between biological and psychological factors is not straightforward. In addition, the condition of phenylketonuria (PKU) shows us that environmental measures can be brought to bear on the expression of inherited disorders. A person with PKU lacks a gene that produces the enzyme that processes a substance called phenylalanine which is found in many proteins. High levels of phenylalanine are toxic to the nervous system and will, over a period of time, produce damage leading to learning difficulties. However, if detected early, a child with PKU can be put on a phenylalanine-free diet and thus be assured of normal psychological development.

The second group of syndromes associated with specific psychological abnormalities identified by Turk and Sales are called *sex chromosome abnormalities*. These include Turner syndrome, Klinefelter syndrome and XYY syndrome. Although people with these conditions often show characteristic patterns of performance on certain psychological tasks, they do not usually show global learning difficulties of the kind under discussion here.

By contrast, two sex-linked conditions that are associated with learning difficulties are Fragile-X syndrome and Lesch-Nyhan syndrome. Fragile-X syndrome is the most common genetic cause of learning difficulties which can range from very mild to very severe, although some children do not develop any learning difficulties. In addition to global learning impairment, Fragile-X is also frequently associated with autistic features such as ritualistic behaviours, repetitive speech, hand flapping, gaze avoidance and attentional deficits. Lesch-Nyhan syndrome is due to a deficiency of an X-located gene which results in severe learning difficulties accompanied by severe self-mutilation.

Turk and Sales identify a third group of disorders that have a suspected but unproven genetic cause. These include Rett syndrome, which involves developmental deterioration accompanied by characteristic motor movements, Cornelia de Lange syndrome which is usually accompanied by severe learning disability, self-injurious behaviours, autistic features and hyperactivity, and Sotos syndrome which is characterised by difficulties with peers, tantrums and attentional difficulties.

The frankly biological focus of the last few paragraphs should not be taken to mean that, as genetic and neuroscientific techniques become more sophisticated, the role of psychology in helping us to understand learning difficulties is destined to be diminished. Indeed, this is far from the case. Although it is tempting to think that there is a simple, one-to-one relationship between genes and behaviour, this is not so. Even the inheritance of physical characteristics is more complex than the simple example of eye colour given earlier would suggest; the organism's phenotype, whether physical or behavioural, is the result of a complex interaction between different genes, the organism's environment and changes in that environment over time (Rutter, 1996). In this respect, not only is the physical environment important, but the social one as well. For example, a simple biological trait such as the amount of certain pigments in skin can, given the wrong social and political environment, be highly disadvantageous for an individual. It would be mistaken to conclude that the poverty experienced by individuals in the old South Africa was *caused* by the gene that gave them black skin. Similarly, although there may be genetic conditions that make it more difficult for an individual to learn adaptive behaviours, such a difficulty poses more problems for someone born into a technological rather than an agrarian society.

The identification of behavioural phenotypes, although an important step forward in our understanding of learning difficulties, also poses new questions, some of which fall squarely in the psychological domain. If a given genetic condition, such as Williams syndrome, produces 'visuo-spatial and motor problems', what exactly does this mean? Visuo-spatial skills cover a wide range of competences ranging from one's ability to navigate through a familiar town, through being able to predict the direction of rotation of a particular gear in a gearbox, to being good at jigsaw puzzles. Among the questions we need to ask when we find a group of people with a recognised gene abnormality and impairments of one or more of these skills is whether all visuo-spatial skills are impaired or only just some? If it is only just some, are the same ones impaired in every affected individual or does the pattern differ from person to person? We also need to ask ourselves about people without the gene abnormality but who nevertheless show similar visuo-spatial difficulties. And most importantly, we need to develop some understanding of how specific deficits relate to general intellectual difficulties. In short, the identification of behavioural phenotypes represents a major development in our understanding of how individuals relate behaviourally to their environments and how such relations may be mediated by brain structures, but there is still a lot of work to do. The temptation of thinking that there is a gene for mental retardation or learning difficulties is one that should be strenuously resisted.

Conclusion

The role of the psychologist encompasses two broad aspects. The first is to provide a systematic understanding of human behaviour and those factors that influence its development and change. The second is to develop applications of that understanding that should aim to improve human welfare. The present chapter has focused primarily on how the first of these functions has provided conceptual frameworks that help us understand why some people experience difficulties in learning to adapt to their environment.

Even in the current climate of increasingly sophisticated techniques in the fields of neuroscience and genetics, the conceptual insights offered by the science of psychology will continue to explain how the physical structure of organisms interfaces with the social structures of the environments they create.

References

Anastasi A (1986) Psychological Testing. 6th edn. New York: Macmillan.

Bandura A (1965) Influence of models reinforcement contingencies on the acquisition of imitative responses. Journal of Personality and Social Psychology 1: 589–95.

Bandura A (1977) Social Learning Theory. London: Prentice-Hall.

Carr J, Yule W (Eds) (1987). Behaviour Modification for People with Mental Handicaps. 2nd edn. London: Croom Helm.

Cipani E (Ed) (1989). The Treatment of Severe Behavior Disorders: Behavior analysis approaches. Washington, DC: AAMR.

Clarke AM, Clarke ADB (1985). Criteria and classification. In Clarke AM, Clarke ADB, Berg J (Eds) Mental Deficiency: The changing outlook. 2nd edn. London: Methuen.

Dockrell J, McShane J (1993). Children's Learning Difficulties: A cognitive approach. Oxford: Blackwell.

Education Act (1981) London: HMSO.

Farr R (1987) The science of mental life: A social-psychological perspective. Bulletin of the British Psychological Society 40: 2–18.

Gardner H (1985) The Mind's New Science. New York: Basic Books.

Kail R, Hagen J (Eds) (1977) Perspectives on the Development of Memory and Cognition. Hillsdale, NJ: Erlbaum.

Kiernan C (1974) Behaviour Modification. In Clarke AM, Clarke ADB (Eds) Mental Deficiency: The changing outlook. London: Methuen.

Lane H (1977) The Wild Boy of Aveyron. Cambridge, Mass.: Harvard University Press.

Lieberman DA (1993) Learning: Behavior and cognition. 2nd edn. Pacific Grove: Brooks/Cole.

Nihira K, Foster R, Shellhaus M, Leland H (1974) Adaptive Behavior Scale. Washington DC: AAMD.

Rosenblith J (1992) In the Beginning: Development from conception to age two. London: Sage.

Rowe H (1991) Intelligence: Reconceptualisation and measurement. Hove UK: Lawrence Erlbaum.

Rust J, Golombok S (1989) Modern Psychometrics. London: Routledge.

Rutter M (1996) Are we controlled by our genes? The Independent, 15th April 1996.

Sparrow S, Cicchetti D (1989). The Vineland Adaptive Behavior Scales. In Newmark CS (Ed) Major Psychological Assessment Instruments, Vol II. Boston: Allyn Bacon.

Turk J, Sales J (1996). Behavioural phenotypes and their relevance to child mental health professionals. Child Psychology and Psychiatry Review 1: 4–11.

Warnock M (1978) Special Educational Needs: Report of the Committee of Enquiry into the Education of Handicapped Children and Young People. London: HMSO.

Zigler E, Hodapp RM (1986) Understanding Mental Retardation. Cambridge: Cambridge University Press.

Chapter 2

Interventions with Children who have Learning Difficulties: Contributions from Clinical Psychology

SARAH LISTER BROOK AND DERMOT M BOWLER

Introduction

Psychologists have contributed in a variety of ways to our conceptual understanding of learning difficulties. Within this century psychological theory and principles have been rigorously applied to our practices in everyday life. Two fields of applied psychology have evolved which have had a significant impact on the services provided for children with learning difficulties. These applied disciplines are largely subsumed under the general headings of Clinical Psychology and Educational psychology. This chapter will focus on the contribution of the former, although not surprisingly there is considerable overlap between the two disciplines.

Society as a whole has played an important part in influencing our attitudes towards and our understanding of people with learning difficulties (see Chapter 1). During this century educational reforms have had a particular influence on how we recognise and respond to children with learning difficulties. The Education Act of 1944 defined ten categories of 'handicap' in children for which provision would be made in special schools. However, this system of categories was seen as of little use in describing the needs of children. A government committee was then set up and chaired by Mary Warnock. The central recommendation in the report of the Warnock Committee in 1978 (Special Educational Needs, DES Cmnd 7212) stated that children should be referred to as having 'special needs' if they have a learning difficulty which calls for special educational provision to be made for them (Education Act 1981, s.1 (1)). This central recommendation was given legislative effect by the

Education Act of 1981. Since that Act there has been further legislative reform culminating in the Education Acts of 1988 and 1993. The general trend, however, has been a move away from a conceptual framework which identified and defined children in terms of their deficits in favour of one based on the concept of need.

The role of the clinical psychologist

The term 'clinical psychology' was first used by Witmer in 1896 (in Mackay, 1975) to refer to the assessment procedures which were carried out with 'retarded and physically handicapped children'. Pioneering psychologists in the clinical field were preoccupied with disabled children and assessment was generally accepted to be the primary function of the applied psychologist throughout the first half of this century. Since then the role of the clinical psychologist has expanded considerably. Clinical psychologists still maintain a large investment in the devising of objective clinical assessment procedures. In addition to this they also contribute widely to the development and implementation of educational and treatment programmes for children with learning difficulties.

The settings in which clinical psychologists work

Clinical psychologists working with children who have learning difficulties can be found in a variety of settings. Some are attached to paediatric hospital-based teams and may become involved in the care of neonates, advising on appropriate early stimulation whilst the child is in special care, or counselling parents who have discovered that their child is going to be disabled in some way. Clinical psychologists might also service paediatric teams who are involved in dealing with children who have complex medical problems in addition to their learning difficulties, for example, children who are suffering from Retts syndrome or those who have complex sensory and physical impairments. Clinical psychologists may also work within tertiary referral centres that have an important role in the assessment and diagnosis of children who have very complex patterns of disability or behaviour that are challenging local services so that the children require more specialist assessment and intervention. These specialist centres may be organised through paediatric or child psychiatry services, or through independent organisations such as charities.

Community paediatric services responsible for the monitoring of the development of children with special needs are multiprofessional and utilise the skills of clinical psychologists in the comprehensive assessment of each child's development and in the implementation of therapeutic interventions available to the children. Clinical psychologists have played a large part in the delivery and evaluation of home-based early intervention programmes for children with developmental difficulties (see section on Early intervention programmes p. 31). Within this setting they usually form part of a multidisciplinary team located within a District or Regional Child Development Centre. Clinical psychologists are rarely employed directly by special schools, but there are some exceptions as in the case of residential services for children with very complex needs associated with epilepsy or autism. For the most part clinical psychologists act as external consultants to special schools advising on how to reduce problem behaviour, techniques of behavioural management, the teaching of new skills and ways of enhancing existing skills. They may also contribute indirectly by developing internal or external support systems for the staff.

The role of the clinical psychologist working with children who have learning difficulties therefore varies considerably according to the client need and the service organisation. In most cases the services of a clinical psychologist are called upon when there are concerns about the child's behaviour. These concerns may arise as a result of parents or service providers feeling challenged by new patterns of disruptive behaviour. On the other hand, the presenting behaviour problems may be long standing and those caring for or working with the child may have come to feel that they have exhausted all the resources that have been targeted at modifying or containing the behaviour. Alternatively, the services of a clinical psychologist may be requested when the presenting behaviour is not particularly challenging with respect to its day-to-day management but is hard to make sense of in the context of the child's developmental level or chronological age.

Before any kind of intervention can take place it is essential that a full *functional assessment* of the presenting behaviour problem is carried out. Assessment and intervention will be dealt with under separate headings, but good clinical practice requires that the clinician builds in ongoing assessment as part of any intervention programme that is designed to alter behaviour patterns.

Assessing behaviour problems

In most cases the child under investigation will have undergone or be undergoing a full medical assessment to ascertain where possible any causes of their learning difficulties and/or the treatment requirements of any complicating medical factors. The information available from this assessment will be very helpful in guiding the psychological assessment of behavioural problems as medical factors may be relevant in the triggering or the maintenance of the presenting behaviours (see Oliver & Head, 1990). For example, in the case of episodic rage which is involuntary this may be related to 'frontal lobe seizure', a term that has replaced the vague terms 'subclinical seizure' and 'episodic dyscontrol' (Nunn, 1986; Fraser & Rao, 1991).

Children with learning difficulties may well have complicating neurological conditions or have had neurosurgical intervention for medical phenomena such as intractable epilepsy. The child's neurological status or neurosurgical history will have a bearing on the development of their cognitive abilities and adaptive functioning. Another important consideration is whether or not the child's learning difficulties are genetic in origin. Recent advances within the field of behavioural genetics have identified a host of behavioural phenotypes (Turk & Sales, 1996). This has led to the development of different societies and groups whose purpose is often to provide a focus for collecting and disseminating information related to a particular syndrome. The specific needs of the child with a particular genotype can then become more easily recognised and understood by parents and professionals and those new to the syndrome can very readily tap into a network of existing knowledge. However, as always in the course of assessing any child with a learning disability, it is important to maintain some appreciation of the notion of individual differences. The identification of a particular gene abnormality can lead people into thinking in terms of behavioural stereotypes. For example, the common stereotype of the person with Down syndrome as being very sociable can lead to the failure to recognise that a person with Down syndrome may also have autism (Howlin, Wing & Gould, 1995).

Behavioural observation

Behavioursim has had a strong influence on our understanding of behaviour problems in children with learning difficulties. The general rules governing behaviour that have been identified through animal experimental work have guided the developments in behavioural modification techniques used with children and adults with learning disability. When these techniques are applied and utilised appropriately there is often rewarding success and significant changes in behaviour patterns are made. However, when these techniques are misapplied the consequences can be disastrous for all concerned. The most likely explanation for this less rewarding outcome is that pressures to make changes in behaviour have resulted in a hasty and insubstantial assessment of the behaviour that has been targeted for change. Any kind of behavioural approach, whether it is directed at teaching a simple skill like brushing your teeth or unravelling a complex loop of self-injurious behaviour, requires a proper *functional analysis*. A functional analysis therefore involves the identification of stimuli that might elicit the target behaviour, the situations in which the target behaviour occurs and the consequences of this behaviour. This process is commonly referred to as the

ABC of functional analysis. The 'A' refers to the antecedents, the 'B' refers to the behaviour that occurs and the 'C' refers to the consequences of that behaviour. By using functional assessment techniques information can also be gathered about the form, size and frequency of the target behaviour. The antecedents for the target behaviour, the target behaviour itself and the consequences of emitting that target behaviour can present in many different forms. Functional analysis techniques are not only concerned with identifying overt behaviours but are also concerned with the role of cognitions and internal physiological states in the ABC relationship. Internal emotional states are less available to the observer but a feeling of sadness, for example, could be a potential antecedent for, or consequence of, a problem behaviour. Certain thoughts or cognitions, as illustrated by, 'that person's laughing at me because he thinks I am stupid' can also play a part in triggering or maintaining problem behaviours. A supersensitivity to specific auditory stimuli can result in very distressed behaviour in an individual whose sensory experiences are disrupted by their impaired brain functioning (see Figure 2.1).

Antecedent	Behaviour	Consequence
(Eg. adult brings teaching task to child)	(Eg. child starts to head punch)	(Eg. adult removes task and child is left alone)

Antecedent	Behaviour	Consequence
(Eg. child A decides she wants a friend)	(Eg. child A grabs child B, who pushes her away)	(Eg. child A hits child B and is left feeling sad and disappointed)

Antecedent	Behaviour	Consequence
(Eg. whenever teacher raises her voice)	(Eg. child covers ears and screams)	(Eg. child is removed from lesson)

Figure 2.1 The ABC of functional analysis

There needs to be a comprehensive method of assessing and recording the behaviours within the functional analysis stage. There are three major types of assessment procedure:

1   those that are based upon self-report by the child
2   direct observation of behaviour
3   physiological measures.

The assessment procedures most commonly used with children who have learning difficulties involve direct observation and this is usually carried out in a naturalistic environment. Observational aids like checklists, rating scales and daily schedules are employed to provide a structure for the data gathering process and improve on the accuracy and reliability of the recordings. However, there are some inherent difficulties in using these aids. For example, the observer's presence may directly or indirectly influence the child's behaviour; similarly, the observer's own viewpoint may bias his or her perception of the behaviour, or the observation period might miss critical behaviours. To try and combat these difficulties, analogue situations within a controlled environment are used. This technique has been used extensively in the assessment and treatment of well-established self-injurious behaviour where the web of contingencies maintaining the behaviour is often very complex and unsuccessful treatment interventions have resulted in the 'SIB trap' (self-injurious behaviour trap) (Oliver & Head, 1990).

Cognitive assessment

The early pioneers in clinical psychology were dedicated to devising objective methods for quantifying and defining intelligence. With the developments in behaviourism in the 1950s and 1960s intelligence testing became outmoded. Clinical psychologists as a professional group were anxious to rid themselves of the image of a 'testing technician' whose sole function was to derive IQs for other professionals and who played only a small part in the formulation and classification of mental impairments. However, the 1970s brought another revolution in our conceptualisation of brain-behaviour relationships and so began the cognitive psychology movement. As we have seen in the previous chapter, cognitive psychology reawakened our interest in the internal workings of the mind and how the mind processes and organises information. The birth of cognitive psychology reawakened interest in the craft of cognitive assessment and its contribution to the holistic assessment of the child with learning difficulties. Today, cognitive assessment is essentially 'ipsative', ie. the comparison of a child with learning difficulties to other similar or non-handicapped peers is de-emphasised, and the child's individual profile of strengths and weaknesses is sought (Powers & Handleman, 1984). A normative interpretation of test results has not been totally abandoned since it still allows the clinician to place the child on a developmental continuum which in turn can provide useful information in the overall diagnostic assessment and generate further questions in the assessment process.

There are many reasons why cognitive assessment of an individual child's cognitive functioning may be implicated. For children who show atypical patterns of development but are not globally delayed, cognitive assessment may provide an objective validation of their splinter skills. Such findings will have implications for the child's educational placement and will help identify the most appropriate teaching methods that can be usefully employed to capitalise on their cognitive strengths. For example, the child who is having difficulty in processing language, but is very aware of his or her surrounding environment, may be helped by a very visual learning environment with lots of visual clues to help cue him or her into auditory stimuli. Objective cognitive assessment can also be useful when there is confusion amongst family members and professionals over the level at which a child is functioning. Sometimes people may be overestimating aspects of a child's functioning or even underestimating their functional level. The continuous pressure of unrealistic demands being put on a child with learning difficulties may indeed be the root of a presenting behaviour problem. Alternatively, a child may become difficult to manage because they are bored and not being stretched enough while their skills in certain areas have been unrecognised. Assessments of cognitive skills can also be helpful in revealing additional specific learning difficulties such as dyslexia. Cognitive assessment used appropriately can be of great value in providing a very individualised assessment of a child's abilities to process and organise information available to them in their environment. The results of cognitive assessment combined with behavioural assessment and, ideally, a consideration of the family and community or larger system issues, can then in turn lead to a highly individualised assessment of need. Cognitive assessment has come a long way from the days when test batteries were simply used to categorise whether or not a child was educable.

Psychological tests

There is a range of psychometric instruments available to clinical psychologists and other qualified test users. Psychological tests are like tests in any other applied science, in so far as observations are made on a small but carefully chosen sample of an individual's behaviour (Anastasi, 1986). A psychological test is therefore essentially an objective and standardised measure of a sample of behaviour. Standardised in this instance implies uniformity of procedure in administering and scoring the test. If the scores obtained are to be comparable, testing conditions must obviously be the same for all. Psychological tests have no predetermined standards of passing or failing; performance on each test is evaluated on the basis of empirical data. An individual's performance on a test can therefore be compared with the scores obtained by others on the same test. A norm indicates the normal or average performance.

Like any scientific instrument or precision tool, psychological tests must be properly used to be effective. There are two principal reasons for this: a) to ensure that the tests are used by a qualified examiner; and

b) to prevent general familiarity with the test content which would invalidate the test (Anastasi, 1988). Clinical psychologists are therefore regarded as qualified users of these tests as they are taught how to select tests appropriate to the individual under investigation, administer them with rapport and appreciation of the need for a standardised approach, and interpret test results in the context of the individual's case.

An intelligence test can provide information at various levels. At an objective level it can provide a broad measure of intelligence in the form of an intelligence quotient (IQ). The Full Scale IQ is made up of subtests from the Verbal Scale and Performance Scale. The latter contains subtests that are more dependent on non-verbal reasoning skills. There is an ongoing debate about the clinical significance of Verbal Performance scale discrepancies and the significance of discrepancies between individual subtest scaled scores. However, at a qualitative level, variation in performance would indicate the need for further investigations. A profile on a Wechsler Intelligence Scale characterised by peaks and troughs in performance is commonplace in children suffering from pervasive developmental disorders (Happé, 1994). A qualitative analysis of performance may also provide useful cues about problem solving approaches, conceptual development or cognitive styles. The unusual content of test responses can provide a further source of clues about how the child views the world. There are many different intelligence test batteries which are all aiming to provide a composite score of cognitive functioning; the Wechsler Scales for children are probably those most widely used by clinical psychologists, although the British Ability Scales (BAS) are now probably the most comprehensive test battery in general use. The BAS also have the added advantage that they have been especially developed for children and are not simply a downward extension of an adult intelligence scale such as the Wechsler Scales. They also have greater flexibility allowing the clinician to calculate global IQs and/or test out specific hypotheses regarding a child's relative strengths and needs across ability areas.

Another group of tests are referred to as *criterion referenced tests*. These differ from norm based tests in that they use a specified content domain rather than a specified population of persons as their interpretative frame of reference (Anastasi,1986). Criterion referenced testing has found its major applications in education, examples of which include individualised self-paced instructional systems and broad surveys of educational accomplishment.

Neuropsychological tests were developed to provide indicators of organicity or brain damage. They are used to differentiate children whose difficulties are either functional or organic, to document the extent of neuropsychological involvement, and, in organic conditions, to chart the temporal interactions between on-going development and recovery or deterioration of function (Hynd, 1988). Psychological tests of intellectual impairment are generally based on the premise of differential deficit in different functions. The areas of functioning considered to be most sensitive to pathological processes are those responsible for perception of spatial relations and memory for newly learned material (see the Bender Visual Motor Gestalt Test, commonly known as the Bender Gestalt Test, and the Benton Visual Retention Test). Since the development of these tests, psychologists have increasingly recognised that brain damage may lead to a wide variety of behavioural patterns. No one symptom or set of symptoms need be common to all cases of brain damage; in fact brain damage may produce the opposite behaviour pattern in two individuals. These findings are consistent with the wide diversity of the underlying organic pathology itself. As this wide diversity of organic brain dysfunctions with their accompanying behavioural deficits was recognised, it follows that single tests are even less suited to differential diagnosis. Clinicians frequently use a combination of available tests assessing different skills and deficits. Systematic efforts have also been made to assemble comprehensive standardised batteries that provide measures of all significant neuropsychological skills. There are two such batteries available for use with children: these are the Luria–Nebraska Neuropsychological Battery–Children's Revision (LNNB–CR) and the Halstead-Reitan Neuropsychological Test Batteries for Children and Adolescents. The Halstead–Reitan Batteries are administered along with the Wechsler Scales. The child's age will determine which Wechsler Scale is used. (For a more in-depth discussion of the use of these test batteries with learning disabled children see Hynd, 1988.)

There are other groups of psychological tests not covered in the previous categories that are used with children with learning difficulties. These include tests for the infant and preschool level, tests specifically for sensory and motor impairments and tests used to provide profiles of adaptive behaviour. The psychological examination of young children with learning difficulties requires a coverage of a broad spectrum of behaviours within the motor, social and cognitive domain. Examples of such tests include the Wechsler Preschool and Primary Scale of Intelligence and the British Ability Scales which have already been mentioned, the Gesell Developmental Schedules, Bayley Scales of Infant Development, McCarthy Scales of Children's Abilities and the Merrill–Palmer Scale of Mental Tests. The Leiter International Performance Scale (LIPS) is intended to provide a culture-free, non-verbal means of assessing intelligence, based on primarily abstract concepts. As there are very few verbal instructions necessary in the administration of the LIPS it has proved to be a very useful test to use with children with hearing impairments and/or those with specific language processing difficulties. The Snijders-Oomen Non-verbal Intelligence Tests were also intended for use with children who have impaired verbal communication.

Examples of tests looking at adaptive behaviour include the Vineland Social Maturity Scale (Doll, 1965) and the Adaptive Behaviour Scale (ABS). The Vineland is a developmental schedule concerned with an individual's ability to look after his or her practical needs and it covers an age range from birth to 25 years. It has been found to be most useful at the younger age levels and with children who have learning difficulties. The information required for each item is obtained through an interview with someone who knows the child well. The items fall into eight categories: general self-help, self-help in eating, self-help in dressing, self-direction, occupation, communication, locomotion and socialisation. The Adaptive Behaviour Scale (ABS) is designed primarily for people with learning difficulties. Adaptive behaviour in this instance is defined as 'the effectiveness of an individual in coping with the natural and social demands of his or her environment' (American Association on Mental Deficiency, 1974). This scale can be used from age three years on and is based on observations of behaviour in everyday contexts. It can be completed by anyone who knows the examinee well.

Another group of instruments available to clinicians are in the form of standardised structured interview schedules. Examples of these include the Pre-Verbal Communication Schedule (PVCS) (Kiernan & Reid, 1987) and the Pragmatics Profile of Early Communication Skills (Dewart & Summers, 1988), both of which can be used to identify therapeutic goals and to monitor behaviour change within treatment programmes. Standardised interview techniques have also been used in the differential diagnosis of autism. Interviews are carried out with a person who knows the child well using a schedule of questions that are designed to elicit information about patterns of behaviour which are then rated according to predetermined sets of criteria. Epidemiological work, carried out by Wing and Gould (1979) looking at the prevalence of Kanner autism and related conditions, provided the impetus for the development of these techniques.

Wing and Gould (1979) established that children with learning difficulties could be categorised according to their ability to participate in two-way reciprocal social interaction appropriate to their mental age. There were essentially two groups of children: those who were sociable but who had learning difficulties and those who were socially impaired relative to their overall mental age and who also had learning difficulties. These findings came from a large epidemiological study that set out to look for any one of the behavioural features required for the diagnosis of an autistic disorder in a population of children with severe to mild learning difficulties. The study demonstrated that social impairment could co-exist with any level of IQ, but that if the child showed impairments in reciprocal social interaction they always also showed impairments in their communication and imagination and a tendency to engage in repetitive behaviours. This pattern of behaviour has since been referred to as the 'triad of social impairment' (Wing, 1988). The presentation of the social impairment ranges from the aloof child who interacts with no-one and is always on the periphery of social groups, to the child who is passive in social interaction and allows others to manipulate and manoeuvre him or her. Children at the other end of the range may try to initiate social interaction with others but frequently lack the flexibility in thought and behaviour to adapt to new situations and consequently appear odd and bizarre – the 'active but odd' child. The Handicaps, Behaviours and Skills (HBS) interview schedule (Wing & Gould, 1978) was designed for the epidemiological study so that information about the child's general level of functioning, and in particular their social functioning, could be gathered systematically. As in the Vineland, information is gathered from an informant who knows the child well. The HBS is essentially a research tool and since its creation, in response to growing clinical demand, a similar tool has been developed by Wing and her colleagues which provides a more comprehensive profile of the quality of the child's impairments in social interaction, communication and imagination. The Diagnostic Interview for Social and Communication Disorders can be used to gather data about an individual of any chronological age and any mental age, and allows the clinician to derive a diagnostic formulation based on the criteria used in any one of the diagnostic systems available for the diagnosis of pervasive developmental disorders. It is not yet available for general use but there is ongoing international collaboration examining its reliability and validity as a tool for the differential diagnosis of autism and related disorders. Other examples of similar instruments include the Autism Diagnostic Interview (Lord, Rutter & Le Couteur, 1994) which is essentially a research tool and generates data that enable the diagnostician to systematically apply the *International Classification of Diseases* criteria (WHO) for childhood autism and related disorders.

The majority of clinical psychologists working with children who have learning difficulties, whatever their theoretical orientation, agree that the identification of learning difficulties requires a wide assortment of tests and supplementary observational procedures. The diagnostic problem has many features but these five features are often common to all:

1   the variety of behavioural disorders associated with the presenting condition
2   the individual differences in the particular combination of symptoms
3   the need for highly specific information regarding the nature and extent of the difficulties
4   the need to appreciate the developmental context
5   the need to appreciate that the child is part of a family system and/or a larger education/community system.

Clinical psychologists typically draw upon multiple sources of data in the intensive study of individual cases. Information is derived from interviewing family and teachers and from the case history, and is then combined with test scores to build up an integrated picture of the child. Through this eclectic approach it is then possible to avoid the dangers of overgeneralising from isolated test scores. This type of assessment process is rooted in the scientific-practitioner model of clinical psychology, where the clinician generates hypotheses about why certain behaviours are present and then systematically tests out these hypotheses by engaging in a multifaceted assessment process.

Interventions

In line with a broader approach to the psychological assessment of children with learning difficulties there has also been a move towards a more eclectic approach in interventions with this population. Clinicians work together with other professional groups with the aim of providing a needs-led intervention package for the child and their family. Most clinical psychologists are trained in the use of behavioural analysis and modification techniques appropriate for use with children who have learning difficulties and these methods tend to form the core of their therapeutic skills.

Behavioural techniques have also been adopted by many different professionals, and whilst it is encouraging to see the widespread use of psychological methods that can potentially be very powerful and effective intervention techniques, it is important to be mindful of the fact that all too often there is misuse of these techniques. Through the common usage of behavioural techniques in a 'cook book approach' many of the principles behind the techniques have been misunderstood, behavioural techniques have been misapplied and confidence in these techniques is sometimes irreparably damaged.

A thorough functional analysis should provide the clinician with data which will enable the identification of the appropriate strategies and methods for reshaping the behaviour of the child under investigation. As mentioned previously, children are most likely to be referred to clinical psychology services because there are concerns over the child's negative behaviour. Therapeutic interventions therefore usually involve the devising of specific strategies for decreasing unwanted behaviours and at the same time creating a parallel programme for increasing the rate of more desirable behaviour(s). Good clinical practice should always focus on both these components of intervention to ensure that the child is developing new skills whilst he or she is being helped to 'unlearn' maladaptive behaviours. This two-pronged approach is also to be encouraged to help those who will be working with the child within the programme to maintain a balanced approach in their day-to-day working with the child. For example, a programme that is solely concerned with decreasing unwanted behaviours can lead to a pattern of interaction between the child and parent or staff member that is ostensibly 'punitive' and unlikely to facilitate more positive ways of interacting.

Any intervention should be developed into a programme plan which may incorporate several behaviour modification techniques in unison, and the components of the programme may change over time as the targets for behavioural change are re-evaluated. A programme plan is essential to provide a means of monitoring progress and adjusting treatment goals based upon new data. It also provides a formalised system for communicating who does what, where, when and how. So often, interventions break down because of poor communication between those responsible for designing the programme and those executing it. If an intervention programme is going to be extremely labour intensive and emotionally demanding with the likelihood that the changes in the target behaviour are going to be very gradual, then it is essential that the person overseeing the programme builds in a system of rewarding staff so that the staff themselves can be helped to keep on task. Motivating staff or parents to deliver a programme can be equally as challenging as motivating the child to change his or her behaviour.

In certain instances, interventions focused on decreasing undesirable behaviours may need to take priority over programmes targeted at accelerating the development of other skills if the undesirable behaviours are seriously interfering with the child's learning of appropriate behaviours. For example, a child's tantrums could be happening with a frequency and intensity that makes it difficult to teach basic self-care skills. Deciding on what is an undesirable behaviour has to be carried out in the context of the child's whole behaviour repertoire, possible maintaining organic factors and the impact of the behaviour on other people in the environment (see Figure 2.2).

There are various techniques that have been found to be useful in decreasing unwanted behaviours. They can be classified as follows: 1) restructuring the environment; 2) extinction; 3) punishment; 4) reinforcement of other behaviours (DRO schedules) and reinforcement of low rates of behaviour (DRL schedules). Punishment techniques are not to be confused with 'negative reinforcement' strategies which are intended to strengthen behaviour. Examples of punishment techniques include time out, response cost, overcorrection, restraint and electric shock (see Murphy & Oliver (1987) for a full review of these techniques).

As mentioned previously, any attempts to get rid of unwanted behaviours should always be balanced by the use of other programmes to increase more desirable behaviours. These types of interventions can have very powerful effects when the desirable target behaviour is incompatible with the presenting undesirable behaviour. Sometimes the

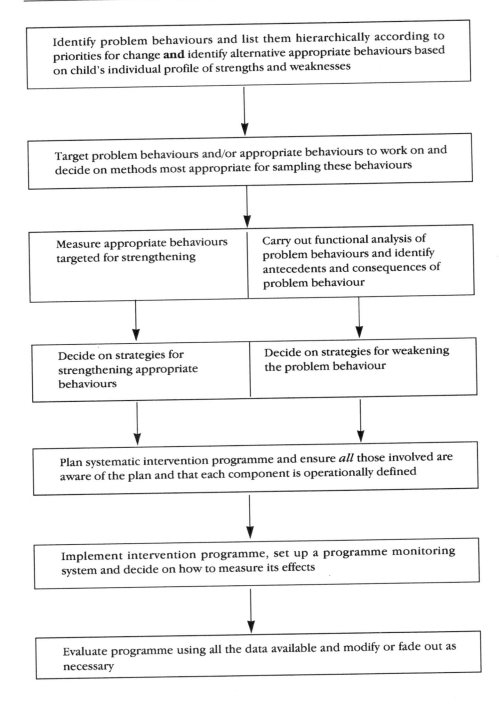

Figure 2.2 Stages of intervention

differential reinforcement of other behaviours incompatible with the undesirable behaviours can be used alone to reduce the frequency of undesirable behaviours if the undesirable behaviours are no longer being reinforced. For further reading on the management of challenging behaviours consult Presland (1989) and Harris and Handleman (1990).

Reinforcement is a behaviour-strengthening strategy. Its use in behaviour modification programmes needs careful consideration with respect to the types of potential reinforcers available and their suitability for a particular child. How will they be presented to ensure that they are contingent upon the target behaviour? What schedules of reinforcement are going to be appropriate, ie. is reinforcement going to be presented continuously or intermittently? Some children with learning difficulties receive little reinforcement in their everyday lives, and may have little expectation of success. In contrast, they may have well-founded expectations of failure or the probability of aversive consequences. By arranging and delivering reinforcers to strengthen appropriate behaviours in children with learning difficulties, the child's opportunities for learning, their social acceptability and enjoyment of life can be enhanced (Hemsley & Carr, 1987). For further reading on these and other related issues consult Yule and Carr (1987) and Carr (1995).

Interventions tackling the reduction of unwanted behaviours all too often neglect the possible communicative function of the presenting behaviour. Work by Edward Carr and colleagues has demonstrated that extreme forms of what appear to be maladaptive behaviours are sometimes emitted for the purposes of communicating basic needs in an individual who has a limited repertoire of communication skills (see Carr & Durand (1985); Carr, Levin, McConnachie, Carlson, Kemp & Smith (1994)).

Early intervention programmes

With the sophistication of techniques for the early identification of children who are developmentally at risk from organic impairments, came the expectation that appropriate stimulation early on in the child's development might help to ameliorate the handicapping effects of their condition and produce significant changes in a child's developmental course. The first early intervention programmes for children showing developmental delay, with associated biological impairment, evolved from the amelioration programmes developed for children who had experienced extreme social deprivation. The Head Start programmes of the 1960s offered teaching and stimulation to environmentally disadvantaged preschool children. Evaluation of the programmes demonstrated clear IQ gains in the first year of the programme: however, these gains in IQ were not maintained. Not surprisingly there was initial disappointment in these findings but the results from the Head Start programmes did seem to indicate that the parent–child relationship was important in the maintenance of the gains that were made. The model of a home-based tutoring programme then came to dominate approaches to early intervention with children who had developmental delay. Probably the most famous example of this kind of approach used today is the Portage programme.

The Portage programme was developed in rural Wisconsin in 1969 and was originally designed for socially disadvantaged children and children with mild learning difficulties. It is an example of a triadic model of service delivery. Portage workers are trained to act as behavioural engineers training parents to teach their own child. Portage workers are then supervised by a behaviour consultant (usually a psychologist). The parent works directly with the child and draws upon the system for guidance and ideas. The Portage model has been taken up uncritically by many intervention services for developmentally delayed children in this country but there has been little sound evaluation of its efficacy (Sturmey & Crisp, 1986).

Probably the greatest potential influence on early intervention practices today are the findings from the pioneering work by Cliff Cunningham and his colleagues. The famous early intervention project involving 181 Down syndrome children and their families in a longitudinal study measured a range of possible outcomes resulting from early intervention. The early intervention programme used in this study was aimed at preventing the typical deceleration of development seen in Down syndrome children. Matched controls were used in this study for a comparison with a group of children who received early intervention in the first two years of life. The children were later followed up between the ages of five and ten. The results indicated significant short-term benefits in the intervention group. However, no long-term effects were to be found on behavioural difficulties or measures of child development. There were, however, differences favouring the intervention group in terms of children's health. They were also more likely to have attended a mixed or mainstream preschool facility and to have had more hearing/sight difficulties reported by their mothers. From this study it was concluded that supportive intervention which started at birth and continued for two years had affected the mothers' attitudes to their child's disability and had made them more aware of potential services which they might call upon for help. This study also revealed that the mother's relationship with the child was significantly correlated with development scores and with the presence or absence of behaviour problems. This prospective study was very important in that it drew attention to the fact that the significant correlates or predictors of later development in these children were: social class, birth order, family size and parental education, which are the same as those found for non-handicapped populations. The overall programme elements seem to have had a limited and short concurrent influence on outcome measures defined in terms of developmental ages but have highlighted the need to consider more parent or family-centred early intervention programmes in the development of future services.

Counselling

The main aim in counselling is to produce constructive behavioural change and personality change. Such change emerges from a relationship of trust, a trust that emerges from confidential conversations between the professionally trained counsellor and the client (Herbert, 1988). This framework of therapeutic intervention has obvious applications in work with families of children with learning difficulties who are experiencing a crisis. Discovering that your child has developmental delay, and that this in turn is going to have a significant impact on his or her schooling and ability to function as an independent adult, is a devastating experience for most if not all parents of a disabled child. In the case of Down syndrome the identification of a disability may occur prior to the birth of the child or shortly afterwards. However, in the case of autism a diagnosis may not be agreed upon until the child is well on into the early school years or even later. Receiving a diagnosis at this stage in the child's development can evoke very mixed feelings of relief, on the one hand that the child's difficulties have been formally recognised, and on the other, immense anger towards professionals for not having identified the child's difficulties earlier. The parents then have to begin a process of grieving for the 'normal' child that they thought they had and make adjustments in their expectations and hopes for their child. Sometimes professional help may be sought when a family is struggling with these issues (Bicknell, 1983).

Individual psychotherapy

In 1980 psychologist and psychoanalyst Neville Symington founded a workshop on psychoanalytical psychotherapy and mental handicap after realising, through his work with a handicapped man, that emotional understanding and intelligence could be intact even where performance intelligence was badly damaged (Symington, 1981). Symington's ideas have since been developed by Valerie Sinason, a child psychotherapist, and Sinason claims that psychoanalytic treatment is proving as relevant a treatment for learning disabled children as it is for other children. Sinason works with children with all kinds of learning disability ranging from those who are mildly affected to those who are multiply and profoundly affected. The work by Sinason and her colleagues has shown that, whilst children with learning difficulties are unable to permanently change their level of functioning through therapy, there have been changes in the level of violent behaviour. The psychotherapy carried out has been essentially unmodified psychoanalytic psychotherapy and through her work with children Sinason identified a phenomenon that she refers to as 'opportunist handicap'. This is essentially the pernicious use of handicap to express hostility and envy. Sinason hypothesised that some children with learning difficulties engage in self-inflicted attack on their own capacities which enables them to remain in a disgruntled angry state in which they can claim there is nothing good in the world (Sinason, 1986; McConachie & Sinason, 1989).

Family therapy

In the assessment of children with learning difficulties it is important to consider the child in the context of the family and the community. The family process model looks at the child in relation to his or her family and how the relationships within the family affect the child's behaviour. Some behaviour problems located within the child might have their source in family behaviour patterns that are faulty or self-defeating (dysfunctional). Even when a child is suffering from mental impairments that clearly stem from organic damage it can be helpful to bring a systems perspective to the analysis of the presenting behaviour problem. A dysfunctional family can play an important role in the maintenance and possible exacerbation of behavioural problems. Alternatively, the family may have become dysfunctional as a result of having to cope with a child who is presenting with extremely challenging and difficult behaviour.

Some argue that the implementation of behaviour modification programmes necessitates a family perspective. Any analysis of antecedents and consequences must assume the potency of contextual (ie. familial) contingencies. The actual process of getting all the family members sitting down together for the purpose of analysing and defining the behaviour problem can often be very therapeutic in itself. Family members may discover that they have different perceptions of the presenting behaviour and consequently have very different ideas about how they should respond to the behaviour being shown by the child. Identifying and recognising these differences may in turn enable them to develop a more united front when tackling the problem behaviour in a crisis situation and could help strengthen their approach in their day-to-day management of it. This will mean that the resources available to the family are harnessed effectively and targeted more efficiently, and because the parents feel they are working together they consequently put more effort into the programme. Parent training as a vehicle for changing families is therefore considered by some to be a legitimate form of family therapy.

Summary

The practice of clinical psychologists working with children who have learning difficulties has been influenced by many different ideological and theoretical debates. This chapter has covered just some of the many different contributions from clinical psychology to the welfare of children with learning difficulties. Since the needs of children with learning difficulties are so varied and complex, clinical psychologists have tried to maintain an eclectic yet critical approach in their work. The current model of clinical psychology practice endorses a scientific-practitioner approach and clinical psychologists undergo a training that enables them to acquire skills in scientific analysis and research as well as skills in clinical assessment and intervention. This places them in a unique position of being able to contribute to the day-to-day care and education of children with learning difficulties and at the same time carry out scientific evaluation of the services that they and others provide.

References

American Association on Mental Deficiency (1974) Adaptive Behaviour Scale Manual. Washington DC: AAMD.

Anastasi A (1986) Psychological Testing. 6th edn. New York: Macmillan.

Bicknell J (1983) The psychopathology of handicap. British Journal of Medical Psychology 56(2): 167–78.

Carr J (1995) Helping Your Handicapped Child: A step-by-step guide to everyday problems. 2nd edn. London: Penguin.

Carr EG, Durand V (1985) The social-communicative basis of severe behaviour problems in children. In Reiss W, Bootzin RR (Eds) Theoretical Issues in Behaviour Therapy. New York: Academic Press. pp 219–54.

Carr EG, Levin L, McConnachie G, Carlson JI, Kemp DC, Smith CE (1994) Communication-based Intervention for Problem Behaviour: A user's guide for producing positive change. Baltimore: Paul H. Brookes.

Department of Education and Science (1978) Special Educational Needs (The Warnock Report). London: HMSO.

Dewart H, Summers S (1988) The Pragmatics Profile of Early Communication Skills. Windsor: NFER-Nelson.

Doll, E.A. (1965) Vineland Social Maturity Scale: Manual of Directions. Revised edn. Minneapolis: American Guidance Service.

Education Act (1981) London: HMSO.

Fraser WJ, Rao JM (1991) Recent studies of mentally handicapped young people's behaviour. Journal of Child Psychology and Psychiatry 32 (1): 79–108.

Happé FGE (1994) Wechsler IQ profile and theory of mind in autism: A research note. Journal of Child Psychology and Psychiatry 35(8): 1461–71.

Harris SL, Handleman JS (Eds) (1990) Aversive and Nonaversive Interventions: Controlling life-threatening behaviour by the developmentally disabled. New York: Springer.

Hemsley R, Carr J (1987) In Yule W, Carr J (eds) Behaviour Modification for People with Mental Handicaps. London: Croom Helm.

Herbert M (1988) Working with Children and their Families. Leicester: British Psychological Society.

Howlin P, Wing L, Gould J (1995) The recognition of autism in children with Down syndrome – implications for intervention and some speculations about pathology. Developmental Medicine and Child Neurology 37(5): 404–14.

Hynd GW (1988) Neuropsychological Assessment in Clinical Child Psychology. London: Sage.

Kiernan C, Reid B (1987) The Pre-verbal Communication Schedule. Windsor: NFER-Nelson.

Lord C, Rutter M, Le Couteur A (1994) Autism Diagnostic Interview–Revised: a revised version of a diagnostic interview for caregivers of individuals with possible pervasive developmental disorders. Journal of Autism and Developmental Disorders 24: 659–85.

Mackay D (1975) Clinical Psychology: Theory and therapy. London: Methuen. p 60.

McConachie HR, Sinason V (1989) The emotional experience of multiple handicap – issues in assessment. Child Care Health and Development 15(1): 75–8.

Murphy G, Oliver C (1987) Decreasing undesirable behaviours. In Yule W, Carr J (Eds) Behaviour Modification for People with Mental Handicaps. 2nd edn. London: Croom Helm. pp 102–42.

Nunn K (1986) The episodic dyscontrol symptom in childhood. Journal of Child Psychology and Psychiatry. 22: 439–46.

Oliver C, Head D (1990) Self-injurious behaviour in people with learning difficulties. International Review of Psychiatry II: 101–16.

Powers MD, Handleman JS (1984). Considerations for standard psychological assessment. In Powers MD, Handleman JS (Eds) Behavioural Assessment of Severe Developmental Disabilities. Tunbridge Wells: Aspen Systems Corporation.

Presland JL (1989) Overcoming Difficult Behaviour. A guide and sourcebook for helping people with severe mental handicaps. Kidderminster: BIMH.

Sinason V (1986) Secondary mental handicap and its relationship to trauma. Psychoanalytical Psychotherapy 2: 131–54.

Sturmey P, Crisp AG (1986) Portage guide to early education: a review of research. Educational Psychology 6: 139–57.

Symington N (1981) The psychotherapy of a subnormal patient. British Journal of Psychotherapy 54: 187–99.

Turk J, Sales J (1996) Behavioural phenotypes and their relevance to child mental health. Child Psychology and Psychiatry Review 1(1): 4–11.

Wing L (1988) The continuum of autistic characteristics. In Schopler E, Mesibov GB (Eds) Diagnosis and Assessment in Autism. New York: Plenum.

Wing L, Gould J (1978). Systematic recording of behaviours and skills of retarded and psychotic children. Journal of Autism and Childhood Schizophrenia 8: 79–97.

Wing L, Gould J (1979) Severe impairments of social interaction and associated abnormalities in children: epidemiology and classification. Journal of Autism and Developmental Disorders 9: 11–29.

Chapter 3

Observation of Play in the Early Assessment and Development of Children with Severe Learning Difficulties

DOROTHY JEFFREE

Overview

Many of the children in a class for those with severe learning difficulties will be developmentally immature, at a pre-formal stage of development and not yet ready for a formal curriculum. For these children, the stage of development they have reached needs to be assessed through structured observation. Appropriate games will then help to establish the foundations for later learning, ie. turn taking, imitation, joint attention, anticipatory sets and symbolic function. Once these are established, the games can be expanded to further language development, numeracy, literacy and social interaction.

Introduction

Some children with severe learning difficulties pose extra problems for their teachers. Their chronological age is no guide to their level of development, which is often very uneven; for instance, their language development may lag behind their motor coordination. Also, some children may be extremely apathetic and difficult to motivate while others are overactive and lacking in concentration. Vygotsky (1978) described the role of the teacher as being concerned with the *zone of proximal development*. This zone is a narrow band of abilities which a child has reached but has not yet mastered completely. For maximum learning to take place it is important to pinpoint this zone in each area of development. In this chapter some objective ways of doing this will be described which need not be very time consuming.

It is important to face the fact that some children may not have advanced beyond the infant stage of early development. Teachers and even parents are often unaware of the detailed stages of development ordinary babies pass through. This lack of detailed knowledge can lead to completely inappropriate handling of the situation. For this reason we have included information on normal child development from birth to two years in this chapter.

The leading questions for teachers, having accurately assessed the level their pupils have reached in each area of development, are where to go from there and how to enhance further learning. The developmental charts will suggest the content of development for those who still need to lay the foundations for later learning. The National Curriculum is inappropriate at this stage of early development. In this case the teacher's role is neither active nor passive but proactive. At this stage we probably need a re-evaluation of the play ethos (Smith, 1988) and a reconsideration of the Plowden Report which stated that play was 'the principle means of learning in early childhood'. Smilansky (1968) has described the effects of play tutoring by modelling, verbal instruction, thematic fantasy training, imaginative play training etc. The next section will describe how such playful intervention, together with appropriate playthings, can encourage early development and lay the foundations for the introduction to the subjects in the curriculum.

This will be followed by detailed descriptions of more specific intervention in the areas of language development, literacy, numeracy, social interaction and survival skills.

Early assessment of developmental levels

It is a truism that no one can run before they can walk. Similarly, in other areas of development, there is a logical order which each child goes through. Each of these hierarchical stages is built on the one before. The observational methods of assessment outlined in this chapter owe a great deal to Piaget's theories of intellectual development (Ginsburg & Opper, 1969). The period from birth to two years Piaget named the sensori-motor period and divided it into six substages. Uzgiris and Hunt (1975) have based a series of observational techniques on Piaget's theories. One of the easiest to administer and of the greatest practical relevance is the assessment of object permanence. Administration of this scale simply involves giving the child a series of objects one at a time for two or three minutes and noting what he or she does with them. For the very young it is a good thing to involve a parent and to sit the child on the parent's knee before handing out the objects. A maximum of ten objects should be used and those suggested below have been chosen to evoke a repertoire of different behaviours.

The materials are:

- a soft toy such as a cloth dog
- a few one or two-inch cube bricks with a container such as a beaker
- a baby's rattle
- a small sheet of silver foil
- a string of nursery beads long enough to go over the head
- a small toy car
- an attractive doll of reasonable size, with clothes that can be removed.
- a kelly doll or any kind of sound-based doll which returns to the vertical when knocked over and makes a sound
- a cup or a mug
- a piece of cotton wool.

Ideally every teacher of young children with learning difficulties should practise using this scale on several infants who are developing normally. The scale has also been found invaluable for speech and language therapists in training. As each object is presented to the child the observer will note what he or she does with it and credit the child on the form provided. The twelve developmental stages are described below and a form is included in which to enter the credits and total them up (see Table 3.1).

The stages of behaviour are as follows:

1 Holding (1-2 months): the child holds the object which has been put in his or her hand for about half a minute or more.
2 Mouthing (2 months): the child grasps the object and brings it to his or her mouth.
3 Inspection (3 months): the object is grasped and held motionless in front of the child who looks at it intently.
4 Hitting (4 months): the child hits the object with his or her hand or bangs it on a surface.
5 Shaking (5 months): the object is shaken or moved from side to side, usually by movement of the lower arm.
6 Examining (6 months): this is a more complex form of inspection. The object is held by the child and turned around in an exploratory fashion.
7 Complex or differentiated behaviour (7 months): the child may display a range of differentiated behaviour appropriately towards each object including tearing, stretching, rubbing and sliding, eg. tearing paper, stretching elastic, rubbing a teddy and sliding a toy car along the table. These complex behaviours (6 and 7) are in contrast to the simple manifestations of hitting and shaking which may be applied indiscriminately to all objects.

Table 3.1: Object schemes based on Uzgiris & Hunt (1975)

Child
Rater

D.o.b   D.o.t   C.A.

	Dog	Bricks	Rattle	Foil	Beads	Car	Doll	Kelly doll	Cup*	Cotton wool	Total objects
Hold											
Mouth											
Inspect											
Hit											
Shake											
Examine											
Complex											
Drop											
Throw											
Social											
Show											
Name											
Total schemes											

*If the child puts the bricks into a container (eg. a beaker) make a note of this. Alternatively, offer a spoon or brick with the cup (after the cup has been presented on its own). Do not verbally encourage the child until the child has had the opportunity to show the behaviour unprompted.

8   Dropping (8 months): this involves intentional dropping of objects, looking where they fall and waiting for someone to pick them up or listening to the sound of impact.

9   Throwing (9 months): this energetic movement involves the release of the object. The child will observe the trajectory of the objects he or she has thrown.

10 Socially instigated behaviours (10 months): these behaviours reflect social influences regarding the function of any particular object. They include building with bricks, pretending to drink out of a toy cup, 'driving' a toy car, trying to dress a doll or making it 'walk', or putting a string of beads over your head. This stage reflects the social milieu of the child and also indicates a degree of delayed imitation and a categorisation of objects which may facilitate the subsequent attachment of verbal labels to those objects or expressive language.

11 Showing (14 months): this complex social behaviour is shown when a child initiates interaction with another person by proffering a toy or other object to them. The intention seems to be to 'show' the object rather than to give it up. If the other person attempts to take the object it is often withdrawn.

12 Naming (18 months): this is a sign of object recognition, often using a childish name.

To get a true picture of the child's developmental status, he or she should not be given a model or verbally encouraged to carry out any of the actions. Simply note what the child does with each object and give one credit for each different action. For instance, a child may hold the toy dog, take it to his or her mouth and hit it against the table. This would be a total of three actions under 'dog'.

Proceed similarly with the other nine objects. When the test has been completed and the total number of schemes added up together with the number of objects used, the highest scheme the child has reached should be noted as well as the scheme which has received the most credits. This level would indicate the zone of abilities which the child has mastered. Abilities below this level will also be manifest as they are not lost. A few manifestations of abilities above this level will indicate what the child is starting to be able to do but has not fully mastered. Opportunities should be provided to encourage these emerging abilities.

Observations of the child during this procedure can be very valuable. The observer should note whether the child has a hand preference and which hand it is. It should also be noted whether the child has reached the stage of visually directed reaching (at three to four months normally). Even a young child has preferences and these may be quite strong. A child may systematically push one toy or object away while clinging on to another object and be unwilling to part with it. Teachers and others will know how to gear new experiences and new learning around the preferred toys.

Developmental charts

The observations we have described will provide a guide to the level of object awareness the child has reached and give an average developmental level for the child. You will have noted that the last item to be included is 'naming'. Although naming is the last item in the list all the other items have been building up to this language level. We can rightly say they are all precursors of expressive language. Although such observations are very informative they do not cover all aspects of child development, such as mobility, self-help in feeding and social and language development. To get a complete picture, all these aspects of development must be taken into account, especially where children with learning difficulties are concerned and whose development is often so uneven.

In the past many developmental charts were for professionals only and closed to all but psychologists with permits to use them. It is now realised that primary carers such as parents, guardians, teachers and classroom assistants need to be able to understand, assess and evaluate normal child development. Lansdown (1984) in his book *Child Development Made Easy* has included an overview of development by age in the appendix. He includes a warning to readers that there are wide individual differences between normal children and any such chart can only be a rough guide. When running workshops for parents of children with severe learning difficulties, it was realised that if parents filled in a simplified chart of their child's development it would be easier to advise them and it would also give them practice in observation of their child. A version of these charts has been published (*PIP. Developmental Charts*, Jeffree & McConkey 1976). The charts are divided into five sections of development: physical, social, eye–hand, play and language. Each section is further subdivided. One of the subsections under 'play' is Section 14: Imitative play, reproduced here (see Table 3.2).

These charts have been devised to save unnecessary time and if the child passes the boxed item there is no need to assess him or her on the other items below that level. You will also note that the average age in months at which a child displays a particular form of play is included in brackets against that item. These age norms are only rough estimates which may help when you are comparing one child with another or, perhaps more importantly, when comparing a child's performance in one area of development, say gross motor, with another area such as development of language. Any disparity should give pause for thought and raise

Table 3.2: Section 14: Imitative play

If YES, Go to section 15 - Make believe play	(30)	Imitates correctly a *sequence* of actions in housework, eg. brushes up dust in pan and empties it.		NO
	(24)	Imitates a *single* action in housework, eg. dusts the table.	YES	NO
	(18)	Briefly imitates kissing a doll, reading, etc.	YES	NO
	(12)	Imitates tapping a pencil.	YES	NO
	(10)	Waves bye-bye and plays pat-a-cake.	YES	NO
	(9)	Rings a bell purposefully in imitation.	YES	NO
	(7)	Imitates beating on table with hand.	YES	NO
	(5)	Imitates sticking tongue out.	YES	NO

further questions, eg. does the child have an additional handicap such as hearing loss or motor impairment?

Teachers may find difficulty in filling up some items – on self-help skills for instance. No opportunity should be missed to collaborate with parents or primary carers in the completion of the charts.

The symbolic function and the significance of symbolic play

As soon as a person wakes up they will become active. At breakfast they will probably discuss the programme for the day, possibly write a list of items to be remembered, read the paper and look at the clock to tell the time. The ability to carry out these activities may seem 'child's play' to the normal adult. We forget that all these activities depend on symbolic function. When we let something present stand for something which is not present this is symbolic. For instance, a sequence of sounds making 'BUS', spoken in the present, stands for the vehicle which is not present but which we hope to catch later. Similarly, marks on a piece of paper (eg. 'BUS') can also stand for something not present. When we draw a map to show someone how to get to work this is also symbolic.

A child is not born with this symbolic ability but it usually develops in the first 18 months or two years. As its development is an important

prerequisite to so much further development and learning, it is important to be able to observe and record the child's present ability. By
watching a child at play we can see the gradual development of symbolic
or 'pretend' play. A child who kisses a doll in play, or puts it to bed in a
box, is demonstrating an early stage of symbolic activity. S/he is using the
doll (which is a piece of material stuffed) to represent or be the symbol
of a real live baby. Children vary a great deal in this ability to be imaginative; some may need a lot of props and others can create a rich story or
situation with very little. Children with autistic features find it difficulty
to 'pretend' but take everything literally. If told it is raining cats and dogs
they may look in vain for the animals coming down from the sky.

As symbolic ability is a prerequisite to most of the subjects on the
National Curriculum it is important to measure its emergence. In the last
twenty years there has been a growing interest in the measurement of
the level of symbolic play in infants; for instance, a test of symbolic play
has been devised and standardised by Lowe and Costello (1976). In this
chapter a simple observational test of the level of symbolic play will be
described which was developed by McConkey and Jeffree (1979). In this,
a standard set of toys is prepared and the child is invited to take them
out of the box and play with them. It is best to have toys which are not
too familiar in order to gain the child's interest. The following collection
has proved effective:

- doll with clothes that take off and with jeans and short hair so that
  it could represent a boy or a girl
- doll's bed to scale with bedclothes
- table and a chair
- toy cup and saucer
- plate and knife
- fork and spoon.

To give scope for the child's own imagination, the best kind of doll is a
stuffed doll with minimum features who could be thought of as any character.

For this observation schedule, play has been classified into five stages:

1   *Exploratory play* in which the child plays with one toy at a time
    and mouths, shakes, examines, throws, feels, rubs or drops it
    deliberately.
2   *Relational play* in which the child relates two objects together,
    either by banging them together or putting one object in, on, or
    under another, or relates them by usage (eg. putting a spoon in a
    cup, a pillow on bed, etc).
3   *Self-pretending* in which the child relates objects to him or herself

and feeds self with toy spoon or cup, combs hair, tries to sleep on doll's bed or sit on doll's chair.

4   *Simple pretending* in which the child uses the doll and relates it to another object (eg. pretends to feed the doll with spoon or cup, combs doll's hair, washes doll, lays doll down on bed, sits doll on chair or sits the doll alone, will kiss the doll or make it walk, dance or jump etc).

5   *Sequence pretending* in which the child may repeat an action with different subjects (eg. feed doll from cup and then feed self, adult, teddy or other child). Similarly, he or she may pretend to comb the doll's hair and then his or her own hair. Another example is the sleep sequence – pillow on bed; doll on bed with head on pillow; cover doll with sheet (a sequence of three actions).

In Table 3.3 (below) there is a checklist which can be completed for each child.

Table 3.3: Pretend play checklist (McConkey & Jeffree)

Child's name	Age	D.o.b		
Length of session	Date	Observer		
Comments				
Stage	**Tick each new action**		**Total**	**%**
1 Exploratory play				
2 Relational play				
3 Self-pretending				
4 Simple pretending				
5 Sequence pretending	No. of actions in sequence			
(1) same action				
(2) same theme				
• imaginary object				
	Total overall			

*Actions with imaginary objects are ticked but not included in the total as they will usually occur in a sequence.

McConkey R, Jeffree DM (1979) First steps in learning to pretend. Special Education: Forward Trends 6(4): 13–17.

A ten minute session is usually sufficient for each child so long as they are relaxed and enjoying it.

When the playlist has been completed it is important to add up the items for each stage and then turn them into a percentage, and it is also important to note the highest stage a child has reached.

A developmental profile

From the information gathered from the observational assessments (Uzgiris, McConkey, PIP Charts) on each child, individual profiles can be recorded (see Table 3.4). These profiles highlight strengths and weaknesses and give an indication of where to start with each individual child. In the following section, suggestions will be made for interactive play, games and toys which can further the progress of the child whose development is on or below the 18 month level and has not yet reached the stage where formal education would be appropriate.

Marking a start

Some of the children, though chronically older, may be at an immature stage of intellectual development. The first 'toy' for these children will be their own fingers and toes. They may begin to repeat their own arbitrary movements and sounds playfully and intentionally. This can be encouraged with mobiles arranged strategically so that they respond to the child's gestures. However, the most important plaything at this stage is the mother or caretaker who plays with the child. Peek-a-boo and other traditional baby games might have to be continued for a long period for the child with severe learning difficulties. In such games, the foundations are laid for turn-taking, imitation, joint attention and anticipatory sets (Milosky, 1990) before any toys are introduced. Sometimes early 'asking' behaviour occurs when a child is enjoying being 'bounced' on someone's knee and suddenly the 'bouncing' stops. A child may ask to be picked up by raising his or her arms in anticipation.

At first, little children hardly need any 'bought' toys at all. Boxes, saucepans, wooden spoons and buckets are not only fascinating but can have educative value as shown. For instance, hiding games using an object and a duster or cardboard box are not only helping concentration and joint attention but are also consolidating the idea of object permanence. Before this idea is consolidated, any toy which is out of sight is also out of mind. As soon as a child begins to relate one object to another, for instance, putting a toy spoon into a toy cup, then he or she will enjoy having a box to put toys into and to take them out again. This activity can be repeated in sand and water play. A child at this stage also likes to pile toys on top of one another. At first, they will only be able to make a pile of one or two toys; small boxes can be used to make a pile.

Table 3.4: Developmental profile chart

CA	Feeding	Cognitive	Social	Imitation	Imagination	Books	Gesture	Speech	Comprehension	Phonology
60m	–	–	Play with rules	–	Sequential role play	Recognises phrases in story books		Uses correct grammatical sentences	Can follow 2 part instruction	
48m	–	–	Simple cooperative play	–	Role play – postman etc.	Joins in repetitive lines in story	–	Uses telegraphese. Asks questions	Can fetch 3 objects from another room	Consolidation of consonant clusters 'cr', 'pl', 'st', 'scr', etc.
36m	–	–	Joins in play with one person, kicks ball etc.	Imitates action sequence	Sequential doll play	Enjoys being told stories from picture books	–	Uses 3-word sentences and plurals	Follows directions with prepositions 'in' and 'on'	
24m	–	–	Shares toys with others	Imitates mum sweeping	Puts doll to bed etc.	Can identify 7 pictures and photos of family	Will pull person to show toys etc.	Uses 2-word sentences		Consolidation, begins to use 'h', 'f', 'v', 's', 'z', 'sh', 'w', 'y', 'l', 'th', 'ch', 'j', 'r'
18m		Searches for lost toy, etc.	–	–	Pretends to feed self	Recognises a few pictures	–	Jargon and many single words	Responds to 'Give me the ball' if ball is in sight	

Table 3.4: (cont)

CA	Feeding	Cognitive	Social	Imitation	Imagination	Books	Gesture	Speech	Comprehension	Phonology
15m		Picks up small objects	Rolls ball to adult	–	Hugs doll, kisses teddy	–	Points to objects	4–5 single words	Points to familiar person when named	
12m	Feeds self with fingers	Finds toy hidden in box	Cooperates in pat-a-cake etc.	Waves bye–bye	Pushes toy car along	–	Shakes head for 'No'	Babble and 1 or 2 words	Responds to words eg. 'Where's Daddy?'	Words using consonants 'b', 'p', 't', 'd', 'm', 'n', 'k', 'g' and open vowels
9m	Chews biscuit	Looks for dropped toy	Peek-a–boo	Rings bell in imitation	Plays with two toys, brick in box etc.	–	–	Tuneful repeated babble	Responds to own name	
6m	Soft food	Looks for toy rolled just out of sight	Enjoys being lifted and swung etc.	–	Treats all toys, bangs, shakes, etc.	–	Puts up arms to be lifted	Coos to self	Turns to mother's voice	
3m	Liquid food	Shows interest in toes	Smiles at mother	–	–	–	–	Throaty noises	Turns to sound	Consonants and vowels, 'bababa', 'nanana'

As the child becomes more adept, bricks can be used. Soft bricks can also be piled one upon the other, and if a string is sewn to the bottom brick a slight pull will bring them all tumbling down. The child is now ready to benefit by being given a simple box and objects which can be dropped into it through a hole. This could be a medium sized cardboard box with a hole cut in the bottom. The dramatic participation of an adult will encourage anticipation of the moment when the box is suddenly lifted and behold – the hidden object reappears! Now is the time to think of providing a stock of versatile toys which will last the child for many months or even years. Here are some suggestions of versatile toys to buy.

Versatile toys

We are fully aware that teachers nowadays are inundated with catalogues of educational toys and programmes which may be a source of help and ideas. However, the teacher needs to be extremely discriminating. Obviously the budget will not stretch to cover all our needs and some apparatus is too specific, with its use limited to a single activity once the child has mastered that skill. Similarly, in toy shops and specialist shops such as Early Learning, one of our criteria must be the flexibility of the toy or apparatus. How soon does the child outgrow it? There are a few toys that can be used in so many different ways that they are never completely outgrown. The ball is a very good example. Babies play with balls but so do elderly men on the golf course. You will also find that the age range for which toys are suitable is often printed on the box. This should be used as a very rough guide only, especially when you are teaching children with learning difficulties. I cannot resist a cautionary tale here. I was on the train and two little boys were given boxed motor cars with which they were, at first, delighted. Then the older one let out a sad cry and said, 'It says on the box that this car is for children from 2 to 4. I shall be four in a week's time and won't be able to play with it any more'.

Posting boxes

Several different types of posting box are available commercially and some of these will be listed where appropriate, but in practice it has been found that the function of some of these educational toys is too specific, eg. posting boxes with geometrically shaped slots in the lid for posting triangular, square and circular bricks which are provided. These posting boxes are fine, but their use is very limited. The orientation of these bricks is quite skilful and it is frustrating for the child who has not mastered this skill; once the skill has been mastered there is nothing more of interest to do. This specific posting box has no built in incentive and the child may soon become bored. Of course, the names of the pieces can also be introduced and the child asked to post the triangle from a display of all the shapes, or name the shape he or she has just posted.

As an alternative, a simple box of cardboard or wood can be upturned and a hole of about two inches in diameter cut in the bottom. The version illustrated was custom made and proved its worth (see Figure 3.1). If at any time a smaller hole is required then a new top can be stuck over the original one. A collection of miniature common objects should be collected for use with this box. The popularity of this box is not so much inbuilt, but depends upon the enthusiasm and imagination of the adult, who may keep a child in suspense after an object has been posted by wondering where it has gone and then suddenly lifting the box off the floor to reveal the contents.

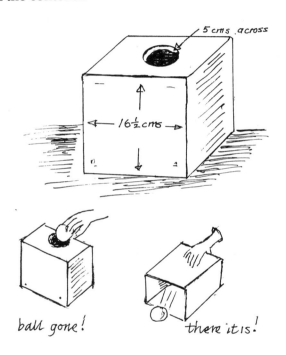

Figure 3.1: Simple posting box

Another type of posting box that is not as yet available commercially but can easily be made at very little cost is shown in Figure 3.2. It has inbuilt reinforcement, for when the pullout shelf is pulled back by the adult the posted object will suddenly appear. A panel above the posting hole is for slotting in pictures or words should you want to encourage the child to match these with the objects to be posted. As before, you could make a collection of miniatures of common objects which will fit through the hole and keep them with the box for use with many of the suggested games.

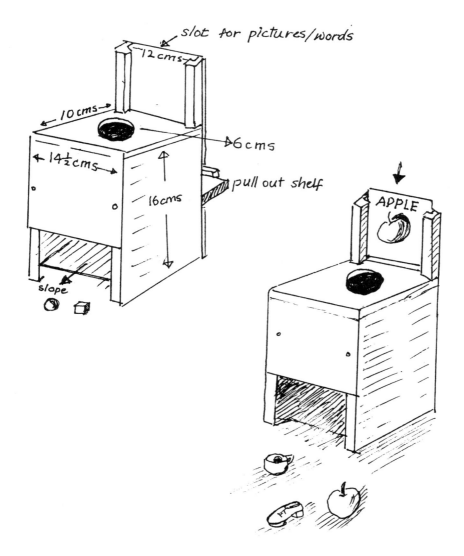

Figure 3.2: Second posting box

One-armed bandit

This posting box is now commercially available from Toys for the Handicapped. Although the initial outlay may seem rather high, the box is well worth it as it is extremely versatile. The handle, which is like a fairground one-armed bandit, can be manipulated by the children by themselves so that the contents of the box come sliding out. This toy has proved popular with a wide range of ages. It is also very sturdy and lends itself to floor play and can be used by the player with additional physical handicaps. It can be used with somewhat larger objects than the other boxes and more objects can be posted before being retrieved. This makes it ideal for memory or classification games.

Posting games and learning

Posting boxes are extremely versatile and also very motivating. They are useful initially to increase the attention span of children who are hyperactive or find concentration difficult. They can be allowed to play with the one-armed bandit on their own sometimes, to get them used to posting objects and seeing them reappear in a dramatic fashion. Children with very different levels of ability can play together with the bandit and so learn to wait and to take turns. Joint focus of attention will probably also occur in the initial free play sessions. Posting objects, especially in the first box described, and then seeing them reappear almost immediately, will help the child who has not as yet attained object permanence. Earlier in this chapter we mentioned the early development of relational play when a child learns to cope with more than one object at a time and relate them together by stacking things and putting one object into or under or over another: the posting boxes are excellent for encouraging and developing such relational play.

A few suggestions follow to indicate how the adult can add to the dimensions of the game and facilitate further learning. The adult should have a bag or box of well selected objects for different levels of development and will find that creative use of these comes with practice.

Searching

Once a child has sufficient concentration span to amuse him or herself by picking up objects and posting them, the adult can encourage searching by placing some objects further away from the box or even partially hidden under a cloth for the child to find.

Two years and over

A child who is at the developmental level of a two to four year old will be ready for more specific games which lead on to formal learning. Some will be described in this section.

Early comprehension, naming, imitation and putting two words together

Start with a very few common objects and one of the posting boxes. Take turns with the child in posting the objects but do not worry if he or she is sometimes out of turn. When it is your turn, add a little drama and suspense to simple posting; hold the object above the hole for a little while and suddenly release it with the word 'gone'. At first the child may start to imitate your rather exaggerated action, but if you continue the ritual he or she may start to imitate 'gone!' as well. Even if he or she does not say anything, he or she will be starting to connect language and speech to the situation. Similarly, when the object reappears you could greet it with a dramatic 'There it is!'. Soon you will be ready to name objects you have been posting, eg. ball, cup, car. As the child picks one up to post, you should name it at first, and later see if the child can pick the right object when it is named before anything is picked up. You can gradually increase the number of objects you use until the child can identify five or six and is attempting to name them him or herself. Next you can begin to model putting two words together and demonstrate dramatically as before, with 'Ball...gone!' as it disappears. How soon the child will be copying you in two-word utterances will vary, but it is no use trying to go too fast.

Classification

A child whose vocabulary has increased so that he or she is able to identify and name a great many single objects and actions may be ready for a classification exercise. Again, only a few objects should be present to begin with, spread around the box, eg. chair, ball, brush. The child now has to find the 'one we sit on', or the 'one we throw' or the 'one we brush with' – and so on.

To encourage further classification, carefully select some more toys and objects, eg. chair, table, spoon, fork, toy duck, cat, dog, sheep, and lay them out at random around the posting box. This time the instruction should be 'post furniture' or 'post an animal'.

Colours

Coloured balls, beads or bricks can then be substituted for the toys and the child asked to post the blue one, etc. This can then be made more difficult by having bricks, balls and beads available and asking the child to post the yellow ball, for instance, or the red brick.

Memory

Once children are able to name the objects they have posted in the box they can play the memory game which is a version of Kim's Game. Remember that with all these games it is important to start off with very few objects (three at the most) and gradually build up the number used: this ensures success at the outset. To play the game the child is asked to post a number of objects in the box. He or she is then asked to name the objects in the box. This game is self-checking as the child can then pull the lever or the slide and see how many he or she got right. Some children will work up to a good score with this game. Two children may enjoy playing the game together. They do not need to be at the same level of achievement: one could be given extra points at the start of the game. You could keep a record for each child of the number of items remembered.

Early numeracy

Before they start school many children show evidence of numerical ability so long as only small numbers are involved. They will be able to count out a small number of items, eg. three bricks, and the games that follow will demonstrate that many children will also understand taking an item away or adding another item (addition and subtraction). However, as Hughes (1983) has demonstrated, although a child can tell you that one brick and another brick is two bricks, he or she will not be able to tell you that one and one make two. It is very important to remember that any introduction to numeracy must be with actual objects or people.

A simple posting box like the first one described above can be used to extend this ability to add and subtract. For numerical work it is best if all the items to be posted are the same kind, eg. all bricks or all balls. The adult starts the game by posting a few bricks, eg. three, in the box, and the child counts them as they go in. The adult then checks that the child can say how many bricks are in the box, and then lets the child see that one more is being posted and asks him or her to guess how many bricks are in the box now. Plenty of practice at this level is invaluable, then gradually the number of bricks in the box can be increased.

Simple subtraction games can also be played. A few bricks are posted in the box and then the adult checks that the child knows how many are in the box before taking one or two out, showing them to the child and asking him or her to guess how many are left in the box. The child then checks to see whether he or she got the answer right. Gradually the number of objects in the box can be increased and, even more gradually, increase the number of items subtracted. It is illuminating to see how children record numbers of objects spontaneously.

Hughes (1983) played another game with under-fours. He had four tins and the children watched while he put three objects in one tin, two in the next and one in the next. One of the tins he left empty. The tins were then shuffled and the children had to guess which tin had three bricks in, which two, etc. The children quite enjoyed this game although it was a matter of chance if they got any right. Once they had grasped the idea of the game, Hughes gave them an opportunity to help themselves by sticking a label on each lid, giving each child a pencil so that they could indicate how many were in each tin. The way in which they labelled the tins fell into distinct categories. These were idiosyncratic, pictographic, iconic and symbolic. The idiosyncratic response was a variety of scribbles which, while perhaps meaningful to the child at the time, did not aid in the recognition of the correct tin later on. The pictographic representations consisted of attempts to draw the bricks or even to draw around them, and the child who had used this mode was able to identify the tins correctly in the guessing game. In the iconic mode, the children used tallies to indicate the number of bricks in the tins (strokes, or circles, etc). In the symbolic mode the children either used numerals, 1, 2, 3, or spelled out the numbers, one, two, three. The only mode which was unsuccessful was the idiosyncratic mode. By interacting with the children in this way, Hughes was able to pitch any further instruction at the right level of difficulty.

Jeffree (1993) has suggested more games that can be played to help numerical ability. At this stage some of the children are only able to add and subtract numbers of actual objects in context, but school arithmetic demands an abstract understanding and also the use of the symbols plus + and minus –. Magnetic numerals are usually available at shops like Early Learning as well as plus and minus signs, and equals signs. These magnetic numerals, which can be handled and arranged and played with, provide a bridge to the abstract way in which numeracy is treated at school. Children can also be asked to use the numerals in the tins game. One of the problems may be in the understanding of the numeral nought (0).

Hughes has demonstrated how much you can learn of the child's ability by allowing him or her to sort the numerals out as he or she thinks best. At one point Hughes laid out the numerals in order, 1, 2, 3, 4, 5, 6, 7, 8, 9; he then covered up the first three numerals and asked the child how many were under his hand.

Matching and pre-reading

A posting game can be played to improve a child's ability to match objects. An object is held up and the child has to find one the same and post it (but make sure you have two of each object). Once the child is able to play this game, make it a little harder by using a picture of the object that you wish the child to post in the box. The second posting box described above has a slot in which you can put the pictures for this game. Later on you could print the word on the back of some of the picture cards and see if the child can recognise the printed word and post the correct object. If he or she does not recognise the word let him or her turn the card over and look at the picture, then turn it back to the word side. Gradually introduce a few more sight words in this way.

Joint attention

It is often difficult to get the attention of young people with learning difficulties. Direct confrontation may have a bad effect and it has been found that they are most likely to join in if they are ignored and the adult busies himself or herself with some intriguing occupation.

The child will then probably start watching and gradually joining in when he or she is ready. The child can learn a great deal from these sessions if they are properly planned. Two examples will be given here but the same principles can be used for many other activities such as painting or brass rubbing.

Paper houses

Houses are usually a source of interest to most people young and old. These paper houses can be made with the minimum of equipment and will give instant satisfaction (see Figure 3.3). One of the most important lessons to be learnt with this activity is joint attention. It can also lead to skilful use of paper, scissors, paste and colouring materials. The houses are a source of discussion, imagination and choice, so that any language introduced can be both appropriate to the child's level and also to the subject discussed.

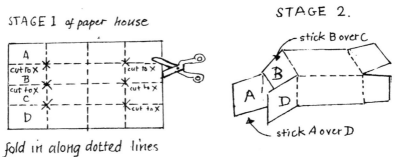

Figure 3.3: Making a folded paper house

Materials needed are:

- rectangles of paper (ten by eight inches is a good size)
- pairs of safe scissors with rounded ends
- adhesive such as Pritt stick
- paints, brushes and water for decoration
- if a village is being contemplated, extra materials such as pieces of loofah could be collected to make trees, etc.

To make the houses

1 Fold the paper crisply in half lengthwise and then fold sides to middle (see Figure 3.3).
2 Flatten out and then fold the paper in half widthwise and fold sides to middle.
3 Flatten paper again and cut as shown in the figure.
4 Stick flap B over flap C to form the gable and stick Flap A over flap D for the end wall. Form gable and wall at the other end of the house in the same way. Colour the house or add doors and windows as you think fit.

Cork animals

With a collection of corks of all sizes, stiff card, wooden skewers, adhesive and wool the children will be able to make a variety of animals, both farm animals and wild animals, etc.(see Figure 3.4).

Figure 3.4: A cork horse

Learning through joint activity

In these activities the adult will be modelling many different actions and fairly sophisticated imitation will arise from the child. As the adult demonstrates the moves he or she can, quite naturally, keep up a running commentary on what they are doing or are about to do or have done. Such joint reference is an aid to comprehension and later to production of language. Such sessions could also have a more specific objective as the following examples show:

- practising and extending the use of colour names (as decisions have to be made when painting the walls, roofs, doors, etc.).
- practising and extending the use of adjectives by making comparisons, eg. town house, small house, country house, wooden doors, glass windows or bigger windows, smarter, roomier, etc.
- counting the number of houses in a row or the legs of the animals, etc.
- referring to the past, present and future in planning sessions.
- narrative and story telling about the people who live in the houses or own the animals can also be added as the model making proceeds.

Symbolic functions

The necessary foundation for human learning is the strength of our symbolic function. It is a measure of abstraction that we can let something in the present – a sound or gesture or mark on paper – stand for something else which may not be present. For instance, in language a string of phonemes such as C-A-T stands for an actual animal which may not be present; In arithmetic a series of symbols can stand for real objects, eg. 5 for the fingers on one hand. In the written word we are even further removed from the concrete reality, a series of marks on the paper stands for a word or sentence and this again stands for language which indicates actual objects and events. Similarly, the symbolic function is the essence of all branches of learning such as algebra, physics, etc. Small children live in the present and their understanding of their world depends largely on being able to manipulate it and to see, hear, smell, taste and touch it directly. It is important to recognise this so that we do not introduce tasks which depend upon this symbolic function before it has fully developed. One of the signs of the developing symbolic function is the emergence of imaginative or pretend play where one object, such as a teddy, is treated as if it were a real person who can be fed, bathed and taken for a walk. This kind of play normally develops alongside the development of language at around eighteen months or two years and some people consider that it may be a necessary precursor to language acquisition.

It is important to encourage pretend play and imagination with children with learning difficulties who may be slow to develop this type of play. Some of them may even be discouraged if they are older children as some adults may think that such play is no longer appropriate. Children with autistic tendencies are particularly lacking in this respect and are inclined to take things literally. Children who have not yet begun to pretend may indeed have a limited repertoire of language, but this has usually been learned parrot fashion, eg. bye-bye, mummy. They are unlikely to use language creatively to express their own individual wishes or ideas, eg. ball gone, milk gone, teddy mine. Some children with autistic tendencies are deceptive in this respect and may have phenomenal auditory memory and are able to reproduce longish sentences and social greetings such as 'How are you, it's very nice to see you'. These remarks may be appropriately timed and appear to be original. However, those who are with the young people for any length of time will realise that they are constantly repeated and come about through delayed imitation.

You are probably wondering whether imagination can be taught, and the answer is probably not. However, if after administering the observation tests on play and finding that the child is just at the stage of relational play and is using toy cups and spoons appropriately and pretending to drink or feed him or herself with them, then you can encourage more elaborate pretend play in two or three ways. Firstly, you can provide toys which lend themselves to pretend play such as the doll's furniture, dolls and teddy bears described in the test. Secondly, you can encourage and model pretend play by joining in and sitting the doll down, feeding it, giving it a bath or whatever seems appropriate to the particular child. Thirdly you can provide time and space in which the child can pretend. For older children the pretending can take the form of acting out with glove puppets. Paper hats and other props can be provided for role play and a screen in the corner of the room makes a simple house corner or play shop, etc.

Sources of pretend and dramatic play and socio-dramatic play

One of the favourite pretend games for most children is playing mothers and fathers. At one time they found a rich source for their imagination in the adult activities around the home. They were in the midst of cooking, cleaning, washing and hanging out to dry, sewing and knitting, gardening and carpentry, at least as spectators. In many households much of this has changed. Many of the chores are done by machine and all that is to be seen is buttons being pressed. Not only this, but many children spend much of their waking hours in playschool, nurseries or in school. Here they do not see adults engaged in household tasks and so they have few models on which to base their pretend or dramatic play. Often the activities which do take place in the house are potentially dangerous for children who must therefore be kept 'out of the way'. They may be being occupied in passively watching television.

Further play with a purpose (The next stage from 3-5 years)

Numeracy

On visiting a special school the author was fascinated by one pupil who was bent over a pencil and paper task; she was doing addition and subtraction sums and getting them correct. Being a child with some autistic features who loved repetition, she was happy to continue her occupation until home time. However commendable this activity may have been in its own right, it was doing little to promote real numeracy as the child in question was unable to tell the teacher the total number of pens in a pile of four and a pile of six. A child with true mathematical ability *must* be active. At first this activity will be concerned with real objects which can be felt and held, assembled and reassembled. Then a link must be made between these activities, which are concrete, and abstract numerical ability. The child needs to be able to move freely from the concrete to the abstract, eg. one apple, one pear and a bunch of grapes related to the sum of $5 + 6 + 8 = 19$ pence.

Hughes (1986) has thrown much light on this problem. Many games and activities can give the child this practical numerical ability. For instance, dartboards made with safe darts are available for children of different ages and with them totals can be computed. Board games were once popular in the home and were played by adults with their children. As most of them are games of chance then the child has a equal opportunity of winning. However, even a simple game such as snakes and ladders is too complex for many of children with learning difficulties; it also takes too long to finish and so gets boring, especially for children with a short attention span. Several authors have suggested starting with a very simple race game with board and dice (Hughes, 1986; Jeffree, 1989; Moyles, 1994). These can consist of a piece of stiff card divided into a grid of four by eight squares. Four players can then play a simple race game with a dice and counters. Another problem encountered may be the conventional small dice but this can be overcome easily if small square bricks are used with low numbers represented by stick-on dots on each face, eg. just one, two and three spots to start with.

If a child has difficulty with simple numerical puzzles using actual objects, he or she may need further practice in matching, naming, sorting and classifying which all underlie mathematical concepts. Griffiths (1958), Liebeck (1984) and Graham (1985) all suggest games to play to help your child at this stage. The posting boxes mentioned earlier can all be used for matching, naming, sorting and classifying. For instance, an adult can hold up a red counter and ask the child to post one of the same; or he or she could pick out an animal from a mixed collection of objects and then ask the child to pick out and post another animal. The child could be asked to post three objects in the box and then be asked how many had gone in, checking them when they were revealed again.

The concept of more or less is also gained through practical experience and is often helped through the matching of dissimilar objects, which nevertheless belong together through use, eg. egg cups and eggs, cups and saucers, milk bottles and pupils. To start with, the objects will need to be laid out together and matched with one another, but later the child can guess whether there are enough egg cups for the number of eggs they have counted, or enough bottles of milk for the pupils in the class. Many activities include this kind of matching and one-to-one correspondence; another example is making a necklace of two different coloured beads.

With older pupils you may have young people who can count up to a hundred and correctly fill in the right numbers in addition and subtraction 'sums', yet are unable to use any numerical skill in solving day-to-day problems such as putting out the right number of milk bottles, deciding how to share out a cake or some sweets, or buying the right number of buttons for a jacket. There are probably two major reasons for this kind of difficulty. One is what Hughes calls 'translation'. There is no point in being able to calculate sums on paper if you cannot translate this ability to dealing with concrete examples. On the other hand, as well as dealing with concrete instances, you need to know how these can be recorded on paper for future reference. The second difficulty with many pupils is that they cannot see the point of school arithmetic; it is something they do to please the teacher, or even enjoy in its own right; but it has no real point as far as they are concerned. As well as having no point, there is also no element of personal choice. A sum when concluded is either right or wrong; if it is usually right you may get some satisfaction from the exercise, but if it is usually wrong, you may form a mental block which prevents further progress. It is obvious that playing games with the pupils can introduce an element of choice and also of purpose. Many teachers are rather conventional in their introduction to sums and choose the easier way out, giving out pre-printed or written examples. Even here choice can be introduced and instead of giving pupils a series of 'sums' such as $5 + 5 = ?$, $7 + 3 = ?$, you could give them a collection of 10 tokens and see how many sums they could record in their book using these tokens.

Social interaction through games

Much of what we learn in later life is learnt from other people, through cooperation with another person or with a group. A small baby is not a cooperative individual but seems at first mainly aware of himself or herself, his or her own body and perhaps a caretaker who gives him or her sustenance and reassurance. This is also mirrored in play which begins by being solitary, even when other children are present. Later there will be parallel play in which children play side by side and may even be influenced in their choice of toys by a playfellow, but it will be quite a time before they are able to play cooperatively.

Temperamentally some people tend to be comparatively solitary and learn by handling and constructing solutions to the situation and by thinking about what they are doing. This attitude should be respected, but there are some pupils with learning difficulties who find any sort of social contact very difficult. Children with autistic tendencies are an extreme example of this. Partly due to their early upbringing, many children with learning difficulties do not mix with their peers as much as normal children. The situation worsens the longer it goes on but we have found that when parents are aware of the importance of acceptance by the peer group and make sure their children can play out with others and attend clubs or classes, they find a great difference in the social development of their children.

Of course, just putting young people together is not enough. Activities should be provided which require cooperation. For instance, at a young level, games with balls to be rolled or thrown to a partner are useful. Imaginative games, such as playing with a tea-set, have been found to encourage cooperation. A child who pours an imaginary cup of tea naturally looks for someone to drink it. In the playground see-saws require cooperation as well as skipping with two people turning the rope. Parents in particular should be aware of the effect of modern trends in the home and whether they are encouraging social skills or not. Television is in many ways a boon for young people who have learning difficulties, but if watched to excess it leaves little time for social interaction. Normal children usually find their own friends and do things with them, but children with learning difficulties often need positive extra help. A short time in the day could be given to family activities such as table games. These could be very simple at first, eg, picture dominoes, or elementary race games played with the simple dice described earlier. Games such as hunt the thimble can also be graded with the thimble being 'hidden' in a very obvious place at first. 'I spy' can be played at first with short descriptions used instead of initial letters, eg. 'I spy with my little eye something you put on your head'.

We all know parents and teachers who have a flair for pretending with children and bringing humour into the situation, and others who are very seriously concerned with the curriculum and prefer the children not to spend time 'playing about' when they could be 'doing some work'. Probably we have to strike the happy mean; the teachers who can get absorbed in the game must also be aware of its purpose. Those who are over serious will have to convince themselves that their pupils do develop mathematical, literacy and scientific concepts when the play has been well chosen and planned.

References

Ginsburg H, Opper S (1969) Piaget's Theory of Intellectual Development. London: Prentice-Hall.

Graham AT (1985) Help your Child with Maths. London: Fontana.

Griffiths R (1994) Mathematics and play. In Moyles JR (Ed) The Excellence of Play. Buckingham: Open University Press.

Hughes M (1983) What is difficult about learning arithmetic? In Donaldson M (Ed) Early Child Development and Education. Oxford: Basil Blackwell.

Hughes M (1986) Children and Numbers. Oxford: Basil Blackwell.

Jeffree DM (1980) Let Me Read. London: Souvenir Press.

Jeffree DM (1983) Unpublished M.Ed. thesis, Manchester University.

Jeffree DM (1989) Let Me Count. London: Souvenir Press.

Jeffree DM (1993) Teaching number concepts. In Harris J (Ed) Innovations in Education of Children with Severe Learning Difficulties. Chorley: Brothers of Charity.

Jeffree DM, McConkey R (1976) PIP Developmental Charts. London: Hodder and Stoughton Educational.

Lansdown R (1984) Child Development Made Easy. London: Heinemann.

Liebeck P (1984) How Children Learn Mathematics. London: Penguin.

Lowe M, Costello AJ (1976) Manual for Symbolic Play Test. London: NFER.

McConkey R, Jeffree DM (1979) First Steps in Learning to Pretend. Special Education: Forward Trends 6(4): 13–17.

Milosky L (1990) The role of world knowledge in language comprehension and intervention. Topics in Language Disorders 10(3): 1–13

Moyles JR (1994) The Excellence of Play. Buckingham: Open University Press.

Smilansky S (1968) The Effects of Socio-Dramatic Play on Disadvantaged Pre-School Children. New York: John Wiley.

Smith PK (1988) Children's play and its role in early development: A re-evaluation of the 'play ethos'. In Pellegrini AD (Ed) Psychological Bases for Early Education. Chichester: John Wiley.

Uzgiris IC, Hunt J McV (1975) Assessment in Infancy: Ordinal Scales of Psychological Development. Illinois: University of Illinois Press.

Vygotsky LS (1978) Mind in Society. Cambridge: Harvard University Press.

Chapter 4

Developing Communication: Early Intervention and Augmentative Signing from Birth to Five Years

JANET GOMPERTZ

Introduction – The changing climate in attitudes

Parents of a child with learning difficulties have the same aspirations as any parents: that their child will grow up to be independent, to be a valued member of society, to gain useful employment, to be happy, to form successful and lasting relationships and to fulfil his or her intellectual potential, whatever that may be. Until relatively recently such aspirations would have been deemed unrealistic by those who base their judgements solely on adults with learning difficulties seen in the community today – those who have been segregated in institutions for the formative part of their lives. The majority of these learning-disabled adults, who have not had the advantage of early intervention in their childhood, have very limited communication and are unable to make decisions for themselves.

The dramatic change in attitude over the past forty years, from segregation to integration for severely learning-disabled people, has affected the way the individuals present themselves and the way society views them. The United Nations policy for equal opportunity for disabled people (United Nations, 1986), can only be implemented if people with severe learning disabilities are able to make and express choices. With this emphasis on self-advocacy comes a recognition of the central role played by the development of language and communication. Earlier access to communication through very early intervention and augmentative signing gives children with learning difficulties the confidence to interact with other children and adults and the possibility of entering mainstream education. While this is still a contentious issue, the opportunity for typically developing children to learn alongside their disabled peers may be helpful in reducing prejudice and promoting a better understanding of people with learning disabilities.

Intervention – When is the right time to start?

As it is now possible to identify some genetic causes of intellectual impairment *in utero*, mothers who decide to proceed with their pregnancy when they discover they are carrying a child with Down syndrome usually start off with a positive attitude and are ideal candidates for early intervention from birth, or even before birth.

For other parents who only learn of their child's disability at or after birth, it is a different story. The way the news of disability is broken to parents is thought to have a crucial bearing on the parents' attitude to their disabled child and to intervention (Worthington, 1982; Ormerod & Huebner, 1988).

In order to know when and how to commence intervention it is vital that interventionists, such as speech and language therapists, be aware of the differing emotional reactions and phases parents can pass through in coming to terms with the shock and realisation of severe disability. Various phases have been identified (Ingalls, 1978; Cunningham, 1979; Hornby, 1991) but not all parents experience all of the phases; they may also oscillate between the phases described below:

Shock phase

When the parents first receive the news of severe disability most report being so stunned they experience 'post-traumatic amnesia'. Any advice or words of encouragement imparted by the paediatrician at this time are unlikely to be retained. Their shock may be manifested by emotional disorganisation, confusion, paralysis of action and disbelief.

Denial phase

Some parents react by refusing to accept the diagnosis, thinking or hoping there must have been a mistake. This may lead to a frenzied search for additional expert opinions in the hope that a different explanation can be offered. Other parents react by adopting a 'head in the sand' approach: they carry on as if nothing had happened in the belief that the child is 'normal' and they resist all offers of help. Such parents need to be allowed this space and time. Intervention offered at this phase is unlikely to be implemented.

Isolation phase

Most parents report a feeling of isolation, particularly from couples with typically developing children.

Adaptation phase.

This is the stage at which parents request reliable and accurate information. While they may be coping on a practical level at this stage, they may not yet be coping emotionally. Fathers often find it more difficult to adapt to their child's disability (Hornby, 1989), leaving the onus on the mothers, especially during this early period. It may therefore appear that there is an obvious need for counselling at this stage, but the majority of parents are unable to make use of the service and may only seek it many years later, if at all.

Sorrow and mourning phase

Nine months expectation of having a 'normal' child cannot be eradicated the moment the diagnosis of disability is made. Most parents go through a period of mourning for the child they did not have. In some cases parents may not experience this phase until the child has reached his or her teens, when comparison with 'typical' teenagers serves to emphasise the differences.

Orientation phase

This is the point at which parents spontaneously seek help and advice and begin to plan for the future.

Acceptance phase

This phase is identified when the parents can realistically accept and accurately appraise their child's abilities, disabilities and potential for an independent life including his rights as an individual.

Guilt

Most parents report feelings of guilt at having a severely disabled child, although it is not always easy to understand why. Parents ask themselves, 'why should this happen to me?' This inevitably leads to an irrational conclusion that it is retribution for some previous misconduct or neglect. Guilt may emanate from conflicting emotions, the parents oscillating between feelings of love and the wish that their child had failed to survive.

Over-protection

Some parents are over-protective in their concern that no one else will recognise their child's needs. Other possible explanations may be that they are compensating for feelings of guilt; or as a process of denial, they are keeping their child a baby so that less will be demanded of him or her and the level of his or her disability will be concealed.

In an ideal world all parents would reach the 'Acceptance phase' within their child's first months and the interventionist's job would be rendered relatively easy. In the real world, however, many parents never reach this stage. Some parents cope very effectively, even at the 'Adaptation phase', by adopting 'a day at a time' approach, dealing with the issues as and when they arise and seldom looking too far into the future. This can therefore be a suitable time for intervention to commence. Some would argue that parents may be too depressed to be involved in early intervention which involves time, energy and commitment. However, depression is unlikely to be alleviated by playing a waiting game. By keeping parents busy through involvement in their child's progress, they have less time to worry about the future. The fact that even the most severely disabled children develop and improve over time usually provides parents with the encouragement and impetus to keep going.

Communication – Why is it important to intervene early?

The human brain displays its greatest plasticity early in life and any process of adaptation is likely to be cumulative. The earlier the intervention process begins the greater the gains (Serpell & Nabuzoka, 1991), but intervention is usually only considered once a problem has occurred. In the case of a baby with a medical history suggestive of potential 'learning difficulties', it is possible to anticipate some of the problems and therefore to intervene, even before the learning difficulties have become apparent. Whatever the specific nature of the disability, the development of language and communication will inevitably be affected and is invariably more severely delayed and impaired than any other area of development (Gibson, 1978; Cunningham, Glenn, Wilkinson & Sloper, 1985). Early speech and language therapy intervention must therefore be viewed as a priority.

Communication, by definition, cannot only be confined to the child. Intervention needs to address the other parties in the communication as well as the child's language environment. Styles of mother–child interaction and communication are laid down very early in a child's life and these habits are difficult to change once they are firmly established (Tiegermann & Siperstein, 1984). It is therefore essential that the optimum conditions for communication development are established at birth, or very soon afterwards. Interactive difficulties can be substantially reduced through preventative or early remedial intervention (Berger & Cunningham, 1983a; Mahoney & Powell, 1986; Giralometto, 1988) and parental depression and stress levels can also be reduced (Burden 1980; Sloper, Cunningham & Arnljotsdottir 1983). There is a strong case therefore for involving a speech and language therapist at this pre-verbal stage of development.

Most children with learning difficulties develop 'challenging' behaviours (such as object throwing, head-banging or biting) at some stage in their early development. These behaviours, which may arise from frustration, can become entrenched and resistant to modification once they become a habit. It is therefore essential to intervene immediately they emerge by advising parents how best to manage them. Additionally, the incidence of challenging behaviours is often reduced in children who can communicate their needs early by the use of sign.

Moreover, with regard to augmentative signing, there is growing evidence that signed input appears to have its greatest impact during the prelinguistic and early stages of linguistic development (Abrahamsen, Cavello & McCluer, 1985; Kouri, 1989).

Finally, if children with severe learning difficulties can learn to communicate early there is more chance they will cope and integrate in school.

Is the communication environment of children with learning difficulties different?

There is some evidence to suggest that the communication environment of children with severe learning difficulties is quantitatively and qualitatively different, in some respects, from that of typically developing children (Berger, 1990; Owens, 1993). This is partly due to factors connected with the child's disability itself and partly due to the reactions of the immediate family and society towards the disabled child.

The children's disabilities often result in reduced opportunities to interact with those in their environment, not least because they tire easily and consequently spend more time sleeping than do typically developing children. Those with Down syndrome are more prone to upper respiratory tract infections and conjunctivitis which cause them to feel unwell and to be unresponsive. Parental depression may also give rise to difficulty in bonding with their severely disabled child. A child who has feeding difficulties, and whose poor muscle tone makes him or her floppy and unrewarding to pick up and cuddle, may exacerbate further parental rejection and depression.

The earliest communications and essential precursors for language acquisition are eye contact, smiling and the visual and vocal 'turn-taking' interactions between mother and child. It is generally assumed that both partners are innately prepared for these, but babies with learning difficulties and particularly those with Down syndrome, are slower to acquire these abilities and to respond. This can result in the mother getting out of step with her child's responses, making it more difficult to establish and sustain mutual understanding and reciprocal communication

(Berger & Cunningham, 1981, 1983a,b, 1985). Although over time the mother and child become more in tune with one another, this process can be accelerated by early intervention (Giralometto, 1988).

It is consistently found that parents of atypical learners are more directive in their interactions with their child, in the increased use of imperatives (Buium, Rynders & Turnure, 1974), demands, commands and requests (Marshall, Hegrenes & Goldstein, 1973) and in initiations in dialogue (Conti-Ramsden, 1990). This directiveness may be the parent's natural response to the children's passivity in conversational interaction (Bryan, 1986) and their failure to initiate. In this desperate attempt to hold the child's attention and to maintain the conversation, the parents become ever more directing and initiate even more (Conti-Ramsden, 1994). While this parental 'directiveness' is generally negatively regarded, future researchers may recognise a useful purpose for this behaviour.

It has also been observed that parents simplify their linguistic input to children with learning difficulties (Buium et al, 1974) and that this simplification is determined more by the children's productive language levels than by their cognitive levels (Matey & Kretschmer, 1985). Gallaway and Woll (1994) propose that 'the continuing use of simplified speech may not provide an unfacilitative linguistic environment', but could in fact 'be supportive and reduce the load for a still incompetent speaker.'

It is not clear to what extent parents' and society's reduced expectations of children with learning difficulties may affect their communication development. Additionally, carers' knowledge of their routines and preferences often obviates the need to communicate and could partly explain the children's failure to initiate conversations (Fischer, 1983). As the children's early communication attempts are often unintelligible to their listeners (Hyche et al, 1992), it is unlikely that they will be rewarding for the children. There is then a danger that both the speaker and the listener will eventually give up trying.

Different early intervention approaches

While it is beyond the scope of this chapter to discuss in detail the advantages and disadvantages of the various intervention approaches in existence, it is necessary to refer to certain ones to explain the philosophy which underpins the particular approach that I have adopted.

'Naturalistic / Transactional' versus 'Direct'

Speech, language and communication intervention approaches currently used in clinical practice fall into one of two main categories: 'naturalistic' and 'direct', each based on different theory and principles (McCormick & Schiefelbusch, 1990).

'Naturalistic' intervention or facilitation approaches are based on a developmental/cognitive/social model and rely on the natural environment for cues and intervention content and focus on the primary carer's responsiveness to the child. 'Direct' approaches, on the other hand, are based on a behavioural model, which incorporates modelling, reinforcement, shaping, chaining, fading and prompting-cueing strategies. While 'direct' approaches can occur in naturalistic settings, the methods they use are highly structured (Ratokalau & Robb, 1993).

A prime example of a 'direct' approach in a natural setting is the Portage Home Intervention Scheme (Bluma, Shearer, Frohman & Hilliard, 1976), which originated in Portage, Wisconsin, but has been widely used in the UK since 1980. Portage invites criticism by attempting to address all the main areas of development (motor, social, self-help skills, cognitive and speech and language) with the same learning theory approach. Proponents of the 'naturalistic' approach argue that while a behaviourist structure can be highly effective in dealing with aspects of social behaviour, such as challenging behaviours, it does not lend itself to the development of cognition and communication, which require a more interactive framework.

'Naturalistic' approaches, or 'transactional' as they are sometimes referred to (Sameroff & Chandler, 1975; McLean & Snyder-McLean, 1978), are based on the premise that development results from a continual interplay between a changing organism and a changing environment, so that both the individual and their settings experience change. Thus in the case of families with disabled children, the families affect and are affected by their children as the child passes through different developmental stages. In a 'transactional' approach to intervention the impairment is not viewed as a static impediment to developmental progress (Guralnick, 1982), but as a constantly changing, evolving and diminishing one.

Fine examples of 'transactional' communication approaches are the Hanen Early Language Parent Programme (Manolson, 1983), and the first year of The Swedish Early Language Intervention Programme (Johansson, 1994), both of which involve informal teaching to parents to be more responsive to their child by following the child's lead in play, encouraging child participation and turn-taking.

The Swedish Early Language Intervention Programme is of particular interest because it a) can be commenced at birth, b) includes the use of an augmentative sign system and c) employs a highly controversial auditory bombardment technique, whereby the baby is frequently exposed to the phonological units of sound which make up his or her native language. During the first year the programme focuses on 'developing performative communication' (the child's deliberate and conscious use of communication to manipulate people in his or her environment to achieve certain goals), by the use of augmentative signing. The following five years of the programme use a combination of 'direct' and 'naturalistic/transactional' methods to promote the growth of symbols, and to develop simple syntax, morphology and phonology.

A study carried out in Sweden by Johansson (1990), on 65 children with Down syndrome (29 of whom received this Swedish Programme, while the remaining 36 controls received conventional speech and language therapy), produced some interesting results. Using the Sequenced Inventory of Language Development (SILD) (Hedrick, Prather & Tobin, 1970), it was found that there were high scoring children in the intervention group whose scores were similar to children of normal intelligence. While there were also high-scoring children in the control group, their test results were similar to the low-scoring children in the intervention group. Although her study lacks statistical analysis, Johansson claims that children with Down syndrome who are given structured and repeated language intervention from an early age, perform higher on the SILD than children given conventional speech and language therapy. It is interesting to speculate whether similar results could be achieved by using only certain aspects of the programme, e.g. the augmentative signing component. The whole programme involves the daily practising of routines and activities which occupy the primary carer for 30 minutes every day, for the first six years of the child's life, with weekly visits by a speech and language therapist to the home or nursery school, to ensure effective adaptation of the programme to the individual's needs.

The majority of home intervention schemes are successful to a greater or lesser extent by effecting desirable change and progress probably as the result of the high levels of commitment, determination and investment of time and effort that they demand of the primary carers. Those intervention schemes that present as 'programmes', which involve daily exercises and routines, can result in over-loading parents who are already highly stressed and exhausted, causing them to feel guilty and anxious if they fall behind when either they, or their child has an 'off day' or is ill. Moreover, ensuring carry over, from a contrived exercise to a natural context, is time consuming .

'Naturalistic/transactional' interventions can be incorporated into daily living from the outset, so they are practised whenever the natural contexts occur, obviating the need for deliberate generalisation. Thus they become part of the child's and adult's natural repertoires seemingly effortlessly and unconsciously.

Augmentative signing

The reasons why it has been decided to focus on the use of early augmentative signing in this chapter are twofold: firstly, it has been found to be the single most important tool in developing communication in young children with severe learning difficulties and secondly, while the benefits of early introduction of augmentative signing to learning-disabled children are often recognised, many therapists do not know how to introduce it to young babies in a transactional way. Moreover, little has been written on the most effective ways of introducing and using augmentative signing with this client group.

What is augmentative signing?

The term 'augmentative signing' refers to signing which 'augments' or is 'added to' speech. It does not refer to sign systems or sign languages which are used as an alternative to speech. It is important here to differentiate between the severely learning-disabled and the profoundly hearing-impaired, for although both populations may use the same sign system, they use signing in different ways and for different purposes. In the context of this chapter reference is made to the temporary use of an augmentative sign system to facilitate the development of communication of children with severe learning difficulties in the first five years of their life. Only the key words in the phrase or sentence need be augmented by sign, but which 'key words' to augment by sign will change as the child develops. Moreover, it is important to stress that when they sign, parents should speak in a normal manner to their babies, using full grammatical phrases and sentences with the appropriate rhythm, stress, vocal intonation and facial expression.

Will the use of an augmentative sign system from birth deter the development of speech?

Contrary to common misconception, the use of an augmentative communication system does not deter development of speech (Kahn, 1977; Konstantases, Oxman & Webster, 1977; Reich, 1978; Abrahamsen, Cavello & McCluer, 1985; Gibbs & Carswell, 1988; Kouri, 1989; Buckley, Emslie, Haslegave & Le Prevost, 1993; Owens, 1993).

The majority of children with severe learning difficulties automatically stop using signing as soon as they can communicate adequately via speech. In cases where augmentative signing was introduced during the first year of the baby's life, the children often began talking by the age of three and dispensed with signing before they were five. Moreover it is thought that the early introduction of augmentative signing actually facilitates spontaneous verbal communication (Kahn, 1977; Konstantases, et al, 1977; Reich, 1978; Schaeffer, 1980; Daniloff & Shafer, 1981; Abrahamsen, et al, 1985; Buckley, et al, 1993). For the very small minority of children who also have other problems which deter the development of spoken language, such as severe articulatory dyspraxia and/or a profound hearing loss, the use of an augmentative sign system is invaluable as their only means of communication (Owens, 1993; Le Prevost, 1993).

Why is it beneficial to augment speech with sign?

There are many reasons why the early introduction of augmentative signing is thought to be beneficial to children with severe learning difficulties (see Figure 4.1).

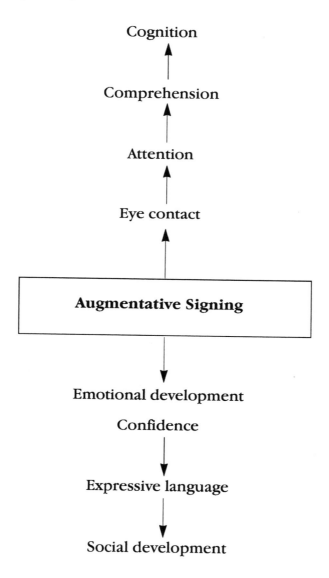

Figure 4.1: Possible impact of augmentative signing on a child's development

The impact of augmentative sign on language and thought

Firstly, and perhaps most importantly, augmentative signing facilitates the development of eye contact, visual attention and selective listening (Abrahamsen, Romski & Sevcik, 1989; Le Prevost, 1993; Hurd, 1995), which are essential prerequisites for language acquisition and cognition. It is noticeable that children who have been signed to from an early age are more visually alert and look up to adults more frequently for information. The fact that only certain words in sentences are augmented by sign, helps children focus their attention on the most salient words in the speech stream. Initially the words that are signed convey the semantic information thereby facilitating the development of verbal comprehension and cognition. As the child gets older augmentative sign can be used to highlight certain syntactic features in sentences, thus impacting on verbal comprehension and expressive language development.

The visual nature of augmentative signing helps counteract the negative effects on language development brought about by hearing loss, which is experienced by 80% of children with Down syndrome (Balkany, Downs, Jafek & Krajicek, 1979; Cunningham & McArthur, 1981; Davies, 1985) and around 40% of learning-disabled non-Down children (Jerger, 1970). Children with severe learning difficulties also have profound short-term auditory memory and auditory processing problems (Mackenzie & Hulme, 1987; Broadley, MacDonald & Buckley, 1995). Augmentative signing may be effective by circumventing these auditory processing deficiencies because visually presented information is more permanent and less transient than auditorily presented information. Augmenting speech with sign forces the speaker to slow down, thereby giving the child longer to process the incoming information. It has also been suggested that children at a prelinguistic stage may process visually based linguistic information more effectively than auditory information (Kouri, 1989).

Sign appears to facilitate internal representation of thoughts and ideas; children with learning difficulties are often observed signing silently to themselves by way of commentary when playing alone, looking at a book or watching television. The kinaesthetic sensation experienced by the child when he or she signs adds to the multi-sensory input afforded by augmentative signing, which is likely to make the learning condition more salient. Augmentative signing may act as a mediation device to facilitate learning (Clark, Remington & Light, 1986), in a similar way to the part played by verbal rehearsal to aid memory, in children who can speak (Broadley et al, 1995).

The impact of signing on emotional development and expressive language

Children with severe learning disabilities experience particular difficulties with expressive language which are more severe than could be predicted on the basis of their cognitive levels alone (Beeghly, Hanrahan, Weiss & Cicchetti, 1985; Cardoso-Martins, Mervis & Mervis, 1985), and this discrepancy increases with age. Speech intelligibility is invariably affected and appears to be particularly resistant to intervention. In a study by Buckley and Sacks (1987) on the speech of teenagers with Down syndrome, only 45% of girls and 10% of boys were reported by their parents to be intelligible to strangers.

The ability of young children to express themselves by sign at an earlier age than learning-disabled children not exposed to augmentative signing (Kahn, 1977; Konstantases et al, 1977; Daniloff & Shafer, 1981; Abrahamsen et al, 1985), does much to reduce frustration and the incidence of behaviour problems. This early communication advantage impacts on their social development and these children are noticeably more confident in their interactions with adults and other children, even before their speech develops (Le Prevost, 1987). As most of the children go on to develop speech (Reich, 1978; Schaeffer, 1980; Daniloff & Shafer, 1981; Abrahamsen et al, 1985), it would appear that sign may serve as a vehicle to accomplish the transition from no speech to refined oral language (Jago, Jago & Hart, 1984). Furthermore, for the small minority of children who also have articulatory dyspraxia, and therefore encounter particular difficulties with speech, sign can be additionally advantageous by taking the pressure off speech, and in doing so, it often helps to elicit the word.

The early ability of children with learning difficulties to communicate intelligibly by sign affords their parents valuable insights into the way their child perceives the world and alerts parents to their many auditory and visual perceptual errors. Le Prevost (1983, 1993) cites numerous examples of children with Down syndrome signing 'tea' for 'tree' (auditory discrimination error), and signing 'comb' for 'fork' (visual discrimination error). The parent's ability to monitor and to correct such errors early impacts on other areas of the child's development.

This ability of children to be able to sign what they see and hear, also permits earlier testing of vision and hearing and consequently earlier identification and correction of impairment.

Is iconicity useful to children with severe learning difficulties?

It has been proposed that augmentative signing may be beneficial to children with severe learning difficulties because many of the signs look like the object or concept they represent and are therefore 'iconic' (Daniloff, Lloyd & Fristoe, 1983; Luftig, Page & Lloyd, 1983). If this were true, iconic signs would be learned faster than non-iconic signs. This was not, however, found to be the case (Reichle, Williams & Ryan, 1981; Dennis, Reichle, Williams & Vogelsberg, 1982; DePaul & Yoder, 1986).

Comparison between signs for 'drink' and 'biscuit', in British Sign Language (BSL), provides a good example. Both signs can be highly motivating and require relatively little manual dexterity. Learning-disabled toddlers invariably learn the sign for 'biscuit' (a non-iconic, abstract sign which involves tapping the elbow), before they learn the sign for 'drink' (an iconic sign which involves mimicking the act of drinking). It may be that the ability to use iconicity as a mnemonic device is language dependent, which would explain why it is so useful to us but not to those who have not yet acquired language.

Which sign system?

Much time is spent weighing up the arguments for and against the use of a particular sign system. Time spent in this way is as useful as debating whether it is easier to learn French or English as a first language. The important thing is that children have access to communication via a sign or symbol system and its specific nature is of relatively minor importance. In the early 1970's it was argued that young children with severe learning difficulties would be unable to use particular manual sign systems because they lacked the manual dexterity. While this may be true for some babies who also have cerebral palsy, this is not so for other learning-disabled young children (Abrahamsen et al, 1985; Gibbs & Carswell, 1988; Kouri, 1989; Le Prevost, 1993). Indeed it would seem that the use of manual sign systems may actually facilitate the development of fine motor co-ordination. British Sign Language (BSL), a two-handed sign system, is no more difficult for learning-disabled young children to use than American Sign Language (ASL), a one-handed sign system.

BSL is used currently by over 70,000 deaf people and by increasing numbers of people with severe learning difficulties, making it the most commonly used sign system in the UK. 'The Makaton Sign Vocabulary' (Walker, 1980, 1985), the 'See and Say Manual of Signs' (Le Prevost, 1990) and 'Signalong' (Grove, Kennard & Hall, 1992-1996) are all selected vocabularies of BSL signs, particularly for use by learning-disabled people.

A transactional approach using an augmentative sign system

The approach described below exemplifies how augmentative signing can be used in a transactional way with the parents of children with severe learning difficulties. It must be stressed that it is not a 'programme' but an 'approach' to very early intervention. The term, 'transactional', does not preclude working in a structured way. The structure is applied to the way in which one works and how the significant people in the child's life interact with him or her. Instead of attaching the structure to specific times, places and equipment for assessing and 'teaching' language (Price & Bochner, 1991), the assessment and intervention take place whenever the baby or child interacts in a meaningful and communicative manner.

The method described is truly 'transactional' in the sense that it has evolved and is continually being modified through trial and error, and through observation of children with learning difficulties and their interactions with those in their natural environments. The strategies described are not all the author's; many of them have evolved through the sharing of ideas with others who work in a transactional way.

This chapter cannot deal comprehensively with all aspects of augmentative signing and will therefore focus on how parents and therapists can facilitate important transitional stages in the baby's and young child's communication development with the use of augmentative signing.

A transactional approach to assessment

A transactional speech and language therapy assessment and intervention usually take place in the child's home where the baby and his or her parents are likely to feel most at ease. Assessment commences by video taping the parent–baby interactions during typical caring routines of feeding, changing and bathing. While the presence of the video may be deemed to be intrusive initially, parents invariably become engrossed in their babies and the activities they routinely perform on them and soon learn to relax and ignore the camera. When the parents and speech and language therapist watch the video together, it is important to ensure that the discussion concentrates on positive features of the parent–child interaction. The opportunity for parents to observe their interactions on video in this more detached manner permits parents to focus on aspects of their baby's behaviour which may have gone unnoticed by them at the time. Similarly, parents can more objectively appraise their own communicative interactions and often comment on their lack of animation or missed opportunities for communication input, thereby obviating the need for the therapist to have to raise them. The opportunity to discuss the central role played by vocal intonation in making speech even more animated, and the use of non-verbal gestural input to gain and maintain the baby's attention, invariably arises spontaneously and paves the way for augmentative signing to be introduced from the outset. As styles of parent–child interaction are laid down very early in the child's life and these habits are very resistant to change, as previously indicated, it is important to capitalise on this early opportunity to introduce augmentative signing.

Signing during daily caring routines

As young babies with severe learning difficulties either sleep for much of the day or are fractious, there are very limited opportunities for language stimulation in the early months. Essential caring routines present ideal opportunities for augmentative signed input because the frequency with which they occur ensures a certain level of exposure to the signs. Any activity is suitable for use with augmentative signing providing it is relatively stress free and enjoyable. It is possible that parents who are tired or depressed perform these routines without spoken commentary and the therapist needs to pick up on this early in intervention.

In such instances it may be useful to recommend they start with 'body-signing' (Morgenstern, 1981), which serves to remind parents to provide their baby with a spoken commentary whilst also helping the baby to anticipate events. It simply involves making the sign on the appropriate part of the baby's body which will alert him or her of an impending sensory experience and simultaneously telling him or her what's going to happen next. As well as helping the child 'prepare' for the experience it also helps the carer empathise with baby's sensory experiences. Whereas typically developing babies quickly learn to associate and interpret environmental clues, such as the sound of bath water running, babies with severe learning difficulties are often shocked by being plunged into water without warning. 'Body-signing' is also useful for children who are blind or who have cerebral palsy.

Which words need to be augmented with sign in the initial stages?

Analysis of the video sample collected always illuminates situations which lend themselves naturally to sign and conform to words which would be stressed in ordinary parent–child interactions. Phrases such as '<u>Up</u> you come !' 'Do you want some <u>more</u> (milk)?' 'Are you tired, do you want to go to <u>bed</u>?' are ideal for signing. In each phrase, only the word underlined need be signed at this stage. It is important to select only a very small lexicon of signs initially as the main aim is to maintain a natural interactive style. About half a dozen signs are sufficient at the beginning, so that for each activity the parent need learn only one or two signs.

Is sign accuracy important in the initial months?

The parents will invariably feel inhibited or self-conscious to begin with and are often over-concerned about the accuracy of their signing. It is vital to reassure the parents that sign accuracy is not important at this stage in their child's development; it is more important that the interaction be lively and enjoyable for both parties. Young babies concentrate on faces and animated voices in their first months (Berger, 1990), and signing accentuates these even though the babies will not yet gain meaning from the actual signs. It is vital that the parents use this period to practise signing during the daily caring routines so that they will have acquired a certain level of natural sign fluency by the time the child is ready to benefit from it.

An additional advantage of introducing signing during the child's first year is that there is no expectation for the babies to sign back so early in their development. This relieves the pressure and affords parents and their baby the opportunity to concentrate only on input.

Gaining the baby's auditory and visual attention via augmentative signing

Synchronising signs with speech requires much practice but its mastery is vital. Timing appears to be the key to the way augmentative signing facilitates many other areas of the child's development.

1   In order to sign, the parents first need to learn how to gain their baby's visual attention, which is not easy. The face should be in a good light and they should use animated voice and facial expressions. In the baby's early development it is often appropriate to encourage him or her to look up to his or her parent for information via a sign. Later on it is advisable for parents to wait and to time spoken and signed input to the moment when the child looks up spontaneously. If the child does not look up it may be necessary for the parent to move his or her own position, or to move the child's position or to move objects in order to manipulate the child's focus of attention. Once the child has learned to follow moving objects with his or her eyes, two fingers can be passed in front of the child's face and slowly moved towards the parent's own face to encourage the child to watch. This method is preferable to tapping the child to gain attention.

2   Parents need to learn how to time their signs to the baby's fleeting gazes and moments of visual attention. This forces the parents to closely scrutinise their child's changing behaviours and permits them to capitalise on optimum periods for interaction.

3   Timing signs to speech serves to highlight for the baby or child the important words in phrases.

4   Signing rhythmically (to mimic the syllable structure of the words) helps gain the child's auditory attention and raises his or her awareness that words are of different lengths, eg. da-dee (Daddy), sau-sa-ges, bed , ta-ble, di-nner (see Figure 4.2). Action nursery rhymes can be a valuable resource for helping parents sign rhythmically to the words and the children usually derive much pleasure from them too!

5   Stopping the sign the moment the word ends is most important. Some parents continue to sign a word long after the word has finished. This only confuses the child and is counter-productive to the way augmentative signing facilitates listening and understanding.

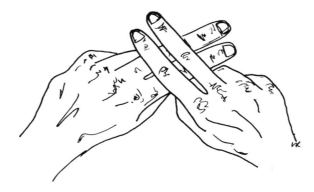

Figure 4.2: Signing 'Da-dee' (daddy). The sign is made by tapping twice, in time with the spoken syllables. This facilitates the baby's auditory attention and awareness that words are of different lengths

Resolving practical issues related to signing

Parents often comment that it is difficult to sign during an activity because their hands are otherwise occupied. It is essential to resolve these practical problems early. Many BSL signs can be made using one hand only. While breast feeding a baby the mother can use her free hand to sign eg. 'light' (if the light should happen to catch the child's attention by suddenly being switched on during the feed). The few BSL signs which require the use of both hands can be reserved for times when the child is supported in a sling, chair, or baby bouncer (see Figure 4.3). Sometimes it is not even necessary to free both hands, eg. the BSL sign 'more?', which is made by placing the palm of one hand on top of the fist of the other, can quite easily be signed while holding a spoon in one hand and a yoghurt pot in the other, with the child seated opposite in a chair (see Figure 4.4).

Cause and effect relationships

The relationship between cause and effect is fundamental to the development of cognition and communication. While typically developing children quickly realise they can gain attention and initiate dialogue by the use of body language and vocalisation, children with severe learning difficulties seem to be unaware of their power to manipulate people and events. In order to facilitate this awareness they need to be helped in stages which are linked to their cognitive and motor development. The baby learns how to use purposeful behaviour to gain what he or she needs by noting that certain, spontaneous, reflexive behaviours elicit a

Figure 4.3: Mother's hands are free to sing and sign to the baby. The baby's visual attention is easy to gain and maintain at this height while supported in a 'baby bouncer'

Figure 4.4: It is not always necessary to free the hands in order to sign. Mother asks the child if he wants 'more', with a yoghurt carton in one hand and a spoon in the other

satisfying response. The baby cries because he or she feels thirsty and is given a drink. Similarly he or she may reach towards an object that interests him or her and someone hands it to him or her. In this way he or she learns that his or her behaviour can influence events. Here are some suggestions for promoting the very early stages of cause and effect in play:

a)   When the baby is lying on his or her back, a band can be placed round his or her ankle with a bell attached to it. He or she learns that movement of his or her foot causes the sound.

b)   A vibrating pad can be placed near any moving part of the baby's body.

c) A baby will move or press anything which makes something interesting happen.

d) To encourage the baby to realise he or she can control external events by vocalising, one fun idea is the use of 'dancing flowers' which are activated by voice.

Eliciting communication from the baby – Encouraging the baby to take the initiative.

The most useful cause and effect activity is the one which 'teaches' the child that he or she can communicate. Turn-taking games provide an excellent framework for eliciting a baby's first deliberate communicative signals and help parents be more aware of their baby's early attempts.

In an enjoyable turn-taking game, such as blowing a raspberry on a baby's hand, the parent first needs to familiarise the baby with the routine of blowing raspberries on the hand, waiting, and then asking the baby if he or she wants 'more?' (using the 'more?' sign). The idea of the game is to invite the baby to 'ask' for 'more' with his or her body language or by vocalising, long before he or she has the ability to sign or say the word or has any awareness that his or her behaviour is influential. At this stage his or her behaviour is interpreted 'as if' an intention exists. As soon as the baby responds even by keeping still or giving an expectant look, the parent immediately blows a raspberry on the baby's hand and the game is repeated. This behaviour helps the baby appreciate his or her role in communication.

Cautionary note: In turn-taking routines timing is crucial to success. In the author's experience, parents invariably fail to wait long enough, and reward the child by blowing a raspberry on his or her hand before the child has had the opportunity to request the recurrence. This inevitably results in interaction 'clashes' and the communication benefit from this game is lost. This apparent inability of parents to wait may simply be an expression of impatience or their failure to accommodate their child's slow reaction times. Alternatively, it may emanate from a real anxiety that the child will not be able to respond, so they obviate the problem by proceeding prematurely. Therapists need to talk parents through this often unsubstantiated fear and demonstrate that waiting for much longer will finally be rewarded (see Figure 4.5). Viewing video recordings is the most powerful means of demonstrating such points.

Early sign lexicon

It is advisable that parents' early sign lexicons include concepts which are salient for the child, or ones which are communicatively useful to him or her. Highly motivating signs, such as 'up', 'more', 'again', 'biscuit', 'drink', have a greater chance of being comprehended and used

Figure 4.5: Ben enjoys being rolled. His mother asks if he wants to be rolled again. She needs to be patient to accommodate his slow reaction times until Ben asks for 'more' with his body language

by the child early in his or her development. Signs such as 'light', 'telephone', 'bed', 'dog', 'car' are often among the first signs the child makes, perhaps because they represent salient concepts which cause change to the child or his or her environment.

Once a core vocabulary of single signs has been established, in which nouns will invariably predominate, it is important to add new signs (eg. adjectives and verbs), which permit the possibility for two-sign combinations eg. 'the cat's gone', 'the dolly's broken', 'the dog's eating', 'where's the ball?', 'do you want more milk?'.

When introducing signed concepts to children, consideration needs to be given to salience. It is not advisable to 'teach' a concept such as 'dirty' by contrasting it with 'clean', as this serves only to confuse children with learning difficulties. Moreover, as 'negative' concepts such as 'dirty', 'empty', 'broken' 'all gone', 'No!' are more salient to children, it is better to introduce such signs first, long before their contrasting counterparts.

Encouraging young children to make signs. To mould or not to mould?

Many therapists encourage parents to mould their children's hands to 'help' them make the signs. It is unclear why they should think this could be helpful, when most of them would not recommend manual manipulation to facilitate articulation in a child having difficulty with speaking. Moreover, this procedure is likely to interfere with the child's sensory and kinaesthetic feedback and the children are often resistant to having their hands moulded in this way. In this context much can be gained by watching how deaf signing mothers encourage their children to sign, by making their sign on the child (Harris, Clibbens, Chasin &

Tibbitts, 1989). This technique can be highly effective for children with severe learning difficulties.

For example, if a parent wants to sign 'lady' to the child, he or she would first gain the child's attention and then model the BSL sign to him or her (by gently drawing his or her right index finger down the right side of his or her own cheek), while saying the word 'lady'. He or she would then do the same movement with his or her index finger, but on the child's cheek this time (see Figure 4.6.i), repeating the word 'lady' as he or she does so. In this way the child learns to associate the sensation (feeling the sign on his or her face) with the word, and before long the child spontaneously makes the sign on his or her own face (see Figure 4.6.ii)

Many signs can be signed on the child in this way and facilitate the child's ability to make the signs himself or herself through this sensory experience.

How long does it take before children sign back?

Clearly there is much individual variation among children with severe learning difficulties. Some children with Down syndrome, who do not have additional complications, begin to use signs themselves about a year after first receiving augmentative signing, providing it was commenced shortly after birth on a regular daily basis, and that as many people as possible in the child's environment have been augmenting their speech with sign. It is important to be aware that children's earliest attempts at sign are likely to pass unnoticed because their signs are so

Figure 4.6.i: Encouraging the child to make the sign himself. Mother displaces the sign by signing 'lady' on the child's face

Figure 4.6.ii: The sensory experience facilitates the child's ability to make the signs

unrefined at this stage and often bear no resemblance to the target sign. It is only the consistency with which the child uses a particular action or gesture for a particular situation which permits parents and therapists to recognise that the child is signing. Children spontaneously modify and refine their signs over time until they can sign clearly, just as typically developing children refine their speech.

Giving children choices

Children with learning difficulties do not always know that they have choices. Those who do may not know how to indicate their preferences. This ability develops through awareness of cause and effect. Initially the child looks at something he or she wants; this is interpreted as a signal by the parents and so becomes purposeful. It is therefore essential that parents provide their child with the opportunities to make reasonable choices. Initially the choices may need to be ones the child can look at or point to and where one option is known to be more attractive than the other, eg. 'Do you want a glass of orange juice or a glass of water? These contrived 'choices' are vital to the child's awareness that he or she is signalling preferences (Gunning, 1983). They are precursors to real choice-making, eg. 'Do you want a drink or a biscuit?', where the options are equally attractive. Once the child can sign, the possibilities are endless. 'Do you want to look at a book or watch a video?', 'Do you want to wear your red socks or your yellow socks? ', 'Shall we put your vest on first or your pants?', 'What shall we put on now?'

Delay in walking – effects on language development

Parents are often unduly concerned with their child's delay in walking and this can predominate over their concern for his or her language development. It is important to remind parents that while most learning-disabled children walk, many never talk. Speech and language therapists may view this tardiness in developing mobility more positively, as it provides a longer period for developing language and attention skills, while the child is a 'captive' audience. When they do start walking their language abilities can be expected to plateau for up to six months, in a similar way to that observed in typically developing children.

Joint focus of attention and augmentative signing

With the child's developing interests and increasing mobility, the chances of encouraging him or her to watch his or her mother's face diminish. There will be times when the child is already attending to another activity and distracting him or her in this way would be counter-productive. In this situation the child can still be provided with a signed commentary, but the parent needs to displace the signs so that the sign is made within the child's existing focus of attention and in the child's visual field (see Figure 4.7.i) or on the child (see Figure 4.7.ii), thereby obviating the need for the child to divert his or her gaze.

Establishing a common focus of attention between child and adult is essential if the adult is to facilitate a child's language learning. Children who receive augmentative signing need to learn how to divide their attention between the signed input and the context to which the language refers. The signer can facilitate this by first getting the child to attend to the signer's face, then simultaneously saying and signing the word. The signer then needs to catch the child's gaze with two fingers together (the index and middle finger), and slowly direct the point towards the object, ensuring that the child is continuing to follow the fingers all the way towards the object. The signer then needs to make the sign again in this displaced position between the child and the object towards which he or she is looking, while simultaneously saying the word. While this may sound complicated it very quickly becomes part of the parent's repertoire.

Child-centred language activities with augmentative signing

Mastery of the technique described above is quite liberating for the parents because they suddenly realise that they can talk to the child

Figure 4.7.i: 'Where's........' The mother signs in the baby's visual field

Figure 4.7.ii: 'The pussycat ?'. Mother displaces her sign by making the sign, 'pussycat', on the baby's face, thereby obviating the need to divert the baby's visual attention

about anything that catches the child's interest. Additionally, this child-centred approach serves to extend the parents' vocabulary for signs to cover the limitless conversations that ensue. (The BSL Dictionary of Signs (BDA, 1992) is most useful at this stage.)

Books

Books are a most valuable resource because they expose children to a wider set of experiences while at the same time permitting frequent exposure to augmentative input in the same order each time they are 'read'.

Parents often comment that it is difficult to sign the content of a book with the child seated on their lap because the child's face is turned away from the parent and towards the book. This is also a situation where displacing the signs, by making them in the child's visual field or on the child, is most useful (see Figure 4.8). Alternatively a simple solution is to read the book facing a mirror so that the parent's signs can be easily seen by the child whilst also looking at the book (see Figure 4.9).

It is important to ensure that books are carefully chosen with a view to interesting visual and verbal content. Children quickly tire of books which depict a different animal or object on each page and offer only limited language possibilities. Books such as the 'Maisy' Pop-up Series by Lucy Cousins (1990 onwards) are particularly useful for signing because many of the moving pictures coincidentally mimic the BSL signs. Their simple story line serves to fill this intermediate stage, until children are ready for proper story books..

Figure 4.8: The mother displaces the sign so that the child can see and feel the 'horse' sign without having to divert his or her gaze

Figure 4.9: 'and the little girl was sad'. The use of the mirror permits the child to simultaneously look at the book while also seeing the mother's signs and facial expressions

Videos and signed television programmes for children

There are an increasing number of videos and television programmes which use augmentative signing. Adults appear to derive as much pleasure from them as the children. Videos, such as the Makaton Nursery Rhymes Video (MVDP, 1991), with Dave Benson Phillips, are particularly useful. The facility to play them repeatedly provides children and their parents with the opportunity to join in and the practice they need to become more fluent signers.

Developing symbolic play

The ability to play symbolically is an important precursor to developing more sophisticated language structures. Acting out scenarios with small toys together with augmentative signed commentary facilitates the development of symbolic play.

Sign babble

Children who have been exposed to augmentative signing often go through a phase of 'sign babble' when they sign phrases and sentences to themselves when looking at books or thinking about something. This is encouraging because it signals that speech is imminent, just as 'jargoning' is a precursor to speech in typically developing children.

First words

A child's first word is invariably supported by the corresponding sign, and is always cause for celebration. Soon afterwards the child will spontaneously dispense with the sign when he or she no longer needs it. This is not a cue to adults, however, to cease augmentative signing to the child. The child will still be dependent upon augmentative signing for his or her learning and especially for acquiring new vocabulary.

Groups to establish social skills

Attendance in a small group can act as a useful rehearsal for entry to playgroup or nursery school and is an ideal forum for the development of social skills and social language. Augmentative signing within the group context can facilitate comprehension of social rules such as possession of objects, eg. 'This is my biscuit – that's yours'.

Certain language structures are difficult and sometimes dreary to 'teach' in a one-to-one situation because the children need so much exposure to the structures in order to learn them. They are often best learned by example from the other group participants in a 'fun' situation. One example of this is learning to affirm and deny accurately. This can be done by drawing a variety of common objects from a bag one by one. Each time an object is drawn from the bag, the adult will name the object, sometimes giving it the correct name and sometimes an incorrect one. The game involves the children affirming or denying, by sign or word, whether what the adult said was correct. Children with learning difficulties all too readily accept that what adults say is always correct and learning to question statements is clearly important for their cognitive development.

Challenging behaviours

Children with severe learning difficulties invariably display challenging behaviours at some point during their first five years, although such behaviours appear to occur less frequently or less persistently in those who have access to augmentative communication. It is not always clear why children fling objects, pull hair, bite themselves or others or head bang, and frustration may only be part of the problem. Sometimes the behaviour is sparked off by genuine, but ill-timed laughter, and before long the behaviour has become a habit. The biting of a parent's toe can be amusing the first time it happens! It is essential that these unwanted behaviours be dealt with as soon as they arise because once they have become established, they are very difficult to modify or eradicate. The most effective way to do this is to determine what triggers or causes them. In this regard Portage Behaviour Sampling (Bluma et al, 1976) may provide useful insights. This requires the parent to log incidence of occurrence of challenging behaviours on a chart along with the antecedent and consequent events (see Figure 4.10). The value of this approach is that it sometimes reveals a consistent pattern of events which appear to exacerbate or reinforce the unwanted behaviours but were not apparent to the parents at the time of the occurrence. Video recordings provide opportunity for objective analysis.

In Figure 4.10 it can be seen that the head-banging behaviour always occurred when Tim was unoccupied and alone and towards the end of the day. Telling Tim to 'stop it', an expression he was known to understand, appeared not to be successful. Systematic sampling over the next weeks revealed that the behaviour was not due to boredom or a desire for company but simply an expression of tiredness.

Lisa pulled hair and drove her mother to a 'crew cut' in desperation. Analysis of the behaviour sample revealed that the victim's consequent squeals and screams were reinforcing the behaviour and reprimanding her appeared to be an additional reinforcement. Quietly removing Lisa's fingers from the hair while exercising maximum self-control eradicated the problem over the ensuing months.

Andrew threw bricks. Analysis of the sample revealed no pattern of events. It was concluded that he was probably throwing bricks because he was not very successful at stacking them and there was nothing else interesting to do with them. Throwing bricks at playgroup had quite a dramatic effect! Many of the difficult behaviours children display may emanate from boredom because of their limited play repertoires and lack of resourcefulness. Showing them how to play and use the same objects in a variety of ways appears to be a most effective strategy.

Some behaviours, such as teeth grinding, are more difficult to modify or eradicate. It may be helpful to refer to suggestions for their management in the Portage Manual (Bluma et al, 1976).

Playgroups and nursery school

The majority of children with learning difficulties who have early access to augmentative signing are often ready to attend mainstream playgroups and nursery school by the time they are three or four years of age. The experience of mixing with typically developing children is usually an enriching experience for them and has considerable impact on their language and social development.

School

Although some children are able to talk well by the time they go to school and have dispensed with using signs, it continues to be a valuable support system for introducing new vocabulary and language

Day & Time	What did Tim do?	What do you think provoked it?	Where did it happen?	What did you do?	What happened as a result of your efforts?
Thurs 16.20	*Repeatedly banged head on carpet*	*I don't know, I was in the kitchen*	*In the lounge*	*Told him to "stop it"*	*He continued until I picked him up*
Thurs 20.00	*Head-banged*	*Tiredness?*	*In the bathroom*	*Told him to "stop it"*	*He looked at me then continued to bang head on carpet*
Fri 18.05	*Head-banged*	*Appeared bored, probably hungry*	*In the lounge*	*Told him to "stop it"*	*Looked at me, paused, continued – so I picked him up*
Sat 17.55	*Head-banged*	*Tired? Bored? Attention seeking?*	*In the lounge. I was talking to a friend*	*Told him to "stop it"*	*Paused, then continued until I picked him up*
Sun 15.50	*Head-banged*	*Tired and irritable*	*In the lounge*	*Told him to "stop it"*	*He stopped!*
Tues 19.10	*Head-banged*	*Very tired, irritable. Wanted a cuddle*	*In the lounge*	*Told him to "stop it"*	*Held arms up. He wanted a cuddle. I cuddled him*

Figure 4.10: Challenging behaviour data sheet

structures and for the teaching of reading. For those children with severe learning difficulties whose speech is still unintelligible, augmentative signing is often their only chance of making themselves understood.

Conclusion

The benefits of augmentative signing to people with severe learning difficulties have been recognised for twenty years, yet few speech and language therapists introduce it during the child's first year of life. This may be because those who refer children for speech and language therapy may not be aware that augmentative signing has its greatest impact on the child's development during his or her pre-verbal period. This chapter argues a case for early intervention soon after birth using augmentative signing in a 'transactional' way. Augmenting speech with sign requires parents to time their speech to moments when their child establishes eye contact and attends, thereby capitalising on times for optimum learning. This results in earlier access to communication and speech and impacts on all areas of the child's development. The child is enabled to act on his or her environment in a dynamic way, which also influences the way society views people with learning difficulties. The best argument for early intervention with augmentative signing is expressed by the children themselves.

References

Abrahamsen AM, Cavello M, McCluer J (1985) Is the sign advantage a robust phenomenon? From gesture to language in two modalities. Merill-Palmer Quarterly 31(2): 177–209.

Abrahamsen AM, Romski MA, Sevcik RA (1989) Concomitants of success in acquiring an augmentative communication system: Changes in attention, communication and sociability. American Journal of Mental Retardation 93: 475–96.

Balkany TJ, Downs MP, Jafek BW, Krajicek MJ (1979) Hearing Loss in Down's Syndrome. Clinical Paediatrics 18 (2): 116–18.

BDA British Deaf Association (1992) Dictionary of British Sign Language / English (BSL). London: Faber and Faber.

Beeghly M, Hanrahan A, Weiss B, Cicchetti D (1985) Development of communicative competence in children with Down Syndrome and non handicapped children. Paper presented in April 1985 at the Biennial Meeting of the Society for Research in Child Development. Toronto, Canada.

Berger J (1990) Interactions between parents and their infants with Down syndrome. In Cicchetti D, Beeghly M (Eds) Children with Down Syndrome: A developmental perspective. Cambridge, UK: Cambridge University Press.

Berger J, Cunningham CC (1981) Development of eye contact between mothers and normal versus Down Syndrome infants. Developmental Psychology 17: 678–89.

Berger J, Cunningham CC (1983a) Early social interactions between infants with Down Syndrome and their parents. Health Visitor 56: 58–60.

Berger J, Cunningham CC (1983b) The development of early vocal behaviours and interactions in Down Syndrome and non-handicapped infant-mother pairs. Developmental Psychology 19: 322–31.

Berger J, Cunningham CC (1985) Aspects of the development of signing in young infants with Down Syndrome. Child: Care, Health and Development 12: 13–24.

Bluma S, Shearer M, Frohman A, Hilliard J (1976) Portage Guide to Early Education. Windsor, UK: NFER-Nelson.

Broadley I, MacDonald J, Buckley S (1995) Working memory in children with Down's Syndrome. Down's Syndrome: Research and Practice 3 (1): 3–8.

Bryan T (1986) A review of studies of learning disabled children's communicative competence. In Schiefelbusch RL (Ed) Language Competence: Assessment and intervention. London: Taylor and Francis.

Buckley S, Sacks B (1987) The Adolescent with Down's Syndrome: Life for the teenager and for the family. Portsmouth, UK: Portsmouth Polytechnic.

Buckley S, Emslie M, Haslegrave G, Le Prevost P (1993) The Development of Language and Reading Skills in Children with Down's Syndrome. Portsmouth, UK: University of Portsmouth.

Buium N, Rynders J, Turnure J (1974) Early maternal linguistic environment of normal and Down's Syndrome language-learning children. American Journal of Mental Deficiency 79: 52–8.

Burden RL (1980) Measuring the effects of stress on the mothers of handicapped infants: must depression always follow? Child: Care, Health and Development 6: 111–25.

Cardoso-Martins C, Mervis CB, Mervis CA (1985) Early vocabulary acquisition by children with Down Syndrome. American Journal of Mental Deficiency Research 90: 177–84.

Clark S, Remington B, Light P (1986) An evaluation of the relationship between receptive speech skills and expressive signing. Journal of Applied Behaviour Analysis 19: 231–9.

Conti-Ramsden G (1990) Maternal recasts and other contingent replies to language impaired children. Journal of Speech and Hearing Disorders 55: 262–74.

Conti-Ramsden G (1994) Interaction with atypical learners. In Galloway C, Richards BJ (Eds) Input and Interaction in Language Acquisition. Cambridge, UK: Cambridge University Press.

Cousins L (1990) Maisy goes to Bed. London: Walker Books.

Cousins L (1992) Maisy goes to the Playground. London: Walker Books.

Cunningham CC (1979) In Craft M (Ed) Tredgold's Mental Retardation. 12th edn. London: Balliére Tindall.

Cunningham CC, Glenn SM, Wilkinson P, Sloper P (1985) Mental ability, symbolic play and receptive and expressive language of young children with Down's Syndrome. Journal of Child Psychology and Psychiatry 26(2): 255–65.

Cunningham C, McArthur K (1981) Hearing loss and treatment in young Down's Syndrome children. Child: Care, Health and Development 7: 357–74.

Daniloff J, Lloyd L, Fristoe M (1983) Amer-ind transparency. Journal of Speech and Hearing Disorders 48: 103–10.

Daniloff J, Shafer A (1981) A gestural communication program for severely and profoundly handicapped children. Language, Speech and Hearing Services in the Schools 12: 258–67.

Davies B (1985) Hearing problems. In Lane D, Stratford B (Eds) Current Approaches to Down's Syndrome. London: Cassell.

Dennis R, Reichle J, Williams W, Vogelsberg T (1982) Motoric factors influencing the selection of vocabulary for sign production programs. Journal of The Association for Persons with Severe Handicaps 7: 20–32.

DePaul R, Yoder DE (1986) Iconicity in manual sign systems for the augmentative communication user: Is that all there is? AAC Augmentative and Alternative Communication 2: 1–10.

Fischer MA (1983) An analysis of preverbal communication behaviour in Down's Syndrome and non-retarded children. Unpublished Ph.D. thesis. University of Oregon.

Gallaway C, Woll B (1994) Interaction and childhood deafness. In Gallaway C, Richards BJ (Eds) Input and Interaction in Language Acquisition. Cambridge, UK: Cambridge University Press.

Gibbs ED, Carswell LE (1988) Early use of Total Communication with a young Down Syndrome Child: A procedure for evaluating effectiveness. Paper presented at the Council for Exceptional Children Conference, Washington, DC. USA. March 1988.

Gibson D (1978) Down's Syndrome: the Psychology of Mongolism. Cambridge, UK: Cambridge University Press.

Giralometto LE (1988) Improving the social-conversational skills of developmentally delayed children: an intervention study. Journal of Speech and Hearing Disorders 53:156–67.

Grove T, Kennard G, Hall L (1992–1996). SIGNALONG Basic Vocabulary Phase 1 (1992), Phase 2 (1993), Phase 3 (1994), Signalong at Work. Introduction to the Work Place (1995), Phase 4 (1996). Communication and Language Centre, All Saints Hospital, Magpie Hall Rd. Chatham, Kent ME4 5NG.

Gunning M (1983) Alternatives to Speech in Cerebral Palsy. Facilitating communication in young non-speaking children at Cheyne Centre for Cerebral Palsy. Paper presented at a workshop on communication in Gottenburg, Sweden: October 1983.

Guralnick MJ (1982) Mainstreaming young handicapped children. A public policy and ecological systems analysis. In Spodek B (Ed) Handbook of Research in Early Childhood Education. New York: Free Press.

Harris M, Clibbens J, Chasin J, Tibbitts R (1989) The social context of early sign language development. First Language 9: 81–97.

Hedrick DL, Prather EM, Tobin AR (1965) and (1970). Sequenced Inventory of Communication Development. Seattle: University of Seattle.

Hornby G (1989) Effects on Fathers of Parenting a Child with Down's Syndrome. Education Section, Annual Conference 1989.

Hornby G (1991) Parental involvement: Ch. 8 in D Mitchell, RI Brown (Eds) Early Intervention Studies. London: Chapman and Hall.

Hurd A (1995) The influence of signing on adult / child interaction in a teaching context. Child Language Teaching and Therapy 11(3): 319–30.

Hyche JK, Bakeman RA, Lauren B (1992). Understanding communicative cues in infants with Down Syndrome: effects of mother's experience and infant's age. Journal of Applied Psychology 13, 1–16.

Ingalls RP (1978) Mental Retardation–The Changing Outlook. New York: John Wiley.

Jago JL, Jago AG, Hart M (1984) An evaluation of the total communication approach for teaching language skills to developmentally delayed preschool children. Education and Training of the Mentally Retarded 19(3): 175–82.

Jerger J (1970) Clinical experience with impedance audiometry. Archives of Otolanyngology 93: 311.

Johansson I (1985) Mongoloida barns jollerutuecklings provning av en analys modell. 22: 1–23. Dept. Phonetics, Umea University, Sweden.

Johansson I (1990) Early Intervention in Down's Syndrome. Translated by E Thomas. Speech Therapy in Practice. May 1990. UK.

Johansson I (1994) Language Development in Children with Special Needs-Performative communication. Translated by E Thomas. London: Jessica Kingsley.

Kahn J (1977). A comparison of manual and oral language training. Mental Retardation 15: 21–3.

Konstantases M, Oxman J, Webster C (1977) Simultaneous communication with autistic and other severely dysfunctional nonverbal children. Journal of Communication Disorders 10: 267–82.

Kouri T (1989) How manual sign acquisition relates to the development of spoken language: A case study. Language, Speech and Hearing Services in Schools. American Speech-Language-Hearing Association. USA.

Le Prevost P (1983) Using the Makaton Vocabulary in early language training with a Down's baby: a single case study. Mental Handicap 11 (March): 28–9.

Le Prevost P (1987) Pre-play groups aid language learning. Speech Therapy in Practice, September: 23–4.

Le Prevost P (1990) See and Say Manual of Signs. Speech and Language Therapy Dept., Slade Hospital, Horsepath Driftway, Headington, Oxford OX3 7JH. UK.

Le Prevost P (1993) The use of signing to encourage first words. In Buckley S, Emslie M, Haslegrave G, Le Prevost P (Eds) The Development of Language and Reading Skills in Children with Down's Syndrome. Portsmouth, UK: University of Portsmouth.

Luftig R, Page J, Lloyd L (1983) Ratings of translucency in manual signs as a predictor of sign learnability. Journal of Childhood Communication Disorders 6(2): 117–34.

McCormick L, Schiefelbusch R (1990) Early Language Intervention: An Introduction. 2nd edn. Columbus, OH: Merill/Macmillan.

Mackenzie S, Hulme C (1987) Memory span development in Down's Syndrome, severely subnormal and normal subjects. Cognitive Neuropsychology 4(3): 303–19.

McLean J, Snyder-McLean L (1978) A Transactional Approach to Early Language Training. Columbus, OH: Merill/Macmillan.

Mahoney G, Powell A (1986) Transactional Intervention Programme: Teacher's guide. Farmington CT: Pediatric Research and Training Center, University of Connecticut Health Center, USA.

Manolson A (1983) It Takes Two to Talk. Toronto: Hanen Early Language Resource Centre.

Marshall NR, Hegrenes JR, Goldstein S (1973) Verbal interactions: Mothers and their retarded children vs. mothers and their non-retarded children. American Journal of Mental Deficiency 77: 415–19.

Matey C, Kretschmer R (1985) A comparison of mother speech to Down's Syndrome, hearing-impaired and normal-hearing children. Volta Review 87: 205–13.

Morgenstern F (1981) Teaching Plans for Handicapped Children. London: Methuen.

MVDP Makaton Vocabulary Development Project (1991) Makaton Nursery Rhymes Video with Dave Benson Phillips. Felgate Productions Ltd. Virgin Vision Ltd. Available from WH Smith, UK.

Ormerod JJ, Huebner ES (1988) Crisis Intervention: Facilitating parental acceptance of a child's Handicap. Psychology in Schools 25(4).

Owens, RE Jr (1993) Mental Retardation: Difference and Delay. Environmental influences on the language of individuals with mental retardation. Ch. 12 in DK Bernstein, E Tiegermann (Eds) Language and Communication Disorders in

Children. Columbus, OH: Merrill/Macmillan.

Price P, Bochner S (1991) Mother–child interaction and early language intervention. In Mitchell D, Brown RI (Eds) Early Intervention Studies for Young Children with Special Needs. London: Chapman and Hall.

Ratokalau NB, Robb MP (1993) Mental retardation: Difference and delay. In Bernstein DK, Tiegermann E (Eds) Language and Communication Disorders in Children. 3rd edn. Columbus, OH: Merrill/Macmillan.

Reich R (1978) Gestural facilitation of expressive language in moderately/severely retarded preschoolers. Mental Retardation 16: 113–17.

Reichle J, Williams W, Ryan S (1981) Spoken words and manual signs as encoding strategies in short-term memory for the mentally retarded. TASH Journal 6: 48–56.

Sameroff AJ, Chandler MJ (1975) Reproductive risk and the continuum of caretaking casualty. In Horowitz FD (Ed) Review of Child Development Research. Vol. 4. Chicago: University of Chicago Press.

Schaeffer B (1980) Spontaneous language through signed speech. In Schiefelbusch RL (Ed) Nonspeech, Language and Communication: Analysis and Intervention. Baltimore, USA: University Park Press. pp 421–46.

Serpell R, Nabuzoka D (1991) Early intervention in third world countries, Ch. 5 in D Mitchell D, Brown RI (Eds) Early Intervention Studies for Young Children with Special Needs. London: Chapman and Hall.

Sloper P, Cunningham CC, Arnljotsdottir M (1983) Child: Care, Health and Development 9: 357–76.

Tiegermann E, Siperstein H (1984) Individual patterns of interaction in the mother–child dyad: implications for parent–child intervention. Topics in Language Disorders 4: 50–61.

United Nations (1986) Manual of Equalization of Opportunities for Disabled Persons. New York: United Nations.

Walker M (1980) Makaton Vocabulary Development Project, 31 Firwood Drive, Camberley, Surrey GU15 3QD.

Walker M (1985) Revised Makaton Vocabulary. Makaton Vocabulary Development Project, 31 Firwood Drive, Camberley, Surrey GUI5 3QD. UK.

Worthington A (1982) Coming to Terms with Mental Handicap.Huddersfield: Helena Press,UK.

Chapter 5

The Role of Sensory Reinforcement in Developing Interactions

KAREN BUNNING

Sensory stimulation has been employed as a key factor in many approaches and for a variety of purposes with learning disabled children and adults. It has been used in the pursuit of appropriate, educational and leisure opportunities, and as an artefact of behaviour modification programmes. Therapists and teachers frequently employ sensory stimulation techniques as part of a broader approach to arouse improved attention and self-awareness, particularly amongst those children with severely restricted communication skills who are largely dependent on significant others to supply their personal and social needs. Amongst its various applications are: the reinforcement of a desirable behaviour emitted by an individual; the encouragement of a relaxed state; and the general stimulation of an individual so that interactions with people and objects in the environment occur.

The multi-sensory approach has had significant influence over curriculum planning and educational equipment over recent years. Long-horn (1988) developed a multi-sensory curriculum for children with profound and multiple learning difficulties. Her reasoning for such an approach was the 'awakening' of the senses to facilitate a greater understanding of the world. Her work is a collection of practical ideas which has, more recently, been expanded to integrate with some National Curriculum subjects in selected special schools (Cavet & Mount, 1995).

There are a variety of commercial companies that manufacture and market equipment that is associated with the multi-sensory environment or associated approaches. A collection of devices and objects are on offer which provide stimulating or relaxing sensory experiences. Most of the equipment has been designed specifically for use by people with profound and multiple disabilities (Cavet & Mount, 1995), although some of the items that produce visual effects have originated from discotheques, eg. strobe lights etc.

Many schools have created their own 'sensory environments' by adapting available space for the display of multi-sensory stimuli for access by students. However, many questions are posed regarding the precise and consistent use of such equipment. What is the purpose of the child's presence in such an enriched environment? Who will benefit from an approach that uses sensory stimulation? What response outcomes can be expected from a client? By what process are the most appropriate and motivating items selected for the individual? What is the role of the teacher or therapist in support of the client's responses? These questions all point to the need for a clear rationale for using sensory stimulation techniques with severely learning-disabled children.

Contingent and non-contingent stimulation

Definition

Sensory stimulation can be divided into contingent and non-contingent forms. Contingent stimulation is defined as an effect that is dependent on the operational activity of the individual, thereby providing consequences said to be reinforcing. The person performs an action, usually motor in type, which results in sensory feedback. Information is provided about the qualities of the item or person in relation to the behaviour emitted. Furthermore, if the sensation produced by the child's action is pleasurable to the individual, it is likely to encourage repeated emissions of the action in search of the motivating consequence, as in the establishment of cause–effect. Indeed, contingent reinforcement in behaviourally based programmes has been used increasingly for the purpose of establishing new response modes amongst individuals.

Non-contingent stimulation occurs independently of the actions of people. It is present within the environment and it is possible for the individual to receive sensations whilst remaining passive to the process. The importance of non-contingent stimulation has long been pointed out by developmental psychologists (Bowlby, 1953), whilst highlighting that a lack of environmental stimulation may lead to a depression in skills acquisition. Other researchers have commented on the positive effects of an enriched environment on the behaviours of children (Berkson & Mason, 1964; O' Brien, 1975).

However, it does not necessarily follow that non-contingent (unconditional) stimulation is sufficient in itself to produce skill development in children with a learning disability (Clarke & Clarke, 1974). There are a number of variables that must be considered in examination of 'What constitutes a stimulating environment?'. The child needs to be considered in relation to the following:

(i)   available skill set in relation to environmental contingencies;
(ii)   the frequency and intensity of non-purposeful behaviours, including stereotypes, aggression, self-injury, or high levels of neutral behaviour which may represent challenges to those trying to establish patterns of interaction with the individual;
(iii)   the presence of additional sensory and motor impairments which may influence both the assimilation of incoming sensory information and the resulting organisation of adaptive responses.

The child

Who are we talking about and what are the presenting difficulties?

There are some learning-disabled children who experience extreme difficulties in the areas of personal, cognitive, communicative and social development. These are the children who have a more severe degree of learning disability which may be further affected by additional sensory or motor impairments. They are largely dependent on significant others for support. A number of challenges are presented for the parent, teacher or therapist working with these children, not least of which is how to establish a meaningful form of contact with the child who does not seem to admit other people for purposeful interactions, nor to allow a variety of objects for examination and creative activity.

These children with severe learning disabilities who are not yet intentional communicators may appear isolated from or oblivious to their immediate environment. Sometimes words are simply not enough for the success of a communication act and may even be surplus to a meaningful interaction. Providing appropriate support and facilitation for communicative attempts can prove difficult due to the limited nature of responding behaviour. Significant others frequently need to be good observers of minimal behaviours and to fulfil an interpreting role based on their familiarity, knowledge and experience of the person (McLeod, Houston & Seyfort, 1995). They also require considerable skills in the use of facilitative language techniques, such as joint attention, turn-taking, and for the 'reading' of client responses. The question of how to motivate the child to a state of optimal responding is central to the concerns of the professional, together with the selection of preferred reinforcement for the individual's adaptive behaviour.

The level of environmental stimulation, both in terms of quantity and quality, in relation to surroundings, activity and interaction opportunities is important. A lack of stimulation may negatively influence levels of purposeful activity and may even effect a rise in non-purposeful behaviour. This is consistent with the view of Presland (1991) who suggested that a 'lack of materials and activities of interest' may lead to the emergence of stereotypies as a 'way of passing the time' (p.67).

It is acknowledged that the environment has a role to play regarding the engagement levels of learning-disabled children and a lack of stimulation may lead to depressed levels of purposeful activity. The television reports from Romania at the end of the 1980s showed children in barren institutions displaying classic examples of stereotyped behaviour. However, the simple *presence* of stimuli may not be sufficient to affect the levels of non-purposeful behaviour. Jones, Walsh and Sturmey (1995) cite a study by Dehaven, Rees-Thomas and Benton (1980), where little difference was shown in the high levels of stereotypy emitted by participants who were moved from institutional units to rooms with toys and minimal social interaction. Therefore, the indiscriminate presence of stimuli had no effect on the levels of stereotypy. The contingency of the stimulation, the role of the communication partner and the type of reinforcement offered are likely to be significant factors.

Engagement levels

The engagement levels and the presenting characteristics of the learning-disabled population have frequently been documented. The problems seem to be associated with limited purposeful engagement and the prevalence of problem behaviours, ie. stereotypies. Stereotypic behaviour has been defined by Berkson (1983) as: 'immature voluntary behaviours in the repertoire for a long time, and out of synchrony with "normal development", whose patterns tend to be unresponsive to environmental change.' (p. 240).

High levels of stereotypic behaviour have been reported amongst those children with a more severe degree of learning disability (Jones et al, 1995). Felce, Kushlick and Mansell (1980) found that, from a cross section of severely learning-disabled children resident in two hospital villas, the average purposeful activity per day was 31%, and from a similar cross section of adults in three hospital villas, 39% of the day. Jones, Favell, Lattimore and Risley (1984) looked more specifically at the independent and active use of leisure materials amongst residents with profound learning disabilities plus multiple handicaps. They found that less than 13% of the available time was spent in active engagement with the stimuli. Storey, Bates, McGhee and Dycus (1984) observed that self-stimulatory behaviour, defined as stereotypic and repetitive, was prevalent amongst the developmentally delayed population. Repp, Felce and Barton (1988) concluded in a review of documented surveys that stereotypic and self-injurious behaviours were indeed common forms of maladaptive responding amongst severely handicapped persons.

Others have suggested that there is a correlation between communication difficulties and behavioural problems (Chamberlain, Chung & Jenner, 1993). They concluded that the more able clients, having the skills to verbalise their feelings and internal judgements in a common code of reference with their staff, experienced comparatively reduced problem behaviours. It appears that the individuals who are unable to inform others of activity choice, or to send or respond to verbal communications, demonstrate a limited ability to initiate purposeful engagements with the constituent elements of the environment, ie. person, object and person–object.

Additional sensory and motor impairments

Naturally, the potential presence of additional sensory or motor impairments must be determined by significant others who are in contact with the learning-disabled child, particularly when a sensory approach to stimulation is being considered. This is important for the clinical decisions regarding:

1   The selection of stimuli;
2   The identification and targeting of the child's responses;
3   The provision of appropriate interactions in support of the child's responding behaviour.

The prevalence of additional sensory impairments is generally known to be higher amongst the more severely learning-disabled population (Dupont, 1981; Kropka, Williams & Clements, 1984; Yeates, 1992a,b). Furthermore, a lack of reliable assessment data may lead to a deficiency in essential personal and environmental adaptations, which may in turn *further* negatively influence engagement levels. It has also been suggested that the incidence and severity of present impairments increases with the degree of learning disability (Dupont, 1981). The relationship between non-purposeful behaviour, in particular stereotypies, and additional sensory impairments has been variously documented (Eyman & Call, 1977; Stainback & Stainback, 1980). More specifically, Jones et al (1995) cite studies that relate stereotypic behaviours to individual types of impairment: eye pressing and light gazing in children with visual impairments (Jan, Freeman, McCormick, Scott, Robertson & Newman, 1983); and multiple stereotypies including self-injury, tongue chewing, hand flapping and putting fingers in mouth, in deaf-blind children (Aurand, Sisson, Aach & Van Hasslelt, 1989; Myrbakk, 1991) amongst others.

So, we see that individuals who are severely developmentally delayed are likely to engage in non-purposeful behaviour characterised by stereotypies and others. The ability level of the child, the environment in terms of the quantity and quality of available stimulation, and the presence of additional sensory and motor impairments, are all important factors for the consideration of the teacher or therapist.

Types of sensory stimulation

Contingent and non-contingent

Contingent and non-contingent forms of sensory stimulation are currently available via a number of contexts. These are roughly divided into two main areas. The first focuses on the provision of sensory-based leisure environments that incorporate both types of stimulation. The second emphasises the role of sensory stimulation in more objectively designed therapy programmes for the purposes of learning and change in response repertoires. This also takes into account the phenomenon of sensory reactivity and its importance to the responding behaviour of individuals.

Snoezelen

'Snoezelen' is a sensory environment that has originated from Holland (Hulsegge & Verheul, 1987). The word 'snoezelen' is a contraction of two separate words: 'sniffing' and 'dozing'. This is said to identify the two important aspects of Snoezelen, the activation or exploration of the environment, and the passive or restful surroundings. Snoezelen has been defined as:

> '...a selective offer of primary stimuli in an attractive setting.
> '...a primary activation of severely mentally handicapped people, espe-cially aimed at sensory perception and experience, by means of light, sound, touch, smell and taste.' (Hulsegge & Verheul, 1987, p.31).

Hulsegge and Verheul (1987) stress the importance of personal experi-ence facilitation for those people who are 'different', through the provi-sion of fixed environments comprising a variety of sensations and activities. Sensory stimulation is a mixture of non-contingent and contin-gent reinforcement. So far there have been few objective evaluations of Snoezelen to assess its impact on users, other than the anecdotal evidence provided by some staff. The Dutch Snoezelen workers have declined to formally evaluate its effects, arguing that its purpose is one of leisure, and an objective assessment of user outcomes would shift the environment into a therapeutic and skills development dimension. Hulsegge and Verheul (1987) mention that Snoezelen may give rise to therapeutic opportunities but that is *not* its primary purpose.

Effectiveness

An initial investigation into the effects of Snoezelen on the concentra-tion and responsiveness of eight people with profound learning disabilities was conducted by Ashby, Lindsay, Pitcaithly, Broxholme and

Geelen (1995). Assessments took place immediately after the cessation of each therapy session. Two participants showed significant improvement in their concentration levels with smaller gains in four others. Due to the limited sample size and the multiple variables present in the therapeutic condition, as Snoezelen is an environment containing multiple forms of sensory stimulation, the results were inconclusive.

Others have been concerned with the nature of user experiences in this environment, focusing more specifically on the client–carer relationship, positive expressions of pleasure and relaxation time spent in Snoezelen. Haggar and Hutchinson (1991) reviewed the use of a Snoezelen suite in a long-stay hospital for the learning disabled, and concluded that it provided a valuable leisure resource for the residents, influencing an increase in the amount of time spent off the wards. However, its success is probably dependent on it being the sole opportunity for recreational pursuit within the hospital context, because alternative openings were severely restricted.

To date, there has been little evidence in support of the idea that the provision of a multi-sensory approach optimises the learning process in severely learning-disabled children or adults. Cavet and Mount (1995) stress the need for some rigorous research to evaluate the effects of multi-sensory environments. They identify a number of questions in relation to the introduction of such environments, some of which demand the specific address of the following issues:

1 Justification for the choice of equipment;
2 Establishment of compatibility with the philosophy of social role valorisation in adult settings;
3 Rationalisation of specific need for this approach, ie. could normal, everyday activities provide the client with the same opportunities for responding?;
4 Recording method of individual responses and progress;
5 Measurement of effectiveness over time; and
6 Training of significant others for the support of focal people.

Leisure or therapeutic opportunity

For the practising teacher or therapist, consideration of the purpose in using the Snoezelen environment is required. If it is to be used according to its stated aim of leisure (Hulsegge & Verheul, 1987), and not as a focal provider of therapeutic or educational opportunities, the role of the teacher or therapist will vary accordingly. For the purposes of providing a leisure facility, the significant other enacts the role of facilitator to the child-directed activities. This may involve assisting the individual to move in the environment, to position him or herself for optimal sensory effect and to help in the operation of contingent stimuli.

Naturally, therapeutic opportunities will arise but this is more a consequence rather than an objective of the whole experience.

If the main purpose of the sensory environment is for the creation of educational and therapeutic opportunities, the role of the significant other in relation to the child requires operational clarification. Consideration needs to be given to the following:

1   What type of sensory opportunity is appropriate to the individual's skill set and produces a positive response;
2   How each sensory opportunity is presented to the child;
3   What communicative signals are used to attract the child's attention, ie. verbal, touch or visual signal;
4   What responses are expected of the child as an active participant of the process.

A system of clinical decisions is required to guide an approach to sensory stimulation with this population: one that makes explicit the components of the therapy procedure so that teachers and therapists may devise sensory opportunities that are appropriate to the individual's skills and motivation.

Contingent sensory reinforcement

The role of sensory reinforcement in the changing of old behaviours and the learning of new ones has long been of interest. Kish (1966) initially drew attention to the potential usefulness of sensory reinforcement and its effect on the behaviour of animals. In conclusion of his investigations, Kish recommended that 'various forms of stimulation may function as reinforcers even though unrelated to the usual organic drive conditions.' (p.150).

A more extensive investigation was conducted by Olds and Milner (1954) who looked at the behaviour of rats when electrical stimulation was applied to some areas of the brain, later referred to as 'pleasure areas' (Campbell, 1973). It was hypothesised that these brain domains might also be made electrically active by nerve impulses originating from stimulation of peripheral receptors. Obviously, for practical and ethical reasons, direct stimulation of the human brain presents difficulties. In the 1960s research into non-invasive procedures incorporating contingent reinforcement was carried out. Murphy (1982) reported on the positive effects of contingent sensory stimuli on the responses of young non-handicapped children.

A study by Pace, Ivancic, Edwards, Iwata and Page (1985) reported the successful facilitation of adaptive skills through the presentation of stimuli known to be reinforcing to the subjects concerned. Sandler and

McLain (1987) investigated the reinforcing properties of vestibular stimulation on multiply handicapped children and as a result suggested that vestibular stimulation was the preferred reinforcer over food, praise, visual and auditory stimulation. They concluded that the type of stimulation is important to the therapeutic effect. Other studies have concentrated on drawing comparisons between sensory stimulation and other types of reinforcement, such as edibles (Jones, 1980; Goodall, Corbett, Murphy & Callias, 1982), and social reinforcers (Johnson, Frith & Davey, 1978). It was concluded that sensory reinforcement with some individuals can be at least as effective as food (Jones, 1980; Goodall et al, 1982) and more effective than social rewards (Johnson et al, 1978; Goodall et al, 1982). Kiernan (1974) suggested that the provision of a sensory event was the most effective form of reinforcement as its satiation level could not be reached quite so easily as that of others, ie. food and drink.

Use of vibration

Vibration is a form of stimulation that has frequently been used in behavioural management programmes based on the differential reinforcement of an incompatible behaviour (DRI); the differential reinforcement of the other behaviour (DRO); or the differential reinforcement of an alternative behaviour (DRA) (Jones et al, 1995). These schedules have been used specifically to effect a reduction in levels of stereotypies, aggression and other aberrant behaviours (Repp et al, 1983; Walsh, 1986; Jones, Baker & Murphy, 1988).

Studies supporting the use of vibration have been reported in the literature. One of the earliest reports on its application to humans was by Shaefer (1960) who observed that a seven-month-old child tended to prolong contact with an electric hair cutter by head movements at the end of each hair cutting stroke. Further observations of the child's engagement were recorded upon the presentation of an electric toothbrush. The child held the brush at different times in his lap, against his knee, in his mouth, and most frequently, but for shorter durations, against his head. As many as 150 responses were recorded during one 30-minute session. Shaefer later used the toothbrush to reinforce the co-operative taking of medication.

Contingent vibration has been used to reinforce purposeful behaviour whilst effecting a change in the identified incompatible behaviour (Meyerson, Kerr & Michael, 1967; Bailey & Meyerson, 1969, 1970). Exploratory work on its effects on skill set acquisition of children with multiple handicaps has been conducted. Byrne (1979) provided structured and consistent vibro-tactile input to the environment of a 12-year-old girl who had been diagnosed as deaf-blind. By means of a range of vibro-tactile devices the child was provided with feedback about her actions on the environment and thereby, reportedly learned to stand, walk, dance, swim, feed herself, and help with bathing and dressing – all within a six week period.

A review of the literature has specifically revealed skill acquisition in the following areas, when vibratory reinforcement has been contingent in the learning schedule:

- taking medication (Shaefer, 1960);
- switch operation (Meyerson et al, 1967; Rehagen & Thalen, 1972)
- performance on discrimination tasks (Johnson et al, 1978);
- interaction with others (Byrne, 1979; Jones, 1980);
- exploring and manipulating objects (Jones, 1980; Murphy, Carr & Callias, 1986)
- a reduction in undesirable behaviours including stereotypies and self-injury (Bailey & Meyerson, 1969; Nunes, Murphy & Ruprecht, 1977; Jones et al, 1988).

The inclusion of vibro-tactile stimulation in the repertoire of therapies and reinforcements for use with learning disabled people has been recommended (Prosser, 1988). It has been reported to have a clear advantage over edibles in its contingent nature (ie. access to food is non-contingent and there may be ethical concerns over its inclusion in a stimulus-reinforcement programme). Satiation level may also be reached quite quickly. Kiernan (1974) proposed that the most effective reinforcement is a sensory event which may be applied immediately, maintaining the response-contingent model.

Having recognised the importance of contingent reinforcement needs in the therapy procedure as a prime facilitator of response change in clients, consideration is now given to the concept of stimulus reactivity.

Sensory reactivity

The differential effects of object reactivity and certain toys on the play and social responses of non-handicapped children have been observed (Quilitch & Risley, 1973; Hendrickson, Tremblay, Strain & Shores, 1981). Additionally, some evidence has been submitted to suggest that toys with reactive qualities can substantially influence children's toy manipulation (Corter & Jamieson, 1977).

Reactive toys are said to be highly responsive to a child's manipulation. Hooper and Wambold (1978) described reactive toys as those items which, when acted upon, temporarily sustained motion and/or produced auditory, visual or tactile feedback. *Non-reactive toys*, on the other hand, were said to possess limited potential to provide sensory feedback as a consequence of manipulation during the normal course of play.

Thomas, Phemister and Richardson (1981) found that both non-handicapped and severely learning-disabled children interacted more with a 'novel' object that produced both a visual and tonal effect when manipulated than with three other non-reactive toys typically found in a nursery class. Bambara, Spiegel-McGill, Shores and Fox (1984) compared the effects of three commercial reactive toys and three non-reactive toys on the estimated amount of time three children with severe learning disabilities engaged in manipulative activity and visual attention with the toys. The non-reactive toys were identical to the reactive ones, but were modified to eliminate or restrict their sensory feedback features of sound and sustained motion. They concluded that in comparison to the non-reactive toys, the reactive toys had a substantially greater influence on the amount of time each of the three participants engaged in manipulative activity.

Murphy et al (1986) examined the quantity and quality of toy contact in twenty children with a profound learning disability. They used specifically adapted toys which made extra stimuli available as a reinforcer to manipulations in one of the two experimental conditions, and none in the other. They concluded that the children were more actively engaged with the adapted toys than the control toys, and also exhibited fewer stereotypies whilst playing with the special toys.

The concept of reactivity potential as an influential factor in child engagements is important to the creation of social interaction opportunities where sensation is employed as a conducting agent between the person's self and people/objects in the environment, ie. the different effects of reactive objects and person contact on the engagement levels of severely learning-disabled children compared to those of non-reactive stimuli.

The studies reported here provide empirical support for the use of reactive objects for stimulating activity. A number of recommendations may be made based on these research findings:

1   Items which provide sensory feedback that is contingent on child activity/manipulations are preferred over non-contingent reactivity, or those which sustain activation after only one motor response. The latter are thought not to stimulate the active responding of the individual.

2   Individual differences in preferences for sensory feedback should be taken into account, as supported by Rincover, Newson, Lovaas and Koegel (1977); Guttierrez-Griepp (1984).

3   Consideration should be given to selecting reactive objects/items which are commensurate with the skill set level of the individual.

The development of a suitable approach, where the underlying aim is to increase the purposeful responding behaviour of focal subjects, must necessarily pay attention not only to the reinforcing qualities of the material used, but also to the process by which targeted behaviours may be rewarded. Briefly, intervention should aim to encourage individual responses by the provision of motivating consequences, in order that purposeful behaviours are increased. It therefore follows that the resulting rationale must include: the principles of contingent sensory reinforcement as demonstrated in behaviour modification programmes; and the use of sensory based activities that are reactive to participant behaviour and provide reinforcing feedback.

Rationale for a sensory-based intervention

Opportunities

In consideration of a sensory-based approach to intervention, the provision of social opportunities needs to be explored in detail. A child's lack of social participation may be representative of inappropriate opportunities rather than limited, individual potential. Consideration must be given to the level of environmental stimulation, both in terms of quantity and quality, in relation to the surroundings, activities and interaction opportunities. A lack of stimulation may negatively influence levels of purposeful activity and may even effect a rise in non-purposeful behaviour.

The significant other is concerned, therefore, with the provision of opportunities for the child's social responding, both in terms of their frequency and their quality in relation to the child's skill set. An approach that focuses specifically on the provision of interaction opportunities is Intensive Interaction (Nind & Hewett, 1994). It was developed as an approach to establish the basics of communication with people with severe learning disabilities, focusing on the creation of spontaneous interaction opportunities for the individual. It was devised in the 1980s at the Harperbury Hospital School where a large amount of curriculum development work was being undertaken. A range of informal interactive games were devised for use with pre-verbal clients who '...were experiencing extreme difficulty in learning and in relating to others and who were demonstrating ritualistic and challenging behaviours.' (Nind & Hewett, 1994, p. 8).

Its practical application has been described as '...spontaneous and responsive rather than pre-planned.' (p. 9). Although its emphasis is on the organisation of interaction opportunities, it provides little, if any, defined detail for the potential practitioner regarding specific therapy objectives, stimuli details, facilitative strategies, and response criteria for reinforcement. It is perhaps more accurate to view it as a philosophy to guide spontaneous interaction with this population. It may ultimately say more about the development of a positive attitude to the disabled person than it does about the operationalisation of a therapeutic technique.

In summary, the provision of opportunities for responding is considered crucial to the child's social development. The constituent elements of those interaction opportunities must be explored if the individual is to gain access to available environmental contingencies which may otherwise be restricted by the child's own skill set. The child's self is the centre of his or her universe; there is person(s); object(s); and event(s) (person–object) which provide possible contact/interaction points. The objective is to work to the strengths of the individual and to use each person's skill set in an effective and realistic way.

Communication partnership

The second important area that requires consideration is the communication partnership between the child and his or her significant others. The role of the significant other is critical to any potential outcomes in the client's responding behaviour where sensory stimulation is employed as part of the therapeutic procedure. This is the first major decision area for the therapist in devising suitable sensory-based opportunities for the individual: What degree of responsibility for the success of the interaction is assumed by the child and by the therapist? The difference between a leisure experience and an educational or therapeutic one may be defined by the clarification of the roles in the communication partnership.

Increased interest in the influential role of the communication partner has been shown by a number of researchers. MacDonald and Gillette (1986) criticised the traditional language programme approach with children for its neglect of interactional skills. They also pointed out that the predominantly active communication role of the adult in these programmes may in fact encourage the role of respondent in the child. Furthermore, their own study of adult–child interactions led them to suggest that communication skill set match is infrequently achieved.

The development of intentional communication and the assignment of responsibilities within the communication act, between the role of sender and the role of receiver, is viewed as crucially important to the communication partnership. This is so that the interactive opportunities offered to the client are not only motivating but also represent appropriate demands of the client's skills. The opportunities provided through the communication partnership of the sender (client) and the receiver (therapist) change to reflect the developing skills of the individual. The assignment of roles within this partnership is not only relevant to the intervention process, but also to the daily communication acts which are on offer. In order to facilitate a greater success rate in communicative exchanges between client and carer, the various responsibilities of the partnership need to be understood, so that appropriate modifications may be made.

Three areas within the developing continuum of intentional communication have been identified for the realisation of the therapist's role.

1 Pre-intentional communication – from reflexive to reactive:

The earliest stage of pre-intentional communication has been characterised by the *reflexive* and later *reactive* responding of the individual (sender). Early *reflex* responses to both internal and external stimuli gradually become more selectively *reactive* to certain events and people in the environment, as the ability to discriminate incoming sensory data develops. The role of the therapist is crucial for the assignment of communicative intent and meaning to the sender's signals. In the earliest stages, the therapist draws heavily on his or her own knowledge base of the client (sender) and proceeds as interpreter through trial and error, ie. 'the guessing game'. As the child's responses become more specifically reactive to constituents in the environment, so the role of the therapist in 'inference of intent' changes (Gibb-Harding, 1983).

2 Pre-intentional communication – proactive:

Proactive responding emerges as the sender starts to act purposefully on people and objects in the environment, such that these acts 'become signals' to the receiver (Coupe & Joliffe, 1988). Vocalised dialogues between sender and receiver occur, comprising both spontaneous and imitated sound sequences. Eye contact and routines of joint attention and joint action start to emerge, allowing the sender to anticipate each contact in the routine. The sender searches and reaches for desired objects, engages in non-specific actions with objects, ie. hitting, shaking, manipulating, etc.

In response to the actions of the sender, the receiver becomes increasingly selective. Indeed, the consistent reactions of the receiver are a major influence on the development of intentional communication. The role of assignment of meaning and intent is reduced by the discriminating signals emanating from the sender. The receiver is a good observer of the client's behaviour for the construction of an appropriate response in support.

3 Intentional communication from basic to conventional and referential:

Intentional communication has been referred to as *basic (or primitive)*, *conventional* and *referential* forms of responding. The *basic* level is characterised by the context of the communication. There is emerging evidence of event knowledge, as the sender starts to eye gaze alternately between the receiver and a desired item. Frequently, the movement of objects occurs whilst looking at the receiver (Bruner, 1978). Sometimes the receiver is moved to a desired object or location. The receiver recognises the sender's actions in context and uses the cues of the situation to interpret the sender's meaning.

The *conventional* level sees the emergence of signals in the forms of gestures; vocalisations (ie. jargon); verbalisations (ie. protowords); and first words (Coupe & Joliffe, 1988). Communications begin to have purpose and functions emerge: requestive; responding; informing about self and world; greeting; protesting; rejecting people, objects and events (Roth & Speckman, 1984a,b). The receiver is supported in the interpretation role by the *contextually mobile* signals of the sender, pointing out people and objects in the environment to the receiver.

The *referential* level is characterised by speech or a formalised alternative, such as signed communication. These have been described as 'signal bearers' of the intended meanings (Coupe & Joliffe, 1988). Both functions and meanings are expanded. The demands of the interpreting role are reduced significantly as a common code of communicative reference is employed in the intentional communication act.

This developmental continuum provides direction for a number of components considered important to the development of a sensory-based intervention:

1   It highlights the changing role of the therapist as receiver in a communication partnership with a client and the need for a systematic realisation of that role, ie. a hierarchy of support cues to reflect the various levels identified on the continuum of intentional communication development.
2   It provides the basis for the definition of the constituent areas of the interaction or engagement, namely person, object and person–object.
3   It establishes the direction of the intervention or the ultimate goal of therapy towards more clearly defined signals of communication, where there is less emphasis on the inferential role of the significant other and more on the role of the client as sender of communicative messages.

Motivating consequences

In order to attract the client's attention to the properties and functions of environmental constituents, whether object or forms of person contact, the intervention is concerned with forms of sensory stimulation that provide motivating consequences for the individual. The premise is that an environment which is stimulating to the individual will engender their purposeful responses to it. This supports the ideas expressed by Kielhofner (1985) who commented that adaptive behaviour '...is not an automatic or passive response to the environment. Before the system intakes it must have a reason for doing so, thus the built in, or acquired, purposes or goals of the system are critical.' (p.7). In short, it is the responsibility of the therapist or teacher to establish the immediate goal of therapy by the provision of a desirable stimulus or event.

Three major sensory systems have been most frequently targeted by researchers. These are the tactile; vestibular; and proprioceptive systems. Although these systems are emphasised more importantly, the other four main sensory systems (visual, auditory, gustatory and olfactory) are considered because of the nature of sensory interdependence which exists in the central nervous system of the human organism. Also, it would be practically impossible to omit any one sensory system at will! The main reasons for the selection of the tactile and vestibular systems are as follows.

Tactile stimulation

The use of the tactile and vestibular modes of stimulation has been recommended for use with learning-disordered children by Sensory Integration Therapists (Ayres, 1972, 1979). Sensory Integration is 'a theory of brain-behaviour relationships' (Fisher, Murray & Bundy, 1991, p.4) supporting the notion that the human organism possesses networks of neurones that feed back and feed forward sensory information, and are so constructed that every time we engage in any action, we simultaneously provide ourselves with sensory input arising from the action, ie. feedback. Therapy is sensory-based and involves '.....sensory stimulation and adaptive responses to it according to the child's neurologic needs. Therapy usually involves full body movements that provide vestibular, proprioceptive and tactile stimulation....... The goal of therapy is to improve the way the brain processes and organises sensations.' (Ayres, 1979; p.184).

The importance of tactile contact in the early social development of the infant has been stressed. Day (1982) explored the content of parent–infant interactions and found them to be mainly tactile in type. Also, tactile stimulation represents a more immediate form of environmental contact which does not require symbolic representations such as spoken words, iconic gestures or formal sign communications for its occurrence. The stimulus-response demands are reduced in touch contact. Complex encoding or decoding is not required at a cortical level. Incoming tactile information appears to be modulated at the level of the spinal cord and this process is dependent on information descending from higher levels of the central nervous system (Fisher & Dunn, 1983).

Vestibular stimulation

Vestibular stimulation represents either an excitatory form of arousal, ie. rotation which is angular stimulation of the semi-circular canals, or a calming form of stimulation, ie. rocking, which is linear stimulation of the semi-circular canals. The excitatory nature of angular stimulation focuses on changes in the rate and direction of the rotations. The calming influence of linear stimulation focuses on a slow, rhythmic pattern of rocking, and toddlers through to adults engage in many vestibular based activities, such as skate boarding, swings, ski-ing and driving fast cars. There are few adults who can resist turning a revolution or two in one of those executive swivel chairs!

Proprioceptive feedback

Of course, the third sensory modality of importance is the propriocep- tive channel, or the route by which our brains are informed of our actions in the world. Since most of the responses produced by clients are likely to be motor ones, this crucial link must be included in the feedback loop (Tickle, 1988).

Choice of sensory reinforcement

What governs the selection of sensory stimuli needs to be addressed. Is it the responsibility of the therapist or teacher to choose or is the selection based on what is known about the client's responses to reinforcing sensory experiences? Is the choice of stimuli solely client-directed or is the supporting role of the therapist crucial to the responding behaviour, ie. how the stimulus is presented to the individual? Mason, McGee, Farmer-Dougan and Risley (1989) observed a greater effect in on-task performance using client-selected reinforcing stimuli, although this may have been a consequence of the experimental procedure, ie. a superior assessment procedure was used compared with the second condition using teacher-selected reinforcing stimuli. A reinforcer assessment package based on a range of stimuli to which participant approach behaviour had already been observed, made for a higher quality inter- vention, rather than the randomly teacher-selected version of the other condition.

The personal evaluations of the individual need to be considered when building up appropriate opportunities for sensory stimulation. There would be little point in enforcing a sensory experience on a reluc- tant customer. Therefore, the therapist acknowledges those sensory events that provoke an aversive reaction by the individual, and accord- ingly omits them from any subsequent therapy activities. Therapy oppor- tunities focus on the sensory preferences of each child, thereby representing motivating consequences to the individual. However, the therapist or teacher is *instrumental* in taking the decisions regarding the selection of appropriate stimuli.

Distinctive feedback features

In order to ascertain those stimulus properties that are motivating to the individual, the distinctive feedback features of each item need to be examined. Then it may be possible to identify features in common for detecting those which provoke an aversive response from the individual and those which engender purposeful responding by their motivating consequences. Because a child has responded positively to certain items sharing the same properties, it should be possible to generate new ideas for stimuli that provide similar feedback. Bambara et al (1984) performed a dimensional analysis on sensory stimuli used in their study comparing the effects of reactive and non-reactive toys on the manipulative play of disabled children. For the analysis of feedback features, they used the dimensions of: a) sound production; and b) sustained movement (which related to the effects of object manipulation). Three more dimensions are suggested for inclusion in such an analysis: c) tactile feedback; d) visual qualities; and e) vestibular feedback.

Table 5.1 provides some examples of this sort of dimensional analysis on a selection of sensory stimuli (Bunning, 1996).

Response-contingency of therapy

The child is an active participant in the course of intervention. The sensory stimulation is dependent on the child producing the target response, and provides reinforcement for that response. The voluntary behaviour of the individual is modified by, and through, the manipulation of its consequences and in relation to the reinforcer preferences exhibited by the individual. Consideration needs to be given to the determination of individual preferences. Thus the principles of operant conditioning in the learning process are intrinsic to the intervention schedule. This relates directly to the provision of social opportunities and motivating consequences for the frequent emission of target responses by the client. This process is illustrated in Figure 5.1 below.

Clinical decision-making

Planning intervention

In order to devise an approach to therapy that will reflect the needs and sensory preferences of the individual, the systemisation of clinical decisions is recommended as highlighted by Gerard and Carson (1990).

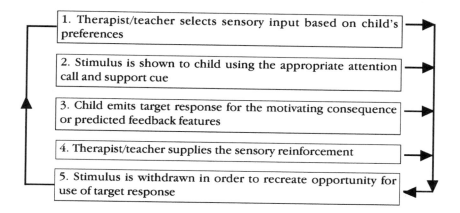

Figure 5.1: Response-contingent procedure for the application of sensory stimulation

They were principally concerned with the ordering of clinical decisions based on an integration of assessment data relating to child performance and environmental factors. The therapist formulates a series of hypotheses based on assessment findings and this represents the first stage in the planning process. Materials and activities are selected, facilitation strategies are invoked, in order that the appropriate setting or opportunity is created for the testing out of the hypotheses. A central question for the therapist making decisions for a client's intervention must be: what type and degree of information is provided by the assessment battery and how can it be integrated into a programme of intervention? Or, how does the assessment data relate to an intervention plan? It is perhaps at this point that the therapist has the major responsibility for identifying the clinical decisions and then for taking them.

As well as the assessment data regarding communication skill set level, a number of extraneous variables inform the therapist's clinical decisions, such as: age of the child; cognitive functioning level; presence of additional sensory or motor impairments; medical condition; service context or setting for the realisation of therapy targets; and the role of significant others. The therapist would usually plan the client's intervention based on an informal review of the interaction of the significant factors with the assessment findings.

Step-by-step approach

The central aim of the sensory-based intervention is to establish some points of contact between the child and the constituents of his or her

Table 5.1: Dimensional analysis of feedback features of a selection of sensory stimuli

Stimulus	Description	Feedback features
1. Fan	Silk-screen fan with wooden hand hold - manipulated by vertical or horizontal wrist/hand movements.	(i) Tactile sensation: wafts of cool air on skin at various rates and intervals, of differing forces. (ii) Visual content: white silk-screen with small picture design, moved in short, regular strokes - up and down - in participant's visual field.
2. Brush materials	Soft bristled make-up brush; • chamois leather; • fur; • flannel mitt.	(i) Tactile sensation: soft, repetitive strokes in circular motions - brushing of skin. • slightly abrasive. (ii) Sound production: quiet, stroking sound in contact with skin.
3. Facial massager (PIFCO)	Hand-held battery massager with soft brush head, which rotates when 'on' switch is depressed.	(i) Tactile sensation: soft, circular, brushing of skin. (ii) Sound production: emits motor-generated sound when 'on' switch is depressed.
4. Talcum powder	Ordinary, cosmetic, non-perfumed talcum powder.	(i) Tactile sensation: light, dry touch - gradually massaged into hands. (ii) Sustained movement: floats on air and can disappear.
5. Body massager (CARMEN)	Hand-held, electrical body massager with a choice of 4 interchangeable heads. Emits vibrations with dual speed control.	(i) Vibro-tactile sensation: emits vibrations at two different rates when placed in contact with skin. (ii) Sound production: emits motor-generated sound.
6. Executive swivel chair	Swivel chair with high back and arms, that rotates by manual application.	(i) Vestibular sensation: angular stimulation of semi-circular canals - rotation, of varying rate and direction. (ii) Visual content: contents, colours, lights of room, move round the person's visual field.
7. Rocking chair	Ordinary rocking chair with cushioned seat, high back and arms, that rocks by manual application.	(i) Vestibular sensation: linear stimulation of semi-circular canals - rocking, in a smooth, regular pattern. (ii) Visual content:changing perspective of visual field, as moving to and fro.

Table 5.1: (cont.)

Stimulus	Description	Feedback features
8. Water ball	Strong, rubberised balloon, filled with cold water.	(i) Sustained movement: inconstant form that adapts according to manipulations. (ii) Tactile sensation: cold, smooth feedback. (iii) Sound production: makes glugging sound when being manipulated or in contact with other surface. (iv) Visual content: dull, red colour of approximately coconut size.
9. Paint sandwich	1 square of cling film, squirts of 2 different colour poster paints in the centre, and a second square of cling film covering it, and sealed at the edges.	(i) Tactile sensation: smooth, soft, dry and squidgy feeling. (ii) Visual content: dual colour which changes according to manipulations, and leaves no visible mark on participant.
10. Cornflour paste	Cornflour mixed with water and food colouring to paste.	(i) Tactile sensation: dry to the touch, but smooth and wet; sticky to manipulate. (ii) Sustained movement: inconstant form - flows or drips according to manipulations, or appears solid. (iii) Visual content: brightly coloured substance - shiny liquid in appearance.
11. Finger paints	Viscous, primary coloured paints applied to paper with fingers.	(i) Tactile sensation: wet, sticky substance that adheres to paper and hands. (ii) Sustained movement: responsive to manipulations - if dropped on page or squeezed through fingers. (iii) Visual content: primary colours of wettish, viscous appearance.
12. Foam	Viscous, cosmetic foam (either shaving foam or baby lotion mousse).	(i) Tactile sensation: wet, light, smooth, of varying consistency according to manipulations: foam-lotion. (ii) Sustained movement: alters form according to manipulations.

Table 5.1: (cont.)

Stimulus	Description	Feedback features
13. Sensory tray	Coloured, plastic tray, filled with one of the below: a) liquid (water) b) powder (flour) c) fine granular d) coarse granular e) dough THEN - 1 beaker; 2 beakers; 3 containers + lid.	(i) Tactile sensation: a) wet, warm fluid; b) dry, light touch; c) dry, fine grains; d) dry, coarse beans; e) moist, solid, pliable (ii) Sound production: a) pouring/splashing; b) light patter; c) light clatter; d) heavy clatter; e) thudding sound. (iii) Sustained movement: rate, direction, flow or form is controlled by manipulations. (iv) Visual content: mainly neutral colours apart from the trays and beakers.
14. Vibro-bubble	Dome-shaped plastic bubble with metal sensors on the surface which when touched cause the bubble to vibrate. Different rates of vibration from different sensors.	(i) Tactile sensation: emits varying rates of vibrations when surface sensors are touched. (ii) Sound production: emits motor-generated sound when touched.
15. Vibro-cushion	Buff coloured, soft cushion in a corded cover.	(i) Tactile sensation: emits vibrations when surface is depressed. (ii) Sound production: emits low motor-generated sound when activated.
16. Vibro-tube	Turquoise coloured 'bendy' massage tube which vibrates when end switch is activated.	(i) Tactile sensation: emits two rates of vibration according to position of end switch. (ii) Sound production: emits a low motor-generated hum when activated.

environment. In this way, the child is prepared for the available environmental contingencies. The following steps are identified in relation to the main clinical decisions.

Step 1: What are the stimulus preferences for the individual regarding the sensory feedback features?

In order to determine the appropriate reinforcement dimensions that represent a motivating consequence for the individual, the significant other needs to complete an analysis of distinctive feedback features that are present, ie. tactile and vestibular properties. This informs the therapist/teacher of the amenability of stimuli in the context of the child's responding.

Step 2: What is the response repertoire of the individual?

In order that the child may gain access to present stimuli and so that the appropriate support for responding may be offered by the teacher/therapist, the child's current responding potential needs to be identified. This enables the therapist to create suitable opportunities and to target meaningful responses of the individual. If one is to reinforce the appropriate responding behaviour of this population, it therefore follows that the individual's response repertoire, however minimal, should be recognised and supported in a meaningful way. In short, the significant other, whether parent, therapist, teacher or other, should be a good observer of the child's behaviour in relation to the antecedent and consequential events of each situation. This is so that the effects of different stimuli may be properly evaluated in relation to the child's response repertoire. Then appropriate feedback features may be selected for use in the individual's own schedule of sensory activities.

An assessment procedure that focused on early communication behaviours for use with the severely learning disabled was developed by Coupe, Barton, Barber, Collins, Levy and Murphy (1985). They established a theoretical framework for their 'Affective Communication Assessment'. The procedure aimed at providing a structure for the observation of differential responses by focal clients to sensory opportunities provided by the assessor. It provides a useful format for informally recording observed behaviours, but neglects other important variables of the interaction such as the behaviour of the significant other presenting the stimulus and the sensory feedback features of stimuli.

A framework for use by the teacher or therapist in observing the responding behaviours of the individual in relation to sensory events is suggested in Table 5.2. It provides a focus for the antecedent behaviour of the significant other (therapist or teacher), the distinctive feedback features of the stimulus and the consequential behaviour of the child.

Step 3: What is the procedure for presenting sensory stimulation to the individual?

A response-contingency model is employed such that the child is required to act in order for the motivating consequence to occur. Sensory stimulation is dependent on the child's overt responses to it. He or she is not passive to the process but is an active participant. For the provision of optimal opportunities for client responding, the stimulus needs to be withdrawn frequently. This is so that the individual must

Table 5. 2: Framework for observing client's responses to sensory input

Antecedent Behaviour of Significant Other	Stimulus	Properties of Stimulus				Consequential Response(s) of Child
		Tactile	Vestibular	Sound	Visual	

once more emit the target response to receive the motivating consequence. Satiation level is also avoided. An example is given in Figure 5.2.

Step 4: What support cues or help is required by the individual in order that he or she might receive the motivating consequence?

How might the stimulus be presented to the client for the triggering of an appropriate response? This is to determine the amount of help required by the child to notice and respond to the focal sensation or stimulus. It also follows that if the aim of therapy is to organise incoming sensory stimulation, then verbal input must also be structured. There is little point in providing controlled tactile stimulation to an individual if they are simultaneously receiving verbal bombardment. It is very tempting, in the face of little or no verbal output from the client, to comment on each sensory experience as it arises. However, a core vocabulary of essential meanings may benefit the client more, particularly

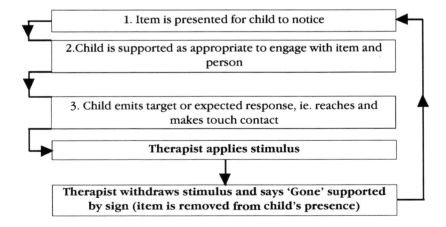

Figure 5.2: Example of response-contingent procedure establishing repeated opportunities for the emission of the target response(s)

where the concepts are introduced in a setting that offers relevance/significance of meaning to the individual, specifically relating to actions and objects. This bears out the comments of Coupe, Barton and Walker (1988) who observed that the teaching of comprehension and expression tended to focus on object labels and identifications, rather than intended effects of communication.

An example of a core vocabulary is shown in Table 5.3 below.

Table 5.3: A core vocabulary of six items based on their functional utility in a sensory-based therapy session

VOCABULARY ITEM	MEANING	USE (with reference to Halliday, 1975)
NAME (participant's name) LOOK	EXISTENCE (noting the existence of another person)	• regulate attention • inform of event
GONE	NON-EXISTENCE or DISAPPEARANCE (noting the disappearance or withdrawal of an item)	• regulate attention • inform of change in event
GO STOP	ACTION/CESSATION OF ACTION (observable change of activity or state)	• regulate attention • inform of change in event
MORE	RECURRENCE (requesting repetition of action or object)	• regulate attention • direct stimulus presentation

Sensory impairment

The sensory status of the individual must be taken into account in order to determine the necessary adaptations to support cues. Signal enhancers are recommended variously for the attention call of the child, to inform of the presence of a stimulus, and to signal its withdrawal. They are employed to bridge the gap between the environment and the child's central nervous system. The decision points are identified as shown in Figure 5.3.

Single case examples

Some examples of sensory events provided to children are now presented in Tables 5.4, 5.5 and 5.6. The first two cases demonstrate the

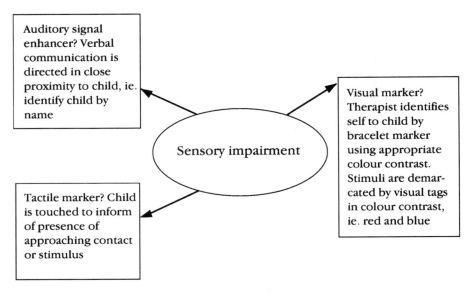

Figure 5.3: Decision points regarding signal enhancers for support cues

use of signal enhancers to meet the sensory needs of the individual. The third case illustrates an approach to a child with particular behaviour problems.

Step 5: How are the appropriate opportunities to be structured such that the optimal responding of the individual may be achieved?

The therapeutic environment identifies the crucial, main constituents, for the individual's engagements. The child's self is the centre of his or her universe; there is person(s); object(s); and event(s) (person–object)

Table 5.4: Child A: Has a profound hearing impairment; touch signal used

Antecedent Behaviour of Significant Other	Stimulus	Properties of Stimulus			Consequential Response(s) of Child
		Tactile	Sound	Visual	
Touch signal to gain child's attention. Show item's approach. Demonstrate item on self.	Body massager (cordless)	Vibrates at two rates; generates heat.	Motor-generated hum.	Displays infra-red lights on vibrating surface.	Arm reach to massager; touches item; relates item to self; vocalises; moves finger-tips over massager surface.

Table 5.5: Client B: Uses a wheelchair, has a profound hearing impairment and is registered blind, although has limited residual vision in left eye; visual and tactile signal enhancers used

Antecedent Behaviour of Significant Other	Stimulus	Properties of Stimulus		Consequential Response(s) of Child
		Tactile	Visual	
Enhanced visual signal to gain child's attention, ie. red bracelet marker on wrist presented to left visual field. Tactile signal follows to gain child's attention. Item's approach is shown by visual enhancement, ie. red on blue background. Demonstrate item briefly on child and withdraw slightly.	Soft brush.	Dry, soft touch. Ticklish sensation on inner surfaces of body, ie. wrists.	Red against blue felt cloth as table covering.	Body move to stimulus; arm reach; grabs item; relates to face; vocalises, holds close to left eye; smiles.

Table 5.6: Child C: Exhibits some problem behaviours; strikes self and others; aversive reaction to close presence of others and direct touch; graduated approach used.

Antecedent Behaviour of Significant Other	Stimulus	Properties of Stimulus				Consequential Response(s) of Child
		Tactile	Sustained Movement	Sound	Visual	
Verbal signal to gain child's attention, ie. call child's name. Visual signal at a distance to gain child's attention, ie. wave. Item's approach is gradual. Demonstrate item briefly on self whilst in adjacent proximity to child.	Silk screen fan.	Cool wafts of air. Strength varies according to closeness, strength and rate of fanning.	Fan moves in visual field.	Flapping sound similar to a light tap on a drum skin.	Brightly coloured: red, yellow and blue.	Body move to stimulus; arm reach; hand moves in air stream; looks at therapist manipulating item; vocalises; smiles.

which provide possible contact/interaction points. It is acknowledged that person and object occur separately before they are conjoined in an event (person–object). Therefore, the opportunities provided should reflect a hierarchy of increasing complexity. Additionally, it is recognised that differences may exist amongst individuals regarding favoured constituents for interaction. This should influence the design of the person's therapeutic programme. The objective is to work to the strengths of the individual and to use each person's skill set in an effective and realistic way.

The role of social interaction and schemes as they apply to the constituent elements of the environment is considered in the therapeutic environment. The development of social interaction describes how we interact with, learn about, and therefore communicate about, our environment. Early in the developmental process, an increasingly complex pattern of social interactions between person and significant other emerges. During the sensorimotor phase of development, as defined by Piaget (1952), there is an increasing awareness of the properties and functions of objects. Six major domains of development have been summarised by Hogg and Sebba (1986): object permanence; spatial understanding; time; intentional behaviour and means-end relations; causality; and imitation. Therefore, the nature of our conceptualisation of objects, and the pattern of our social interactions with significant others, must be acknowledged in the sensory-based intervention.

Outcomes

Access to environmental contingencies

A central question in consideration of the potential benefits of a sensory-based approach must be: Does the sensory reinforcement of the social interaction opportunities provided prepare the child to access other available, environmental contingencies? To answer this, the objectives of the sensory-based intervention must first be reviewed:

1   To establish and expand the purposeful response repertoires of individuals by targeting each child's preferred sensory reinforcers. Thus, the child may be helped in his or her discrimination of environmental stimuli by use of an expanded response repertoire.
2   To reduce the non-purposeful response repertoire of the individual, including stereotypic, self-injurious and other problem behaviours.
3   To introduce the child to the contingent reinforcement available in the natural environment. The experience of structured activities that provide desirable sensory feedback renders the individual more amenable to stimuli in the natural setting (Eason, White & Newsom, 1982). A connection between a purposeful behaviour and a motivating consequence is established.

Assessment of outcomes

The measurement of outcomes must be viewed in the context of these three main objectives. In short the therapist or teacher needs to assess the child's response repertoire across a variety of settings. It is not enough to focus on outcomes within the sensory-based setting as this will only provide information in relation to a specially structured event. The child's interactions in the created opportunity of sensory reinforcement must be observed in tandem with those occurring in the natural environment. Only then can the success of the intervention s objectives be measured.

References

Ashby M, Lindsay WR, Pitcaithly D, Broxholme S, Geelen N (1995) Snoezelen: Its effects on concentration and responsiveness in people with profound multiple handicaps. British Journal of Occupational Therapy 58: 303–7.

Aurand JC, Sisson LA, Aach SR, Van Hasslelt VB (1989) Use of reinforcement plus interruption to reduce self-stimulation in a child with multiple handicaps. Journal of the Multiply Handicapped Person 2: 51–61.

Ayres AJ (1972) Sensory Integration and Learning Disorders. Los Angeles: Western Psychological Services.

Ayres AJ (1979) Sensory Integration and the Child. Los Angeles: Western Psychological Services.

Bailey J, Meyerson L (1969) Vibration as a reinforcer with a profoundly retarded child. Journal of Applied Behavioural Analysis 2: 135–7.

Bailey J, Meyerson L (1970) Effect of vibratory stimulation on a retardate's self-injurious behaviour. Psychological Aspects of Disability 17: 133–7.

Bambara LM, Spiegel-McGill P, Shores RE, Fox JJ (1984) A comparison of reactive and nonreactive toys on severely handicapped children's play. Journal of the Association for Persons with Severe Handicaps 9: 142–9.

Berkson G (1983) Repetitive stereotyped behaviors. American Journal of Mental Deficiency 88: 239–46.

Berkson G, Mason W (1964) Stereotyped behaviours of chimpanzees: Relation to general arousal and alternative activities. Perceptual Motor Skills 19: 635–52.

Bowlby J (1953) Child Care and the Growth of Love. London: Penguin.

Bruner J (1978) Learning how to do things with words. In Bruner J, Gurton A (Eds) Wolfson College Lectures 1976: Human Growth and Development. Oxford: Oxford University Press.

Bunning KT (1996) Development of an Individualised Sensory Environment for Adults with Learning Disabilities and an Evaluation of its Effects on their Interactive Behaviours. Unpublished PhD thesis. London: City University.

Byrne DJ (1979) Vibrator becomes a motivator for the mentally handicapped. Teaching and Training 17: 137–9.

Campbell HJ (1973) The Pleasure Areas. London: Eyre Methuen.

Cavet J, Mount H (1995) Multi-sensory environments: An exploration of their potential for young people with profound and multiple learning difficulties. British Journal of Special Education 22: 52–5.

Chamberlain L, Chung MC, Jenner L (1993) Preliminary findings on communication in learning difficulty. British Journal of Developmental Disabilities 34: 118–25.

Clarke AM, Clarke ADB (1974) Mental Deficiency: The Changing Outlook. London: Methuen.

Corter C, Jamieson N (1977) Infants' toy preferences and mothers' predictions. Developmental Psychology 13: 413–14.

Coupe J, Barton L, Barber M, Collins L, Levy D, Murphy D (1985) The Affective Communication Assessment. Manchester: Education Committee.

Coupe J, Barton L, Walker S (1988) Teaching first meanings. In Coupe J, Goldbart J (Eds) Communication Before Speech: Normal development and impaired communication. London: Croom Helm.

Coupe J, Joliffe N (1988) In Coupe J, Goldbart J (Eds) Communication Before Speech: Normal development and impaired communication. London: Croom Helm.

Day S (1982) Mother–infant activities as providers of sensory stimulation. American Journal of Occupational Therapy 36:, 579–81.

Dehaven ED, Rees-Thomas AH, Benton SV (1980) Research implications: The use of omission training to reduce stereotyped behavior in three profoundly retarded persons. Education and Training of the Mentally Retarded 15: 298–305.

Dupont A (1981) Epidemiological studies in mental retardation: Methodology and results. International Journal of Mental Health 10: 56–63.

Eason LJ, White JJ, Newsom C (1982) Generalised reduction of self-stimulatory behaviour: an effect of teaching appropriate toy play to autistic children. Analysis and Intervention in Developmental Disabilities, 2: 157–69.

Eyman RK, Call T (1977) Maladaptive behaviour and community placement of mentally retarded persons. American Journal of Mental Deficiency 82: 137–44.

Felce D, Kushlick A, Mansell J (1980) Evaluation of alternative residential facilities for the severely mentally handicapped in Wessex: client engagement. Advanced Behavioural Research and Therapy 3: 13–18.

Fisher AG, Murray EA, Bundy AC (Eds) (1991) Sensory Integration Theory and Practice. Philadelphia: FA Davis.

Fisher AG, Dunn W (1983) Tactile defensiveness: Historical perspectives, new research: a theory grows. Sensory Integration Special Interest Section Newsletter 6: 1–2.

Gerard KA, Carson E (1990) The decision-making process in child language assessment. British Journal of Disorders of Communication 25: 61–75.

Gibb-Harding C (1983) Setting the stage for language acquisition: Communication development in the first year. In Golinkoff R (Ed) The Transition From Prelinguistic to Linguistic Communication. New Jersey: Laurence Erlbaum.

Goodall E, Corbett J, Murphy G, Callias M (1982) Sensory reinforcement table: An evaluation. Mental Handicap 10: 52–5.

Gutierrez-Griepp R (1984) Student preferences of sensory reinforcers. Education and Training of the Mentally Retarded 19: 108–13.

Haggar LE, Hutchinson RB (1991) Snoezelen: An approach to the provision of a leisure resource for people with profound and multiple handicaps. Mental Handicap 19: 51–5.

Halliday M (1975) Learning How To Mean: Explorations In The Development Of Language. London: Edward Arnold.

Hendrickson JM, Tremblay A, Strain PS, Shores RE (1981) Relationship between toy use and the occurrence of social interactive behaviours by normally developing preschool children. Psychology in the Schools 18: 500–4.

Hogg J, Sebba J (1986) Profound Retardation and Multiple Impairment: Volume 1 – Development and Learning. London: Croom Helm.

Hooper C, Wambold C (1978) Improving the independent play of severely mentally retarded children. Education and Training of the Mentally Retarded 13: 42–6.

Hulsegge J, Verheul A (1987) Snoezelen, Another World. Chesterfield: Rompa.

Jan JE, Freeman RD, McCormick AQ, Scott EP, Robertson WD, Newman DE (1983)

Eye-pressing by visually impaired children. Developmental Medicine and Child Neurology 25: 755–62.

Johnson D, Frith H, Davey GCL (1978) Vibration and praise as reinforcers for mentally handicapped people. Mental Retardation 16: 339–42.

Jones C (1980) The uses of mechanical vibration with the severely mentally handicapped; part II: Behavioural effects. Apex Journal, British Institute of Mental Handicap 7: 112–14.

Jones RSP, Baker LJV, Murphy MJ (1988) Reducing stereotyped behaviour: The maintenance effects of a DRO reinforcement procedure. Journal of Practical Approaches to Developmental Handicap 12: 24–30.

Jones RSP, Walsh PG, Sturmey P (1995) Stereotyped Movement Disorders. Chichester: John Wiley.

Jones ML, Favell JE, Lattimore J, Risley TR (1984) Improving independent engagement of nonambulatory multihandicapped persons through systematic analysis of leisure materials. Analysis and Intervention in Developmental Disabilities 4: 313–32.

Kielhofner G (1985) A Model of Human Occupation: Theory and Application. Baltimore: Williams and Wilkins.

Kiernan C (1974) Behaviour modification. In Clarke AM, Clarke ABD (Eds) Mental Deficiency: The changing outlook. London: Methuen.

Kish GB (1966) Studies of sensory reinforcement. In Honig WK (Ed) Operant Behaviour: Areas of research and application. New York: Appleton-Century-Crofts.

Kropka BI, Williams C, Clements M (1984) The deaf and partially hearing in mental handicap hospitals in England and Wales. A national questionnaire survey sponsored by the British Institute of Mental Handicap (S. Western Division).

Longhorn F (1988) A Sensory Curriculum for Very Special People. London: Souvenir Press.

MacDonald J, Gillette Y (1986) Communicating with persons with severe handicaps: roles of parents and professionals. Journal of the Association for Persons with Severe Handicaps 11: 255–65.

McLeod H, Houston M, Seyfort B (1995) Communicative interactive skills training for caregivers of nonspeaking adults with severe disabilities. International Journal of Practical Approaches to Disability 9: 5–11.

Mason SM, McGee GG, Farmer-Dougan V, Risley TR (1989) A practical strategy for ongoing reinforcer assessment. Journal of Applied Behavioural Analysis 22: 171–9.

Meyerson L, Kerr N, Michael J (1967) Behaviour modification in rehabilitation. In Bijou S, Baer D (Eds) Child Development: Readings in experimental analysis. New York: Appleton-Century-Crofts.

Murphy G (1982) Sensory reinforcement in the mentally handicapped and autistic child: a review. Journal of Autism and Developmental Disorders 12: 265–78.

Murphy G, Carr J, Callias M (1986) Increasing simple toy play in profoundly mentally handicapped children, II: Designing special toys. Journal of Autism and Developmental Disorders 16: 45–57.

Myrbakk E (1991) The treatment of self-stimulation of a severely mentally retarded deaf-blind client by brief physical interruption: A case report. Scandinavian Journal of Behaviour Therapy 20: 41–9.

Nind M, Hewett D (1994) Access to Communication. London: David Fulton.

Nunes DL, Murphy RJ, Ruprecht ML (1977) Reducing self-injurious behaviour of severely retarded individuals through withdrawal of reinforcement procedures.

Behaviour Modification, 1: 499–516.

O'Brien DV (1975) The use of stimulation as an alternative treatment of self-injurious behavior in an institution for the retarded. Dissertation Abstracts International, 2481–B.

Olds J, Milner P (1954) Positive reinforcement produced by electrical stimulation of septal area and other regions of rat brain. Journal of Comparative and Physiological Psychology 47: 419–27.

Pace GM, Ivancic MT, Edwards GL, Iwata BA, Page TA (1985) Assessment of stimulus preference and reinforcer value with profoundly retarded individuals. Journal of Applied Behaviour Analysis 18: 249–55.

Piaget J (1952) The Origins of Intelligence in Children. New York: International Universities Press.

Presland JL (1991) Problem behaviours and people with profound and multiple handicaps. Mental Handicap 19: 66–71.

Prosser G (1988) Vibratory reinforcement in the field of mental handicap: A review. Mental Handicap Research 1: 152–66.

Quilitch HR, Risley TR (1973) The effects of play materials on social play. Journal of Applied Behavioural Analysis 6: 573–8.

Rehagen NJ, Thalen MH (1972) Vibration as positive reinforcement for retarded children. Journal of Abnormal Psychology 80: 162–7.

Repp AC, Felce D, Barton LE (1983) Basing the treatment of stereotypic and self-injurious behaviours on hypotheses of their causes. Journal of Applied Behaviour Analysis 21: 281–9.

Rincover A, Newson C, Lovaas IO, Koegel R (1977) Some motivational properties of sensory stimulation in psychotic children. Journal of Experimental Child Psychology 24: 312–23.

Roth F, Speckman N (1984a) Assessing the pragmatic abilities of children, Part 1: Organisational framework and assessment parameters. Journal of Speech and Hearing Disorders 49: 2–11.

Roth F, Speckman N (1984b) Assessing the pragmatic abilities of children, Part 2: Guidelines, considerations and specific evaluation procedures. Journal of Speech and Hearing Disorders 49: 12–17.

Sandler AG, McLain SC (1987) Sensory reinforcement: Effects of response-contingent vestibular stimulation on multiply handicapped children. American Journal of Mental Deficiency 91: 373–8.

Shaefer HH (1960) Vibration as a reinforcer with infant children. Journal of Experimental Analysis of Behaviour 3: 160.

Stainback S, Stainback W (1980) Educating Children with Severe Maladaptive Behaviours. New York: Grune and Stratton.

Storey K, Bates P, McGhee N, Dycus S (1984) Reducing the self-stimulatory behaviour of a profoundly retarded female through sensory awareness training. American Journal of Occupational Therapy 38: 510–16.

Tickle L (1988) Perspectives on the status of sensory integration theory. American Journal of Occupational Therapy 42: 427–33.

Thomas GV, Phemister MR, Richardson AM (1981) Some conditions affecting manipulative play with objects in severely mentally handicapped children. Child Care, Health and Development 7: 1–20.

Walsh PG (1986) An evaluation of a DRO reinforcement procedure for controlling the rate of body rocking in a severely mentally handicapped individual. Journal of Practical Approaches to Developmental Handicap 10: 13–18.

Yeates S (1992a) A District Project for the Identification and Rehabilitation of People with Severe Learning Difficulties and Hearing Loss. Paper presented at New Directions Conference on Audiology Services for People with Learning Difficulties, Optimum Health Services, 27th October 1992.

Yeates S (1992b) Have they got a hearing loss? A follow up study of hearing in people with mental handicaps. Mental Handicap 20: 126–33.

Chapter 6

Social Skills Training for Adolescents with a Learning Disability

ALEX KELLY

Introduction

Many children and adolescents lack the skills which are important for success in social interactions. As Hitchings (1992) states, 'people with learning disabilities often have communication difficulties which affect their ability to interact in groups and this ability to interact well in group settings has an effect on their quality of life' (p.31). Walker, Todis, Holmes and Horton (1988) also stress the importance of effective social skills in relation to school-aged children: 'social competence within the specific domains of peer-related, adult-related and self-related social skills are extremely important to school success and long term adjustment for adolescents in general' (p.1). Implications for adolescents with the additional difficulties of a learning disability are obvious.

Speech and language therapists have an important role to play in social skills training, as this is one way in which the clients can be helped to learn the skills necessary to communicate more effectively in a variety of group settings, thus having a profound effect on the quality of their lives.

In this chapter, we will address the following areas: what are social skills?; the assessment of social skills; self-awareness; structuring therapy; the practicalities of running a group; and running groups in a school setting. An example of a social skills group with aims and a session plan is given. This chapter is aimed primarily at working with adolescents with a learning disability and the word 'client' is used throughout.

What are social skills?

Communication is complicated and as Rustin and Kuhr (1989) say, 'many processes are involved and there is no unitary measure or single theory of communication skill/social skill that would encompass all aspects of social communicative behaviour' (p.3) (Rustin & Kuhr, 1989).

They go on to say that social skills training evolved to 'meet the needs of those who lacked adequate models and learning opportunities to function more appropriately within society'. Social skills training therefore aims to 'increase the client's behavioural repertoire and awareness of social situations and offer him (or her) a wide variety of behavioural alternatives from which he (or she) is free to choose as, and when, he (or she) so wishes' (Wilkinson & Canter,1982, p.7).

Social skills can therefore be seen as the ability to communicate appropriately and effectively. Communication needs to be appropriate not only to the situation but also to a person's age, sex, race, status etc. and communication needs to be effective in that a person can communicate what he or she wants to communicate. However, what are these 'social skills'? Spence (1977) says that they may be defined as 'those components of social behaviour which are necessary to ensure that individuals achieve their desired outcome from a social interaction... or as appropriate social behaviour within a particular social situation' (p.9). These components or elements of social behaviour can be grouped in a variety of ways, but we will consider them under the three headings of non-verbal, verbal and assertiveness behaviour.

Non-verbal behaviour

'Non-verbal communication is unavoidable in the presence of other people' (Wilkinson & Canter, 1982, p.10). The authors go on to say that 'a person may decide not to speak, or be unable to communicate verbally, but he (or she) still gives messages about himself (or herself) to others through his face and body'.

Non-verbal behaviours have various functions. They can 'replace words, repeat what is spoken, emphasize a verbal message – especially the emotional type–regulate interaction or contradict what is being said, revealing a true feeling' (Hitchings, 1991, p.32). People form impressions of others based on their non-verbal behaviour and are often more likely to 'believe' the non-verbal behaviour if it contradicts the verbal content. For example, if someone says they are happy but their facial expression and posture 'say' they are unhappy, the non-verbal behaviour will be taken as the truth.

Non-verbal behaviour can be described in terms of the following skills and these can be subdivided into body language and paralinguistic skills.

Body language

Body language is the way we use our bodies to communicate feelings, personality, social roles, likes and dislikes. It incorporates the following eight aspects:

1   eye contact
2   facial expression
3   gesture
4   distance
5   touch
6   fidgeting
7   posture
8   personal appearance.

Paralinguistic skills or vocal cues

These are concerned not with the content of speech but the way in which the words are spoken. They affect the meaning of what is said and how it is received. They include:

1   volume
2   rate or speed
3   clarity
4   intonation
5   fluency.

Verbal behaviour

The main form of verbal communication is conversation and the form the conversation takes will obviously vary depending on the situation and people involved. As Spence (1977) says 'it is important for all individuals to be able to cope adequately at a very basic level of conversation' (p.13). If they have difficulty in this area they are likely to find it hard to make friends or deal with a number of everyday situations.

Verbal behaviour can be described in terms of the following conversational skills:

1   listening
2   opening a conversation
3   taking turns
4   asking questions
5   answering questions
6   relevancy
7   repair
8   ending a conversation.

It is important to remember that a conversation cannot consist of verbal behaviour alone but includes non-verbal behaviour as previously mentioned. Therefore a person's non-verbal behaviour will have an effect on their verbal behaviour.

Assertiveness behaviour

Assertive behaviour has been defined as 'behaviour which enables a person to act in his own interests, stand up for himself (or herself) without due anxiety, and to express his rights without denying the rights of others' (cited by Wilkinson et al, 1982, p.20). Assertiveness can therefore be seen as self-expression and includes a number of skills including the ability to communicate feelings to others, to express friendship and affection, annoyance and anger, joy and pleasure, grief and sadness, and to both give and receive compliments. If a person is unassertive it means that they are denying their needs and failing to express their feelings and opinions effectively.

Being assertive does not mean being aggressive. The aggressive person, as well as the passive person, needs to learn to be assertive. The following are the most common situations in which we need to be assertive and with which clients have most problems:

1   expressing feelings
2   standing up for yourself
3   making suggestions
4   refusing
5   disagreeing
6   complaining
7   apologising
8   requesting explanations.

It is important to remember that assertive behaviour includes non-verbal and verbal skills and therefore a person's ability to be assertive will be greatly affected by their ability to use their body language, paralinguistic skills and conversational skills appropriately.

Assessment of social skills

Rustin and Kuhr (1989) state that 'the goal of assessment is to measure social skills competence in order to define changes required in the client's social interaction' (p.57). There are many ways of assessing social skills; the most relevant and common to this client group are the following:

1 Interview

The interview is the traditional method of assessing social skills and assumes that the client is potentially the richest source of information about himself or herself. When working with adolescents with a learning disability, the interview is more an opportunity to observe the client interacting on a one-to-one basis and to give the client 'the opportunity to express the aspects of themselves which they perceive to be of most importance' (Rinaldi, 1992, p.18). It is also a valuable source of information about the client's self-awareness and awareness of others around him or her.

Talkabout (Kelly, 1996) and *The Social Use of Language Programme (SULP)* (Rinaldi, 1992) both include a short client interview as part of the initial assessment procedure.

2 Observation

Information can be obtained about the client's behaviour in his or her own environment by observing him or her in actual social interactions. This can be achieved by *in vivo* observation, structured or staged interactions, or role play. The information gained is then usually transferred onto a rating scale.

3 Rating scales

Rating scales are an extremely useful measure of change and they can be filled in by one or more people, including the client where appropriate. Rating scales use numbers and sometimes descriptions to rate each skill.

The *SULP* (Rinaldi,1992) includes several rating charts which are designed to be completed either from structured observation over a period of time and in different social contexts, or from the client's self-assessment. Rinaldi uses a 4-point rating scale (0–3), where 0 = appropriate or 'no difficulty' and 3 = inappropriate or 'very difficult'. She uses descriptions as well as a number rating. For example in the 'Communication Skills Rating Chart', the rating 1 for 'rate of speech' is described as 'fast but not difficult to follow'; 2 is 'too fast, difficult to follow'. In the other two rating charts, Rinaldi uses one description for each rating, for example 0 = no difficulty.

The Personal Communication Plan (PCP) (Hitchings & Spence,1991) has a social communication skills section which assesses each skill on a 5-point rating scale. Each number has a description and results are transferred to a pictorial summary in order to quickly identify areas of strength and need (see Figure 6.1).

Talkabout (Kelly, 1996) has an initial rating scale for the client and carer to complete prior to therapy in order to establish how aware they are of their own communication strengths and needs. In addition, clients assess themselves on a 4-point rating scale throughout therapy to increase their self-awareness of communication. This assessment uses pictures (cartoons), 'smiley' faces and group exercises to help clients assess their own skills and identify their own strengths and needs (see Figure 6.2).

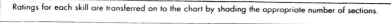

Ratings for each skill are transferred on to the chart by shading the appropriate number of sections.

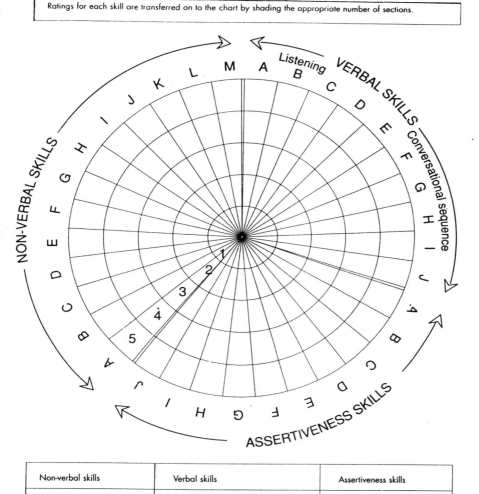

Non-verbal skills	Verbal skills	Assertiveness skills

A Eye contact
B Facial expression
C Hand gestures
D Proximity
E Touch
F Fidgeting
G Posture and gait
H Personal appearance
I Volume
J Intonation
K Rate
L Clarity
M Fluency/hesitations
	A Listening – Focusing
	B Listening – Reinforcing
	C Listening – Responding
	D Opening a conversation
	E Maintaining a conversation
	  – Turn-taking
	F Maintaining a conversation
	  – Asking questions
	G Maintaining a conversation
	  – Responding to questions
	H Maintaining a conversation
	  – Relevancy
	I Maintaining a conversation
	  – Repair
	J Ending a conversation
		A Compliment giving
		B Compliment receiving
		C Expressing feelings
		D Standing up for self
		E Making suggestions
		F Refusal
		G Disagreeing
		H Complaining
		I Making apologies
		J Requesting explanations

Figure 6.1: In the *Personal Communication Plan* (Hitchings & Spence, 1991), ratings for each skill are transferred on to the chart by shading the appropriate number of sections

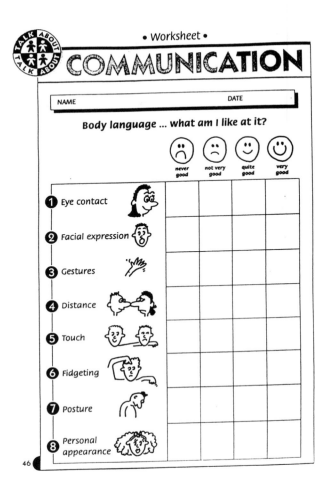

Figure 6.2: Communication worksheet (A Kelly, 1996)

Self-awareness

Good self-awareness is undoubtedly an asset to the client in social skills training, but how much should it be part of the therapy itself? Rustin and Kuhr (1989) emphasise the importance of self-awareness and self-monitoring by saying 'clients need to have a better understanding of their behaviour...If clients are trained in self-monitoring, self-reinforcement and other self regulation procedures, they will be better able to accomplish the complex underlying rules of appropriate interaction' (p.38).

In *SULP* (Rinaldi,1992) self/other awareness is seen as an important and integral part of therapy and is worked on alongside the interactive process of communication. The self- and other-awareness activities are graded according to degree of difficulty, starting with physical attributes, interests, strengths and weaknesses in Part 1 and moving on later to feelings, opinions and friendships in Part 2.

In *Talkabout* (Kelly, 1996) self- and other-awareness are seen to be starting points for therapy and a pre-requisite for success. The author found through evaluating numerous social skills groups with adolescents with a learning disability that the clients' success was directly related to their awareness of their communication strengths and needs, ie. clients with a poor awareness of their needs did not do as well in therapy as those clients who did have good awareness. In addition, it was found that success in improving clients' awareness of their communication strengths and needs was directly related to their self- and other-awareness, ie. clients with poor self- and other-awareness did not do as well at improving their awareness of their communication as those clients who had a good basic awareness of themselves.

The first two levels of *Talkabout* therefore work on these issues. Level 1 (Talkabout Me and You) aims to improve basic self- and other-awareness and looks at the topics of physical appearance, personality, people in our lives, likes and dislikes, strengths and needs and simple problem solving. Level 2 (Talkabout Communication) aims to explore what is meant by communication and enables clients to assess their own communication strengths and needs through improving their awareness of individual skills. In addition, clients are encouraged to decide what skills they need to work on next, for example, body language.

Structuring therapy

It is essential to structure the social skills therapy so that certain skills are taught first and more complex ones taught last. Rustin and Kuhr (1989) describes foundation skills, which include non-verbal skills and a few others, as the 'basic skills and... fundamental to the development of more sophisticated social interactions... clients need to be well versed in these skills before they can proceed to more complicated skills' (p.77). They go on to say that in some cases, for example in severe learning disability, social skills training may be entirely directed at this basic level. They describe 'interaction skills', which include verbal skills, as 'more complex than foundation skills as they require the combination of two or more skills being in operation at the same time'. They then move on to 'affective skills' and then 'cognitive skills'. A hierarchical approach is obviously necessary if social skills training is to be effective and this structure, with the inclusion of self-awareness and awareness of communication, forms the basis of *Talkabout* (see Figure 6.3).

Each level has therapy aims, a suggested process for therapy and worksheets to cover all topics. Using *Talkabout*, therapists are able to

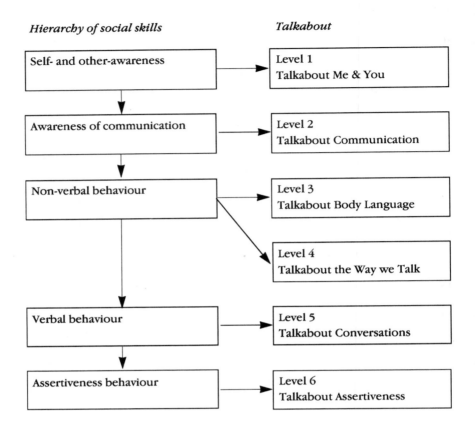

Hierarchy of social skills   *Talkabout*

Figure 6.3: The hierarchical approach used in *Talkabout* (Kelly, 1996)

structure therapy so that clients start at a level that is appropriate to their needs (following assessment) and progress up the levels to reach their full potential.

The *SULP* is also divided into three parts and enables therapists to progress through the stages as appropriate. In Part 1, clients become aware of and practise using skills of the 'interactive process of communication' in game activities and simple conversation tasks, and work on basic self/other- awareness. In Part 2, clients apply the skills they learnt in Part 1 to a range of social contexts which they practise in the classrooms, and work on further self/other-awareness. In Part 3, the clients practise 'assignments' in real life settings.

It is obviously important to build up self-confidence through social skills training. If therapeutic goals are set appropriately and therapy is therefore structured according to their level, clients are not going to fail because of unrealistic demands being put on them, but will naturally reach their full potential at some stage.

Practicalities of setting up a group

Setting up a group

The size of the group should ideally be 6–8 not including the group leaders. It is important to remember that a great number of clients find it difficult to communicate and attend in larger groups. Where this is unavoidable, it may be necessary to consider splitting the group into two for some of the session.

Social skills groups run better with two leaders, especially as we need to model behaviours, work video cameras and facilitate group discussion, sometimes all at the same time! It is also important for carry over, so the co-worker should ideally be someone from the clients' everyday environment, eg. their school or college.

A group contract is often important to set up and agree on and can include membership, time, place and duration of the group, and rules. For examples, see *Talkabout* (p.154) or Hitchings (1992, p.39).

Running a group

The format of the session will vary from time to time but there are general guidelines which apply to most groups:

1 Group cohesion activity

This is an essential part of the group. It brings the group together and helps them focus on the other group members and the purpose of the group. The activity should be simple and stress free and all members should participate and feel part of the group. An example of this activity might be throwing a ball to someone and asking how they are.

2 Revision of previous session

In order to ensure cohesion between sessions, it is important to recap on relevant aspects of the previous sessions. It may also be appropriate to recap on the aims and rules of the group, and change the session plan if something has occurred that needs attention. This is also the time when homework is discussed if appropriate.

3 Introduction to session theme

The theme for that session is introduced. This can be done through discussion, brainstorming, playing a game etc.

4 Main activity

This may include modelling of a new skill followed by role play by the clients and feedback and replay where necessary. The use of video has been found to be invaluable in enabling the clients to accurately monitor their own skills and it is also a good record of progress.

5 Summing up

This may include setting homework which Rustin and Kuhr(1989) consider to be an important feature of generalisation: 'Homework assignments are carried out in the real world and indicate to the therapist how well clients are able to generalize their newly acquired skills' (p.39).

6 Finishing activity

Each session should end with a group activity to bring the group back together again. Once again the activity should be fun, simple and stress free.

Evaluating a group

It is important to consider the following questions when evaluating groups throughout a social skills training programme:

The session:
     How did the session go?
     What were the problems?
     What went well?
     Are there changes that need to be made in future sessions?
The skills:
     Were the activities at an appropriate level?
The clients:
     Did they enjoy the session?
     Did they learn anything?
     Are they improving?

At the end of therapy, we are obviously most interested in whether the clients have improved and if not, why not. If rating scales have been used to assess the clients initially, then a re-test gives a clear indication of success. It is also valuable to gain some insight into whether or not the clients think they have improved. *Talkabout* (Kelly, 1996) has several evaluation forms for this purpose.

Running groups in a school setting

The majority of work with this client group will be through schools, and a constant problem for the speech and language therapist is trying to fit groups in around their existing timetables. Staff often have to withdraw children from important lessons and single them out as children with 'speech problems'. This can sometimes *increase*, rather than decrease, difficulties in their ability to interact with their peers! Adolescents are, more than most of us, markedly affected by their peer group. Rustin and Kuhr (1989) say that 'no behaviour will transfer and be maintained if it is not reinforced in real life... the primary motivating factors for young children are their parents, whereas adolescents are more influenced by their peers' (p.39).

Another problem facing the speech and language therapist in running social skills groups in a school is how to decide which children would benefit from such a group. As Spence (1977) says 'there may be many children attending regular school classes who would benefit greatly from social skills training. If inadequacy in social and interpersonal skills leads to further problems such as anti-social behaviour, depression or anxiety, then there is a good point to be made for using social skills training in a preventative fashion' (p.8). The problem could therefore be seen as being one of deciding which children would not benefit from such a group!

If schools are motivated and encouraged, it is possible to put social skills on to their curriculum by using an existing lesson. For example, in a school in Redbridge, social skills took over from one of year 7 and 8's PSE periods (Personal, Social and Emotional development), of which they had four each week. Each year was assessed and re-grouped according to their social skills, and teachers who normally taught them PSE were the leaders or co-workers for the social skills lessons. There are the obvious problems: it is a massive administrative task and needs to be shared by the therapists and teachers; a strong commitment from the school is essential; therapists need to be committed to a particular time and this has to be planned a term in advance to enable the school to make necessary arrangements.

The drawbacks are far outweighed by the benefits. Clients are learning how to be more effective communicators with their peers; they are not singled out; teachers and children both enjoy the change to their normal timetable and as a result seem more motivated; teachers are able to run groups and learn about this type of therapy; and carry-over is more likely to occur.

Conclusion

In conclusion, it is obvious that social skills training is an extremely important area of the speech and language therapist's work with adolescents who have a learning disability. However, the success of therapy is often dependent on the ability of the therapist to assess the clients effectively and structure the therapy and groups appropriately.

As this chapter has pointed out, it is important to assess the self-awareness of the client and in some cases, especially with clients who

have a more severe learning disability, to work on this area of self-awareness prior to moving on to actual social skills training. It is also necessary
to structure therapy so that the complexity of the skills is graded and
clients are not 'set up' to fail by trying to teach complex skills when they
do not have the foundation skills necessary.

Finally, the advantage of running social skills groups in a school
setting with the client's peers, and as part of the weekly timetable, needs
to be carefully considered. If social skills training is able to have an effect
on a client's ability to interact successfully with their peers and with
adults, then we have the ability to affect the quality of the rest of their
lives.

EXAMPLE GROUP

Name of group	The Body Language Group
Members	Seven clients – all 15 year olds. Two group leaders.
Aim of group	To explore all aspects of body language and improve skills in relevant areas, in particular: eye contact, facial expression, distance and touch, fidgeting and posture.
Therapy contract	1 hr 15 min sessions weekly for 1 term. Total of 8 sessions.
Aim of session	To improve awareness of distance and touch. To consider why we touch people and when we touch. To help the group decide how to get it right and what to do if we get it wrong.

Session Plan

3.00   *Group activity*: 'Change place wink' (leader directs others to change places
        in the circle by winking).
3.10   *Revision*: Recap previous sessions.
        Each group member recalls one aspect of body language they need to work
        on.
3.15   *Introduction to session*: Distance and touch
        Homework feedback: clients watched 'Eastenders' on TV and looked at how
        close people got to each other. Watch short clip from video and discuss.
3.30   *Main activity 1*: Distance. Group leader writes up three headings on board:
        'who can you get really close to?',
        'who can you get quite close to?' and
        'who should you not get too close to?'
        Everyone gives one idea.
        Give worksheet 'Distance....don't get too close!' (*Talkabout* p.79). Clients fill
        in one idea in each box.
3.40   *Main activity 2*: Touch.
        Two small groups: Group 1 discusses 'when can we touch people?' and other
        group 'when should we not touch people?'. Feedback and group leader fills
        ideas in worksheet 'To touch...or not to touch' (*Talkabout*, p.80) to give to
        members next week (See Figure 6.4).

3.50   *Main activity 3*: Getting it wrong.
        Group leaders role play short scenario. Group members notice what
        happened to person being touched. Discussion... What could the person
        touching do if he notices that he has made the other person feel awkward...?
        Re-play and add in ideas from group to rectify the problem.
        Give worksheet 'Distance and touch...getting it right' (*Talkabout*, p.81). To
        be completed next week as recap.
4.10   *Finishing activity*: Change 3 things (observation game).
4.15   End of session.

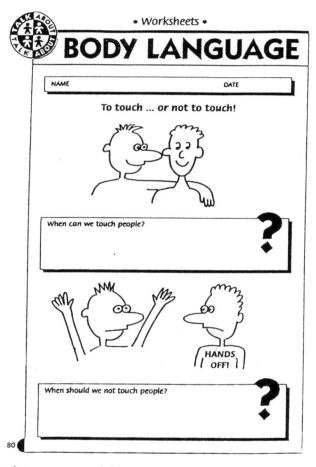

Figure 6.4: Body Language worksheet

References

Hitchings A (1992) Working with adults with a learning disability in a group setting.
    In: Fawcus M (Ed) Group Encounters in Speech and Language Therapy.
    Kibworth: Far Communications Ltd.
Hitchings A, Spence R (1991) The Personal Communication Plan for people with a
    learning disability. Windsor: NFER-Nelson.

Kelly A (1996) Talkabout: A social communication skills package. Bicester: Winslow Press.

Rinaldi W (1992) The Social Use of Language Programme. Windsor: NFER-Nelson.

Rustin L, Kuhr A (1989) Social Skills and the Speech Impaired. Basingstoke: Taylor & Francis.

Spence S (1977) Social Skills Training with Children and Adolescents. Windsor: NFER-Nelson.

Walker HM, Todis B, Holmes D, Horton G (1988) The Walker Social Skills Curriculum. Texas: Pro-ed. (Distributors: NFER-Nelson,Windsor.)

Wilkinson J, Canter S (1982) Social Skills Training Manual. Chichester: John Wiley.

Chapter 7

Occupational Therapy and Children with Learning Disabilities

CHIA SWEE HONG

Introduction

This chapter introduces some of the models, assessments and therapeutic considerations which underlie the practice of occupational therapy with children who have learning disabilities. It offers by examples a range of therapeutic strategies and work undertaken in schools, child development units and at home.

Developments in occupational therapy practice have been influenced by the:

- increased life expectancy of children with severe health problems as a result of better health care;
- variety of programmes and facilities for children with special needs;
- expansion of theory and practice in psychology, the neurosciences, human development and occupational therapy;
- impact of twentieth century technology on diagnosis, treatment and care of children (Pratt & Allen, 1989);
- legislative acts, eg. the Education Act, 1981, place a great focus on a child's needs and abilities rather than his or her disabilities.

A coherent structure for occupational therapy

A continuing debate within occupational therapy is the need for a framework that is sufficiently flexible to incorporate the philosophical, theoretical and applied aspects of the discipline. Such a framework would include an overall view of the nature of the profession, the different schools of thought coexisting within it, and the models used to translate theory into practice.

According to Kortman (1995), there are four major types of models. A professional model is applicable across various clients with different needs and practice settings and is often considered as a professional 'blue-print'. A delineation model identifies principles and seeks to delineate occupational therapy approaches to a specific group of clients, while an application model clearly describes specific assessment and therapeutic techniques and is linked closely to a delineation model. The fourth type is a personal model which acts as a filter which occupational therapists use before translating the other models into practice.

Philosophy for practice

Professional model

Pratt and Allen (1989) consider that a child's capacity to purposefully affect his or her own world of self, culture and environment is the result of, firstly, the ability of the human brain to formulate and symbolise concepts and, secondly, the ability of the human hands to translate concepts into action. The child's awareness of these abilities and continuing interactions with the environment promote the will for purposeful activities.

Purposeful activities are broadly defined as 'the goal-directed use of an individual's time, energy, interests, and attention in interactions with his or her environment'. A child spends most of his or her time engaged in various kinds of purposeful activities that enhance performance of chosen occupational roles. Occupational roles and the supportive occupational activities are distinguished from other kinds of purposeful activities by two characteristics: namely the use of hands and tools to explore and manipulate the environment and the direct or indirect relationship of occupational activities to culture. This includes the development and use of:

- self-maintenance activities including self-care, sleep, leisure and other activities directed toward the preservation of the individual;
- play such as sensorimotor exploration and symbolic activities in art and drama, crafts and games. Skills acquired through play enable the individual to be a competent and creative adult;
- work as the economic function of human beings. Work includes school and prevocational activities of the child in addition to the vocational and home management activities of adulthood.

In a healthy state, the individual is able to adapt and achieve a satisfying life and is able to function adequately in chosen personal, social, and occupational roles.

Delineation model

The model which the author adopts is based on the works of Reed and Sanderson (1983). They propose that an individual adapts or adjusts through the use of various occupations. By occupations is meant those activities and tasks which an individual does as part of daily life and which engage his or her time, energy and attention. Such adaptation or adjustment should be viewed as two-directional. Through occupations, an individual may adapt to the environment or adapt the environment to the individual. Both provide the means toward successful adaptation that will meet the individual's needs and provide satisfaction.

The principal assumption is that occupations can be used to enable an individual to adapt and fulfil his or her needs. Occupations can be divided into three areas – self-maintenance, productivity and leisure – which in turn are comprised of three skill components – sensorimotor, cognitive and psychosocial. Therapy is aimed at evaluating the occupational areas and skill to determine what adaptation is not occurring and which needs are not being met. The needs can then be addressed through an intervention programme that will enable the individual to interact in the environment to promote adaptation and gain functional independence.

In essence, the practice of occupational therapy must be directly related to each child's overall mastery of age-appropriate occupations and must also support the achievement of goals and balance in the broader scope of self-maintenance, productivity and leisure.

Application models

Most occupational therapists subscribe to the following models, examples of which are illustrated in the activity sheets later in the chapter.

Behaviour modification is an approach for changing observable behaviour, based on Skinnerian principles of learning. Some of the basic principles include: that both adaptive and maladaptive behaviour are learned; that the results of a child's actions, or behaviour, determine whether or not he or she repeats that behaviour; that reinforcers are used in a systematic way to either increase or decrease the occurrence of a behaviour, and that tasks are easier to learn if they are broken down into small steps and taught separately and then chained together (Clancy & Clark, 1990). Behaviour modification has been discussed in more detail in Chapter 2.

Developmental play therapy. The aim of this therapy is to enable the child, within the context of the therapeutic relationship and with the use of therapeutic play to achieve his or her appropriate level of emotional development for his or her chronological age. This method of therapy is based on developmental theories that suggest, for a development of healthy personality to occur, the child needs to progress through each stage of emotional development successfully before tackling a further phase (Jeffrey, 1990).

The Bobath Concept is based on the recognition of two factors: normal brain maturation has been interfered with by the lesion resulting in (a) retardation of motor development with (b) abnormal patterns of posture and movement present. The main aim of intervention is to encourage and increase the child's ability to move in an 'efficient' and 'as near normal' a way as possible. Therapy involves the specialised handling techniques of inhibition and facilitation. The techniques are used to prepare the child for functional activities, allowing the child the possibility to experience and learn from the sensations of more typical movement patterns. By giving the child a variety of movement experiences, he or she is helped to use his or her feedback-feedforward system, allowing him or her to generalise the sensations of movement necessary for a better quality of functional ability (Schoen & Anderson, 1993).

Sensory motor stimulation. In this concept, the young child is considered to develop from a stage of input sensation to that of sensation-perception. Until the age of two, the infant develops his or her vision by looking at, recognising and responding to his or her mother's smile and gradually developing an interest in people and in objects. The body is the instrument for the child's kinaesthetic-tactile impressions. Finger feeding gives the infant the sensation of different textures and shapes. The baby plays with his or her own body and also with his or her mother. This provides the opportunity to establish inner language and the beginning of body image which forms the basis of spatial concepts such as left-right, in front and behind. As a meaning is given to sensation this becomes perception. Intervention consists of stimulation work to help the child become aware of his or her own body and his or her basic senses (Seifert, 1973).

Perceptual motor function approach. This is defined as perceiving information, responding with a judgement, followed by a coordinated motor response. Cratty (1969) assumed that there was an interrelationship between judgement and motor expression and that both are related to the intellectual growth of the child and have a positive effect on intellectual abilities. Intervention consists of gross motor activities, including structured games, balancing activities and motor planning action and some components of academic work. The rationale seems to be that if one can continuously stimulate motor activity during which the child is making judgement and decision, then intellectual abilities will also be stimulated and will result in improved performance in academic areas (Chia, 1984).

Sensory integration is the process of organising sensory information in the brain to make an adaptive response. An adaptive response occurs when a child successfully meets an environmental challenge.

Of particular importance to sensory integration is an understanding of the vestibular, proprioceptive and tactile systems. Intervention that involves several sensory systems and requires intersensory integration is more effective than intervention that uses just one system. Therapeutic equipment includes materials with which children readily engage yet perceive as fun and challenging and these include skate boards, a trapeze and a hammock. Therapy needs to be individually based because the child's responses must be watched continually and modifications must be made in therapy (Kimball, 1993).

Social role valorisation (or normalisation). Wolfsenberger (1983) believed that individuals with a learning disability should be given the same basic human rights as others in the community based upon a shared humanity. Central to his thinking was the concept of integration. All people should relate to one another as equals and have mutual respect. Individuals with a learning disability should experience integration in all spheres of life.

John O' Brien's (1987) five accomplishments help to extend further the concept of integration. He suggests the following:

- Community presence to ensure that individuals with a learning disability are present in the ordinary places used by other citizens for leisure, worship etc;
- Support individuals with a learning disability to make informed decisions about their lives;
- Competence to enable service users to develop and maintain skills which will increase the independence of individuals with disabilities and acceptance by others;
- Respect to give dignity to individuals with a learning disability; and
- Community participation to support and enable individuals with a learning disability to make and maintain relationships with their families and the community.

Dolan (1995) said that activities and goals selected should reflect 'normal life' demands, and wherever possible, activities should take place in ordinary, easily accessible, community facilities where the client can be given the necessary support to achieve access.

Assessments in occupational therapy

Given the diagnosis, our assessments are concerned with occupations – self-maintenance or self-care, productivity or work activities, leisure or play activities and occupational skills which consist of sensorimotor, cognitive and psychosocial skills. If appropriate, occupational therapists prefer to do joint assessments with professionals from other disciplines.

Briefly, the aims are to:

- establish a baseline of present occupational function and occupational performance skills;
- identify areas of occupational need(s);
- contribute data for differential diagnosis;
- decide appropriate models for therapy;
- help in selecting goals for a programme of therapy in order to help individuals to learn or relearn skills needed to perform the occupations that are needed by them;
- provide a measure of progress (Reed & Sanderson, 1983; Peck & Hong, 1994).

Three types of assessment are carried out. Firstly, global assessments are made which are designed to assess the general level of function of each child eg. using the Bereweeke skill-teaching system (Mansell et al, 1983). Secondly, it is necessary to analyse the skills needed to perform specific occupations for example of feeding and dressing. Thirdly, the child and the parents are asked to complete a self-assessment which may consist simply of two statements:

I can ....

(eg. hold a spoon – thus identifying activities the child can do)

and

I would like to ....

(eg. learn to use a fork and knife – thus identifying activities the child would like to learn to do).

An initial assessment usually consists of interviews with the child and his or her parents and observations of his or her performance in carrying out basic occupations and occupational skills. This is illustrated in Table 7.1 below in the form of a 'Structured Observations Schedule' (our headings are correlated with Reed and Sanderson's Model which are in bold type).

After the observations, consider the points in Table 7.2a and the example shown in Table 7.2b.

Table 7.1: Structured observations schedule

If possible, observe, assess and interview child, his or her parents, carers and teacher (and other professionals) What are their concerns?

When using the schedule, bear in mind the following (put a tick or a cross or write comments):

- Can the child complete tasks adequately?
- How much prompting does he or she need to achieve the task?
- What is he or she good at?
- What does he or she enjoy doing?
- Which aspects of the curriculum/life skills is he or she good at?
- Is he or she using any equipment to carry out the task?

1   *Social interaction and communication* (**Self-maintenance/self-care: functional communication**).
- Does child initiate and maintain interaction and communication?

2   *Physical ability* (**Self-maintenance/self-care: functional mobility**)
- What is child s posture?
- What is his or her basic tone?
- Can he or she change from one position to another – and maintain it?
- Is his or her movement fluid and rhythmical?
  (**Motor skills: hand skills**)
- Can he or she imitate reaching and touching – top of head, back of neck, hand to mouth, opposite shoulders, chin and ear, tummy, knee, feet, nose, and fingers and thumb?
- Can he or she reach, grasp for and release objects? Eg. unscrewing jar, removing bricks and building a tower, cutting using scissors, putting the picture into an envelope, holding utensils and undoing/doing up buttons.
- Which hand is dominant?

3   *Attention and strategies for learning* (**Cognitive span: attending behaviour**)
- Is child able to attend? For how long at a time? For which activity?
- Is he or she easily distracted? If so, by what?
- How does he or she approach a task/organise his or her work?
- How does he or she manage with sequencing activities? Eg. sequencing and threading a string of beads.

4   *Sensory/Perceptual motor abilities* (**Occupational performance skills: sensory motor skills: sensory processing/sensory sensitivity**)
- Can child see? Can he or she look and follow an object?
- Can he or she hear? Can he or she listen?
- How does he or she respond to smell, taste and touch?

  Body awareness (**Proprioceptive sense – body scheme**)
- Does he or she use both sides of his or her body?
- Can he or she cross the midline of his or her body? (**Motor skills: crossing the midline of the body**)
- Can he or she name/point to parts of his or her body and with his or her eyes closed identify them when they are touched Eg. head, neck, hand, mouth, shoulders, chin, ears, tummy, knee, feet, nose, thumb and fingers.

  Spatial awareness (**Visual sense – spatial relationships**)
- Does he or she know his or her front and back, left and right?

- Can he or she imitate gestures?
- Can he or she complete a formboard?
- Can he or she copy 3D designs?

5 *Self-care abilities* (**Occupations: self-maintenance/self-care**)
- How does he or she manage with self-care skills?
- Does he or she need special positions or equipment for eating, drinking, toileting, washing, dressing and undressing?

6 *Psychological state* (**Psychosocial skills: psychological skills**)
- Is child co-operative? (**Self-control**)
- What is his or her mood like? (**Mood/affect**)
- What is his or her self-esteem like? (**Self-concept**)

7 What is child's leisure interest? (**Leisure: play/occupation**)

8 What is child's family/environment like? (**Environment**)

Table 7.2a: Therapy plan – Summary of observations

Strengths	Needs	Outcome
Can child complete tasks adequately? Which aspects of the curriculum/life skills is he or she good at? What does he or she enjoy doing?	What tasks does child still need help with or find difficult that he or she would like to learn or achieve? Which aspects of the curriculum/ life skills does he or she need help with?	What existing experience/activities is child engaged in to promote his or her learning? If none, consider assessments and techniques and identify activities and experiences which can be used to enhance his or her learning.

Table 7.2b: Example of summary of observations for Nicky's fine sensory/perceptual motor/play development

Strengths	Needs	Outcome
Visually, Nicky is alert. Looks at and follows toys. Turns head towards a drum banged out of her sight 3 feet away. Hands are open and not fisted. Can use palmar or pincer grasp. Can transfer objects from one hand to the other. Can take toys out of a container and is now beginning to put them into a box.	Develop play skills	Encourage Nicky to watch environment and when you talk to her. Provide Nicky with a box containing toys for looking: mobiles; listening: music box; tasting: food; smelling: spices; feeling: finger games; reaching and grasping: feely bags. Devise an activity sheet

Therapeutic practice

Practice settings

Most occupational therapists who work with children and adolescents with learning disabilities are based in child development units or in community teams for individuals with learning disabilities.

The aims of the teams are to:

- provide a comprehensive service for individuals with learning disabilities through multi-disciplinary assessment and treatment;
- offer guidance and advice to individuals, families and groups;
- encourage and maintain independence within the community by offering support and specialist skills;
- provide training and education to parents, carers, members of other professions and volunteers;
- offer support and advice to other services, thus enabling individuals with learning disabilities to make the fullest use of them;
- contribute to the planning of services for individuals with learning disabilities (Chia, 1987).

The team meets regularly to discuss referrals and to allocate key workers who can act, for example, as an advocate for a family. Joint visits enable a better understanding of each profession's skills and the contribution that each can offer, thus forming a valuable foundation for team work.

The benefits of teamwork include the following:

- ease of access for individuals and carers;
- improved communication leading to a sharing of knowledge, consistency of approach and improved care;
- mutual support in times of stress (Dolan, 1995).

Core skills of occupational therapy

The following are processes that are generic to occupational therapy practice (see Penso, 1987; Pratt & Allen, 1989; Clancy & Clark, 1990 and Peck & Hong, 1994).

Therapeutic relationship is a unique interaction between the child and the occupational therapist with the principal aim of one assisting the other to meet his or her needs in a more satisfying way. In the therapeutic relationship, the child is at the centre. It is the mutual understanding of feelings, needs and aspirations which is the focus in the relationship.

Occupational activities – The dynamic interaction between the occupational therapist and child and the activity brings about change. The activity becomes a change agent. Activities can facilitate change because they enable a child to acquire new skills, develop interests and learn to use his or her time effectively. Occupational activities are selected from age appropriate play, work and self-maintenance categories.

Individual or group work

Individual work gives more time and concentration to the child who will be able to concentrate on the activity with minimum distraction. It is particularly useful for certain activities such as teaching attention control, early sensory and perceptual motor skills.

Group work enables children to be seen together at the same time (see Figure 7.1).

Figure 7.1: Group work gives children an opportunity to tackle a challenge together

It provides opportunities for interaction, social skills and learning skills such as taking turns and working together. It eases the pressure on children and enables a wider range of games and activities to be used. It also enables the children to practise and generalise skills taught on a one-to-one basis giving them the opportunity to achieve by tackling challenges. In an individual session, a child may feel under pressure; group work can ease this.

Adapted techniques and equipment

Some occupations can be graded eg. by changing the position of the child or his or her working surface. The activity process itself may be modified by breaking down tasks down into their component parts. Occupational therapists use a large variety of tools, materials and equipment to enhance the ability of each child.

Pre-school children

Occupational therapists prefer to work with pre-school children and their parents at their home where the child is on familiar ground. Observations and therapy can then take place in a natural and realistic environment. On the other hand, when parents have to take their child to a child development unit, they are able to meet others with similar needs. Their child will join in groups where he or she will be able to develop his or her attention, coordination and socials skills.

In either setting, the occupational therapist can help the family by giving them the time to talk about their feelings, sharing useful publications, inviting them to contact societies, developing intervention programmes and supporting and encouraging parents in their efforts to help their child.

According to Whitaker (1985), the following are some of the factors which need to be taken into account before asking parents to work with their child:

- If parents are instructed in an appropriate manner then social class or educational attainment makes very little difference as to how they work with their child.
- Daily demands upon parents such as preparing meals have immediate consequences, whereas working with the child may only produce very slow change. Consequently, some parents need help in organising their days in such a way that time can be given for specific activities with the child.
- If parents are thought to be suffering from eg. anxiety or a depression, help must be given to deal with this before trying to get them to work with their child, as any consequent failure with the child may aggravate their condition.
- It is also wise to see how the parents view their own abilities to cope with the home teaching programmes for their child and whether they regard the home programme as an effective method of increasing their child's development. If parents, views on either of these points are negative, it will probably be necessary to spend extra time demonstrating to them that the child can learn new skills as a result of their involvement.
- Finally, it is important to give parents the necessary knowledge and skills to cope with their child and avoid overdependence upon the home adviser.

School-age children

The Education Reform Act (1988) provides for the establishment of the National Curriculum for all pupils of compulsory school age in mainstream schools in England and Wales. Implementation of the National Curriculum began in 1989 with the core subjects: Mathematics, English and Science. The aim of the National Curriculum is to prepare individuals for the opportunities, choices, responsibilities and experiences of adult life. Frampton (1994) asked: 'What opportunities does the National Curriculum offer? What skills do children need to begin to access these learning opportunities? What part can the paediatric therapists play? How can we use the National Curriculum to broaden and enhance what we offer? The National Curriculum offers many opportunities for learning but many skills are needed to access these learning situations'. She gave examples demonstrating the relationship of independence skills to the National Curriculum (see Table 7.3).

Table 7.3 The relationship of independence skills to the National Curriculum

Activity/Concept learning content	National Curriculum references
Dressing:	
linking garments to part of body –	
which order of putting on garments	Science at 2 (Life and Living Processes)
pushing arms in, pull arms out	Maths at 4 (Shape and Space)
reinforce body awareness and movement	Science at 4 (Physical Processes)
done in exercises	
Grooming:	
improving body awareness, hands and face	Science at 2 (Life and Living Processes)
choosing and grasping brush	Science at 2 & 3 (Reading & Writing)
encouraging correct item for purpose	Maths at 1 (Using and Applying Maths)
exploration of textures water/wet	Science at 1 (Scientific Investigation)
soap/slimy; face cloth/soft, warm, wet	Science at 3 (Materials and their Properties)
	Maths at 4 (Shape and Space)

Therapeutic work may be divided into two categories – face-to-face and non-face-to-face therapy.

In the former, each child is seen for intensive therapy on a regular basis either individually or in a small group. In the latter, the children are seen by the teaching staff who use programmes devised jointly with the occupational therapist. This enables the occupational therapist to disseminate the skills amongst a larger group of pupils than would have been possible using a face-to-face approach.

The following examples illustrate the range of therapeutic work undertaken by occupational therapists in schools, child development units and at home. A list of useful books about some of the following activities can be found in Chia et al (1996).

Self-maintenance occupations are those activities and tasks which are done routinely to maintain an individual's health and well-being in the environment (Reed & Sanderson, 1983).

Activity sheet for individual work – Example A

Name of child: Ali

Date:

Task: Taking off handkerchief

Long-term aim: Ali will learn to dress and undress independently.

Current aim: Ali will grasp and pull a handkerchief from his head.

Equipment: Large handkerchief

Procedure: Take Ali to a quiet room. Ask him to sit on a chair. You sit facing him. Place the handkerchief over Ali's head. Say, 'Ali, take it off'. If he pulls the cloth away from his face, say, 'Good boy, Ali' and stroke his head. Mark a tick on the chart.

If Ali does not attempt to remove the handkerchief after 30 seconds, repeat request. Guide his hand to the handkerchief and prompt him to grasp it. Physically, guide him to pull the handkerchief away from his face. Say, 'Good boy, Ali' and stroke his head. Mark a tick with a circle on the chart.

Results: See Table 7.4.

Table 7.4 Results for Activity A

5	⊘	✔	✔	✔	✔	✔	✔
4	✔	✔	✔	✔	✔	✔	✔
3	⊘	⊘	✔	✔	✔	⊘	✔
2	⊘	⊘	⊘	⊘	✔	✔	✔
1	⊘	⊘	⊘	⊘	✔	✔	✔
	Mon	Tues	Wed	Thurs	Fri	Sat	Sun

Comments: Ali likes this activity. He enjoys the one-to-one contact. He is now ready to learn to undress ie. remove jumper from his head.

Activity sheet for individual work – Example B

Name of child: Betty

Date:

Task: Playing with toys

Long-term aim: Betty will be able to maintain head control to gain stimulation from her environment.

Current aim: Betty will maintain head control for 5 minutes at a time on request.

Equipment: Chair, prone board, pencil and some papers.

Procedure: Place Betty over a prone board. Place the paper on the table. Encourage her to grasp the pencil and draw some pictures (See Figure 7.2). After about 10 minutes, change her position. Sit her in the chair. Continue to ask her to draw the pictures. Encourage her to maintain her head control in each position. If she does, praise her. Note the length of time she is able to maintain her head control. Count 1, 2, 3 etc. softly to note the length of time. If she does not maintain control, repeat request and help her to maintain her head control by firmly holding her shoulders. Praise her.

Figure 7.2: Specialised equipment will help a child to maintain control eg. of head, allowing him or her to concentrate on the task

Results: Betty is able to maintain her head control for at least 5 minutes when she is seated in the chair. She finds it difficult to hold her head for more than 3 minutes when she is standing on the prone board. We need to adjust the angle of her prone board.

Comments: Betty's parents are encouraged to place Betty in various positions for a few minutes at a time, particularly on a wedge at home.

Activity sheet for group work – Example C

Names of children:

Date:

Task: Making pastry

Long-term aim: Each child will be able to prepare simple meals.

Current aim: Each child will learn to make pastry.

Equipment: 1 sieve, 1 mixing bowl, 1 table knife, 1 tablespoon,
Ingredients: 200 g plain flour, 100 g margarine, pinch of salt, 2 1/2 table-
spoonfuls of cold water

Procedure:
1 Wash hands and put on an apron.
2 Sift flour and salt into mixing bowl.
3 Cut margarine into small pieces and add to flour and salt.
4 Rub fat into flour, using finger tips until the mixture looks like breadcrumbs.
5 Add exactly 2 ½ tablespoons of water to flour mixture and mix in with a knife.
6 Gently gather the mixture together with hands to make a firm dough.

Results: The results cannot be quantified but indicate the amount of prompting each child needs to carry out the above tasks, such as sifting flour.

Comments: The session runs on a modular basis; once the group are taught basic skills and recipes such as making pastry, they will learn to make savoury dishes such as cheese pasties or sausage rolls and jam tarts. Recipes are standardised wherever possible, for example, most recipes use 200 g flour. Recipes are simplified by cutting out unnecessary steps eg. all vegetables are boiled for 15 minutes in one saucepan. Oven and hot plate temperatures are simplified by giving everything a low, medium or high rating – low being at the beginning of the dial and high being as far as the knob will turn.

The group is also given practice in weighing, making shopping lists and shopping for ingredients.

Productivity occupations.

These refer to those activities or tasks which are done to enable the individual to provide support to the self, family and society through the production of goods and services to promote health and well-being (Reed & Sanderson, 1983).

Activity sheet for individual work – Example D

Name of child: Elliot

Date:

Task: Threading chamois leathers

Long-term aim: Elliot will be able to work in training centres.

Current aim: Elliot will thread ten pieces of chamois leather.

Equipment: Some chamois leather and a knitting needle with a string attached.

Procedure: Tell Elliot to sit at a table with his peers. Place ten pieces of chamois leather on his left and the needle on his right. If he picks up and threads, praise him. If he does not, repeat request and help him to pick up a piece of leather. If he picks up more than one piece, tell him to put the rest back on the table. Help him to 'move' the leather to the end of the string. Praise him. Continue with the rest of the leather pieces until he has threaded the tenth piece.

Record daily. Mark a tick if he completes task without any prompt. Mark a tick with a circle if he needs a prompt or if he picks more than one piece of leather at one attempt. Mark an 'E' if he eats any pieces of leather.

Results: See Table 7.5.

Table 7.5: Results for Activity D

	Mon	Tues	Wed	Thurs	Fri
10	E	✔	✔	✔	✔
9	E	✔	✔	✔	✔
8	E	E	✔	✔	✔
7	✔	E	(✔)	✔	✔
6	(✔)	(✔)	✔	(✔)	✔
5	✔	(✔)	✔	(✔)	✔
4	(✔)	(✔)	✔	✔	✔
3	(✔)	✔	✔	✔	(✔)
2	(✔)	✔	✔	✔	(✔)
1	(✔)	(✔)	✔	✔	(✔)

Comments: This is a part of the pre-work programme. We have chosen this activity to start with because Elliot likes threading. As he could thread beads, it would be purposeful if he could thread chamois leathers with an end result – a washing up mop!

Elliot likes this activity. He is looking forward to completing the mop and using it to wash his parents' car.

Eventually, Elliot will join a group of four children at a table. Each child will be responsible for one of the following tasks: cutting leather to specific sizes, piercing the leather over a spike, enlarging the holes using knitting needles or threading the pieces and tying off the finished work. The work moves around the table in an anticlockwise motion.

Activity sheet for group work – Example E

Names of children:

Date:

Task: Growing cress (see Figure 7.3)

Figure 7.3: Growing cress

Long-term aim: Each child will be able to work in the local horticultural centre for individuals with special needs.

Current aim: Each child will plant cress seeds.

Equipment: Cress seeds, empty yoghurt pots, cotton wool and water.

Procedure: Sit at a table. Explain the purpose of the session. Show an example. Look at and hold the cress seeds, empty yoghurt pots, cotton wool and water. Ask the children to put some cotton wool in the yoghurt pot, water the cotton wool so it is damp and sprinkle the cress seeds on top. Keep the yoghurt pots in a dark, warm place for a few days until the seeds sprout.

Results: Results cannot be quantified but note the amount of prompting each child needs to carry out the above tasks, such as when watering the cotton wool.

Comments: This is an excellent activity as it gives quick results.

Activity sheet for group work – Example F

Names of children:

Date:

Task: Growing tomatoes

Long-term aim: Each child will be able to work in the local horticultural centre for individuals with special needs.

Current aim: Each child will be able to grow dwarf tomatoes.

Equipment: pots filled with seed compost; seed tray; tomato seeds (dwarf tomatoes); water drainage tray.

Procedure:
1   Arrange the pots in the seed tray.
2   Put one or two seeds in the centre of each pot.
3   Push a little of the compost over the seed.
4   Water gently.
5   Place pots on the drainage tray in a warm place, covering with plastic.
6   When the seedlings grow, remove the plastic and place the tray on a sunny windowsill.
7   Water when necessary.
8   Transplant into big pots, preferably 12 cm, filled with potting compost.
9   Plant out in June.
10 Grow in a sunny spot – tomatoes need plenty of sun to build up their food storing parts.

Results: Results cannot be quantified but note the amount of prompting each child needs to complete the above tasks eg. putting seeds into each pot.

Comments: Unlike growing cress, this activity requires some time before the children can see the produce. The seeds are sown in April and grown indoors on a sunny windowsill until the plants can be planted outside in early June.

Leisure occupations
Leisure occupations are those activities or tasks done for the enjoyment and renewal that the activity or task brings to the individual which may contribute to the promotion of health and well-being (Reed & Sanderson, 1983).

Activity sheet for individual work – Example G

Name of child: Fay

Date:

Task: Playing with electronic toys

Long-term aim: Fay will be able to operate electronic toys for play, school work and leisure.

Current aim: Fay will place her hand on the pressure switch of the robot toy as she completes the movement in rolling.

Equipment: Robot

Procedure: Place Fay on a mat on the floor. Place the switch at shoulder height to the side of the robot, at her right side, so it will move in her field of vision. Hold her right leg straight with light pressure on the knee using your left hand, with your right hand bend her left knee and bring it over her right leg so starting the rolling movement. When her knee touches the floor, hold it there. Then hold your left hand near the switch and say, 'Fay, give me your hand'. If she brings her hand over and places it on the switch say, 'Good girl' and let her watch the robot move.

If Fay does not bring her hand over, return her to supine and begin the movement again. Again holding your left hand near the switch say, 'Fay, give me your hand'. Then with your left hand bring her right hand over and help her press the switch. Say, 'Good, girl' and let her watch the robot move. Repeat it five times per session.

Results: Fay is normally able to place her hand on the pressure switch of the robot toy after the third trial.

Comments: Fay and her parents are encouraged to borrow electronic toys from the local toy library.

Occupational performance areas

These include the ability and skill to perform in each of the performance areas of sensorimotor, cognitive and psychosocial skills. Each individual does not have to perform each and every possible skill which is needed to complete the requirements in each part of the repertoire of occupational areas in self-maintenance, productivity and leisure. (Reed & Sanderson, 1983)

Sensorimotor

Motor skills include the level, quality and/or degree of range of motion, gross muscle strength, muscle tone, endurance, fine motor skills and functional use.

Sensory skills include the level, quality and/or degree of acuity, range, perception and integration of the sensory systems.

Activity sheet for individual work – Example H

Name of child: George

Date:

Task: Learning some basic perceptual concepts

Long-term aim: George will be able to incorporate some basic concepts into daily living tasks.

Current aim: George will learn to use the concepts of 'in' and 'on' using a self-help task.

Equipment: Mat, saucer, cup and spoon.

Procedure: Ask George to sit in the play room. After giving the objects, one at a time, ask George to carry out the task in the following sequence:

1   'Place the mat on the table'
2   'Place the saucer on the mat'
3   'Place the cup on the saucer'
4   'Place the spoon in the cup'
5   Ask him to stir and drink his cup of imaginative tea.
6   The next stage is to ask him to return the objects to you.
7   'Give me the spoon'
8   'Give me the cup.
9   'Give me the saucer'
10 'Give me the mat'

If he completes each task successfully praise him and mark a tick on the chart. If he does not, repeat request and hold his forearm to complete the task. Mark a tick with a circle on the chart. Record daily.

Results: See Table 7.6.

Table 7.6: Results for Activity H

	Mon	Tues	Wed	Thurs	Fri
Place mat on table	✔⃝	✔	✔	✔⃝	✔
Place saucer on mat	✔⃝	✔⃝	✔	✔	✔
Place cup on saucer	✔⃝	✔	✔⃝	✔	✔
Place spoon in cup	✔⃝	✔⃝	✔	✔	✔
Give the spoon	✔	✔	✔	✔	✔
Give the cup	✔	✔⃝	✔	✔	✔
Give the saucer	✔⃝	✔	✔	✔	✔
Give the mat	✔⃝	✔	✔⃝	✔⃝	✔

Comments: This is a useful self-maintenance activity which is done in school and at home. George has been practising with plastic play utensils prior to the session.

Activity sheet for group work – Example I

Names of children:

Date:

Task: Perceptual motor activities

Long-term aim: Each child will enhance his or her movement awareness.

Current aim: Each child will develop his or her body and perceptual awareness.

Equipment: Bean bags, skittles, tennis balls, large bats, a collection of wooden and plastic objects, chairs and tables.

Procedure: Begin the session by asking the children to move their limbs starting from their heads eg. turning the head from side to side.
Ask the children to swing their arms and walk round the room as quickly as possible. After a few minutes, ask the children to walk as slowly as possible.
Ask children to work in pairs, the first to pull the second by his or her ankles across the room. Take turns.
Sit in a large circle. Ask each child to use his or her right hand to rub parts of his or her body eg. rubbing knees.

Create an obstacle course for the children to:

1   crawl under and climb over a row of tables
2   knock down skittles with bean bags
3   climb over a row of chairs
4   bounce a tennis ball with a large bat
5   identify and write down the names of all the wooden objects on the right and plastic objects on the left side of the room.

Close the session by getting the children to lie down on the floor. Get each child to tense and relax starting from the head eg. press the head on the floor and relax.

Results: The results cannot be quantified but note the amount of prompting each child needs to complete the above tasks.

Comments: This is run on a modular basis. The programme of activities is initially done in conjunction with the teacher who continues to implement the activities on a weekly basis.

Activity sheet for group work – Example J

Names of children:

Date:

Task: Making jam

Long-term aim: Each child is given the opportunity to experience a variety of stimulations.

Current aim: Each child's hearing, vision, sense of touch, movement, smell and taste is stimulated.

Equipment: Choose a theme. See props required.

Procedure: Set up the room in advance to represent country lanes and fields. Ask group to identify a jar of strawberry jam when held up. Ask what is needed to make the jam. Suggest making 'jam' by going to the country, picking fruits, taking fruits to the factory, etc.
Content can be simplified or made more difficult by shortening or lengthening sequences, or by adding questions of varying complexity; can be purely imaginative or related to actual experience (see Table 7.7).

Tidying away should be part of the natural progression of the activity and therefore the ending can be part of the overall activity – bringing jam home and tasting it at teatime.

Results: Results cannot be quantifed but note the amount of prompting each child needs to complete the above tasks.

Comments: This is a creative way of using activities based on the work of Action Space (see Figure 7.4).

Figure 7.4: Making jam

Cognitive skills

Cognitive skills are the level, quality and/or degree of comprehension, communication, concentration, problem-solving, time management, conceptualisation, integration of learning, judgement and time-place-person orientation (Reed & Sanderson, 1983).

Table 7.7: Props and songs required for acting out jam-making sequences

Sequences	Props required	Songs
Introduction/presentation		
1 Walking into the country to find the farm where the strawberries grow	Tables and chairs covered with green material or paper to resemble country lanes and field	
2 At the farm, go into the strawberry field and pick the fruit	One section of green material with red shapes stuck onto it. Small punnets or boxes for everyone.	'This is the way we pick the fruit'
3 Load the picked fruit into van to take to factory	A small trolley into which everyone can empty their basket of fruit	Move round the room in lorry formation singing 'Drive, drive, drive the van quickly down the road, merrily, merrily, merrily, merrily with our heavy load' to the tune of 'Row, row, row, your boat'.
4 Arrive at factory, unload and wash the fruit, then put it into a big cooking pot	Part of room set aside possibly with 'Factory' sign and a large pan or bucket to put the fruit into.	
5 Add the sugar and stir the jam	Pour imaginary sugar into the pot and stir the jam. Use as many spoons as required	'Stir the berries into jam' all together to the tune of 'Michael, row the boat ashore'
6 Bottle the jam	Use jugs or ladles to pour the imaginary jam into pots	'This is the way to pot the jam' to the tune of 'Mulberry Bush'
7 Put the pots of jam in the store, counting the number made.	Cupboard or shelving space. One pot of 'real' jam. Invite everyone to taste the 'real' jam.	

Activity sheet for group work – Example K

Names of children:

Date:

Task: Textures

Long-term aim: Increase tactile awareness

Current aim: Experience of different textures

Equipment: Box of different textured materials such as cotton wool, bricks, soft pot scourers, sponges, silk, plus some towels and blankets.

Procedure: Divide children into two groups, each group sitting around a box of different textures. Each child chooses a texture to rub with on his or her elbows, forearms and hands.
    Ask the children to feel or identify materials which are:

soft eg. cotton wool;
hard eg. bricks
rough eg. soft pot scourers
smooth eg. a piece of silk
pliable (bendy) eg. sponges.

Roll up the child in a big towel or blanket and pretend it is a Swiss roll or a sausage roll. Roll him or her along; pat the 'Swiss roll' to put on icing sugar, or stroke the 'sausage roll' to put on ketchup.
    Lay a child with no or few clothes on different textures such as sheep-skin or bubble plastic. Roll the child along this surface and if appro-priate, encourage him or her to crawl or walk along.
    Ask the child to lie on his or her back and smooth him or her with the flat of your hands using body cream. Blow raspberries on his or her feet, hands, back, tummy and face.

Results: Record the response of each child to different textures.

Comments: This session links to art eg. making a collage with different textures.

Activity sheet for individual work - Example L

Name of child: Henry

Date:

Task: Finding objects

Long-term aim: Henry will develop object permanence.

Current aim: Henry will find half-hidden objects.

Equipment: A teddy bear and a towel

Procedure: Partly cover the teddy bear with a towel so that its feet, head and ears remain visible. Encourage Henry to pull the towel. If he does, praise him and mark it on the chart. If he doesn't, help Henry to pull the towel away. Praise him and mark a tick with a circle on the chart. Do it five times per session.

Results: See Table 7.8.

Table 7.8: Results for Activity L

	Mon	Tues	Wed	Thurs	Fri
5	✔	✔ⓒ	✔	✔	✔
4	✔ⓒ	✔	✔ⓒ	✔	✔
3	✔ⓒ	✔	✔	✔	✔
2	✔ⓒ	✔ⓒ	✔	✔ⓒ	✔
1	✔ⓒ	✔ⓒ	✔	✔	✔

Comments: Henry's parents are encouraged to play activities such as hiding things and hide and seek.

Psychosocial skills

Psychosocial skills comprise self-identity, self-concept, coping skills and dyadic and group interactions skills (Reed & Sanderson, 1983).

Activity sheet for individual work – Example M

Name of child: Intan

Date:

Task: Eye contact

Long-term aim: Intan will build up relationships with her parents and peer group.

Current aim: Intan will look on request.

Equipment: Bag of crisps, a quiet room and two chairs.

Procedure: Take Intan to a quiet room. Sit Intan on a chair. Sit facing her. Keep the reinforcers ie. crisps, in your hand. Give her a few minutes to settle down. Say, 'Intan, look at me', twice. If she looks at you, say, 'Good girl, Intan' and give her a crisp. Mark a tick on the chart. If she does not look, repeat the request and turn her head gently towards you. If she looks at you, say, 'Good girl, Intan' and give her the crisp. Mark a tick with a circle on the chart. Do it 10 times per session.

Results: See Table 7.9.

Table 7.9: Results for Activity M

	Mon	Tues	Wed	Thurs	Fri
10	(✓)	✓	✓	✓	✓
9	(✓)	✓	✓	✓	✓
8	(✓)	✓	✓	✓	✓
7	(✓)	(✓)	✓	✓	✓
6	(✓)	(✓)	✓	✓	✓
5	(✓)	(✓)	(✓)	✓	✓
4	(✓)	(✓)	(✓)	✓	✓
3	(✓)	(✓)	(✓)	(✓)	✓
2	(✓)	(✓)	(✓)	(✓)	✓
1	(✓)	(✓)	(✓)	(✓)	✓

Comments: Other activities are suggested to encourage Intan to look, eg. looking at bright objects, mobiles and mirrors. Singing simple rhymes also helps.

Activity sheet for individual work – Example N

Name of child: Jim

Date:

Task: Developmental movement

Long-term aim: Jim will establish a relationship with his peer group.

Current aim: Jim will co-operate with the following activities ie. being rocked, or dragged along on a rug and will climb over a bridge.

Equipment: Rug, large hoop

Procedure:

1   Encourage Jim to sit on the floor with his legs straight out in front of him. Sit close behind him and put your arms around him. Try to contain him with your body. Rock him gently from side to side. Encourage him to relax and rest his weight on you. Accompany rocking with humming or singing.

2   Encourage Jim to lie down on a rug. Gently drag him along the ground.

3   Crouch down to form a 'bridge' ie. on hands and knees. Make sure your hands and knees are fairly wide apart. Encourage Jim to crawl in between your arms and legs in the tunnel you have formed. Change over.

4   Lie down on the floor opposite each other so that the soles of your feet are touching. Both of you should lift your legs up off the floor, but keep pressing the feet, and start to cycle against each other. Do it slowly at first and gradually speed up until a rhythmical motion is maintained.

5   Tie yourself up like a package by crossing your legs, folding your arms and getting into a shape like a ball. Ask Jim to unwrap this package eg. by tugging at your arms.

6   Make a bridge shape on the floor with your feet and knees placed inside a large hoop. Ask Jim to guide the hoop from the knees to the hands and back again, without touching your body. Change over.

Results: Despite his initial reluctance, Jim is taking a more active part in the session. He is becoming more co-operative and seems to enjoy the activities.

Comments: As Jim shows interest in physical contact, he is being asked to join some self-defence classes in the community.

Activity sheet for group work – Example O

Names of children:

Date:

Task: Social skills training

Long-term aim: Each child will improve his or her social skills.

Current aim: Each child will be able to introduce himself or herself.

Equipment and procedure: This is the introductory part of a package to social skills training. The topic deals with 'Introducing yourself'.

1   Explain what the group is going to do and what is expected of everyone.

2   Sit round in a circle and ask each child to tell his or her name to the others.

3   Ask the children to take turns to think of a food which has the same initial letter as their first name eg. 'My name is Swee and I like strawberries.'

4   Ask the children to be aware of each other by taking photographs of each other in different poses, eg. sitting or laughing. A Polaroid camera is useful.

5   Invite each child to describe himself or herself in whatever way he or she wishes eg. name, age, build, height, eye colour, hair colour, hobbies etc.

6   All the children are shown an example of how to greet another person. A bad example is shown first followed by a good one. The children are reminded of the following:

   • appropriate eye contact – too much eye contact may be considered as being impolite while too little eye contact may be seen as a reluctance to make any interaction.

   • posture – a very tense posture conveys anxiety while a listless posture can be perceived as boredom.

   • gesture – too much may give confusing messages while lack of appropriate gestures may be perceived as being unwilling to respond.

   • proximity – too close may cause unease while too far may indicate unwillingness to have contact.

   • touch – too much may be interpreted as being over familiar while too little can be perceived as being rather cold.

   • listening – too much can result in jumping to conclusions while too little may result in missing the full sense of what is being said.

7   Encourage the children to practise this in pairs. Ask them to imagine they are meeting someone whom they have met a couple of times before. Praise is given and, where necessary, guidance. Each pair can show their exercise to the group.

8   Offer this activity as homework to be done by parents which is checked next week: How did each child get on with his or her work?

Results: Results cannot be quantified but note when a child needs support in this activity.

Comments: Homework provides an opportunity for the child to try out his or her newly learned behaviours in real-life situations which is likely to produce rewarding consequences. This will enable the skills acquired in the training session to be transferred to the child's own environment.

This programme is designed for six children. The sessions last for forty-five minutes and the group meets on a weekly basis. The sessions consist of:

- Starting a conversation
- Holding a conversation
- Non-verbal skills
- Verbal skills
- Listening skills
- Decision making

Environment

The environment includes:

- the physical environment – the inanimate, non-human aspects of the environment which include objects, space, weather and other elements;
- bio-psychological environment – the individual self or being, including the body and mind which form the human being;
- sociocultural environment –the other individuals with which the individual relates, including the customs, roles and laws which individuals use to organise behaviour (Reed & Sanderson, 1983).

The environment in which intervention takes place is crucial to the success of any intervention. There is little point in using an intensive programme for any child if the general environment in which he or she lives and works restricts opportunities to use and practise the skills being taught. Equally, it is also pointless to use application models if the same results might be obtained by reorganising or changing the environment. The ideal environment is one which prompts and reinforces appropriate responses and behaviours and offers varied opportunities for the child to engage in age-appropriate activities.

Before choosing any piece of equipment, the occupational therapist, the teacher and the parents need to address the following questions:

- Could the child be helped to do the task without special equipment?
- If special assistance is required, could a normal piece of equipment be adapted for the child?
- Will the equipment be used temporarily or permanently?
- Is the equipment clean, safe and functional?
- Is the environment suitable for the suggested equipment?
- Who will monitor its use and make modifications when necessary?

Sometimes, in order to help children – and in particular those with physical disabilities – to become more independent, occupational therapists assess and may recommend major adaptations to the environment and/or supply equipment such as a special spoon, a toilet seat or a special chair (see Figures 7.5, and 7.6).

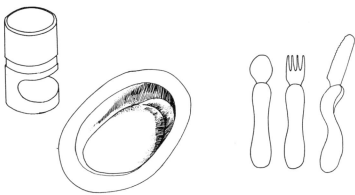

Figure 7.5: Have all the items ready to hand to the child one at a time

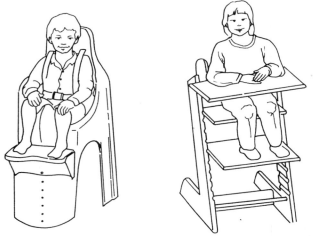

Figure 7.6: Adjustable seats are a great help to children with learning difficulties

The provision of a special chair will enable the child to feel secure against the effects of gravity, overcome the abnormal patterns of movement, develop his or her head and trunk control, free his or her hands for play and work and prevent the development of contractures. Consequently, the child will be able to sit upright and maintain his or her concentration with the task on hand

Evaluation and keeping records

According to Bradley (1985), 'Evaluation is a process of collecting, providing and analysing information that will be useful for making decisions and judgements about a course'. Evaluation can indicate which session or parts of the session work well and where improvements can be made. The evaluation process should lead to a better understanding of the aims and activities of the group and the child's needs. The way each member of staff carries out the sessions determines to a certain extent whether the child succeeds or not.

A useful method of evaluation is to carry out pre- and post-testing for individual work. The child is given a pre-test, for example by giving the child a sock and telling him or her to 'put on your sock'. The child is given opportunities to try several times, with the therapist keeping track of what he or she does. His or her errors are noted so that the occupational therapist knows which parts of the activity must be worked on the most.

Example of a pre-test

Give the child a sock, and indicate that you want him or her to put it on. Help the child only as much as necessary, letting him or her do as much as he or she can by himself or herself. Keep a record of the results (see Table 7.10).

Table 7.10 :Results of pre-test

	Always	Sometimes	Never	With Help
Holds the sock correctly for putting it on				
Puts the sock on over his or her toe				
Pulls the sock on over his or her heel				
Pulls the sock all the way up				
Takes the sock off				
Puts the sock on by himself/herself				

Repeat the pre-test procedure at frequent intervals to measure the child's progress in this activity.

Evaluation of group work

Here is an example of a group work and evaluation record sheet as suggested by Chia (1995) (see Table 7.11).

Table 7.11: Group work evaluation and record sheet

Results of students' overall performance during session

Each student's overall performance is rated as indicated in the key below

Name	II	IG	A	P	C	Comments
Anthony	3	3	3	3	3	Excited about the session
Betty	2	2	2	2	2	Showed extreme delight when she identified the objects by touch
Christine	2	2	2	1	2	Appeared shy and withdrawn today
Dorothy	2	2	2	1	2	Imaginative, asked to do 'pass the movement'
Elliot	2	2	2	2	2	Enjoyed building the bricks and knocking them down

General Comments
It was a good introductory session for all of us. Everybody showed interest, took part in earnest and seemed to enjoy the session.

KEY TO GROUP WORK PLAN/RECORD SHEET
II= Interaction with individuals IG = Interaction with group
A = Attention P = Participation
C = Co-operation

Interaction
Interaction with individuals
1 = Resists contact with other students, for example, when approached, moves away
2 = Responds to another student if prompted
3 = Responds to another student if not prompted
4 = Establishes and maintains contact/relationships with students

Interaction with group
1 = Resists joining in with group
2 = Joins group when prompted but remains passive
3 = Joins group when prompted and plays an active part
4 = Joins group without prompting and plays an active part

Attention
1 = Attends for less than a quarter of the time
2 = Attends for between a quarter and half of the time
3 = Attends for between half and three quarters of the time
4 = Attends for more than three quarters of the time

Table 7.11: (cont)

Participation - participates mainly with:
1 = Physical prompt
2 = Gestural prompt
3 = Verbal prompt
4 = No prompt

Co-operation
1 = Is actively unco-operative - resists help in tasks or refuses to co-operate
2 = Is passively co-operative, for example, allows him/herself to be helped but does not take an active part in helping
3 = Is co-operative, for example, helps in simple tasks
4 = Is actively co-operative, for example, follows simple instructions when asked, or initiates own activities and needs little guidance as to what is the appropriate action in most circumstances

Evaluation of creativity sessions

The following evaluation sheet for dance movement therapy session is useful for sessions which focus on creativity as suggested by Payne (1990).

Date:

Session no:

Children present:

Children absent:

1   *Time and length of session*:
2   *Setting*:
3   *Population*:
4   *Props/music used and reasons*:

5   *Themes predominant (movement and psychodynamic)*
    a) Themes you arrived with:
    b) Themes evolving from group:

6   *What happened overall (including structures used, responses and group dynamics)?*

7   *Any changes noted?*

8   *Any specific expressions?*
    a) verbal:
    b) non-verbal:

9   *Assessment (include socialisation skills related to objectives; objectives achieved; future objectives for next session)*

10   *Any other comments?*

11   *Your own process recording (What happened for you? Include any ideas, images, memories, feelings which emerged for you before, during and after this group session.)*

The following checklist, adapted from Mansell et al (1983) can be used for evaluating staff performance:

- Did staff have all the materials prepared at the start of the session?
- Did staff tell the children what they would be doing for the session?
- Did staff give time for children to explore and develop for example a movement?
- Did staff praise each child's efforts?
- Did staff give adequate help to students who needed it?
- Did the staff encourage the children to put things away?

Conclusion

The process of occupational therapy with children who have learning disabilities has been outlined. Occupational therapists have an important role to play in the assessment and implementation of individually designed programmes in order to help each child to develop to his or her maximum potential.

References

Bradley J et al (1985) From Coping to Confidence. Windsor: DES/FEU/NFER.

Chia SH (1984) Occupational therapy for children with perceptual motor disorders: A literature review. British Journal of Occupational Therapy 47: 39–42.

Chia SH (1987) Occupational therapy and mental handicap. In Bumphrey EE (Ed) Occupational Therapy in The Community. Cambridge: Woodhead Faulkner.

Chia SH (1995) Evaluating groups in learning disabilities. Nursing Standard 10: 25–7.

Chia SH, Gabriel H, St John C (1996) Sensory Motor Activities for Early Development. Bicester, Oxon: Winslow.

Clancy H, Clark MJ (1990) Occupational Therapy with Children. Melbourne, Australia: Churchill Livingstone.

Cratty B (1969) Perceptual Motor Behaviour and Educational Process. Springfield USA: Charles C Thomas.

Dolan J (1995) The challenge of community integration for people with learning difficulties. In Bumphrey EE (Ed) Community Practice. Hemel Hempstead: Prentice Hall/Harvester Wheatsheaf.

Frampton L (1994) The Relationship of Independence Skills to The National Curriculum for Children with Profound and Multiple Learning Difficulties. National Association of Paediatric Occupational Therapists Newsletter Summer: 17–20.

Jeffrey LIH (1990) Play therapy. In Creek J (Ed) Occupational Therapy and Mental Health. Edinburgh: Churchill Livingstone.

Kimball JG (1993) Sensory integrative frame of reference. In Kramer P, Hinojosa J (Eds) Frames of Reference for Paediatric Occupational Therapy. Baltimore USA: Williams and Wilkins.

Kortman B (1995) The eye of the beholder: Models in occupational therapy. British Journal of Occupational Therapy 58: 532–6.

Mansell J, Felce D, Jenkins J, de Kock U (1983) The Bereweeke Skill Teaching System. Windsor: NFER-Nelson.

O'Brien J (1987) A Guide to Lifestyle Planning. In Wilcox B, Bellamy GT (Eds) A Comprehensive Guide to the Activities Catalogue: An Alternative Curriculum for Youth and Adults with Severe Disabilities. Baltimore USA: Paul H Brookes.

Payne H (1990) Creative Movement and Dance in Group Work. Bicester, Oxon: Winslow Press.

Peck C, Hong CS (1994) Living Skills for Mentally Handicapped People. London: Chapman and Hall.

Penso D (1987) Occupational Therapy for Children with Disabilities. London: Croom Helm.

Pratt PN, Allen AS (1989) Occupational Therapy for Children. St. Louis USA: CV Mosby.

Reed KL, Sanderson SN (1983) Concepts of Occupational Therapy. Baltimore, USA: Williams and Wilkins.

Schoen S, Anderson J (1993) Neurodevelopmental frame of reference. In Kramer P, Hinojosa J (Eds) Frames of Reference for Paediatric Occupational Therapy. Baltimore USA: Williams and Wilkins.

Seifert A (1973) Sensory-Motor Stimulation for The Young Handicapped Child. Occupational Therapy 36: 559–66.

Whitaker S (1985) Can all parents teach their own children? Mental Handicap 13: 49–50.

Wolfsenberger W (1983) Social role valorisation: A proposed new term for the principle of normalisation. Mental Retardation 21: 234–9.

Acknowledgements

The author would like to thank N Spalding, Lecturer, School of Occupational Therapy and Physiotherapy, University of East Anglia, Norwich; N Smith, Head Occupational Therapist, Little Plumstead Hospital, Norwich; M Westwood, Senior Occupational Therapist, Jenny Lind Child Development Unit, Norfolk and Norwich Hospital, Norwich for their critical comments on the manuscript and R Steele, Undergraduate Student, School of Occupational Therapy and Physiotherapy, University of East Anglia, Norwich, for his delightful illustrations.

Chapter 8

The Use of Drama in Working with Children with Learning Disabilities

MYRA KERSNER

WARMING UP TO DRAMA

Introduction

Many professionals, without specific drama training, are interested in using drama techniques when working with children with learning disabilities. With this aim in mind, many have attended courses which I have run[1]. This chapter is intended to enable and encourage all interested professionals, irrespective of specialist training, to use drama in their work. Drama will be discussed in relation to the development of children's skills, and the practical approach presented in the courses will be outlined. This will include specific drama techniques which may be used when working with children with learning disabilities.

From the diversity of comments received when running the courses, it is apparent that drama means different things to different people: 'I always imagined it meant organising a school play'; 'I had not realised that some of the things I am doing already constitute drama'. This, therefore, begs the first question to be addressed and leads us to attempt to decide, within the context of working with this client group at least, just exactly what drama is.

---

[1] The courses referred to in this chapter are Continuing Education courses/workshops on *The Use of Creative Drama with Children with Severe Learning Disabilities*, devised by Myra Kersna and Lesley Kerr Edwards, which have been offered since 1988 through the Department of Human Communication Science, University College London (formerly the National Hospital's College of Speech Sciences). They are attended by teachers; speech and language therapists; careworkers; instructors and other interested professionals.

What is drama?

Responses by course participants to 'what is drama?'

SHARING   COOPERATION   RELATIONSHIPS   ROLE PLAY

EXPLORATION   PROBLEM SOLVING   MOVEMENT   DISCOVERY   GAMES

EMOTIONS   MIME   BODY LANGUAGE   CREATIVITY   IMPROVISATION

COMMUNICATION   SELF-EXPRESSION   STORIES   MIMICKING   PLAY

PERFORMANCE   IMAGINATION   ACTING   ENACTMENT   TRUST   ENJOYMENT

EXPERIMENTATION   MUSIC   DRAWING   GROUP BUILDING

The variety and disparate nature of the words associated with drama in the above list suggest not only the breadth of the subject, but also perhaps the ephemeral and intangible nature of the work. However, there is one aspect on which all generally agree, that drama is more than merely 'acting'.

Drama can operate on many levels, eg. the emotional level, the concrete level and the level at which we may gain insight into ourselves and our actions. Drama encourages us to take on the role of 'another', so seeing the world from a different perspective, and it can help to provide a safe and accepting environment in which children may gain the confidence to experiment and explore areas they might otherwise have avoided (Kersner 1989).

Essentially, however, drama is a shared process which develops through a flow of interaction and reciprocal response (McGregor, Tate & Robinson, 1977). Whether the drama is an end in itself, as in a production, or whether it merely provides a medium through which to work, its interactive nature makes it a natural conduit through which communication may flow.

The origins of drama

The origins of drama may be said to lie in: *ritual, theatre* and *play*, and, through each of these roots, drama has played an essential and intrinsic part in our development – and our everyday life – from the earliest days (Jennings, 1978).

Ritual

Throughout our social and anthropological history we have used ritual ceremonies and rites, such as wedding ceremonies and religious festivals, as a primitive form of theatre. Whether it was a ritual conducted by an individual, such as a priest at a burial ceremony, or a rite involving the whole community, for example the celebration of a harvest festival, such occasions incorporated one of the essential elements of theatre: that of 'actors' communicating with an 'audience', and it is in such religious ceremonies and rituals that the origins of modern day theatre – and drama – may be found (Jennings, 1992).

Theatre

Modern theatre is perhaps the final stage of the development of drama through ritual, but it is ritual stripped to the minimum, for the basic ingredients of theatre are merely an empty space and two people – an actor and an audience (Brook, 1968). In order for there to be 'drama', however, there is no prerequisite of an audience and it is this 'individual' aspect of drama which will be explored in this chapter.

Play

Play is perhaps the most important element in relation to working with children with learning disabilities; for play has an important role in all aspects of the development of young children: physical, psychological, cognitive, linguistic and social. Conversely, play levels are influenced by children's mobility, their gross and fine motor skills, and their cognitive levels of functioning.

Children's play

The development of play

There are different theories regarding the development of play (such as Freud; Piaget) and the stages of play 'which develop in psychological and creative complexity' (Jones, 1996, p.171) are variously classified, for example, by McConkey and Gallagher (1984) and by Jennings (1990). However, there are several factors which are commonly referred to in the literature with regard to the development of play, irrespective of the theoretical stance taken.

The ingredients of play

1   Primarily, there is a state of pre-play activity.
2   There is always a period of purposeful, repetitious activity.
3   Much time is spent on symbolic, pretend play, which extends into make-believe and fantasy play.
4   Finally, there is a period when children play more structured games with rules which involve much sharing and cooperation.

In whatever terms play is described, it seems apparent that in the initial stages children need time for solitary, individual exploration which is centred around the discovery of 'self'. This gradually leads to the inclusion of 'others' in relation to self as well as to the development of the ability to relate to objects. Solitary, parallel play, which includes much manipulation of small toys, as children refine their fine motor skills and develop symbolic understanding, generally opens out until children are able to adapt their play to encompass different kinds of sharing activities and group experiences.

Constant practice, and the comfort seemingly engendered by the frequent, almost compulsive, repetition of certain forms of play, seems to be a feature of many of the stages of play. For example, in young children this may be observed in the constant building up and knocking down of bricks; or in older children it may take the form of endless repetition of rhymes, or refrains.

The role of play

Play is a quintessential function of childhood. It has been described as a way of enabling us to make sense of our experiences (Cattanach, 1994); or as a way of helping us to develop skills and understanding, and of expressing ourselves (Hodgson, 1972). One important aspect of play is to provide a safe conduit for the release of energy. Gordon (1983) suggests that through imitating adult roles, play becomes an unconscious preparation for adult life. However, it was recognised as early as 1954 when Peter Slade first talked of 'child drama', that 'child play' is more than a mere aping of adult behaviour. As Landy (1986) points out, it has its own structure and its own logic based on the experiences of the child.

Through play, children explore their world and find their own personal rhythm (Slade, 1954). Play affords them the opportunity for re-enactment, and harmless manipulation and repetition. It provides a harbour of safety within which there is time and space for exploration so that fantasy and creativity may flourish.

Children also use play to express socially unacceptable emotions or unconsciously act out unspoken problems. In the words of Cattanach (1994, p.134), 'Children play to resolve unsolved problems from the past, to cope with present concerns, and prepare for the future and its tasks'.

As the role of play seems to be not only important but also diverse, lack of opportunities to play must have some detrimental effect on the developing child. This has a specific bearing on children with learning disabilities. As they generally require extended opportunities of experiences in order for learning to take place, there are many aspects of their development which would no doubt benefit from the extended provision of opportunities to play, and these opportunities can be provided through drama activities.

The relationship between play and drama – dramatic play

In the early stages of development, before the development of speech and language, children are only capable of participating in what McClintock (1984) refers to as 'pre-drama' activities which closely parallel the early stages of play. However, once 'pretend play' begins to flourish as receptive and expressive language begins to develop, they are able to engage in *dramatic play*. They are able to take on a role and begin to act out their fantasies.

The most important aspect of dramatic play is that it is interactive – not necessarily between the actor and audience, but between the actors themselves – and through this children begin to understand and learn about the complexities of social interaction (Cattanach, 1994). However, it is this peer interaction which children with learning disabilities often find the most difficult aspect of social exchange.

Drama with children with learning disabilities

What does 'drama' mean when working with children with learning disabilities? This in part may depend on the setting, for drama itself wears many different masks, and may be used for many different purposes.

Drama in education

Since the pioneering work of Peter Slade and Dorothy Heathcote in the 1950s, the use of drama has been developed in schools. Its role in an educational setting, however, is not clearly defined, for at any one time it may be used as, 'a subject, a method of teaching or a method of self-expression' (McGregor et al, 1977); both as 'a way of teaching' and 'a way of learning' (Way, 1967). With children with learning disabilities, it also offers possible contexts in which a teacher may ascertain whether or not children have generalised certain aspects of their learning (Peter, 1995).

Thus, it may appear on the timetable as a lesson in itself, subsumed as part of the Speaking and Listening requirement of the National Curriculum; or, it may be used as a medium though which other subjects of the curriculum may be taught. In special schools dramatic activities may be used to help the children establish basic concepts, or to develop their communicative skills generally. At one end of the spectrum, when working with profoundly disabled children, stimulation through pre-drama activities may contribute to many different aspects of their overall development; towards the opposite end of the spectrum, because of its interactive nature, drama with more able children may be particularly useful in helping them to problem-solve, or to develop social skills. For further reading about drama in education for children with learning disabilities see McGregor et al (1977); McClintock (1984); Peter (1994, 1995).

Drama for performance

In most educational settings drama for performance will feature almost as a ritual, at Christmas or the end of the school year, as staff prepare the children to perform before their families and friends. Each year, children of all abilities prove that they are capable of achieving an acceptable and enjoyable level of public performance (see Kersner, 1987a,b). Drama used in this way may be an important part of these children's education and indeed many of the techniques described below may contribute to the achievement of such a performance. For further reading on this aspect of drama see McClintock (1984); Peter (1994, 1995).

Drama as therapy

The use of drama in a therapy setting with children with speech and language disorders has been reported by Barnes (1988) and Landy (1985). In speech and language therapy the primary aim in using dramatic tasks is the development of communicative skills, although 'drama may have a secondary therapeutic effect on the client's psychological health' (Kersner, 1989).

In *dramatherapy*, the primary purpose of the work is to use drama to achieve a therapeutic effect. Trained dramatherapists use psychotherapeutic and dramatic techniques to enable children to gain insight, so enabling personal growth and development (Kersner, 1989). For discussion of dramatherapy with children with learning disabilities see Brudenell (1987); Cattanach (1992, 1994) Chesner (1995); and Jones (1996).

Drama as a creative art

Drama is essentially a creative art. It requires no audience, the experience of the participants being the primary concern. It is this personal, experiential aspect of drama, which may be referred to as *creative drama*, which is used when working with children with learning disabilities.

Creative drama encompasses the activities used in the development of pre-drama and dramatic play, as well as a variety of dramatic techniques, ranging from sensory stimulation to the use of role play. Creative drama also incorporates other creative arts: music and sounds; art; movement and dance; voice work including speech; language – spoken, written, or signed; all aspects of non-verbal communication; mime; puppetry and play. Creative drama sessions provide a time, space and opportunity in which the children may be creatively spontaneous in a non-judgmental, free-to-experiment medium.

The importance of 'the experience' of creative drama

Whatever the activity, creative drama enables children to enjoy different experiences directly, so making the work more memorable and meaningful (Peter, 1995). The value of the work lies in the nature of the experience, for the drama work itself is fleeting and can only be captured in the resultant feelings and memory of the experience (McGregor et al, 1977). This is particularly important for children with learning disabilities, for drama activities offer them opportunities to experience and make sense of their world in different ways, and to separate what they feel from what they know.

Preparing to use creative drama

Who are the drama leaders?

Anyone working with children may use some form of creative drama. Teachers, non-teaching assistants, speech and language therapists, occupational therapists, therapy assistants, careworkers, instructors or any other carer involved in the education and health care of these children may be the 'drama leader' incorporating creative drama into their work. In-depth specialist training is not necessarily required for the early stages of drama work, although a rudimentary level of knowledge and training in the use of drama, as well as an understanding of working with children with learning disabilities, is helpful.

The importance of the adult in creative drama

Adults play a crucial role when working through drama with children, particularly children with learning disabilities. They are more than mere 'drama teachers' for, as children enter the world of make-believe, the adult provides the baseline model from which the children establish their relationship with the real world. It is important that the adult should be able to give the children confidence in their ability to portray ideas, feelings and events dramatically (Cattanach, 1992).

Dependent upon the abilities of the children, more than one adult may be required to work with a particular group of children, and in the early stages of drama work, particularly with more profoundly disabled children, one-to-one work may be preferable (McClintock, 1984). All dramatic performances, however, benefit from having a director, and sessions involving creative drama are no exception. The director, or drama leader, is essentially a provider of 'space' in which the children may feel 'securely contained' (Watts, 1992). The director/leader may also serve as a stimulus to the child's creativity; acting as a crucial catalyst to the development of dramatic play. Children with learning disabilities often miss out on opportunities to play with children of their own age. As a result they may need the intervention of an adult in order to help them develop and practise the skills which will then enable them to play spontaneously (McClintock, 1984).

Who are the children?

Children with learning disabilities comprise a heterogeneous group and no attempt at a specific definition will be made here. For, as Brudenell (1992) points out, labels may obstruct our objectivity, allowing us to make assumptions – possibly false ones – regarding the children's abilities in terms of drama. In general terms, the tasks described below will be aimed at children whose main difficulties lie in the area of intellectual functioning (Montgomery, 1990), who have been described for educational purposes as having severe learning disabilities (SLD). Suggestions will be made with regard to adaptations which may be considered when working with children with profound learning disabilities (PLD) who may be at a pre-verbal stage of development, or with those with mild learning disabilities (MLD) who may be more able, particularly verbally.

Many of these children described as SLD have adequate functional communication skills, although most will have some degree of delay even if this does not require remediation. Some, of course, may not develop speech at all, and may rely on an augmentative and alternative communication system (AAC), such as a signing system (Makaton, Paget Gorman Signed Speech) or a symbol system (Makaton Symbols, Blissymbolics). Although many may be eager to communicate, they usually do so more freely with adults than with their peers; and their interaction skills are often impaired as is their understanding of communication in a social setting .

One general feature of such children, however, is that they do not easily generalise newly acquired knowledge and skills from one situation to another. Because of the cognitive deficit and overall delay in their development, when they reach each developmental stage they are chronologically older than children who have at least average performance skills. This means that in real terms they have fewer opportunities for practising their skills at each stage (McClintock ,1984).

The importance of creative drama to the children

Drama can make a vital contribution to the education and development of children with wide-ranging learning disabilities both as an active teaching and a learning medium. Within creative drama sessions there is scope for them to integrate their knowledge, skills and creativity. However, it has particular value in the development of communication and social skills where it encourages 'initiative, resourcefulness and empowerment.' (Peter, 1995, p.28).

What qualities and skills are needed by the children?

Course participants have suggested a list of skills in relation to children with learning disabilities and drama.
Skills and qualities required for drama:

AWARENESS AND APPRECIATION OF THINGS; PEOPLE AND ENVIRONMENT
SELF-OTHERS AWARENESS
EXPRESSIVE SKILLS: VERBAL AND NON-VERBAL   ARTICULATION SKILLS
INTERACTION SKILLS   TURN TAKING   EYE CONTACT   CONFIDENCE
WISH TO EXPERIMENT   LISTENING   ATTENTION   FOCUS   OBSERVATION
COMPREHENSION OF LANGUAGE   EMOTION   BODY LANGUAGE
IMAGINATION   CREATIVITY   PROBLEM SOLVING
QUESTIONING   LATERAL THINKING   ABILITY TO CHANGE DIRECTION FAST
BRAVERY TO HAVE A GO   LETTING GO OF INHIBITION
TEAMWORK   COOPERATION   RELATING SKILLS   LEADERSHIP
THINKING   MEMORY   SELF-CONTROL   METALINGUISTIC
BUILDING GROUPS   NEGOTIATION

Few of these qualities or skills are a prerequisite to beginning drama work; rather they are the result of accumulative work which may take place over a long period of time. One additional factor is the ability to perform freely in front of others, and this is not often a problem with children with learning disabilities.

Where does it happen?

Dramatic techniques may be incorporated at any time into a classroom lesson or therapy session. If a specific drama session is being planned, however, it is important to create a space in which the children should feel secure, so that they may feel uninhibited and enabled to reveal their creative best.

The ideal place for such a session would be a quiet, separate space with a carpet and a warm atmosphere, which was free from interruptions; the children would have individual mats on which to work, and an adequate supply of equipment. The reality will, of necessity, be far removed from this ideal; however, it should aspire to fulfil the same aims and to meet as many of these criteria as possible, even though this may stretch the creativity and ingenuity of the drama leader!

What is the time frame?

The length of the drama session will be dictated by the constraints of the school timetable, or the therapy appointment schedule; or it may depend merely on the children's attention and concentration span. Length is not always the crucial factor. The five-minute lesson may be just as important, in some instances, as a longer one (Way, 1967). What is more crucial is the frequency and regularity of the sessions which McClintock (1984) suggests are required in order for maximum benefits to be achieved.

The creative drama group

The decision as to whether drama is to be conducted individually or with a group of children will usually be governed by two criteria: the abilities of the children, and the resources available. For instance, with children with PLD it may be necessary to work individually, either one-to-one or where resources allow, as a group, but with each child working with an individual helper.

When drama is a timetabled activity within a school, the teacher, therapist or other professional will usually run the session for the whole class or for small groups within the class. It may not be possible to match the group members either according to their age or abilities in relation to drama, but working with children of mixed abilities is usually a positive feature.

The importance of communication within the group

The lines of authority between the adults working within the group need to be established. For example, where there is more than one adult it should be made clear to both adults and children who is the group leader. It is particularly important for other adults to understand whether they are acting as co-leaders or as assistants, and to what extent they are expected to participate in the drama activities. The organisation of co-workers is a critical task for the leader as tension between the adults may be unsettling for the children. If the group is conducted within the school by someone other than the class teacher, the children should understand the nature of that person's authority within the group.

The primary task of the group

The primary task of the group should be understood at the outset by the leader, the group members and the co-workers. This may sound like a statement of the obvious, but as the word 'drama' conjures up so many different images for different people it is necessary to spell out what the specific drama sessions will involve and what is the overall aim. It is not uncommon for the children in particular to have a different agenda from the leader. For example, drama to them may be inextricably linked to performance, and they should understand, from the beginning, if this is not to be a feature of the group.

Rules and boundaries

Drama and play may be absorbing so long as there are rules and boundaries – across the dimensions of time, space, group membership and acceptable behaviour. Without boundaries, children may feel unsafe and the resulting uncertainty will not be conducive to their engagement and active participation. This is especially true for children with learning disabilities. Some of the rules may be discussed and negotiated with the group members. If such rules are set at the beginning, reference may then be made to them during the sessions and this may help to avoid ensuing potential chaos (Cattanach, 1992).

As well as the provision of a comfortable space, time boundaries also provide security even though children with learning disabilities may have difficulties regarding the specific concept. It is helpful if the sessions can be at the same time each week, so that they become part of the weekly routine. If they start and end on time, then the children may develop a sense of the sessions fitting into their routine without a sense of flurry, or difficulty. It may be important to establish the number of sessions which will be run and for the weeks to be marked off on a chart. The children will then have warning before the group finishes.

The children should know who the members of the group will be, even if they are not all available for the first session; whether the membership is fixed, or whether they may have to adjust to new members from time to time. Confidentiality may need to be addressed, particularly with older children or MLD children who may be working on more sensitive issues in social skills.

Cattanach (1992, p.94) says that: 'Boundaries are the most important safety mechanism for people who are anxious about their emotional control', and it is certainly important for boundaries to be set regarding 'acceptable behaviour' within the group. Children are always eager to test out discipline boundaries, and basic ground rules must be laid down. Rules regarding acts of aggression, and what may be considered to be other 'anti-social' acts such as swearing, or running out of the room at an inappropriate time, need to be agreed by the members before the group begins.

Similarly, the rules of social interaction need to be made explicit: that they should not all talk at once; that they must not raise their voices or try to shout over one another; that they should listen to each other; respect each other's viewpoint; take turns; share, and work together.

WORKING WITH DRAMA

Structuring the session

Drama sessions may appear to be informal and relaxed, but they can only successfully be so within a carefully pre-planned structure. All sessions should have a beginning, middle and ending which are clearly defined by the leader in terms of aims and activities. The repetition of this structure becomes in itself a ritual. Although there can be no specifically prescribed ratio of time allotted to each of these three sections within the session, Jennings (1986) suggests that approximately half of the session should be devoted to the middle – the main development of the work – and a quarter of the time given to each of the opening and closing sections. (For additional suggestions of activities see Jennings (1986).)

The beginning – warming up

The warm-up enables the children to leave behind their previous activities; to settle into the room; to (re)adjust to the group, and to prepare for the activities to come. It may also help to provide familiarity and security, and act as a reminder of previous work (Brudenell, 1987). For the leader, the warm-up provides an opportunity to observe the group, get a feel for what stage the children have reached (Cattanach, 1992) and to focus on the group and the work.

Some suggestions for warm up activities

1   If the children do not know each other, this is the time for name games, such as passing a ball while saying their own name; eventually trying to name the receiver. How the ball is passed will depend on the motor skills of the children. It may be thrown, rolled or

handed on. Passing a cushion or bean bag may be more helpful if the children cannot grasp a ball.

2   If the children already know each other's names an introductory game of observation and description could be used. The leader asks a child to 'pass the ball to the boy with long hair; the girl with the yellow jumper.' Verbally able children may be able to take over the task from the leader.

3   With children with PLD the leader may say each child's name, naming an item of their clothing, or it may be helpful to sing a 'welcome' song at the opening of every session.

The middle – development of the work

This is the part of the session during which the main bulk of the tasks are performed in accordance with the specific aims and objectives for the group and individuals. Activity suggestions for this section will be included in 'A framework for practice' below (see p.195).

The end – closure

This is a time for reflection, for talking about the children's work together and evaluating the experience (Cattanach, 1992). It is also an important time during which 'the group can make a gradual transition from the focus of the session back to the focus of everyday life' (Jennings, 1986, p.16). It is always necessary to provide time within drama sessions for children to complete the work and disengage themselves from any emotions and feelings which may have been aroused by it. This is particularly important for children with SLD as they do not transfer easily from one activity to the next. Children who are unable to speak also need this time for winding down and transition, even if they are not able to reflect on the process verbally.

Some suggestions for activities for closure

1   The nature of the activities at this stage of the session will be dependent on the needs of the children in relation to the work undertaken during the session. For example, they may need to reflect on the work they have just completed, for example by naming an aspect which they enjoyed/learned.

2   They may make a drawing, symbolising how they feel. This may be done individually or as a group on a large sheet of paper. With more able children, single words of reflection could be used, written or spoken.

3   If the session was particularly strenuous, the children may need a quiet period, with some guided relaxation; or the group could stand in line, making a circle, each giving the person in front a

'well done' pat on the back. If the session has been relaxed, they may need an energetic exercise before they leave.

4   With less able children, a ritual leaving song may help them to mark the ending; or they may join hands and say goodbye to each other by making eye contact.

Developing the aims and objectives

The aims and objectives for the group will be developed by the leader in accordance with the primary task of the group, and for individuals in relation to each child's individual educational plans or therapy programme. However, there are some overall aims and objectives which apply to any drama group:

1   *The children must be engaged.* Situations must be structured; the material must be relevant and pitched at the right level to ensure their continual involvement. It is important that all of them are engaged at least some of time (Peter, 1995). This may require the leader to accommodate to individual needs, and to break up the tasks into short manageable 'bites'. Different activities involving a change of pace will help to maintain the children's attention and restimulate them if their energy levels begin to wane. Working to the strengths of the group – and to their interests – will enhance the opportunities for successful engagement. It might be helpful to incorporate some of the children's own ideas.

2   *The children must be able to understand.* Language must be kept simple so that the children can follow the instructions clearly. In many group situations it does not matter if some of the children merely imitate others: within the drama session, it is important for each child to be able to understand what is required of him or her for each task and to experience each exercise for himself or herself.

3   *The leader must encourage the children's creativity.* The leader should endeavour to create an ambience which will encourage the children to experiment, so fostering creativity and the development of the imagination.

4   *The children need opportunities to explore a range of content* including sensory awareness and feelings, concepts, movement, and social themes.

5   *The children need to be able to develop as individuals.* They also need to learn how to function individually as a member of a group.

Acceptance, praise and judgement

In a drama session the children can 'be themselves'; experiment in safety without fear of censorship. They must be given 'genuine freedom of opportunity' (Way, 1967, p.26) so that their ideas may be '*of* them and *from* them' (Way, 1967, p.27). Thus it is important for the leader to adopt 'an accepting attitude to what is offered by the group' (Watts, 1992, p.41). Potential creativity is often crushed if children are told that they do not conform to someone else's accepted standard.

Within a drama group there is no pre-set standard other than the ultimate objectives set for the group and the individuals. 'In drama there need not be a 'right way' of doing something – indeed, there is often a multiplicity of possible interpretations and representations of a given theme, which gives both legitimisation and scope for pupils of all abilities to work to their respective strengths' (Peter, 1995, p.6). It is for the leader to encourage and develop these strengths, to praise their efforts so that the incentive to improve may come from within the children themselves.

Indiscriminate use of praise has the disadvantage of encouraging the children merely to please the leader. However, used appropriately, praise may help children to take risks with their work so that they may develop their individual creativity.

Group leaders should

- be aware of how they respond to the children's efforts;
- be aware of how they respond to any lack of response;
- praise for effort, rather than achievement;
- 'act as a catalyst rather than a controller' (Jennings, 1986, p.13);
- be accepting of the non-conforming.

Developmental stages of drama

Little has been done to discover the developmental stages of drama (Courtney, 1981). However there is evidence to suggest that certain aspects of physical and cognitive development are prerequisites for successful participation in specific aspects of drama.

For example:

- In order to engage in exploratory play the child must be able to manipulate objects.
- To engage in specific wider aspects of play the child needs to be mobile.
- Levels of symbolic development need to be achieved if the child is to engage in make-believe.
- 'Self' in relation to 'other' must be firmly established if the child is to successfully participate in role play.
- Specific levels of social skills are required if the child is to engage in the process of negotiation required for certain aspects of group work.

Thus the development of drama skills within the dramatic process follows a developmental sequence which is closely linked to other aspects of the child's development.

Some suggested stages of development in relation to the development of drama (with acknowledgement to Courtney's Developmental Drama Check List, 1981)

1   Enjoys sensory experiences including vocal play.
2   Repetition of movements; manipulation of objects.
3   Exploration of environment; sound games; gestures.
4   Begins to develop knowledge of self as separate from others.
5   Begins to understand language.
6   Learns to play with toys; pretend actions.
7   Impersonates; mimics; develops rhythm.
8   Miniature symbolisation.
9   Gives commentaries.
10   Projective play.
11   Pretend; acting 'as if'.
12   Sharing; stories; acting out characters.
13   Development of imagination; games with rules; rituals.
14   Group play; role flexibility; improvisation; social rules.

A framework for practice[2]

In this suggested structure, drama is related to aspects of physical, cognitive and linguistic and emotional development so that the drama work may be directed towards engaging the interest and attention of children with differing levels of learning disabilities; utilising and developing their creativity and dramatic skills (see Figure 8.1).

Pre-verbalisation

I   Sensory experience
II   Developmental movement
III   Contact
IV   Sound

Verbalisation

V   Object play

Creative verbalisation

VI   Word games
VII   Story making
VIII   Improvisation
IX   Body work and emotion
X   Character development
XI   Social skills

Figure 8.1: The Framework

[2] This framework was developed by the author and Lesley Kerr Edwards.

Pre-verbalisation

In order to work at any of the stages included in this section the children require little or no expressive language and limited receptive understanding. Children who are only able to work at this level are younger children, or those older ones who have a greater degree of cognitive and/or physical disability. They will probably have limited motor skills and are unlikely to be mobile. They will generally be self-absorbed and may not easily relate to an 'other'.

Verbalisation

While they are playing, children often engage in solitary verbalisation, such as giving a commentary. For this they need some receptive and expressive language. Older children who need to begin working at this level may have some degree of mobility and gross motor skills, although they are unlikely to have refined fine motor skills. They will generally be able to relate to others, although there will still be much concentration on 'self'.

Creative verbalisation

Children capable of working at this level will need to have reasonable levels of receptive language, concept development and situational understanding, as well as the intention to communicate and some means through which to express themselves. These are prerequisite even for many of the non-verbal activities.

There may be some children who are capable of self-expression, but who may feel too inhibited. Sometimes this may be encouraged through the use of an 'intermediary projective item' such as a puppet.

Children with SLD and MLD who have the cognitive abilities to work at this level, will usually be mobile unless they have a specific physical disability. They will normally have a wide range of gross and many fine motor skills, even though these may not be commensurate with their chronological age. Generally they will be able to relate socially, although their peer interaction may be limited. and behaviourally and emotionally they will probably be immature.

Social development and confidence building

It is important to consider confidence and social development alongside dramatic skills development while work is being planned at any of the stages within this section of the framework. Children need to learn how to 'be' in different social situations; how to react and respond, and how to expect others to respond. Through dramatic play they will have opportunities to interact with their peers; to develop the ability to cooperate and share; and to gain the ability and confidence to develop the negotiating skills required to enable them to work together in small and large groups.

Implications for emotional development

The emotional development of children with SLD is rarely commensurate with their chronological age. They are often more vulnerable than their mainstream counterparts and are more likely to be easily emotionally affected by aspects of drama such as developmental movement or a difficult role play, which may easily trigger an emotional outburst. They may have more difficulty expressing this emotion and their reactions may be manifest in terms of unacceptable behaviour. The drama leader must be aware of this possibility, as time and space may be needed to deal with such problems.

Flexibility of activities

Most of the activities suggested may fulfil more than one aim, and so may be adapted for different purposes for different groups.

Example: a basic trust exercise Working in pairs, one child is blindfold, or closes their eyes. The other then guides the blindfold child carefully on a 'voyage of discovery' around the room. The guide introduces the blindfold child to items of interest, sampling different textures.

Some of the objectives which may be achieved by this exercise include:

- the development of visual observation skills of the leading child;
- the development of tactile observation skills of the blindfold child;
- the development of trust/responsibility;
- sharing and the development of working in pairs;
- the development of peer interaction – encouraging the use of speech and language.

Similarly, the activities need not necessarily be undertaken only by children who are functioning at that stage. For example, with children with more advanced skills, it may be helpful to take them back and forth through the earlier stages, allowing them to consolidate – and extend – some of this work. It will be encouraging for them to begin from a point where they know they can achieve success.

Sometimes activities from one section may be used as a warm-up, or closure, for another. For example, basic contact work might make a good introductory warm-up for a session on improvised movement; or an energetic, demanding session may be closed with sensory work, or relaxation.

Role reversal, allowing the children to become the leader, is a useful way of varying the activities.

All of the exercises suggested below will need to be developed over several sessions and in some instances will require much preparatory work.

Putting it into practice

I Sensory Experience

Although children of all abilities may enjoy working at this level, the exercises are particularly pertinent for children with a greater degree of cognitive and physical disability who may not be able to participate more actively. However, children with PLD are not always able to tolerate physical contact. It is important to approach such exercises sensitively, to assess the child's tolerance levels and to allow the child the opportunity to say, 'No!' to aspects of the activities which are not tolerable.

Some suggested activities

1   Present a series of light smelling aromatic oils, herbs and/or spices and ask the child to indicate preferred smells.
2   Present small pieces of material, or items of different textures, and encourage the child to feel them and indicate preferred textures.
3   Present a small selection of pleasant smelling hand creams. Gently rub a cream of the child's choice into each of the child's hands.

Care must be taken to ascertain beforehand that the child is not allergic to any of the substances presented. Similar checks should be made to ensure that no contra-indicative condition exists before applying creams. Allergies or conditions such as eczema would preclude such sensory approaches.

For any of these activities one adult will need to work with each child. Gentle music played during the session may help to create a relaxed atmosphere. The most important features of each of these exercises are that the children are given choices; that a way is found for them to express their preferences whether by speech, or some alternative method such as sounds, or pointing; and that they are given time to enjoy sensory experiences.

II Developmental movement

These exercises imitate the movements made by young infants. They enable the children to become more aware of their bodies and the movements they can make, and increase their self-image. However, this work must always be approached sensitively, as an emotional response may be prompted by evoked memories of early childhood experiences.

Most of this movement work requires the adults and the children to sit on the floor, preferably on a rug or mat, and to wear comfortable loose clothing. Relaxing music may help to create a calming atmosphere. Working one-to-one, exercises may be included which enable the children to enjoy relating to an adult (or another child) in what Sherbourne (1990) refers to as 'caring relationships'. Sherbourne (1990) lists further exercises and a detailed analysis of developmental movement.

Some suggested activities

1　The child sits on the floor, back between the legs of the adult. The adult supports the child with legs, arms and body, and cradles the child, gently rocking to and fro.

2　The adult gently rolls the child from a supine position first onto one side, then the other, encouraging a relaxed free flowing movement.

3　The adult gently pulls the prone child by the ankles across the mat, or across a slippery floor; or pulls the mat, with the child lying on it, gently across the floor.

III Contact

Once children are independently mobile and have had an opportunity to explore their world for themselves, they may be interested in exploring the effects of their movements in relation to others, the 'shared' and 'against' relationships referred to by Sherbourne (1990). Children of all abilities usually enjoy this type of contact. Contact exercises are not merely intended to be a test of strength, although assertiveness and resistance do feature, but they aim to encourage mutual support and trust.

Some suggested activities

1　*Balancing*: From a standing position, two children lean against each other, shoulder to shoulder (or back to back) experimenting how they can gradually give and take more of each other's weight.

2　*See-saw*: Two children sit on the floor, facing each other, legs splayed – one child's legs may have to rest over the top of the other's. They grasp each other's wrists. Then they take it in turns to help each other lean back till the head and back are touching the floor, then gently pull back upright to a sitting position.

3　*Resistance*: The children sit on the floor back-to-back with knees bent and feet firmly on the ground. Hands, too, should be firmly based on the floor beside them. They then have to push against each other, feeling the strength, stability and resistance.

IV Sound

Sound work may be incorporated into any aspect of drama work, for as part of the developmental process, children need opportunities to play with sounds (McClintock, 1984).

Some suggested activities

1   The children sit in silence for a few moments, then try to identify all the environmental sounds they can hear within the room, from the rest of the building and from the street or garden.
2   Each child chooses some form of stick and explores the room, gently tapping, for example, the radiators, wall and floor to investigate the different types of sounds they each yield.
3   The children experiment with the range of sounds which they can make with their voices and their mouths. They may imitate animal noises or environmental sounds and explore a range of vocal expressions such as grunts, giggles or whistles. They can try blowing through their fingers, or through a comb, with and without their voice.

V Object play

Playing with objects is an important part of the developmental process and children of all ages need this opportunity. With children with SLD such opportunities should continue in relation to their cognitive levels of functioning, rather than their chronological age, as they benefit from repetition. With older children, age-appropriate material may be substituted, such as action toys rather than teddy bears.

Three major stages of object play may be identified.

1   *Exploring, identifying and relating objects*

Some suggested activities

In the early stages of play children need opportunities to explore objects, using all their senses. They need to manipulate them, feel them, listen to them, and to smell them. They then need to explore how objects may relate to one another, for example, banging a spoon against a lid, fitting a small cup inside a larger one.

2   *Recognising and relating miniature representations – symbolic and pretend play*

Some suggested activities

Children need to discover that miniature items may be used to represent 'real things', such as cars, dolls, furniture, and they need opportunities to use them in relation to each other experimentally, so beginning symbolic and pretend play. Taking the child's lead, adults can help the children extend their play, incorporating other items to develop the make-believe.

3 Projecting the qualities of one item onto another

This is an extension of make-believe play when there is no longer a need for an exact representation to be present. The imagination dominates as matchboxes become cars; cruet sets petrol pumps; and attendants are invisible.

Some suggested activities

1   Present the children with everyday household items, such as a sieve (which could become a hat or a microphone); a pencil (which could become a moustache or a conductor's baton); a saucer (which could become a halo; or an ear-ring). Ask them to demonstrate different ways in which they could pretend to use the items.
2   With a group of children sitting in a circle, demonstrate, with or without words, the shape of an imaginary object such as a round ball. Pass 'the ball' to the first child who will then demonstrate another quality of the ball for example, a sticky ball. The next child could make it a large ball. Then they could demonstrate what they do with a ball, pretending to throw, or kick it.

VI Word games

Word games have the intrinsic value of developing expressive language skills and with some exercises, this may be the specific objective.

Some suggested activities

1   *Word association.* The leader begins by saying a word. As a ball, or bean bag is passed from child to child they each have to add a word that is in some way associated with the previous word.
2   *Crossing the river.* The room is divided into two by a 'river' and the group assembles on one side. The leader tells the children that they can only pass to the other side if they possess a specific attribute, such as blue eyes, or are wearing something red. The items chosen will depend on the cognitive level and under-standing of the children. A combination of attributes can be given to more able children. The children pass back and forth as the items change. One of the children may then take over the lead.

3   *Pass the song*. The children sit in a circle. The leader begins by saying the first word of a song or nursery rhyme with which they are all familiar. Going round the circle, each child is only allowed to say the next word. This is more suitable for verbally able children as the word boundaries in familiar verses may be confusing. If children with MLD become proficient, then the activity can be speeded up.

Other word games may be used as a lead-in to story making. These require some level of conceptual development as well as expressive language; for example, an understanding of cause and effect, and some concept of time.

Some suggested activities

1   *Fortunately/Unfortunately*. The children sit in a circle and the leader begins with the opening sentences of a simple story. The next sentence begins, 'Fortunately...' and a specific element of the story is introduced. The next child has to begin, 'Unfortunately...' and add a consequent sentence. The next child continues with, 'Fortunately.' The story passes round the group, alternately beginning 'Fortunately/Unfortunately'. This activity also works successfully with small odd-numbered groups, and children working on their own, particularly older children and children with MLD.

2   *Image blending*. One child describes an image. This may be, for example, a description of their breakfast, or a memory from a recent journey. Another child does the same. Drawings, or other visual representation of these images may prove helpful. The children then try to find a way of relating these two images as part of a simple, imagined story. More images could be added, so that the children are challenged to make a greater number of links, and small groups of more able children, or children with MLD could work on their own, later telling their stories to the rest of the group.

VII Story making

Stories can be used in many ways in different aspects of drama work. The exercises which will be described here are specifically aimed at enabling the children to develop their language skills, their sequential thinking, and their powers of imagination and inventiveness. The stories created could be acted out by the group.

Some suggested activities

1   Several items are placed in the centre of a circle of children. The leader then begins to tell a story. At certain stages of the story the

children, individually or collectively, will be invited to choose an item which they must then weave into the story. This continues until all the items have been used. MLD children may be able to initiate their own stories, solely based on a group of items, each of which must be included.

2   A story is developed by the group, guided by the leader asking questions. For example, 'Who is in this story? How old are they? Where do they live?' The children are invited to create their own characters, the environment and story line. Children with MLD may work in pairs. They agree a theme together, then one of the pair draws 'the place' (such as a desert island, or another planet), while the other draws 'the characters'. They each then question the other regarding what they have drawn so that they continue to develop the place, the characters and the action together. These stories could later be shared by the whole group.

VIII Improvisation

The essence of improvisation is spontaneity, and as such it is often able to tap the children's creative core, stimulating a flow of ideas. However, improvisation work needs to be carefully planned and structured by the leader and the power of the emotions which may be tapped should not be underestimated.

Improvisation can take many different forms, for example, through movement, or acting out situations with or without words. It is often advisable for such improvisations to be short, for, although the children may be initially creative, they may have difficulties in maintaining the theme. Non-verbal improvisations may require great concentration and a high level of situational understanding.

Some suggested activities

1   *Non-verbal improvisation: The group machine.* One of the children stands in the centre of the circle and begins making an action. The leader may need to suggest something specific such as imitating the motion of the wheels of a train with their hands. This movement is repeated continuously. A second child then joins the first, adding a movement of their own which is repeated. The remaining children each add their own repeated action until the group are working like a large 'machine'. Less able children may need much lead-in work to such an activity so that they understand the types of actions which may be suitable. Children with MLD usually enjoy experimenting themselves.

2   *Improvisation using speech in a 'non-real' way.* The children working in pairs are asked to discuss a given topic. However, they

can only use the word 'Rhubarb' (any single word could be used for this, or a sound such as 'baa'). This may be more suitable for older children or MLD children, who are more able to use the full range of intonation patterns in their 'conversation'.

3   *Verbal improvisation – Use the object.* The children work in pairs, each pair working in front of the whole group. They are given an object, for example a pair of scissors. They then have to decide on a place where they could use this object, such as a hairdresser's. They choose who will be which character, and at a given signal they are given one minute to act out a scene in the salon. With younger children there will need to be much preparatory work to set the scene and the characters, and maybe some suggestions from the group as to what might take place during the action. However, where possible the actual scene should be spontaneous and left to the pair themselves. If the children are capable (particularly MLD), the whole group may work in pairs at the same time. Each pair could be given a short, fixed time to decide on their situation and character, and begin at a given signal.

IX Body work and emotion

This more advanced level of body work is a precursor to the characterisation required for taking on the role of 'another'. It aims to increase body awareness and body image, and to enable the children to relate how they are feeling to the 'state' of their body. For example, when feeling angry, the body tenses, poised in preparation for 'fight or flight'; fists may clench, breathing become more rapid, and the face becomes set.

Some suggested activities

1   *Individual body sense.* The children gently rub each of their own arms to get a sense of how long they are, how wide. They do the same with each leg. Then they outline their trunk, shoulders, head. They carefully trace round their own facial features, screwing up their face, then stretching, while feeling the changes with their fingers.

2   *Emotion (i).* The children take up a posture. For example, they might bend over, pretend they are grasping a walking stick, walk with a shuffling gate. Then ask how this makes them feel.

3   *Emotion (ii).* Ask the children to 'think happy'. They then try to take up a position that shows that they are feeling happy.

It is important to take into account the feelings which may be engendered in the children by such exercises, particularly when emotions other than happy ones are expressed. At the end of such activities, the children will need an opportunity to 'shake off' the feelings, physically, and may need a chance to run about for a few minutes so that they may 'become themselves' again.

X Character development

In-depth character development requires a high level of understanding, much training, and concentrated effort to maintain the role, work which may be easier for children with MLD. However, children with SLD often enjoy taking on a role even if the character remains only superficially developed. The ensuing role play enables them to explore situations, roles and ways of being within the safety of a fiction, which they may not be able to experience – or cope with – in the real world (Cattanach, 1992).

Some suggested activities

Characters may be considered along six dimensions:
Their physical appearance: age, how they look, how they walk, what they wear.
Some qualities of character: meanness, seriousness.
Their actions: what kind of activities they like to be engaged in.
What they say: how they respond in conversation; what topics they talk about.
How they interact: who they spend time with and how they relate.
How they might feel.

1   Choose a favourite character well known to the children and discuss in terms of the six aspects outlined above. Then ask the children to think themselves into the character, and to move about and talk as the character.
2   The group help each child to develop a character of their own creation using the same dimensions. In pairs, or small groups, the children interact with each other, in character. They might act out a short improvisation. The emphasis at this stage of the work is on how the characters react, interact and develop rather than developing the improvised story.
3   Children with MLD may work in pairs, each asking questions to help the other develop a character. They could be encouraged to develop a complete history for that character, including education, social habits, family background. A situation is then agreed, where all these characters come together, such as a doctor's waiting room; or a space ship, and in small groups the characters interact in a short improvisation.

De-roling

It is always important for the children to de-role after taking on the role and persona of 'another'; to come back to being themselves, making an affirmative statement that confirms their real status and identity. This is particularly important when the characterisation has been deep, when emotions have been aroused while playing the character. Children with SLD may not enter into a character deeply, but they do not always have a firmly based sense of self, and it is important to make sure that they return to being 'themselves' at the end of such a session before leaving the drama space, by confirming who and what they are.

Some suggested activities

1   Each child in turn sits on an empty chair and makes a statement such as: 'I am not (name the character)'; 'I am (name of self)'. 'I am not going to (name an activity the character was involved in)'; 'I am going to (name the activity the child will progress to)'.

2   Each child in turn stands in the centre of the circle, takes off the imaginary costume of the character and 'throws it away', making a statement such as: 'I am not (name the character) and I am not wearing (name an item the character was supposed to be wearing); I am (name of self) and I am wearing (name an item the child is actually wearing)'.

XI Social skills

Through role play and improvisation in social skills training specific encounters, both old and new, can be experienced and rehearsed, and lessons may be drawn and learned (Brudenell, 1990). Older, more able children with SLD as well as children with MLD are able to benefit most from this aspect of drama work as the ability to take on a role, develop a character, and improvise are prerequisites. Receptive and expressive language skills are also required, whether using speech or AAC.

One of the ways in which social skills may be introduced in drama sessions is by creating a 'performance' in which the actors and the audience together try to resolve a particular problem.

Some suggested activities

1   The leader describes a 'situation' which is discussed by the group, for example, how to find the right platform at the station. The setting and relevant characters are agreed including several subsidiary characters who may help at different times.

2   Roles are assigned and some preparatory work may be done on characterisation.

3   A 'stage' and audience area are marked out, the leader asking questions of the whole group in order to set the scene. Props may be used if available.

4   A short improvised scene is acted out.

5   In order to maintain interest, the audience may be involved in the action. For example, the leader could 'freeze' the improvisation and ask the audience, 'What should happen next?', or 'What should he/she do?' Members of the audience might substitute briefly for the actors, improvising their own suggestions. If too much happened at once on stage the leader could 'freeze' the action only allowing two people at a time to continue.

6   Time must be allocated during closure for discussion regarding the problem, the suggested resolution and any implications this may have for their everyday lives.

De-roling

At the end of such an activity it is important not only to de-role the characters, but also the room. The set should be dismantled and the room is returned to its original state so that it is no longer regarded as 'the stage'.

ON REFLECTION

All good drama sessions end with a 'cooling down' period (Brudenell, 1990), a closing session when there is time to pause, take stock, consider what has been learned, and prepare to move on. This chapter on drama will not be any different and will close with a summary regarding the children and the drama leader and the work they do together.

- Children with PLD may only be able to work within the early stages of the *Framework*.
- Children with SLD should be able to work through all the stages of the *Framework* as they develop, even if this is sometimes only at a superficial level. They may need much preparatory work before fully engaging with each activity, will require much repetition, and their progress will be slow but, as their dramatic skills and group skills develop, so hopefully will their social interactions.
- Children with MLD will be able to work at any of the stages of the framework through verbal and non-verbal activities, at a faster pace, in greater depth and more independently.
- The leader must always be 'on the lookout for ways of adapting and changing methods and techniques to suit the individual needs' (Brudenell, 1990, p.190), and may adapt and extend the suggested activities, and include new ideas to enable the children to develop to their full creative potential.

References

Barnes S (1988) The use of drama as a diagnostic and therapeutic tool with school aged language impaired children. CSLT Bulletin.

Brook P (1968) The Empty Space. Harmondsworth: Pelican Books.

Brudenell P (1990) Dramatherapy with people with a mental Handicap. In Jennings S (Ed) Dramatherapy: Theory and Practice for Teachers and Clinicians. London: Croom Helm.

Brudenell P (1992) Dramatherapy with people with a mental Handicap. In Jennings S (Ed) Dramatherapy: Theory and Practice 2. London: Routledge.

Cattanach A (1992) Drama for People with Special Needs. London: A & C Black.

Cattanach A (1994) Dramatic play with children. In Jennings S, Cattanach A, Mitchell S, Chesner A, Meldrum B (Eds) The Handbook of Dramatherapy. London: Routledge.

Chesner A (1995) Dramatherapy for People with Learning Disabilities. London: Jessica Kingsley.

Courtney R (1981) Drama assessment.In Schattner G, Courtney R (Eds) Drama in Therapy Vol I. New York: Drama Book Specialists.

Gordon R (1983) The creative process: self expression and self transcendence. In Jennings S (Ed) Creative Therapy. London: Kemble Press.

Hodgson J (Ed) (1972) The Uses of Drama. London: Methuen.

Jennings S (1978) Remedial Drama. London: A & C Black.

Jennings S (1986) Creative Drama in Groupwork. Bicester: Winslow Press.

Jennings S (1990) Dramatherapy with Families, Groups and Individuals. London: Jessica Kingsley.

Jennings S (Ed) (1992) Dramatherapy: Theory and Practice 2. London: Routledge.

Jones P (1996) Drama as Therapy. London: Routledge.

Kersner M (1987a) Ali Baba and the 40 Thieves – a play for people with special needs Colchester: Alphabet Books.

Kersner M (1987b) A Space Oddity Play for People with Special Needs. Colchester: Alphabet Books.

Kersner M (1989) Drama in therapy is more than acting. Speech Therapy in Practice 5 (5): pp 8–9.

Landy M (1985) Communication through drama. Child Language Teaching and Therapy 1: p 3.

Landy R (1986) Drama Therapy Concepts and Practices. Springfield IL, USA: Charles C Thomas.

McClintock AB (1984) Drama for Mentally Handicapped Children. London: Souvenir Press.

McConkey R, Gallagher F (1984) Let Me Play. London: Souvenir Press.

McGregor L, Tate M, Robinson K (1977) Learning Through Drama. Oxford: Heinemann Educational.

Montgomery D (1990) Children with Learning Difficulties. London: Cassell.

Peter M (1994) Drama for All. London: David Fulton.

Peter M (1995) Making Drama Special. London: David Fulton.

Sherbourne V (1990) Developmental Movement for Children. Cambridge: Cambridge University Press.

Slade P (1954) Child Drama. London: University of London Press.

Watts P (1992) Therapy in drama. In Jennings S (Ed) Dramatherapy: Theory and Practice 2. London: Routledge.

Way B (1967) Development through Drama. London: Longman.

Acknowledgements

The author would like to acknowledge the help of Lesley Kerr Edwards in developing the Framework and the courses referred to in this chapter; and the editorial support of Dr Jannet A Wright.

Chapter 9

Music Therapy for Children with Learning Difficulties

HELEN TYLER

Introduction

Musical training is a more potent instrument than any other because rhythm and harmony find their way into the inward places of the soul.
(Plato)

Music has been used as a means of healing for thousands of years and its ability to bring about change, both physical and emotional, has been recorded throughout legend, literature and history. From the Bible story of David soothing King Saul by his harp playing, to tales of coma victims waking up to the sound of a favourite singer, music has been recognised as a powerful medium, capable of making inroads into conditions which appear intractable to other forms of treatment.

It is only in the last fifty years, however, that the use of music in this way has developed into a recognised profession with its own training and career structure. More recently still, it has begun to be accepted and valued by the medical profession and the education and social services as having an important contribution to make to the well-being of patients and clients, both adults and children, and there is still a long way to go.

It is, therefore, not surprising that many people working with children with special needs have no direct experience of music therapy, nor a clear idea of what it can offer. In this chapter the author sets out to answer three basic questions, and these in turn provide the areas on which she will focus:

1 What is music therapy?
2 Why does it work?
3 Who can it help and how?

This chapter continues with an overview of the history and background of the profession, followed by a broad survey of music therapy in the UK today. The final section is based on specific examples of music therapy illustrated by case material of children with learning difficulties.

Early history of music therapy – The pioneers

After the Second World War, hospitals in the USA found themselves treating traumatised ex-servicemen whose symptoms did not respond to conventional medication. However, musicians who were brought into the hospital to give recreational concerts seemed to break through the patients' isolation and despair and to assist their return to normality (Ainlay, 1948). At the time, the reasons for these results could only be conjectured, although most people have had the experience of music as being uplifting or 'taking one out of oneself'. Anecdotal evidence of the effectiveness of music used in this way led to a call for research and a methodology to be developed, resulting in the first music therapy training course which was held in Kansas University, Texas, in 1946.

Meanwhile, in Britain, the concert cellist Juliette Alvin had experienced similar results when performing in psychiatric hospitals and playing to children with various disabilities. In her pioneering work she extended her role as a performer into that of a therapist by seeking to draw the patient into shared communication through the music. She wrote:

> The idea which has guided me throughout the work is a conviction that music should be a creative experience and that it should help to discover or exploit to the full any ability which the child may possess, not necessarily in music ....
>
> The seeds of music can yield a rich harvest if their growth responds to a need. The child's individual response to music very often reveals a non-musical need, and shows how he (or she) can be reached and helped. (Alvin, 1965)

Juliette Alvin was responsible for setting up the first music therapy training in Britain, at the Guildhall School of Music and Drama.

Two other influential pioneers of the same period were Paul Nordoff and Clive Robbins. They worked on the now accepted premise that there is an innate responsiveness to music which remains unimpaired by physical disability, learning difficulty or emotional trauma. In their experimental music therapy sessions in 1959–1960 with children with a wide range of special needs, each child was brought to the music room and shown simple percussion instruments, such as drum, cymbal, tambourine and bells. While Clive Robbins facilitated or encouraged the child's participation, Paul Nordoff improvised music at the piano which reflected and responded to whatever sounds and reactions the child produced, whether it was playing, singing, screaming or rocking. The sessions were tape recorded and the results analysed and afterwards they wrote: 'The children were making musical self-portraits of themselves in the way they were reacting. Each was different and it was becoming evident that there must be a connection between the individual's pathology, personality, psychological condition and the musical self-portrait he (or she) revealed.' (Nordoff & Robbins, 1971).

Nordoff and Robbins continued their work as part of a team in a day-care unit for autistic children in Pennsylvania and were able to move beyond their early diagnostic work into showing how the use of improvised music could bring about change, first in the child's response to the music, and then generalised into daily life. Nordoff and Robbins returned to Britain in 1974 to teach on the first Nordoff-Robbins training course.

Key dates in British music therapy

1958 British Society for Music Therapy (BSMT) formed by Juliette Alvin 'to promote the use and development of music therapy.' (BSMT Constitution).

1968 First music therapy training course at Guildhall School of Music and Drama.

1976 Association of Professional Music Therapists formed (APMT).

1982 Career and grading structure awarded by DHSS.

1994 Negotiations begin for full state registration as part of the Council for Professions Supplementary to Medicine (CPSM).

At this point, a formal definition of music therapy may be helpful:
Music therapy is the use of organised sounds and music within an evolving relationship between client and therapist to support and encourage physical, mental, social and emotional well-being (Bunt, 1994).

Further developments

In the course of the development of music therapy, influences from other professions and forms of therapeutic intervention have been vital, both in providing treatment models for the new discipline and in lending a vocabulary with which to describe it. Psychoanalysis, cognitive psychology, behaviourism, Rogerian counselling and the medical model have all been enriching. In addition, the multi-disciplinary teams in which many music therapists work have led to cross-fertilisation between music therapy, the other arts therapies, teaching, speech and language therapy, physiotherapy and occupational therapy. Research into the physical nature of sound has led to the development of vibro-acoustic therapy, while guided imagery techniques have been developed by some music therapists.

While all these contacts have been important and fruitful, as music therapy grows in self-confidence and in the body of research available, it becomes essential for music therapists to find their own language in which to talk about their work. Bunt writes: 'Music therapy will eventually be able to step outside existing frameworks and orientations to establish itself as a unique discipline. Perhaps by a deeper understanding of music and musical processes we shall begin to become aware once again of the central position of music within music therapy.' (Bunt, 1994).

Music therapy training

As the profession developed, so more training courses came into existence and there are now five (1996), with more in the planning stages. The entry requirements vary slightly for each course, as does the orientation of the teaching and clinical work. Normally, music therapy trainees need a degree or diploma from a university or music college, as all the courses are postgraduate. A high standard of musical performance is essential and auditions for the training include the playing of repertoire and improvisation. An intensive interview looks for evidence of the candidate's potential for personal insight and self-awareness, as well as maturity and sensitivity.

Successful completion of the training after one or two years leads either to a Diploma in Music Therapy or a Master's Degree, depending on the length and intensity of the course. Following qualification there is a mandatory period of work under supervision before therapists can be accepted as full registered members of the APMT.

All the courses give students experience of working under supervision with children and adults with special needs, disabilities or emotional problems. Lectures give a background to the medical, psychological and psychiatric conditions of the clients they will meet, and to child development, physical and mental illness and other related topics.

Where music therapists work

There are currently 300 music therapists registered in the UK and the diversity of places in which they can be found is a sign of the growth of the profession over the last fifty years. Music therapists work with babies, very old people, and with all ages in between. Health Service settings include medical and psychiatric hospitals, hospices, child and family centres and special units for drug or alcohol abusers, for young people suffering from anorexia or the results of abuse and people living with

HIV or AIDS.

Within education, music therapy is found at all levels within special schools, from nursery to further education colleges, while mainstream provision focuses on emotionally and behaviourally disturbed young people. In social services, music therapists work in day centres, residential units and as part of the resettlement work with people returning to the community from long-stay hospitals. A recently expanding area of work in music therapy is in forensic psychiatry in prisons, secure units and in centres for young offenders.

Despite all these developments, music therapy provision is very patchy and inconsistent throughout the country, with the majority of music therapists working in London and the South East of England. Funding of posts is also an ongoing concern. Although therapists employed by the NHS have a negotiated pay scale, in other areas employment is less secure; for example, education authorities are reluctant to pay music therapists at an equivalent rate to teachers unless they have a teaching qualification. This means that a highly-trained and skilled music therapist could be paid as an unqualified instructor (Warwick, 1995). The shortfall in funding, especially for work with children, is often supplied by charities such as the Music Space Centres in Bristol and Nottingham, the Nordoff-Robbins Music Therapy Centre in London and the Northern Ireland Music Therapy Trust in Belfast. All these charities fund therapists to work both in their own premises and in outreach programmes in the local communities.

Why music?

No culture so far discovered lacks music. (Storr, 1992)

In all societies music is an integral part of public and private life. Music adds another dimension to occasions of national importance or personal significance and supports or transcends the spoken word in worship, celebration and mourning. Few people would deny the important part that music has played in their lives from infancy to old age and that it is a powerful medium for the communication and expression of emotions.

Music therapists, however, are making use of an even more fundamental connection between music and human beings, one which is innate biologically as well as psychologically. Paul Nordoff, in a BBC interview, described it like this:

> We are rhythmic beings and tonal beings, and rhythm and tone are the basic materials of music. In speaking we use tone and we can use the tonal quality of our voice to make it expressive. We are rhythmic beings as well; in the beating of our hearts and in the relationship between breathing and heartbeat (Nordoff, 1975).

Nordoff went on to describe how in music therapy these 'basic materials' could be the means of communicating directly with the child, despite disability or impairment.

> Now, when a child comes to us, he reveals his musical limitations imposed on him by his pathology; he shows us that he can only beat in one tempo, or that he cannot beat at all; he cannot speak so he does not have a tonal experience. We take these manifestations of pathology and through improvisation we meet them. We meet the tempo of his walking, his head banging, his rocking; we take the sounds he might make, screaming or crying, and we give them back to him in music, so that he has a new experience of what he does habitually (Nordoff, 1975).

These observations were made by Nordoff after fifteen years as a music therapist, based on his experience of working with children and his analysis of tape recordings of their sessions. In another sphere of research, psychologists studying very young babies have made similar connections between tone and rhythm and the development of mother/infant communication.

In the womb the foetus reacts to pitch and rhythm and there is much anecdotal evidence from pregnant women about the response of their babies to different sounds or types of music. In 1980 Shetler set up an investigation into prenatal experience that measured foetal response to music described as either 'stimulative' or 'sedative' . Marked differences in reactions indicated early, and probably innate, musical response (Shetler, 1990).

In the past, it was thought that new-born babies used their voices only to express hunger, pain or distress, but recent research has shown that they also respond communicatively. For example, Ockelford shows that babies less than 24 hours old can turn their heads to the sound of their mothers' voices (Ockelford, 1988). Trevarthen has made an extensive study of 'protoconversation', communication between a mother and a young infant, first thus described by Bateson (1975). He makes an analogy between this early communication and a musical improvisation.

> The improvisation of a performance on two instruments can be used by a trained music therapist to explore and transform the emotions of patients with mental illness (Pavlicevic & Trevarthen, 1989). This is the kind of coherence or confluence of narratives of feeling between subjects that one observes in protoconversation too (Trevarthen, 1993; Bateson, 1975).

Robarts, writing about music therapy for children with autism, also draws a parallel between improvisational music therapy and early communication.

Infancy research, in its investigation of the beginnings of relationship, social interaction and communication, uncovers a spectrum
of rhythmic phenomena and expressive tones that requires
musical terminology to provide accurate and appropriate description. Micro-analytic studies of mother–infant interaction demonstrate in detail the musical improvisatory features and phrased
infra-structures of basic emotional communication, mother and
infant both adjusting the timing, emotional form and energy of
their expression to obtain inter-synchrony, harmonious transi-
tions and complementarity of feelings between them in an
emotional partnership or 'confluence' (Trevarthen, 1993). It is
this very inter-synchrony, flexibility and creative reciprocity that is
absent in the autistic child and which the music therapist seeks to
help the child experience and assimilate to whatever extent she
or he is able (Robarts, 1996).

Stern (1985) writes of 'affect attunement' when referring to the
synchronicity of non-verbal communication between mother and baby.
Many other psychologists have described the same phenomenon, often
using musical terminology, such as timing, phrasing, dynamics and song.
The evidence suggests that these early communication experiences are
vital in the acquisition not only of speech and language but also in the
development of the first relationship, and therefore all subsequent relationships.

Many of the skills intuitively used by mothers to engage their babies
in 'protoconversation' are part of the music therapist's technique;
listening, attuning, attending, waiting, imitating, reflecting, mirroring,
turn-taking, sharing and playing are all part of making a musical relationship with the client, whatever the chronological age. Children who come
for music therapy may have a difficulty with verbal communication,
either because they have not developed adequate language, or because
words are not enough. The music therapist can make contact when the
child is functioning spontaneously at a non-verbal or pre-verbal level
and using improvised music has the flexibility to respond in the moment
to whatever communication the child makes. Then, by extending the
shared interaction which develops, the therapist is able to lead the child
into new experiences and to support the exploration of areas which may
have been unreachable before.

The other element of music which predisposes its use as a healing
agent is that music has an undisputed link with the emotions. Aristotle
was specific in his analysis of the effect of music on the emotions, referring to the modes on which ancient Greek music was built.

Men are inclined to be mournful and solemn when they listen to
that which is called Mixo-Lydian; they are in a more relaxed frame
of mind when they listen to others ...... A particularly equable

feeling is produced, I think, only by the Dorian mode, while the Phrygian puts men into a frenzy of excitement (Aristotle: translated Sinclair, 1981).

Anthony Storr writes as both a psychiatrist and an amateur musician:

> Participating in music not only affords an opportunity for expressing and mastering disturbing emotions, but also opens up new channels of communication between therapist and patient. Anyone who has played chamber music or sung in a choir knows that music reinforces emotional ties with others; for autistic children and other patients whose disabilities make it difficult for them to communicate with their fellows verbally, music can be a life-saver, preventing regression into the hell of total isolation (Storr, 1993).

The greatest poets, writers and philosophers have all agreed that music goes beyond words in its expression of emotion. Music can soothe and lull to sleep, stimulate and stir to action, excite and energise, irritate or bore, and awaken memories, bringing to mind forgotten feelings of sorrow, loss or joy. It is these responses which we are harnessing, together with the biological, psychological and developmental connections with human beings when we use music as therapy. 'Above all, it is the emotional, aesthetic power of music (hard to convey in words) that can offer a depth of shared emotions or 'communion' of the kind that unites people, regardless of abilities or disabilities.' (Robarts, 1996).

Why therapy?

At this point, a question may be raised as to how music therapy differs from other forms of musical activity. At home and in school, music is an essential part of entertainment and education, and the enjoyment gained from listening to and taking part in singing and playing is therapeutic through creating feelings of well-being and enhancing the quality of life. Music therapy practised as a profession, however, has certain features which separate it from more general musical experiences. Central to the therapy is the relationship which is built up between therapist and child. This relationship is based on mutual trust and acceptance and takes place within the boundaries of a therapeutic setting. This means regularity and consistency of time and place of sessions, confidentiality and the identification and pursuit of therapeutic goals. In musical terms the child/therapist relationship is developed largely through the use of musical improvisation, which is the predominant model of music therapy in the UK. The free-flowing exchanges which can be facilitated through clinical improvisation allow the therapist to be the listener, the reflector, the enabler and the supporter of the child, with the flexibility to move into new musical areas as the therapy demands. Although pre-composed and recorded music can be used in therapy, clinical improvisation provides the shared language of the communication. Similarly, therapist and child may speak, either about the music or thoughts and feelings evoked during the session, but the music will retain its position at the heart of the therapy.

Another aspect of music therapy which sets it apart from other musical experiences is the necessity to work with negative and resistant feelings, whether these are expressed musically, verbally or acted out. Nordoff and Robbins, when developing rating scales to evaluate their work with autistic children placed equal value on the 'participation' and 'resistiveness' elements of the child/therapist relationship in the musical activity. They wrote:

> Not all response in therapy was participatory: with autistic or other emotionally disturbed children resistiveness appeared in many forms to impede or influence the development of the relationship. With many, resistiveness was a corollary to participation – a progressive response was immediately preceded and/or followed by one that was resistive in some way (Nordoff & Robbins, 1977).

Whether the therapy lasts for a few months or several years, the therapist will be working to enable inner change, growth, fulfilment of potential and improved quality of life. For each child the gains and experiences will be different, and it is the process through which child and therapist travel together which brings about the changes, rather than the acquiring of musical skills and knowledge or the performance of a piece of music. For this reason, the child does not have to be musically skilled, 'musical' or even to like music to benefit from music therapy.

Music therapists, like other professionals, keep records, make notes, have supervision and think deeply about their case-work. In general, however, they will try to approach each session with an open mind and open ears, without preconceived aims, objectives or programmes. The instruction of Bion to analysts to 'abolish memory and desire' (Bion, 1967) in no way contradicts the fact that therapists work with focus and intent during the session and will assess and evaluate it afterwards.

Music therapy in action - Two case studies

The case studies which follow are taken from the author's work at the Nordoff-Robbins Music Therapy Centre in North London. As the centre is the only one of its kind in the UK, it is not a typical music therapy setting, yet the 200 clients who attend for weekly sessions represent a cross-section of the case loads of many music therapists up and down the country.

The setting for the sessions in these case studies is a large, carpeted workroom with muted colours on the floor and walls. There is a grand piano in the middle of the room, a side drum without snares and a cymbal, while cupboards contain an assortment of small instruments such as tambours, tambourines, wood blocks, claves, bells, maracas, whistles and reed horns. Larger instruments can be brought in from a central store as needed. A microphone embedded in the ceiling records all sessions on audiotape, while video cameras in two of the corners can be operated from a control room when appropriate. A mirror running the length of one wall conceals an observation booth which is used primarily by students in training, although neither of the children in the following case studies was observed.

The author has chosen two children at opposite ends of the continuum of learning difficulties, hoping to show how music therapy as a uniquely flexible medium can meet very differing needs. One is a girl, Susie, who will probably never acquire more than a few words of speech and will need total care all her life, while the other, Joe, is already verbal and articulate, with the potential for leading an independent life in the future. What they have in common is summarised by Nordoff and Robbins:

> Each one is isolated from the course and content of normal human life to a particular extent, frequently the child is unable to assimilate life's experiences; he may be confused because he fails to interpret them, he may even misinterpret them ...... he may live in a vortex of emotion or, conversely, his consciousness may be so remote that it is concerned only with distorted fragments of the realities of existence (Nordoff & Robbins, 1971).

Case study – Susie: Angelman syndrome

Susie was four years old when she was brought to the Nordoff-Robbins Music Therapy Centre for a consultation. While her parents and I talked, Susie lay placidly in her buggy, apparently oblivious of her surroundings. She occasionally moved her arms and legs jerkily or sucked her hands. She did not respond when her name was called, and appeared to make only fleeting eye contact when her mother spoke directly to her. Sometimes she smiled; at other times her eyes closed and her head dropped forward suddenly as though in a brief fit. She was very quiet, making a few soft vocalisations. Her mother described her as generally contented, but said it was difficult to interest her in anything except food. However, she liked musical toys and noisy rattles and her parents hoped that music therapy would help her to respond more and 'to reach her potential' .

Angelman syndrome is a genetic disorder caused by a deletion on chromosome 15 (Clayton-Smith, 1992) leading to global developmental delay. The principal features of the syndrome include the following:

severe learning difficulties
no speech
epilepsy
jerky movements and motor difficulties
gastric problems
feeding problems
sleep disturbance
unprovoked laughter

Susie showed all the signs of the syndrome and could not stand, crawl or sit up unaided. Her mother also said that Susie's hands were very sensitive and that she did not like them to be touched. All this gave me the impression of a very isolated child, cut off from normal development by her disability and with very little motivation or means to reach outside her restricted world to communicate with others. This rather bleak picture contrasted with the external image of Susie as a smiling, contented 'baby', who made few demands and was generally 'good'.

From this consultation it was agreed that Susie should come for weekly half-hour sessions with me and that a co-therapist would also be present to encourage and facilitate Susie's participation.

The account that follows looks at aspects of the first five months of Susie's music therapy, and at how the music was used – initially diagnostically and then as a means of drawing her into an exploration of new experiences.

Nordoff and Robbins express the early work with a developmentally delayed child as: 'the gradual process of dawning awareness and skill development through which the child discovers meaning, satisfaction and some trust and security, through her musical response.' (Nordoff and Robbins, 1977).

My initial clinical aims were to help Susie to increase her self-awareness and also her awareness of herself in relation to the therapists and the music. In the early sessions I therefore experimented with the sounds of different instruments and played in a range of registers, dynamics and tone colours, to find out how Susie would react. I would begin at the point where she was reacting spontaneously with vocal sounds and body movements and, by building musically on every evoked or reflexive response, would heighten her perception and give her a new experience of her habitual behaviour. Video recordings were helpful in assessing the sessions afterwards and in trying to make sense of Susie's sounds, smiles and movements, which appeared to be random and disconnected. I was also interested to notice that in the early sessions she would suddenly seem to fall asleep, only to wake up just as suddenly seconds or minutes later. It was not clear whether this was related to her epilepsy, her medication or other reasons.

Table 9.1 below illustrates some of Susie's responses in her third session.

Table 9.1: Susie's responses in her third session

Therapist and Co-therapist	Susie
Co wheels S in buggy	S apparently asleep
Th silent until S is near	–
Th sings 'Hello Susie' . Music on piano bright, lively, high register.	S opens eyes briefly, turns head towards Th, smiles, closes eyes.
Singing more strongly, 'Hello Susie, music day.'	Opens eyes, waves arms and legs. Smiles, turns head toward Th again.
Co brings wind chimes to S's left side and rings them – bright bell-like sounds.	S turns head away from Th towards chimes, smiling and gurgling.
Co plays wind chime very close to S. Th accompanies on piano, leaving spaces for S's response.	S smiles, looks at chimes but doesn't reach out.
Co gently moves S's arm to make contact with the chimes.	S allows this briefly, then stiffens, withdraws arm, wrapping hands in bib. Head down.

Later

Co shakes the tambourine vigorously. Lively piano music with tremolos and trills.	S becomes excited, laughs and waves arms and legs.
Co moves tambourine rhythmically up and down. Th accompanies with dramatic piano music, following the tambourine's movements.	S tracks the tambourine with her eyes, sustaining her interest for several minutes. Vigorous kicking movements with legs.
Co holds the tambourine by S's foot. Th sings 'kick the tambourine' .	S withdraws feet, draws knees towards chest, serious expression.
Co moves tambourine to make contact with waving hand.	S withdraws hand and drops head forward.
Co and Th continue to play and sing, music becoming lullaby-like in character.	S apparently deeply asleep and remains so for remainder of session.

Key: Th = therapist; Co = co-therapist; S = Susie

Analysis of this session showed that Susie was excited and attracted by high, bright sounds and that she reacted to shiny instruments played strongly, close to her. However, it seemed that she resisted any attempts to involve her directly in the music making, both by her physical withdrawal and by allowing herself to fall asleep. Her frequent small seizures certainly added to her difficulty in sustaining concentration, but our feeling was that Susie was choosing to be a passive spectator, rather than an active participant in her therapy. It seemed that it would be important to address this in the sessions and not collude with Susie by providing a constant diet of attractive, undemanding experiences which did not draw her into participation. Using the Nordoff-Robbins Rating Scales led me to evaluate Susie's progress in terms of the resistive response as well as her level of participation.

Nordoff and Robbins see resistiveness as a necessary and valuable part of developing a relationship. They write: 'resistiveness was seen to move from shutting out the therapy situation to withdrawing from it, then to actively rejecting it and then on to appearing in successively higher forms as evasion, manipulativeness, assertiveness and expressions of competent independence.' (Nordoff & Robbins, 1977).

A similar value is attached to resistant behaviour during the formation of a relationship by Trevarthen, in his description of the communication patterns of a one-year-old. 'Assertive differencing in the form of refusals, antagonistic repulsions, withdrawals etc. is as necessary as compliant or encouraging agreement.... passionate unreasonable insistence on agreement and violent disagreement both threaten relationships .... willing co-operation strengthens relationships.' (Trevarthen, 1993).

In these early sessions when we were still developing a trusting relationship, it was important not to impose on Susie, so we continued to offer the experience of the instruments without insisting on, or even expecting, her participation. However, at this stage it seemed that Susie was most able to enter into a dialogue through her voice. Although her vocalisations were short and unformed, I found that it was possible to engage her in shared interaction through matching and extending even the briefest sounds. The following example is from the beginning of Session 8. The singing is unaccompanied and is soft and intimate in quality:

Susie sounds the note E on a short 'uh' sound.

I answer, on the same pitch and with the same length note.

Susie extends this to a two note phrase; D E.

I answer, reversing it to E D.

Susie extends further to a four note oscillation between D and E, still on an 'uh' sound.

I answer with 'Hello', 'Hello' on D E, E D, developing a lilting quaver/crotchet rhythm.

Susie continues on her two notes, turn-taking with me in the rhythm.

I add a third pitch G, singing 'Hello' on a falling third, G E.

Susie answers exactly on the same pitch G E, and changes her vowel sound to a-o, in a clear approximation of 'Hello'.

This dialogue continues for four minutes, with Susie making frequent, if brief, eye contact, waving her arms and generally seeming excited and stimulated by this close musical/emotional contact.

As Susie became accustomed to the music therapy setting, she allowed more physical intervention. She enjoyed being rocked, or swinging her arms, with the co-therapist's help, to rhythmical music. She also responded with energy to music with a pronounced bass line, showing increased movement in the lower part of her body when the piano was played strongly in the bass register. We used this response to engage her in a 'kicking' activity, and she no longer withdrew from this. She also showed increased tolerance of her hands being touched by an instrument or the therapists.

Table 9.2 shows an example of part of Session 18, illustrating some of Susie's developing responses.

Table 9.2: Susie's responses in Session 18

Therapist and Co-therapist	Susie
Co wheels S into room. Music, high register, 'Hello'.	S apparently asleep. S yawns, stretches, waves arms and legs.
Co plays the cabasa to lively music. Holds it on S's lap. (a cabasa is a small rattle-type instrument covered with shiny ball-bearings)	S allows Co to take her hand so she can feel the movement of the cabasa. After 2 minutes hand and arm go limp. S sleeps.
Th and Co stop the music. Silence for 2 minutes.	S sleeps.
Th plays strong bass rhythm, associated with tambourine. Co brings tambourine to S's feet.	S opens eyes, smiles and kicks legs strongly. S kicks tambourine and is helped to stamp on it.
Th and Co continue with tambourine music.	S seems very alert, allows her hand to be tapped on the tambourine, then her feet again.
Th sings.	S echoes on the same note.
Th sings 'Susie can sing'.	S closes eyes.
Th sings 'Susie can go to sleep and ..... wake up!'	S opens eyes.

Key: Th = therapist; Co = co-therapist; S = Susie

This 'going to sleep and waking up' game is repeated several times, with Susie opening and closing her eyes as if in recognition of the words. I exaggerate the musical contrasts; soft and gentle for 'going to sleep' and sharp and bright for 'waking up'.

Although the musical dynamics may well have played a part in stimulating Susie to open her eyes, we also felt that there was an awareness in her of our direct expression of her avoidance and that in the musical acknowledgement of 'going to sleep and waking up' she was drawn into involvement, despite her reluctance. Her acceptance of the cabasa and the tambourine (as well as bells and the wind chimes) pointed to a development of a new kind of communication. Trevarthen describes the interaction at this stage of development as 'Person–Person–Object' games, rather than the 'Person–Person' games of a younger infant (Trevarthen & Hubley, 1978).

At the end of these five months Susie began to be able to use music therapy as a means of communication, self-expression and the development of all facets of her personality. Her parents commented that in this period she had shown improvements in alertness, concentration, vocalising, and the use of her hands. She was also beginning to make clear choices and to be more assertive.

Case study – Joe: Asperger's syndrome

It was hard work living with Joe. At nine years old he was anxious, noisy and demanding. He was very active but clumsy, with poor concentration, constantly asking questions yet never being reassured by the answers. Rituals, obsessions and fears controlled his life, particularly about burglars, accidents and death. His loud voice and inappropriate comments often caused embarrassment to his quiet parents and well-behaved younger brother, while other children thought him strange and teased him.

When I first met Joe he was struggling to cope in a mainstream primary school with a support teacher for one hour each day. He was a fluent reader but lacked understanding of what he read and number concepts were hard for him. At school he tended to be very quiet and fearful of doing the wrong thing. He found any change to routine, such as a school outing, very alarming, and break times were an ordeal as he did not know how to play with his peers.

Joe's parents contacted the Nordoff-Robbins Centre because at home he would sit for long periods playing the piano and singing, and they felt this had a calming effect on him. Joe attended the centre for weekly half-hour sessions for three years, until he was twelve; he had approximately 125 sessions.

Asperger's syndrome (and autistic states in general) affect the ability to make relationships, interact and empathise and as a result opportunities for leading a full life are restricted. 'Many children with a primary diagnosis of autism can be working and relating at a cognitive, emotional and social level which is much less than their potential.' (Brown, 1994).

As we have seen earlier, a child will reveal his or her limitations and difficulties in the course of the musical improvisation: 'By working to free the person's musical limitations, resistances and defences and by building on the strengths of his or her musical elements, components and structures within an improvisational relationship, we are simultaneously working towards healing the other aspects of her or his cognitive, physical, neurological and emotional being.' (Brown, 1994).

Music therapy did not cure Joe of Asperger's syndrome, nor take away all the symptoms, but enabled him to face his difficulties and struggle with them as they emerged as part of the musical therapeutic relationship.

Year 1. Through omnipotence to play

'Playing takes place in the potential space between the baby and the mother figure ..... it is only in playing that the child or adult is able to be creative and to be the whole personality, and it is only in being creative that the individual discloses the self.' (Winnicott, 1971).

In the early sessions Joe took command of the piano, the largest instrument in the room, and isolated himself by loud, inflexible playing and raucous shouting of nursery rhymes, such as 'Old MacDonald' and 'Here we go round the mulberry bush'. He tested boundaries by swearing at me, banging the piano lid and pushing instruments over. In between playing episodes, he flicked the light switches on and off, or repetitively opened and closed the door. He asked a stream of questions: 'How old are you?', 'Have you got a husband?', 'Has your mum died?', or, more anxiously, 'Can my Dad hear me?', 'Will I die if I jump off the piano?'

At this stage it was important to listen to Joe with full attention while establishing safe boundaries so that he knew he would not be allowed to hurt himself or me, nor deliberately break the instruments, and that we would stay in the room for half an hour with no-one hearing or watching. (Joe regularly checked the video cameras to make sure that they were not on, as indeed they never were.)

Gradually, there were episodes when Joe told me to play the piano while he sang the nursery rhymes and accompanied himself vigorously on the percussion instruments. This was the first sign of his isolating behaviour becoming interactive, although he kept control by shouting 'Stop!' mid-verse and changing the song. Joe was very rejecting of any music I introduced, rubbishing it unless it was something he already knew or commanding me to stop if I strayed from the expected tune. The mood created by songs such as 'If you're happy and you know it clap your hands' was of false jollity, in conflict with the reality of the tension in the room, but it seemed important to allow Joe to use them as 'transitional phenomena' (Winnicott, 1974).

'Pre-composed melody offers a safe starting point from which to explore the potentially unsafe world of music therapy, rather like having a musical hand to hold.' (Flower, 1993).

The rituals felt like a defence against feelings of powerlessness, and asking Joe to stop flicking the light switch had no effect, except to increase his agitation. I then set the flicking to music, to a calypso rhythm at a rather slower tempo than his actions: 'Now it's on, now it's off, now it's light, now it's dark.' Joe adapted the flicking to match the rhythm and seemed delighted with the effect, and after a few weeks was able to relinquish it altogether. This was the first musical suggestion from me that Joe accepted, apart from a goodbye song which I introduced in the first week and which remained throughout the therapy, enabling Joe to make the difficult transition from the therapy room to the outside world.

My support of Joe's choices at this stage was not slavish compliance but attuning, mirroring and matching, always holding on to the possibility of extending creatively when the time was right. To return to the mother/baby analogy with a quotation from Josephine Klein: ' ..... if adults will play the required part for a time, then the baby will have had some actual experience of magical control, of omnipotence.' (Klein, 1987).

Klein then refers to the case of Dibs (Axline, 1964): 'I think it is this which the psychotherapist Virginia Axline practised so perceptively, that when, years later, Dibs, a previously unhappy and disturbed little boy was asked what had helped him, he replied "Everything I did, you did; everything I said, you said" – the essence of support and confirmation.' (Klein, 1987).

After a few weeks, the nursery rhymes diminished considerably and Joe discovered that the music therapy room could also be a play room. He devised a number of games for us to play together, although he remained in control of the rules and the outcomes.

1   *Hunt the instrument*: we would take it in turns to play the piano with our eyes shut while the other person hid the instruments.
2   *Hide and seek*: for weeks on end Joe delighted in hiding and being found, despite the lack of real hiding places in the room.
3   *Guess what I'm saying*: Joe would blow a rhythm into a reed horn, and I had to try to interpret it – an impossible task.
4   *The blind boy*: Joe would walk round the room with his eyes shut. I had to play the piano, but stop if he bumped into anything.

In general, Joe was always 'the winner' in these games, and it was impor-tant to him that I experienced 'failing', 'not understanding' and 'getting it wrong', as he so frequently did in his daily life. All these games could be repeated endlessly so I had to negotiate a 'music time' within the sessions, usually the beginning and the end, to allow for the possibility of musical interaction. Joe cooperated with this, accepting that it was 'music therapy' so we would play and sing some music every week. At this time he frequently wanted to sing a song he knew from school: 'When I needed a neighbour'. In contrast to his often raucous singing, his voice took on a gentler tone in this song and it seemed that he was responding both to the poignancy of the minor key music and to the sensitivity of the words which could be related to his own needs and longings.

> When I needed a neighbour were you there?
> And the creed and the colour and the name won't matter, were you there?
> I was hungry and thirsty, were you there?
> I was cold, I was naked, were you there?
> When I needed a shelter, were you there?
> When I needed a healer, were you there?
> When they put me in prison, were you there?
> Wherever you travel, I'll be there, I'll be there.
> (Carter, 1963)

It was important to Joe that I should accompany his singing on the piano, so I was literally 'there' with him in his travelling. He needed me as a musical support, in the same way that I was necessary to his games. He was thus able to relinquish some of his omnipotence and permit the beginnings of shared play.

Year 2 – From ritual to spontaneity

In the second year of therapy Joe moved to a new class and was increasingly stressed and unhappy. His parents were trying to find a special school which could cater for his emotional and social needs, while allowing him to develop his academic potential.

Joe's anxiety was played out in our weekly sessions in a re-creation of a terrifying school assembly in which Joe, as a sadistic Headmaster, would harangue, humiliate and bully the pupils. The school game included the ritual of counting and naming all the pupils as they entered the imaginary hall. My role was to be the music teacher playing the assembly hymns. Joe's choice was often: 'Let there be peace on earth', or 'Peace is flowing like a river' – words which expressed his deep wish for inner calm, in contrast to the chaos which was his everyday experience. Invariably, during the course of the assembly something would go wrong and the 'Headmaster' would have to threaten punishment. If I reflected the change of mood in the music by breaking up the smooth melody into jagged lines and adding dissonance, Joe would become agitated, demanding, 'Play nice music, happy music, all jolly and nice.' He was very aware that changes in the rhythm, melody and harmony were expressing the feelings in the room and felt uncomfortable hearing them reflected back to him, wanting immediately to revert to a safe musical place and deny the discord.

Part of the struggle in the therapy at this time was to help Joe find an authentic voice to express his emotions, not just through the attacking voice of the 'Headmaster' nor the sweetly compliant tone of the happy hymns, which denied loss and sadness. Joe could not accept spoken comments on what he was doing but increasingly became more tolerant of musical intervention, so I took every opportunity to give expression to what I perceived as Joe's inner state. For example, the 'Headmaster' would often announce a death or disaster that had happened to a pupil or teacher, and Joe would allow sorrowful music at this point, although he would switch rapidly to 'happy music' if he felt it was getting too intense and personal. At this stage it was hard for him to accept disturbing feelings as part of himself, wanting only to identify with the 'nice music'.

The concept of the 'True and False Self' was helpful in understanding Joe at this point (Laing, 1960; Winnicott, 1960). Laing describes the 'True Self' as meaningful, real and spontaneous and the 'False Self' as futile, unreal and purposeless. 'Love is precluded and dread takes its place. What one might call a creative relationship with the other in which there is mutual enrichment of the self and the other is impossible.' (Laing, 1960).

In music therapy there was an opportunity for Joe to experience 'a creative relationship with the other' and to be released from the futility and dread which he so often felt, thus enabling a more authentic expression of the 'True Self'. To illustrate this, I will quote from a session in the middle of the second year of Joe's therapy in which I was working musically to help Joe to stay with the difficult feelings, despite the conflict and struggle which ensued.

The 'Assembly' had begun with 'Morning has broken' which had led to a violent outburst by the 'Headmaster' because the children had all been naughty. I reflected this on the piano with dissonant chords and fragmented music. The melodic line was angular and the dynamics loud and agitated.

Joe: (speaking) Play sad music Helen, like good music, not loud music, like 'Morning has broken'. (Music changes to a minor key, slower tempo.)

Joe: (singing expressively) When we were broken, no-one could come. When we were broken, no-one would ever come.

Helen: *(singing)* No-one could come. When everything's broken, no-one could ....

Joe: *(joining)* ..... come. (Joe continues with lyrical singing, words unclear.)

Joe: *(speaking)* The chorus is quite loud and it is really happy. When I say 'chorus' you've all got to get happy and cheer up and shout. (Music does not change but maintains sad mood.)

Helen: *(singing)* When something is broken.

Joe: *(singing)* No-one can help you.

(Shouting) Here's the chorus, get happy, you've all got to cheer. *(Clapping)* (Music maintains sad mood.)

(Singing) Everything is happy!

(Shouting) Play happy Helen, really loud and happy, can't you read and write?

(Gets agitated and bangs the piano to stop me playing. Music maintains sad mood but faster.)

Joe: *(singing passionately)* When the things are mended

And no-one can help us

We just sit down and watch

(Continues singing, words unclear; music maintains the sad mood.)

Joe: *(speaking)* Thank you children, give the pianist a big clap. *(Claps and cheers.)*

This extract illustrates how Joe constantly split off and denied painful feelings with a resultant sense of chaos and 'brokenness'. Using Bion's concept of a container (Bion, 1967), it could be said that the music contained these unassimilated feelings and Joe, by acknowledging his 'brokenness' was able to allow a true expression of his spontaneous emotions. Jos De Backer (1993) writes: 'The specific contribution of music therapy as opposed to verbal therapies lies in the fact that .... patients can express their chaotic experiences and that the therapist can be there for them without leaving them isolated in their chaos.'

Year 3 – Towards a shared reality

When Joe was eleven, he moved to a special school which was far more accepting of his difficulties and, despite the anxiety that surrounded the change, he began to flourish. The sessions of the previous year had been stormy, emotional and often on the brink of chaos. In the third year Joe was able to let go of some of his controlling behaviours and show a more vulnerable side of his personality. 'Pretend I was dead' was a game in which I could express a sense of sadness, loss and love for Joe, which he could now tolerate, and then he could experience symbolically coming back to life and us both celebrating.

We also made up songs together in which we both contributed the words which were now more direct and personal, for example: 'Sometimes it's hard to know what to do, sometimes it's hard to be Joe,' which reflected his struggles, and 'This is a song about Joe, and all the things he can do,' which was an affirmation of his abilities. These were songs about the 'real' Joe, which he could now share with me. Building a house under the piano became a feature of the sessions and Joe would ask me to play lullaby music for him to go to sleep. This brought a new kind of closeness and trust.

As the end of the third year of Joe's therapy approached, a change came in the content of the sessions. He began to bring in school books to show me; there was pride in his new skill of singing French songs, and in his computer designs. He brought photographs of his family and treasures from home, seeming to value himself and the good objects of his life. I began to think about finishing the therapy.

Just after his twelfth birthday, Joe told me that he could now 'do' music therapy and that he didn't need to come any more. This timing coincided with him clearing out his toys at home and putting away 'childish things' .

It seemed the right time to finish, and we had six sessions in which to say goodbye and explore the mixed feelings that ending would bring. Verbally, this was difficult for Joe, but his musical self-expression at this time made it clear that he was able to use the experience positively. He improvised more freely and spontaneously on the instruments than at any other time, and introduced songs with tellingly appropriate words.

The week after we had agreed that we would shortly finish the therapy, Joe brought his own tape recorder into the session and told me we were going to listen to some music. These are some of the words of the song:

I met a girl who sang the blues
And I asked her for some happy news
But she just smiled and turned away
I went down to the sacred store
Where I'd heard the music years before
But the man there said that the music wouldn't play
And in the streets the children screamed,
The lovers cried and the poets dreamed
But not a word was spoken
The church bells all were broken.
And the three men I admire most –
The Father, Son and The Holy Ghost
They caught the last train for the coast
The day the music died
And they were singing: 'Bye, Bye etc.
(*American Pie*, Don McLean)

As we sat quietly together listening to the song, I felt we had moved a long way from 'If you're happy and you know it clap your hands.'

In the next session Joe wanted to sing 'Jamaica Farewell' , which includes the words 'But I'm sad to say, I'm on my way, won't be back for many a day.' In the chorus he allowed me to change the words to reflect our parting, to: 'My heart is down, my head is turning around, because we have to say goodbye in four weeks time.'

In Joe's last session he remarked that his dog was getting very naughty and out of control, so perhaps he could send it to live with me. I felt that this was a recognition that music therapy had been able to hold and contain the 'out of control' part of Joe during an important period of his childhood. It had certainly helped him to get in touch with and develop his innate creativity and personal strengths, and also eased the limitations imposed on him by Asperger's syndrome.

Conclusion

The case studies above are of necessity personal accounts of the development of two unique relationships and therefore cannot claim to be typical or representative of the work of the profession as a whole. Nevertheless, the author hopes it has been possible to show that music used as therapy is a flexible and accessible medium, with a great deal to offer to children as different from each other as Susie and Joe. Not only can the process be seen as being valuable in its own right, but also as complementing and supporting the work done by all who are concerned with the growth, development and self-fulfilment of children with learning difficulties.

References

Ainlay GW (1948) The place of music in military hospitals. In Bunt L (Ed) Music Therapy: An Art Beyond Words. London: Routledge.

Alvin J (1965) Music for the Handicapped Child. Oxford: Oxford University Press.

Aristotle – The Politics.Translated by TA Sinclair. London: Penguin 1981.

Axline V (1964) Dibs: In Search of Self. New York: Gollancz.

Bateson MC (1975) Mother-infant exchanges: The epigenesis of conversational interaction. In Aaronson D, Rieber RW (Eds) Developmental Psycholinguistics and Communication Disorders. Annals of the New York Academy of Sciences Vol. 263.

Bion W (1967) Notes on memory and desire. Psychoanalytic Forum 2: 271–80.

Brown SMK (1994) Autism and Music Therapy – is change possible, and why music? British Journal of music therapy 8(1): 15–25.

Bunt L (1994) Music Therapy: an Art Beyond Words. London: Routledge.

BSMT (1995) Constitution of the British Society for Music Therapy (revised 1995).

Clayton-Smith J (1992) Angelman Syndrome. Arch Dis Child 1992: 67: 889–91.

De Backer J (1993) Containment in music therapy. In Heal M, Wigram T (Eds) Music

Therapy in Health and Education. London: Jessica Kingsley.

Flower C (1993) Control and creativity, music therapy with adolescents in secure care. In Heal M, Wigram T (Eds) Music Therapy in Health and Education. London: Jessica Kingsley.

Klein J (1987) Our Need for Others and its Roots in Infancy. London: Tavistock Publications.

Laing RD (1960) The Divided Self. London: Tavistock Publications.

Nordoff P, Robbins C (1971) Therapy in Music for Handicapped Children. London: Gollancz.

Nordoff P, Robbins C (1977) Creative Music Therapy. 2nd edn. New York: John Day.

Ockelford EM (1988) Response of neonates to parents' and others' voices. Early Human Development 18: 27–36.

Pavlicevic M, Trevarthen C (1989) A musical assessment of psychiatric states in adults. Psychopathology 22: 325–34.

Robarts JZ (1996) Music therapy for children with autism. In Trevarthen C, Aitken KJ, Papoudi DI, Robarts JZ (Eds) Children with Autism: Diagnosis and Intervention to Meet their Needs. London: Jessica Kingsley.

Shetler DJ (1990) The enquiry into the pre-natal experience. In Wilson FR, Rochmann FL (Eds) Music and Child Development. St Louis, MO: Magna Music Baton.

Stern D (1985) The Interpersonal World of the Infant. New York: Basic Books.

Storr A (1992) Music and the Mind. London: Harper Collins.

Storr A (1993) Foreword: Heal M, Wigram T (Eds) Music Therapy in Health and Education. London: Jessica Kingsley.

Trevarthen C (1993) The self born in intersubjectivity: the psychology of an infant communicating. In: Neisser U (Ed) The Perceived Self: Ecological and Interpersonal Sources of Self-knowledge. New York: Cambridge University Press.

Trevarthen C, Hubley P (1978) Secondary intersubjectivity: confidence, confiding and acts of meaning in the first year. In Lock A (Ed) Action: Gesture and Symbol: the Emergence of Language. London, Academic Press.

Warwick A (1995) Music therapy in the education service. In Wigram T, Saperstern B, West R (Eds) The Art and Science of Music Therapy: A Hand Book. Harwood Academic Publishers.

Winnicott D (Ed) (1960) Ego distortion in terms of the true and false self. London: Hogarth Press.

Winnicott D (1971) Playing and Reality. London: Tavistock Publications.

Winnicott D (1974) The Maturational Processes and the Facilitating Environment. London: Karnac Books.

Chapter 10

Bloody-Mindedness

From a triad of impairment to a quadrant of possibility: towards an applied theoretical paradigm for autism and Asperger syndrome

MIKE BLAMIRES

Introduction

This chapter will explore a range of theoretical perspectives in order to inform an educational understanding of the needs of learners with autism or Asperger syndrome. Our current thinking and action on autism and Asperger syndrome is largely dominated by a clinical view which emphasises diagnosis and classification. While diagnosis may be important, it must place a responsibility on the clinician for an appropriate intervention. A label needs to be a starting point rather than an end in itself. It should be considered as a signpost to an understanding of the individual rather than a limiting stereotype.

Diagnosing autism

Does a diagnosis of autism or Asperger syndrome mean that the individual's horizons become broader through appropriate intervention or do the horizons of one's world begin to close ?

In order to develop an educational approach towards autism and Asperger syndrome, we have to debunk a few myths and partial understandings that have gained ground within the wider community and then impinged upon education. These have developed in part from the media. Examples of the media interest in strange people include Dustin Hoffman's portrayal of a person with autism in the film *Rain Man* and also the press coverage of Steven Wiltshire, a young man with autism and a highly developed ability for drawing architecture. The early conjectures on autism have also been pervasive. The theories of

Tinbergen and Tinbergen (1983) and Bettleheim (1967) relating to defective parenting have permeated into 'common sense' despite the evidence.

The myths

The person with autism:

- is selfish and manipulative –
  The word autism is derived from the Greek word *autos* meaning 'self'. It was used originally by Bleuler (1913) to describe the withdrawal from social contact of schizophrenic patients. People with autism may not be conscious that their actions hinder the intentions of others. They may also have a directness in order to achieve their aims. This is because people with autism can find it difficult to understand that other people have intentions and they may not have the social skills needed to get what they want in a socially acceptable way.
- is totally withdrawn or does not want social contact –
  Clarke and Rutter (1981) found that people with autism can respond differently to different people and to different types of approach. As Clements (1996) suggests 'they know if you don't like them!'. Sigman and Mundy (1989) demonstrate that they are not all 'pervasively aloof' and can exhibit proximity-seeking as well as vocalisations to attract social attention. Capps, Sigman and Mundy (1994) found that, of a group of infants with autism, 40% demonstrated strong attachment to their carers.
- is the result of poor parenting ie. to the lack of bonding; this being due to the coldness of the mother, described by clinicians at the time as a refrigerator mother.
  This was proposed by Eisenberg and Kanner (1956) and taken up by Bettleheim (1967) as an explanation. Sigman (1989) and Rogers and Pennington (1991) demonstrate that children with autism are actually emotionally attached to their carers. There is no evidence for this 'blaming of parents' (Clarke & Clarke, 1976; Schopler, Reichler & Lansing, 1980).
- has some special talent –
  Some people with autism have an islet of ability such that an aspect of their cognitive functioning is unimpaired. They may have a special interest which is highly developed but it can be quite arbitrary. The classic cliché is that of the autistic person very interested in trainspotting – but not all train-spotters are autistic in the same way that not all people who wear anoraks are autistic.

Happé (1994) suggests that theoretical explanations of autism must be clear about the level at which they are operating e.g. psychological, behavioural or biological, and that a course must be steered between 'explaining too much through literal description' and 'explaining too little by attempting to cover too great an area'. Happé's second criterion is suggested as she believes there is a need for a range of small-scale theories to explain the variety of phenomena within autism. This opposition to large-scale theories may be due the bittiness of much of current cognitive psychology which is not yet embedded with an evolutionary consideration of the development of mind. (This is explored extensively in Plotkin, 1994.)

There is also a need to reassess the implications of the different theoretical perspectives for emergent concerns in providing special educational provision. Parental and learner partnerships are becoming more important within legislation for meeting special needs and need to be included (eg. DfE, 1994). A child with autism is more frequently being educated alongside his or her non-autistic peers. The individual with autism is part of our society. His or her parents will want their child to participate in society to the extent that he or she is able.

Gerald Newport (1996), an adult with autism, has suggested a definition of autism:

> Autistic behaviour is composed of almost entirely typical behaviours in young children/people gone haywire. The collection of traits and the degree of them is what makes a diagnosis, and the genetics in terms of traits, personality, temperament, all of that helps shape each individual and produce a person (Newport, 1996).

This appears positive and realistic and it puts the individual at the centre of the syndrome .

The facts may stay the same. It is only the truth that changes

We have a need, in the words of Jordan and Powell (1996), to move 'beyond diagnosis towards intuition', and to develop a paradigm that works for autism or Asperger syndrome within education. Clinical considerations of the subject have yielded a great deal of insight and evidence which has been applied within education with different degrees of success. Clinical models seek a diagnosis and then follow up with individual or group therapy to remove, reduce or ameliorate the symptoms or causes. An educational model similarly assesses the child's needs in order to set targets and implements provision which can then be monitored and evaluated. Educational interventions also stress the viewpoint of the parent and learner within a developing partnership. The educational paradigm for autism or Asperger syndrome must encompass the learner not as a subject or patient but as an active participant in a social/educational activity.

The English Code of Practice (DfE, 1994) states that this is a plus, as do many other countries' special-needs guidelines.

> The effectiveness of any assessment and intervention will be influenced by the involvement and interest of the child or young person concerned. The benefits are practical – children have important and relevant information. Their support is crucial to the effective implementation of any individual education programme.
> Principle – children have a right to be heard. They should be encouraged to participate in decision making about provision to meet their special educational needs. *Code of Practice, 2:340*

Many educationalists stress the difficulty of responding to these exhortations in practice. Children with autism may have no spoken communication. They may not like to make choices. However, if the starting point were based upon the premise that the child should be encouraged to make choices and evaluate his or her learning then there might be fewer children whose learning difficulties have been exacerbated by learned helplessness. They have special needs. These needs are met by others. As new needs arise through development and maturation, they are also met by others. This is not intended as an argument for the withdrawal of support; it is a reminder that inventions need to be strategic and that roles and functions have to be specific and enabling rather than disabling.

Parents contributing to an on-line discussion group on autism have expressed concern about the role of classroom assistants allocated to their children with autism. They fear that their children will grow up with a constant adult shadow over them, working, with the best will in the world, to anticipate needs and avoid confrontations. That the child with autism needs support is unquestioned. It is the nature and long-term aims of this support that need to be clear.

Is the classroom assistant:

- a filter of experience?
  Does the classroom assistant help mediate experiences or does he or she selectively block out opportunities that might be problematical for the child ?
- a translator?
  Does the classroom assistant assist in interpreting what is happening so that the child can engage in activities?
- an advocate?
  Does the classroom assistant ensure that the child is included in activities?
- a minder or safeguard for the rest of the class and the class teacher?
  Does the classroom assistant perform the role of protecting the

other children in the class from this strange and difficult child? (This may be very valid as well as being wrong in some cases.)
- an enabler?
  Does the classroom assistant enable the child to develop skills that he or she can then carry out later without support?
- a cultural attaché from our culture into the world of autism?
  Does the classroom assistant understand and provide insights into the culture of the world of people without autism?

The limitations of technical paradigms within education

Education can be susceptible to theoretical fashions. A particular approach or technique is adopted or modified based upon discrete theoretical underpinnings, eg. Instrumental Enrichment (Feuerstein & Jensen, 1980; Sharron & Coulter, 1994) and Reading Recovery (Clay, 1987). Even when these approaches are not adopted in toto, they influence practice and may enable teachers to diversify their response to learning needs. They may also be applied dogmatically and become divisive, pushing teachers into different camps of believers and non-believers. These technical paradigms can be pervasive. They have specific equipment and approaches backed up with key texts that provide tenets ripe for OHPs. The bell, book and candle may be replaced by the chalked name on board, plastic alphabets or banks of paper exercises. Proponents of an educational model of autism or Asperger syndrome need to be aware that their theory might develop a life of its own!

Functions of a clinical theory of autism

The clinical model has specific roles and interventions. It views individuals with autism as subjects who are being studied or diagnosed by the experts to find common autistic traits. This can lead to a description of autism rather than a theory which has explanative value. For example, the classic diagnostic criteria for autism are based upon Wing and Gould's (1979) 'Triad of Impairments'.

1 *Social impairment*
  – Impaired, deviant and extremely delayed social development; in particular, impaired interpersonal development.
  – A continuum from being solitary and withdrawn, to those who respond in a passive manner but will not initiate interaction, through to those who seek interaction but do not understand how to manage and maintain it.

2   *Language and communication*
    – Impaired and deviant language and communication including verbal and non-verbal communication; ranging from no spoken language to those who have excellent grammar and pronunciation yet have difficulties with functional and social communication. This includes semantics (to do with meanings and pragmatics) relating to verbal and non-verbal rules of social engagement.

3   *Thought and behaviour*
    – Characterised by rigidity of thought and behaviour; a reliance on routine and an absence of or extreme delay in 'pretend play'. There may be difficulty in distinguishing imagination from reality.

These are descriptions of behaviours which help in the identification and diagnosis of autism and the provision of support for the child, parents and educators. The function of the Triad of Impairments criteria is for identification and recognition which may fuel further research. They cannot immediately explain why a person with autism behaves as he or she does.

To well that a child finds it difficult to learn because he or she has a difficulty in learning is a circular argument, and we will get nowhere unless we start to look at the meanings of the words we are using.

- What is *learning*, what has to be learnt, how can it be learnt and where can it be learnt best ?
- What does *difficulty* mean ? What is difficult ?
- What exactly are the *learning difficulties* that learners with autism have?
- Some clearly find it *difficult to work alongside others*.
- Some can deal with *facts and concrete learning* more easily than *problem solving and creative learning*.
- Some prefer to work *visually*, obtaining more information through the eye than the ear.
- Some may be anxious about *changes* to routine and forthcoming events.
- Some tend to learn more easily by *doing* rather than being told what to do.

Any theoretical consideration of autism has to address and explain the behaviour that confounds, amuses or challenges us. For example, for people with autism:

- Why are there routines?

- Why do they have obsessions?
- Why is language elaborate and often inappropriate?
- Why do they find difficulty in abstracting and generalising?
- Why do some have special abilities ?

Descriptions of the phenomena surrounding autism have led on to alternative models which have attempted to provide more insight into the nature of autism which the author will outline below. However, they focus upon the autistic individual and fail to consider the social dynamics of autism.

A clinical theory of autism may serve the further understanding of the nature of autism and the 'normal' development of mind. An applied theory of autism should, in addition, serve the aims of the individual with autism, his or her parents, peers, educators, policy makers and other professionals.

Leekham (1996) has outlined several levels of explanation of autism.

Genetic
Physiological
Neurological
Behavioural
Cognitive/Psychological

These perspectives have been covered extensively (see Frith, 1989; Baron-Cohen, Tager-Flusberg & Cohen, 1993; Happé, 1994; Trevarthen, Aitken, Papoudi & Roberts, 1996).

To this, the author would suggest that we need to acknowledge a number of further levels:

Individual/ Phenomenological
Evolutionary Neuro-Scientific
Sociological
Educational

Where does autism come from?

Although Frith (1989) has attempted to document cases of autism from historical accounts, the identification of autism and Asperger syndrome as syndromes only occurred in the middle of this century. Until then, people with autism must have been accommodated in some other way. A possible example comes from a novel by Wilkie Collins, a protégé of Charles Dickens' who describes a character thus: 'Papa is an extraordinary mechanical genius. You will say so when you see his clock. It's nothing like so large, of course, but it's on the model of the famous clock at Strasbourg. Only think, he began it when I was eight years old; and (though I was sixteen last birthday) it isn't finished yet'.

One could imagine a number of settings in the past where a person with autism could manage or fit in to some degree. For example, a computer in Victorian times was a person trained to do long and laborious calculations. Someone who enjoyed such tasks would obviously be an asset and worth looking after. Today, it is probably more difficult to find niches for people with autism so their diagnosis is more widespread. A recent edition of the trade magazine *Professional Engineer* explored the possible prevalence of people with autism among engineers and their near relatives (Dunn, 1996).

Phenomenological perspective of individuals with autism

Who owns autism?

Recently, the writing of Donna Williams (1996) and Temple Grandin (1995) have contributed to our understanding of autism. Both have been diagnosed as having autism but have been able to write about their experiences and how they have coped with the condition. Donna Williams describes with eloquence the perceptual difficulties she has faced.

> 'Autism' is spoken of by some people as a jigsaw with a missing piece. I experienced my own autism as one bucket with several different jigsaws in it, all jumbled together and all missing a few pieces each, but with a few extra pieces that didn't belong to any of these jigsaws. The first dilemma for me was sorting out which pieces belonged to which jigsaws From there, I had to work out which pieces were missing and which weren't supposed to be in my bucket at all (Donna Williams, 1996).

Temple Grandin has a PhD in animal husbandry. She has written two books on autism and has had the privilege of being interviewed by the neurologist Oliver Sacks (1995). He used her metaphor for what it is like for her to understand social interaction as the title of his book *An Anthropologist on Mars*. Grandin elaborates the problems she faces in dealing with others.

> It has to do, she has inferred, with an implicit knowledge of social conventions and codes, of cultural suppositions of every sort. This implicit knowledge, which every normal person accumulates and generates throughout life on the basis of experience and encounters with others, Temple seems to be largely devoid of.

Lacking it she has to 'compute' others' intentions and states of mind to try to make algorithmic, explicit , what for the rest of us is second nature. She herself, she infers, may never have had the normal social experiences from which a normal social knowledge is constructed (Grandin, 1995).

But can we rely on the insights that people with autism offer us in good faith? Some professionals suggest that anyone who can offer an insight into the nature of autism must by definition have been wrongly diagnosed. However, this would be a denial of the validity of individual experience. It treats diagnosis as a final decision rather than a snapshot of development and it would represent a professional arrogance in which there is only one interpretation of autism. There are now a number of accounts of experiences from people who have disabilities other than autism.

At a day conference where Donna Williams spoke alongside a number of experts on autism, the evaluations from over 400 professionals dealing with people with autism who attended the day stated that Donna Williams' input provided the most insight into the condition and would help them change their approach (Oberheim, 1996).

There are also other autobiographies by people with autism which may cause us more problems in relation to their validity. These tend to be produced by non-vocal people with autism who have used facilitated communication. This is a technique where the person with autism is helped to press keys on a computer or communication aid by a facilitator who interprets and filters the communication. It is a controversial technique and needs very careful implementation and evaluation. It is not the case that facilitated communication can reach across to the normal person on the other side of autism. Facilitated communication may be akin to sharing of the consciousness and unconsciousness of both participants. This means that the resulting communication is open to misconstruction, redirection or misinterpretation without the facilitator being aware. Without the critical application which pays appropriate regard to confirmability and dependability of response, facilitated communication appears to combine the ambiguity of the Rorschach test with the dangerous nonsense of the ouija board. We need to be more than a little wary of biographies from these sources.

For example, Rocha and Jorde (1996) tell the story of a child with autism written through facilitated communication with her mother. The child claims a previous life in which she was burned to death by Cleopatra and therefore requested God to make her autistic in this current life by manipulating neurotransmitters in her foetus. Such accounts make it more difficult for academics to investigate facilitated communication as, in this case, it transcends a technical paradigm and becomes an act of religious faith.

Where our understanding of autism comes from

The clinical work of Kanner and Asperger

In the mid forties Kanner and Asperger contemporaneously published detailed case descriptions of autism and offered theoretical explanations. Both described children who were unable to maintain normal affective relationships. Both initially suggested that the condition was innate, described poor eye contact, isolated and often bizarre interests, and their resistance to change. Kanner's work was more widely distributed as it was undertaken in America whilst Asperger was writing, in German, in Austria at the end of the war. Happé (1994) notes that Kanner's description differs in four ways from that of Asperger:

1   Kanner reported that three of the eleven children never spoke whilst the others did not use the language they had to communicate. Asperger in contrast noted that all of his patients spoke fluently 'like little adults' with 'freedom' and 'originality'.
2   Kanner reported clumsiness in only one of his subjects: 'several of the children were clumsy in gait and gross motor performance, but all were skilful in terms of fine motor coordination.' On the other hand, Asperger reports problems with school sports (gross coordination) and handwriting (fine motor coordination).
3   Kanner believed that autistic children have a specific impairment in social understanding, with better relations with objects than with people, while Asperger proposed that there were disturbances in both areas; 'the essential abnormality in autism is a disturbance of the lively relationship with whole environment' (Asperger – In Frith, 1991).
4   Kanner believed that autistic children are best at learning by rote while Asperger suggested that autistic children 'learnt best when the child can produce spontaneously' and suggests that they are 'abstract thinkers'.

There has been much debate about whether Kanner's syndrome and Asperger syndrome are both part of the same syndrome (Baron-Cohen & Bolton, 1993) and whether Asperger syndrome can be distinguished from High Functioning Autism (Bishop, 1989; Ozenhoff, Rogers & Pennington, 1991). Trevarthen et al (1996) suggest that they 'comprise a continuum of impairment' best described as 'autistic spectrum disorder' (Gillberg, 1992). They propose that diagnosis which uses a multi-dimensional framework to express the different aspects of motivation for attention to the environment, and motivation for attention to persons and to language, might be more useful than attempting to divide the population into two groups. This may be a positive solution to the creation of the highly valued label of Asperger syndrome which is held to be more of a 'blue chip' condition than autism.

Mind blindness – A cognitive explanation of autism

A significant amount of research has been undertaken on the 'Theory of Mind' theory of autism (Frith,1991; Leslie,1991; and Baron-Cohen et al, 1993). This follows the anthropological work with chimpanzees of Premack and Woodruff (1978) who suggested that the ability to represent mental states of self and others would be evolutionary adaptive in that it could be used to predict behaviour in other animals. They suggested that this was not a conscious theory but an innate mechanism. Children without autism around the age of four are able to understand that people have beliefs and desires about the world and it is suggested that is due to their possession of a 'Theory of Mind' (Perner,1990). It is argued by the researchers in this area, that people with autism lack this capacity and that 'The Mind-blindness Theory' seems able to explain the triad (Happé, 1994). A wide number of tests dealing with the representation of mental states, particularly false belief tasks, have been undertaken to demonstrate that people with autism lack a 'Theory of Mind'; eg. by Baron-Cohen et al (1985); Leslie and Frith (1988).

However, Leslie and Thias (1992) and Charman and Baron-Cohen (1992) conducted experiments in false beliefs using the standard Sally-Anne test of 'Theory of Mind'. Subjects verbally report the place where they think someone who is deceived will look for a hidden object; the experiments also tested the ability to represent false beliefs with photographs or drawings. While the subjects with autism failed the standard test, they passed the test when it was translated into a visual medium. Leslie suggests that this is because the subjects with autism could not build representations of mental states themselves but could make use of external (ie. visual) representations. Does this mean that people with autism may be able to recognise external representations of mental states but not be able to generate them themselves?

Happé (1994) provides a number of examples in which the lack of a 'Theory of Mind' is proposed as an explanation of autistic behaviour.

Take, for example, the autistic girl who had a tantrum every time she was told she was going swimming, until someone thought to say, 'we're going swimming – and we're coming back'!

Is this the inability to understand the intentions of others or the inability to mentalise the future ?

Without an understanding of the intentions of speech, communication breaks down, as for the autistic child who, in response to the request 'Can you pass the salt ?' replies in all earnestness, 'Yes'.

Is this solely due to a lack of 'Theory of Mind' on the part of the autistic individual, or is this just part of a more widespread breakdown in social understanding?

An Ethnomethodologist on Earth

It may be illuminating to broaden our consideration of autism and Asperger syndrome to include a social dimension. This will enable us to look at the individual with autism in relation to others. Within sociology, the classic work of Garfinkel (1967) was concerned with the theory of action, the nature of intersubjectivity and the social constitution of knowledge (Heritage, 1984). The process of investigation was termed by Garfinkel as 'Ethnomethodology'. This focused upon the body of 'common-sense knowledge and the range of procedures and considerations by means of which the ordinary members of society make sense of, find their way about in, and act on the circumstances in which they find themselves.' (Heritage, 1984).

Garfinkel conducted a number of investigations which sought to tease out this knowledge, which he termed 'breaching experiments' as they disturbed or upset normal social interaction.

One game involved tick-tack-toe (known as noughts and crosses in the UK). Here, the experimenters asked the subject to make the first move. After this the experimenter erased the subject's mark, moved it to another cell and then made his own mark, while avoiding giving any indication that what he was doing was unusual. Out of 253 of these experiments, 95% reacted in some way and over 75% demanded some kind of explanation. Those who assumed some new game was in progress, that it was some form of practical joke or a new method of play, had abandoned tick-tack-toe as an interpretative framework for the game and showed little disturbance. Those who still continued to assume that they were playing tick-tack-toe showed most disturbance.

Although Garfinkel was wary of generalising from a game setting to 'real life', two findings arose from the experiment. First, behaviours that were at variance with the normal rules 'immediately motivated attempts to normalise the discrepancy', ie. to treat the observed behaviour as an instance of a legally possible event. The second finding was that 'senselessness and disturbance was increased if the subject attempted to normalise the discrepancy while retaining an unaltered view of the rules of the game'.

Does this have implications for our consideration of interactions between people with autism and non-autistic people? Two different games are being played. Each player is using a different set of implicit rules that they have derived from interaction with the world. Initially, the players may interpret that the other is trying to play by the rules in some way. But the more that one player sticks to his or her rules, regardless of the other, the more the other becomes disturbed and lacks sense of what is happening. Unless one accommodates his or her thinking to that of the other, the disturbance will grow.

Although not with an ethnomethodological paradigm, a study of the reaction of peers to children with autism who were integrated into mainstream school suggests Garfinkel findings may have relevance to a consideration of autism or Asperger syndrome. Graziella, Vizziella and Graziella (1994) found that more able peers accommodated to the child with autism by making some form of homespun diagnosis of the child and then implementing compensatory strategies. Less able peers imitated the strange behaviours of the child with autism. From an ethnomethodological perspective, therefore, the 'less able' children took on the rules of the game of the autistic child while the 'more able' children attempted some interpretation of the rules being used by the child with autism and adapted accordingly.

This perspective on autism enables us to go beyond a description of action which must ultimately be evaluative and move towards an acknowledgement of the different ways that people with and without autism make sense of the world.

A further experiment in a more real-life setting was developed by Garfinkel (1963). The experimenters were 'instructed to engage an acquaintance or friend in an ordinary conversation and, without indicating that what the experimenter was saying was in any way out of the ordinary, to insist that the person clarify the sense of commonplace remarks.'

Most people would guess that this experiment would cause trouble. They even might call it an act of 'bloody mindedness' because how people will react is only 'common sense'. It was this 'common sense' that Garfinkel was trying to tease out. He was trying to make the implicit explicit. Whilst Temple Grandin sees herself as 'An Anthropologist on Mars, attempting to make sense of an "alien" culture', Garfinkel was attempting to do the same thing on earth thirty years ago.

The following case studies show some of the results.

Case 1:

The subject was telling the experimenter, a member of the subject's car pool, about having had a flat tyre while going to work the previous day.

S: 'I had a flat tyre.'
E: 'What do you mean you had a flat tyre?'
S: Appeared momentarily stunned. Then she answered in a hostile way; 'What do you mean? What do you mean ? A flat tyre is a flat tyre. That is what I meant. Nothing special .What a crazy question!'

Case 3

On Friday night my husband and I were watching television. My husband remarked that he was tired.
I asked, 'How are you tired? Physically, mentally or just bored?'
- S: I don't know, I guess physically, mainly.'
- E: 'You mean your muscles ache or your bones?'
- S: 'I guess so. Don't be so technical.'
       (After more watching)
- S: 'All these old movies have the same kind of old iron bedstead in them.'
- E: 'What do you mean? Do you mean all old movies, or some of them, or just the ones you have seen?'
- S: 'What's the matter with you? You know what I mean.'
- E: 'I wish you could be more specific.'
- S: 'You know what I mean! Drop dead!'

Case 6

The victim waved his hand cheerily.
- S: 'How are you?'
- E: 'How am I in regard to what? My health, my finance, my school work, my piece of mind, my......'
- S: (Red in the face and suddenly out of control.) 'Look ! I was just trying to be polite. Frankly, I don't give a damn how you are.'

Heritage (1984) notes 'the subjects had expected that the experimenters would, by drawing upon background knowledge that "everyone knows", supply a sense to their remarks that was empirically identical with the sense intended by the subjects.'

More succinctly Garfinkel (1967) states 'much that is being talked about is not mentioned, although each expects that the adequate sense of the matter being talked about is settled.'

If this expectation is breached, it is very noticeable how quickly the communication breaks down, leading to self-righteous indignation being displayed by the innocent party. Garfinkel stresses that the maintenance of this expectation of 'reciprocity of perspectives' is not merely a cognitive task but one in which each participant 'trusts' the other as 'a matter of moral necessity'. Hence the outrage.

Schutz (1962) suggested that individuals develop a personal and shared stock of knowledge about the world. This knowledge assumes a 'common world' which goes beyond an individual's private experience and includes an understanding that people have motives and emotions. This knowledge is sustained and developed through social engagement. Garfinkel has given us evidence of what happens when people refuse to make use of the shared stock of knowledge. Accounts of people with autism or Asperger syndrome show us what happens when people do not have access to this shared stock of knowledge.

Angela Dyer (1994), an educational advisor and autism course tutor, notes:

> Most of us shut off if we listen to foreign language we don't under-stand. A child with autism is the same: if one or two sentences go over their head, he or she shuts off. You need to keep checking that he or she is listening and understanding. (Dyer, 1994)

If too many references are being made to a knowledge base that the child does not have, then it is not surprising that the child 'switches off'. The alternative, to ask questions in order to make the implicit explicit, requires verbal dexterity in the first place, but if the child has the neces-sary verbal skills, it is a dangerous strategy as Garfinkel has demon-strated. The task for the teacher or classroom assistant must involve making the implicit set of understandings that comprise Schulz's stock of knowledge explicit. This has to occur alongside the other educational task of engagement with explicit curriculum knowledge.

Donaldson (1992) suggests that it is difficult to acknowledge these understandings:

> We can know in different ways. Some of our knowledge is explicit, out in the open. We know that we know it. We can give an account of what we know, and sometimes of how we came to know it or how we would justify the claim that it is 'knowledge'. But we also have knowledge that is to varying degrees implicit in the dark – not spoken of, sometimes not able to be spoken of (Donaldson, 1992).

A person without this stock of knowledge or shared understanding will find it difficult to engage in a conversation. He or she has to make every-thing explicit because he or she cannot take short cuts as nothing can be taken for granted. The person sounds very formal and often verbose. This is what a person with Asperger syndrome often sounds like. They will provide lots of superfluous detail in the conversation because they do not know what the other person already knows. They cannot make reference to the stock of knowledge the rest of us have. Baltaxe (1977) describes a 'sense of pedantic literalness' in the language used by five able adolescents with autism during semi-structured interviews. They tended to repeat fully specified noun phrases instead of using pronouns ('it', 'they', 'those') to refer back to items already discussed.

Example 1. A launch into a monologue about Doctor Who

'I have nearly finished my Dalek.'
'Why are you making a Dalek?'

'It is to commemorate the arrival of the new Doctor, Paul McGann. Doctor Who is over thirty years old. I liked the Daleks' appearance in remembrance of the Daleks in 1988 and the Daleks were quite good. You didn't see the Daleks at the start but you just heard the Daleks.'

Example 2. A dialogue about Christopher Columbus

Speech Therapist: 'It says here that archaeologists have discovered a skull of a ten-year-old boy in Italy which they think might be that of Christopher Columbus. Why do you think that might be wrong?'
Child: 'I don't know.'
Speech Therapist: 'What did Christopher Columbus do?'
Child: 'He discovered America in 1642.'
Speech Therapist: 'How old was he when he did that? He must have been grown up?'
Child: 'He was 32.'
Speech Therapist: 'He must have died when he was quite old then.'
Child: 'When he was 52.'
Speech Therapist: 'So could the skull of the boy have been Christopher Columbus's?'
Child: 'I'm not sure.'

The child knows a lot of facts about Christopher Columbus but he cannot link them to common understanding of death and skeletons. Our bodies contain skeletons which grow with us and we only have one. If the child's skull was Christopher Columbus, he would have had to have died when he was a child. It may be that the child has this particular understanding but cannot apply it to this problem. We will examine this possibility later but it may be that he does not have this 'common understanding' that permeates most western culture. Something is missing within the stock of knowledge.

Speakers select from a set of co-referential expressions the one that will express the desired aspect of meaning that they require at that time (Searle, 1969). The use of pronouns can serve this purpose and also avoid laborious repetition.

An example from a steamy soap opera springs to mind:

'How was it for you?'
'It was okay.'

The following playground joke works because it relies on the listener to use it as a backward reference rather than to take 'it' literally.

Question: Mississippi is a very long word. How many letters are in it ?
Answer: There are two letters in 'it'.

Studies of the language of people with autism show abnormalities in their use of stress, intonation, rhythm and prosodic aspects of language (eg. Kanner, 1943; Pronovost, Wakstein & Wakstein, 1966). These are the very ways in which attitudes, emotions and values are applied to the stock of knowledge. Hobson (1993) suggests that all utterances convey nuances of 'speaker's meaning' that will be lost on autistic individuals.

A person from Yorkshire might state 'I wun't give it house room' to be very dismissive of something. This would be totally misunderstood if you were not aware of the scathing emphasis with which the words were spoken and that the person was never contemplating putting (it) in his home.

Irony, metaphor, figures of speech and implicature rely on references to the shared stock of knowledge and are difficult for people with autism. 'Implicature' refers to implicit or contextual assumptions intended by the speaker. Eg.:

Fred: 'What time is it?'
Mary: 'We'd better be going.'

The stock of knowledge can dictate what aspects of the environment people find important. This vital component of functioning has been described in a cognitive model by Sperber and Wilson (1986) as 'relevance theory' the first major premise of which is 'our attention automatically turns to what seems relevant in the environment'. The stock of knowledge subsumes the theory of relevance in that it dictates what aspects of the environment are important.

Frith (1989) suggested that children with autism do not process stimuli for meaning. She states: 'A good decision [about what to attend to] would be based on large amounts of pooled information. If coherence at this central decision making point is weak, the direction of attention would be quite haphazard'.

Frith attempts to explain the difficulty by positing a cognitive deficit in 'central coherence': 'a lack of the drive to pull information together into overall meaning'. An alternative interpretation that doesn't need to refer to 'drives' or potential homunculi, is that people with autism attribute different meanings or ignore stimuli as meaningless based upon a different stock of knowledge about the world from non-autistic people.

A stock of knowledge or culture ?

Schutz (1962) suggests that the stock of knowledge comprises:

- 'type constructs of objects eg. mountains, trees, animals, fellow men'

- 'typified "recipe knowledge" concerning the "how to do it" of all kinds of courses of action.'

These represent two areas of difficulty which people with autism may have in using language. The first is use of semantics in language – the meanings of words which are accrued. The second is the pragmatic use of language which deals with language as a means of social interchange and makes use of semantic language. However, Van Dijk (1977) states that a pragmatic utterance 'should not be characterised in terms of its internal structure and the meaning assigned to it but also in terms of the act accomplished by producing an utterance'. It is functional communication. It is well established that people with autism, and particularly Asperger syndrome, have problems in this area (Frith, 1989).

In an unpublished study of the preparation for and consequent integration of a child with Asperger Syndrome, Rennells (1996) observed the following exchange between a class teacher and a child with Asperger syndrome.

Teacher: 'Peter, would you like to stop talking to Robert and Jenny and get on with your writing?'
Peter: 'No.'

Peter thinks that a semantic transaction of information is a required rather than a pragmatic response and provides what he understands is required. It is a breach of Garfinkel's expectation of 'reciprocity of perspectives' which the author suspects he would be delighted by.

The stock of knowledge has similarities to the term 'culture' as used by some educationalists. Culture here does not mean the valuing of artful artifacts and pristine classical dance and music performances.

> Culture refers to shared patterns of human behaviour. Cultural norms affect the ways people think, eat, dress, work, understand natural phenomena such as the weather, of the passage of day into night, spend leisure time, communicate and other fundamental aspects of human interactions. (Mesibov & Shea, 1996)

Thus this definition of culture is very similar to the stock of knowledge and Mesibov and Shea note that it is not entirely appropriate to consider autism as a culture but in that autism 'affects the ways that individuals eat, dress, work and spend leisure time, understand their world and communicate',... 'in a sense it functions as a culture in that it yields characteristic and predictable patterns of behaviour in individuals with this condition.'

It may be useful to consider autism as a culture especially if you are dealing with groups of people with autism and you are keen to find commonalities between them. If you are attempting to understand an individual with autism among others without autism, it is perhaps more useful to understand and map the differing stocks of knowledge that are implicitly or explicitly used to guide action.

A cultural perspective from Feuerstein

Feuerstein (1976) has documented the problems faced by immigrant children who have lost their own cultural background, and who are attempting to adapt to the culture of their new homeland Israel. He suggests that children who have emigrated with groups who have strong cultural understandings in terms of traditions and ways of doing can adapt more readily. Some children's cultural background had been impoverished either as a result of the holocaust, or because they had come from Morocco where, for example there was a discontinuity of cultural transmission due to economic migration from close knit communities into towns (where the children lost contact with grandparents whose main role had been the teaching and preservation of culture).

Children from an impoverished culture were held to be 'victims of information' (Feuerstein, 1976). They could not make adequate sense of the world. They failed to use and master information for school or their daily lives. They also had difficulties in problem solving and short-term memory because they did not have a way of organising or assigning importance to their experiences, because they had a poor store of experience or culture to make reference to. They tended to be passive and sometimes impulsive.

Feuerstein stressed that culture is important in aiding an individual to make sense of the world and that this was formed through the mediation of meaning with others, particularly parents and relatives. Mediation is the process through which culture grows and is transmitted from one generation to another. It is the imposition of meaning onto otherwise neutral stimuli.

For example:

1   Try this. Isn't it delicious?
2   Don't touch that. It is dirty.
3   Now wash your hands.
4   Oh Roger! What have you done?
5   What's good listening, children?

We can see that there is quite a bit of common ground between a 'stock of knowledge' and the more diaphanous term 'culture'.

Where does our stock of knowledge come from ?

Feuerstein's (1976) description of 'neutral stimuli within the environment gaining saliency through the mediation of others' can perhaps provide us with a developmental framework to consider the development of people with and without autism. It is tempting to picture a growing stock of knowledge, about things, about actions, about self, about others and about thoughts. This is not purely a cognitive description of development. Wrapped up in this development is the emotional growth and the skill to make use of gestures, signs, and symbols. Hobson (1993) suggests that people with autism have primary difficulty with 'I–Thou' relatedness. For example, in infancy they will lack mutual eye gaze and will not engage in turn-taking activities with the carer. This will also impinge upon what Hobson terms the child's 'I–It' cognitive development which is relatively unaffected. They are able to learn about the world or things but they are handicapped by difficulties in interpersonal interaction. They cannot take full advantage of the mediation of their carers in developing their stock of knowledge.

As stated earlier in this chapter, this is not an abnormality of emotion or emotional communication. Rogers and Pennington (1991), in a review of different models of autism and development, suggest that children with autism do have affectionate reactions to key people they know well but 'reciprocal imitation' and joint perspective taking are selectively impaired. These behaviours develop after nine months and become elaborated in the second and third years in normal development and may be central to mediated learning.

The mother of all mediation

Mundy, Sigman and Kasari (1990) note that children with autism or Asperger syndrome may not initiate, respond to or maintain shared attention where the child or mother points at things within the environment. This sharing of attention they suggest is a key factor in the development of the precursors of language. The absence of 'protodeclarative pointing' in which a child will use gestures to make declarations, indications or observations has been also used as an indicator of autism in early years.

This lack of shared attention hinders the natural process of mediation. Whilst language development in humans without impairment is held to be largely the unfolding of innate capacity, (Lenneburg, 1967; Chomsky, 1972; and Pinker, 1994) it needs a support system to develop fully. Carers engage in lengthy, carefully nuanced exchanges with their infants, offering models, seeking repetition and clarification and offering corrections. Some researchers have termed this as 'motherese' for obvious reasons and it develops from the earliest child–carer interactions. Once again a child with autism is not able to take full advantage of this tuition. Trevarthen et al (1996) propose that 'the mother's emotions are used by the child increasingly, to evaluate experiences in the world.'

This 'emotional referencing' (Stern, Hofer, Haft & Dore,1985) plays a 'central role in learning'.

Indeed, carers may adopt compensatory strategies in dealing with the different patterns of communication of their infants with autism. Sigman, Mundy, Sherman and Ungerer (1986) report that they may physically hold their child on task, or they may become directive in their speech, encouraging communication when the child is unresponsive (Papoudi, 1993). Such behaviours are totally natural reactions to an unresponsive infant. Jordan and Powell (1996) have stressed the need to resist these behaviours in order to respond to the agenda set by the child and so gain joint attention. From a stock of knowledge perspective, this can be interpreted as the need to recognise differences between each individual's stock of knowledge and then seek to conjoin them to some degree.

Many people with autism do develop a sophisticated level of understanding and language but it tends to be in areas of thinking which are concrete and do not involve social or interpersonal skills. There are numerous examples of people with autism who have specialised interests as stated earlier. Durig (1993) has suggested that people with autism have a difficulty in carrying out inductive thinking but can be deductive. The areas of special ability include maths, representational drawing, timetables and classification systems which are essentially deductive. Induction is the ability to abstract, to think about thinking. Cognitive theorists term this 'meta-cognition'. It is of central importance as it means that people do not have to be at the mercy of their senses. They can become aware of their senses. They can make sense of things.

An evolutionary perspective

Rozin (1976) suggests that humans differ from many other organisms in that they are able to join together otherwise separate specialised brain mechanisms in order to produce new skills. For example, reading involves a conjoining of phonological and visual processing systems. Gazzaniga (1992) calls this function 'the Interpreter', an executive mechanism which, as a result of his studies of patients who have had 'split brain' surgery, he suggests resides in the left hand hemisphere of the cerebral cortex. 'The Interpreter' develops from infancy and Gazzaniga suggests that it has a crucial role in distinguishing itself from others and then interpreting the intentions of others. Furthermore he stresses the evolutionary advantage of such capabilities.

Edelman (1992) suggests a two-component evolutionary model of consciousness. He suggests that 'consciousness arises as a special set of relationships between perception, concept formation and memory. The first component is the result of the interplay between the limbic system and thalamocortical system. The limbic system is concerned with motivation, appetite, and evolved defensive behaviour patterns, whilst the thalamocortical system is concerned with perceptual categorisation and the production of signals for voluntary muscles. This interaction produces a scene comprising the variety of present stimuli. These stimuli have value ascribed to them either from past experience of from in-built value attachments. Thus an animal with primary consciousness spots things that may be eatable or things that may eat it and responds according to its repertoire of behaviours. This scene is a representation of events in the immediate world. Edelman describes *primary consciousness* as the 'remembered present' because a creature with only primary consciousness is not able to represent the future.

Primary consciousness thus:

> is limited to a small memorial interval around a time chunk I call the present, and it does not afford the ability to model the past or the future as a part of a correlated scene. It lacks a notion or a concept of a personal self, and it does not afford the ability to model the past or future as part of a correlated scene. An animal with primary consciousness sees the room the way a beam of light illuminates it. Only that which is in the beam is explicitly in the remembered present; all else is darkness. This does not mean that the animal cannot have long term memory or act on it (Edelman, 1992, p122).

The implications for autism are tentative. An impairment in one of the systems producing primary consciousness may result in perceptual difficulties with stimuli being attributed with a significance other than would be usual and then resulting in strange behaviour. It could also lead to impulsiveness and extreme defensive behaviours. All these behaviours have been documented in people with autism. Bauman and Kemper (1985) report, in studies of the neurology of people with autism, that there is damage to the amygdala and hippocampus which are part of the limbic system. The amygdala, as well as dealing with aggression and emotion, is also responsive to sensory stimuli such as sounds, touch and smells. A number of people with autism are very anxious about specific sounds and may become so frightened by them they resort to aggressive avoidance strategies. Ritvo et al (1990) have also shown that the cerebellum has reduced numbers of Purkinje cells in the people with autism who were examined. The cerebellum is concerned with attention and inhibition of stimuli. This may be why some people with autism engage in self-stimulation or find it difficult to share attention.

The second component in Edelman's model is *secondary consciousness* which requires primary consciousness plus a symbolic memory. Primary consciousness in fact provides an affective element within this system. Secondary consciousness encompasses the ability to model the world in terms of the past, present and future. It also includes the construction of a socially based self that is aware. Secondary consciousness is linked to the development of language which is in turn dependent upon the development of symbolic thought. The two areas of the cerebral cortex which have evolved to support speech are Wernicke's area and Broca's area. Through secondary consciousness we are aware that we are aware, and we may be aware that others may be wary of us.

Clearly, secondary consciousness encompasses a vast range of cognitive and emotional development. If a person has a limited secondary consciousness, he or she may be reliant upon primary consciousness. They would be trapped in the 'remembered present', unable to represent the future clearly and unable to devise or apply coping strategies. They may well be anxious or keep within set routines where remembered stimuli can be responded to with the range of behaviours available. They would be resistant to change. This would explain why educationalists report that children with autism tend to learn by doing rather than being told what to do (Jordan & Powell, 1996). It might also explain why visual diaries and instruction sheets are also advocated for learners with autism, as it brings the future into the primary consciousness.

(It is tempting to suggest that secondary consciousness is impaired by alcohol and that it is why it is a popular temporary escape route.)

The process of development, maturation and experience have a great effect upon an individual's ability to deal with the world. The preceding accounts and conjectures do not provide an excuse for non-intervention from education. The neurology of the brain is dynamic and dependent upon what an individual experiences. Interventions from the medical discipline may be of benefit (Trevarthen et al, 1996) as might interventions dealing with diet (Williams, 1996). Educational and social interventions are important because they can improve the quality of an individual's life in the short and long term and may produce adaptive changes in the brain that drugs may not be capable of producing.

A psycho-dynamic conjecture

To dismiss Freud for a variety of reasons may be to throw the baby out with the bath water. However, for this discussion we only need to keep a bit of the baby and a little of the bath water that is not too dirty. There is no need to accept all of Freudian theory so that we have to put mum back in the refrigerator. But a little bit of Freud's insight might be illuminating. Freud suggested a three-component model of mind, the *id* which is concerned with primal impulses and drive, the *ego* which is a socially constructed self and the *super ego*, guiding principles and morals derived from society. We can equate primary consciousness with the id, secondary consciousness with the ego, and the super ego with our understandings of culture or stock of knowledge, ie. symbolic memory. Could it be that if our ego is not working properly for a variety of acquired or functional reasons, we could still have a working super ego? The super ego, built for storing nuances, symbols, and symbols of symbols, would have surplus capacity. It could then be used for storing deductive information, 'islets of ability' or special talents that some people with autism have. It might also account for the reported loss or lack of elaboration of these abilities as the individual becomes more socially adept (Autism Discussion Group, 1996). This spare capacity is needed again as the person expends enormous intellectual effort to approach what comes naturally to people without autism: the most precious talent of all, that of interpersonal understanding.

What can these findings offer an educational framework for meeting the needs of learners with autism or Asperger syndrome?

It might be expected that research into autism would result in the uncovering of a range of deficits. Their piecemeal application within education will emphasise what is lacking within an individual. The list of deficits may not suggest what compensatory intervention may be required from others. They may even result in metaphors and guiding principles that limit or even impoverish an individual's world.

For example:

'They are autistic, that is what they do.'
'They lack a sense of humour so avoid jokes.'
'They have mind-blindness so avoid talking about your intentions.'
'They need routine.'

Because a person has difficulties in particular areas does not mean they are incapable of ever learning that behaviour or that they should not have the opportunity to experience or learn these behaviours. This chapter has attempted to put autism into a social and developmental context. It has attempted to dispel old and emerging myths, to move beyond wonderment or consternation towards an understanding of autism, an impairment which hinders the meeting of minds.

From a triad of impairments to a quadrant of possibility

The following are educational/social principles derived from the previous discussion that may be of use in guiding educational interventions with people with autism. These form the four corners of an educational paradigm for autism and Asperger syndrome and represent the best of existing and emerging practice.

1   Find signposts to the individual to help them foster a social self –
     attempting to understand why the individual is doing things
     rather than to describe or excuse it; working with the individual to
     help him or her to seek maximum independence within the
     world.
2   Making the stock of knowledge common –
     making the implicit explicit; explaining and guiding; finding out .
     what they actually know and what we know of the ways the indi-
     vidual with autism copes with the world.
3   Support and enable the use of external representations to explain
     the world –
     using visual materials, including multi-media, to represent the
     world, as well as concepts and understanding about the world; to
     foster understanding.
4   Try to like them.

References

Baltaxe CAM (1977) Pragmatic deficits in the language of autistic adolescents. Journal of Pediatric Psychology 2: 176–80.

Baron-Cohen S, Bolton P (1993) Autism: The facts. Oxford: Oxford University Press.

Baron-Cohen S, Leslie AM, Frith U (1985) Does the autistic child have a theory of mind? Cognition 21: 37–8

Baron-Cohen S, Tager-Flusberg H, Cohen DJ (1993) Understanding Other Minds: Perspectives from autism. Oxford: Oxford Medical Publications.

Bauman ML, Kemper TL (1985) Histoanamatic observations of the brain in early infantile autism. Neurology 35: 866–74.

Bettleheim B (1967) The Empty Fortress – Infantile autism and the birth of self. New York: Free Press.

Bishop DVM (1989) Semantic pragmatic disorders and autistic continuum. British Journal of Disorders of Communication 24: 115–22.

Bleuler E (1913) Autistic thinking. American Journal of Insanity 69: 873–86.

Capps L, Sigman M, Mundy P (1994) Attachment security in children with autism. Development and Psychopathology 6 (2): 249–61.

Charman T, Baron-Cohen S (1992) Understanding drawings and beliefs: A further test of meta-representation in autism. Journal of Child Psychology and Psychiatry 33: 1105–12.

Chomsky N (1972) Language and Mind. New York: Harcourt Brace Jovanovich.

Clarke AM, Clarke ADB (1976) Formerly isolated children. In Clarke AM, Clarke ADB (Eds) Early Experience: Myth and evidence. London: Open Books. pp 27–34.

Clarke P, Rutter M (1981) Autistic children's responses to structure and to interpersonal demands. Journal of Autism and Developmental Disorders 11: 201–17.

Clay M (1987) Implementing reading recovery: systematic adaptations to an educational innovation. New Zealand Journal of Educational Studies 22: 35–8.

Clements J (1996) Personal communication.

Department for Education (1994) A Code of Practice on the Identification and Assessment of Special Educational Needs. London: HMSO.

Donaldson M (1992) Human Minds. London: Penguin.

Dunn J (1996) Like father like son. Professional Engineering Vol 9, No. 9.

Durig A(1993) The Microsociology of Autism. Internet ftp//.syr.edu.information /autism/microsociologyofautism.txt

Dyer A (1994) Information on Autism and Asperger Syndrome for schools. National Autistic Society.

Edelman G (1992) Bright air, Brilliant fire: On the matter of the mind. London: Penguin.

Eisenberg L, Kanner L (1956) Early infantile autism. American Journal of Orthopsychiatry 26: 556–66.

Feuerstein R (1976) Mediated learning experience: A theoretical basis for cognitive human modifiability during adolescence. In Mittler P (Ed) Research into Practice in Mental Retardation Vol.II. Baltimore: University Park Press.

Feuerstein R, Jensen MR (1980) Instrumental enrichment: theoretical basis and instruments. The Educational Forum, May 1980: 401–23.

Frith U (1989) Autism: Explaining the enigma. Oxford: Blackwell.

Frith U (1991) Autism and Asperger Syndrome. Cambridge: Cambridge University Press.

Garfinkel H (1963) A conception of, and experiments with, 'trust' as a condition of stable concerted actions. In Harvey OJ (Ed) Motivation and Social Interaction. New York: Ronald Press. pp 187–238.

Garfinkel H (1967) Studies in Ethnomethodology. New York: Prentice Hall.

Gazzaniga MS (1992) Nature's Mind: The biological roots of thinking, emotions, sexuality, language and intelligence. London: Penguin.

Gillberg C (1992) Subgroups in autism: Are there behavioural phenotypes typical of underlying medical conditions? Journal of Intellectual Disability Research 35: 201–14.

Grandin T (1996) Thinking in Pictures. New York: Doubleday.

Graziella F, Vizziella M, Graziella S (1994) How classmates interact with an autistic child in a mainstream class. European Journal of Special Needs Education Vol 9 No 3.

Happé F(1994) Autism: An introduction to psychological theory. London: University College London Press.

Heritage J (1984) Garfinkel and Ethnomethodology. Oxford: Polity Press in association with Blackwell.

Hobson PR (1993) Autism and the Development of Mind. Hove, UK: Lawrence Erlbaum.

Jordan R, Powell S (1996) Understanding and Teaching Children with Autism. Chichester, UK: John Wiley.

Kanner (1943) Autistic disturbances of affective contact. Nervous Child 2: 217–50.

Leekham S (1996) Presentation given on 'Enabling Entitlement for Learners with Autism Course'. Kent County Council, Canterbury Christ Church College with Foxwood and Stone Bay Schools.

Lenneburg EH (1967) Biological Foundations of Language. New York: John Wiley.

Leslie AM (1991) The 'Theory of Mind' Impairment in autism: Evidence for a modular mechanism of development. In Whiten A (Ed) Natural Theories of Mind: Evolution, development and simulation of everyday mindreading. Oxford: Blackwell.

Leslie AM, Frith U (1988) Autistic children's understanding of seeing, knowing and believing. British Journal of Developmental Psychology. 3: 315–24.

Leslie AM, Thias L (1992) Domain specificity in concept development: Evidence from autism. Cognition 43: 225–51.

Mesibov GB, Shea V (1996) The Culture of Autism. From theoretical understanding to educational practice. New York: Plenum Press.

Mundy P, Sigman M, Kasari C (1990) A longitudinal study of joint attention and language development in autistic children. Journal of Autism and Developmental Disorders 20: 115–29.

Newport G (1996) email contribution to autism discussion group. autism@SJUVM.STJOHNS.EDU.

Oberheim D (1996) Personal communication concerning evaluations of a day conference held by the Kent Autistic Trust.

Ozenhoff S, Rogers SJ, Pennington BF (1991) Asperger's Syndrome: Evidence of an empirical distinction from high functioning autism. Journal of Child Psychology and Psychiatry 32: 1081–1105.

Papoudi DI (1993) Interpersonal play and communication between young Autistic children and their mothers. PhD thesis, University of Edinburgh.

Perner J (1990) Understanding the Representational Mind. Cambridge MA/MIT/Bradford.

Pinker S (1994) The Language Instinct. London: Penguin.

Plotkin H(1994) Darwin Machines and the Nature of Knowledge. London: Penguin.

Premack D, Woodruff G (1978) Does the chimpanzee have a theory of mind? Behavioural and Brain Sciences 4: 515–26.

Pronovost W, Wakstein MP, Wakstein DJ (1966) A longitudinal study of the speech behaviour and comprehension of fourteen children diagnosed atypical or autistic. Exceptional Children 33: 19–26.

Rennells J (1996) Unpublished enquiry submitted as part of post graduate diploma course work. Special Needs Research & Development Centre, Canterbury Christ Church College.

Ritvo ER, Freeman BJ, Pingree C, Mason-Brothers A, Jorde LB, Jensen WR, MacMahon W, Peterson PB, Mo A, Ritvo A (1990) The UCLA–University of Utah epidemiological survey of autism: prevalence. American Journal of Psychiatry 146: 194–99.

Rocha A, Jorde K (1996) A Child of Eternity. London: Piatkus.

Rogers PJ, Pennington BF (1991) A theoretical approach to the deficits in infantile autism. Developmental Psychopathology 3: 137–62.

Rozin P (1976) The evolution of intelligence and access to the cognitive unconscious. Progress in Psycho Biology and Physiological Psychology 6: 245–80.

Sacks O (1995) An Anthropologist on Mars. London: Picador.

Schopler E, Reichler RJ, Lansing M (1980) Individualised Assessment and Treatment of Autistic and Developmentally Disabled Children Vol.2 Teaching Strategies for parents and professionals. Dallas, Texas: Pro-Ed.

Schutz (1962) Commonsense and scientific interpretations of human action in Collected Papers, Vol 1: The Hague: Martinus Nijhoff.

Searle JR (1969) Speech Acts. Cambridge: Cambridge University Press.

Sharron H, Coulter M (1994) Changing Children's Minds. Birmingham: Sharron Publishing.

Sigman M (1989) the application of developmental knowledge to a clinical problem: The study of childhood autism. In Cicchetti D (Ed) Rochester Symposium on Developmental Psychopathology Vol. 1: The emergence of discipline. Hillsdale NJ: Erlbaum.

Sigman M, Mundy P (1989) Social attachments in Autistic children. Journal of the American Academy of Child and Adolescent Psychiatry 28: 74–81.

Sigman M, Mundy P, Sherman T, Ungerer J (1986) Social interactions of autistic, mentally retarded and normal children and their caregivers. Journal of Child Psychology and Psychiatry 27: 647–56.

Sperber D, Wilson D (1986) Relevance: Communication and cognition. Oxford: Blackwell.

Stern DN, Hofer L, Haft W, Dore J (1985) Affect attunement: The sharing of feeling states between mother and infant by means of inter-modal fluency. In Field TM, Fox NA (Eds) Social Perception in Infants. Norwood N.J: Ablex. pp 249–68.

Tinbergen N, Tinbergen EA (1983) 'Autistic' children – New hope for a cure. London: Allen & Unwin.

Trevarthen C, Aitken K, Papoudi D, Roberts J (1996) Children with Autism: Diagnosis and interventions to meet their needs. London: Jessica Kingsley.

Van Dijk TA (1977) Text and Context: explorations in the semantics and pragmatics of discourse. London: Longman .

Williams D (1996) Autism: An inside-out approach. London: Jessica Kingsley.

Wing L, Gould J (1979) Severe Impairments of social interaction and associated behaviours in children: epidemiology and classification. Journal of Autism & Childhood Schizophrenia 1: 256–66.

Chapter 11

Applying the Principles of the Code of Practice to Pupils with Specific Learning Difficulties/Dyslexia

JANET TOD

Introduction

This chapter aims to examine the construct of dyslexia in the context of historical and contemporary educational legislation and in so doing to provide an understanding as to why the educational needs of pupils with specific learning difficulties/dyslexia may not be fully met within the framework of the Code of Practice.

Educational legislation since the Warnock Report of 1978 has aimed to reduce the emphasis on categorisation of pupils according to their difficulties and redirect attention towards the assessment of the pupils' 'educational needs'. Why then do parents and teachers continue to ask whether their child or pupil is 'dyslexic', instead of asking 'What are this child's educational needs'?

The 1988 Education Reform Act legislated that pupils access a national curriculum. This provided the first opportunity for pupils' 'educational needs' to be assessed in relation to a national indicator of educational access and attainment. Why then is the formal task of deciding whether a pupil qualifies for the 'dyslexic' label still allocated to Educational Psychologists who base their decisions on the pupil's response to normatively referenced psychometric and attainment 'tests'?

The 1994 Code of Practice (DfE, 1994) describes a 'staged' response for the assessment and meeting of pupils' special educational needs, and adopts the strategy of Individual Education Plans as an approach for targeting and meeting pupils' individual learning needs. Dyslexia has been included, along with eight others, as a named area for description of difficulties and provision in the Code of Practice (3:60). Two years on from the implementation of the Code of Practice the response from parents of dyslexic pupils and voluntary dyslexia bodies suggests that the Code is failing to satisfy the demand for effective educational provision (Special Educational Needs: The Working of the Code of Practice and the Tribunal,1996). It is anticipated that this dissatisfaction will continue to be reflected via the disproportionate number of appeals on behalf of dyslexic pupils to the Special Needs Tribunal.

How is it that dyslexia remains highlighted by, but largely non-conformist to, post-Warnock educational legislation? Will the Code of Practice succeed in ensuring parity of provision for all Special Educational Needs (SEN) pupils based on need not label? Or will dyslexia continue to be strengthened by ensuring that it is a 'stand alone' special need?

This chapter looks at three topics central to the change in educational provision prescribed by legislation.

Section 1: examines the role of labelling which characterised the pre-Warnock deficit approach to special education;

Section 2: seeks to examine the utility of an educational definition of dyslexia for use in the post-1988 educational context of 'access and entitlement to a national curriculum';

Section 3: describes core elements of the 1994 Code of Practice to assess whether the principles of early identification and Individual Education Plans can be effectively applied to pupils with dyslexia/specific learning difficulties.

SECTION 1: SEEKING A LABEL

'Do you think he's dyslexic?'

This apparently simple question is often asked by parents and teachers when they are seeking to explain why a particular child exhibits a difficulty or delay in acquiring literacy skills. Why then is it such a controversial question?

'Dyslexic' is a commonly accepted term used to describe individuals who exhibit a specific difficulty in dealing with textural materials that cannot be attributed to an overall lack of intellectual ability. The condition has a history rooted in medical settings and was first recognised in patients with acquired aphasia by Kussamel in 1887 (Critchley, 1970) and labelled 'word blindness'. In 1986 Pringle-Morgan and Kerr, in separate reports, cited studies of pupils who exhibited 'congenital word blindness'. The change of reference group from 'adult aphasic patients' to ' pupils' brought with it an emphasis on the 'developmental' aspects of the condition and the notion that dyslexia was an educational problem with a medical cause. Since that time dyslexia has developed a history characterised by research and academic debate which has resulted in both consensus and controversy about the nature of the condition. There is considerable agreement about the core difficulties experienced by sufferers, namely: difficulty in processing, sequencing, retrieving and generating words and symbols which arises as a consequence of delayed or impaired development of the underlying cognitive processes necessary for these activities.

'Symptom lists' characteristically include:

- a discrepancy between intelligence and the ability to learn basic literacy skills;
- difficulty with processing language quickly;
- difficulty with auditory perception;
- difficulty with visual processing;
- directional difficulties such as confusion between right and left;
- weak short term memory;
- difficulties with fine motor coordination;
- sequencing problems:

Dyslexia has retained its original definition of being characterised by a specific difficulty in handling information that is coded into a different format eg. sounds into written symbols, oral language into text, etc. In addition, a 'causal' explanation has been attributed by the observation that sufferers exhibit a relative weakness in areas of processing which involve short term memory. Dyslexia is therefore traditionally assessed by reference to a 'discrepancy' (between observed and expected attainment in literacy) 'deficit' (in short term memory processing) definition.

The plight of dyslexia sufferers provided impetus for the development of a plethora of support organisations. Many of these developed as a consequence of researchers and practitioners taking ownership of their own causal explanations and 'treatments'. One example is the Orten Society, founded in 1949 in the USA, and named after an American psychiatrist who pioneered teaching methods for 'specific reading disability'. On the basis of his work with 1000 dyslexic children, Orten offered explanations and flexible guidelines that would be supported by many present-day researchers and practitioners. He assumed, for example, that dyslexia was a problem of linguistic development, and that in some children symptoms could be attributed to delay in the development of cerebral dominance with accompanying 'neurological' symptoms. He emphasised the need to observe carefully the child's individual profile of abilities, to note the significance of 'instructional errors' (miscues), to pay attention to the child's emotional reaction and to provide an individually tailored and responsive intervention programme. Other organisations were developed by charities in response to the need to provide specialist help for sufferers, such as the Invalid Children's Aid Association *Word Blind Centre for Dyslexic Children* which opened in London in 1963. Voluntary local dyslexia organisations were set up mainly by parents of dyslexic children, and in 1972 *The British Dyslexia Association* (BDA) was formed and is now a registered charity. The BDA is a voluntary body which represents an umbrella group for all dyslexia organisations and is consulted, along with other voluntary bodies, by the Department for Education and Employment (DfEE) when changes in educational legislation are proposed. The Dyslexia Institute runs recognised accredited training courses for qualified teachers and other professionals and offers facilities for diagnostic assessment by qualified educational psychologists. Specialist research centres were developed either specifically for dyslexia or housed within hospital paediatric settings or multi-disciplinary 'learning disabilities' centres. An increasing number of private schools offered specialist help for dyslexic pupils. Public and professional interest in the field has been evidenced by an ever increasing number of publications from a range of sources.

Given this consensus of opinion concerning the existence of the condition, the agreement about core difficulties, and the development of research, treatment, and supportive networks, why is there such controversy about the label?

Whilst there is no one answer to this question there are some points worth noting. The first is that whilst there is consensus of opinion concerning observable features of dyslexia, ie. we can observe that some otherwise able pupils have a very real difficulty in acquiring literacy skills, there is much less consensus about the interpretative aspects of the condition. This has resulted in an eminent researcher in the field recording '...in popular usage dyslexia tends to be accepted as a shorthand that allows communication between parents and professionals. The aetiological, prognostic, and resource implications of the term remain a communicative quagmire, frequently unrecognised until misunderstandings have developed' (Pumphrey & Reason, 1992, p. 20). There is little doubt that difficulties have been encountered because dyslexia has historically been viewed as an educational problem with a medical cause. Any condition born and nurtured in a medical setting carries with it the implicit sequence of events described as 'observation of symptoms – diagnosis – cause – treatment'. Educational difficulties in contrast traditionally follow the pattern 'assessment – identification – remediation'. Intrinsic to the dyslexia classification is a list of varying 'symptoms' which may be categorised as neurological (eg. no established laterality), physical (eg.difficulty with eye–hand coordination), cognitive (eg. weak short term memory), and emotional (eg. low self-esteem). Trapped in a medical model, the problem for dyslexia is that individuals who develop behavioural responses which conform to the classic descriptive definition of the condition (ie. a discrepancy between attainment in written language and intelligence) do not show the same conformity in sharing 'symptoms', 'aetiology' or 'prognosis'. A class teacher expecting the arrival of a 'dyslexic' pupil would thus be able to predict little more about that individual other than the fact that the pupil is very likely to exhibit specific under-achievement in written language. Thus dyslexia has inherited from its medical roots such problems as:

- how *many* of the dyslexic 'symptoms' does an individual need to evidence before he or she can be afforded the label 'dyslexic'?

  'He's got some of the features of dyslexia but he is not classic and I'm not sure he'd get the label if we referred him. The LEA Educational Psychologist wouldn't give him the label but an independent one might. He could be referred for a private assessment but I don't want to suggest it to his parents – he does need help – but I don't want them to be disappointed.' (Classroom teacher)

- If a child has developed strategies to cope with underlying dyslexia and thus can read, write and spell, but may not be able to do all three simultaneously or may take longer or use more effort, is he/she still dyslexic? That is, do the symptoms or the behavioural response to the symptoms, carry equal diagnostic weight?

  'When we asked his head teacher, he said that Robert could read as well as the other children in his class, and that "if we thought Robert was a problem we should see some of the other pupils!" But we know that it takes him ages to read, and he can't remember what he's got to take to school. He knew exactly what his science was all about because he told us, but he spent two hours writing a few lines for homework. I don't think he will be able to cope at secondary school, but no one believes us.' (Parent of 10-year-old boy)

- Are the 'symptoms' relative to the individual or relative to an age referenced norm? Eg. if a pupil exhibits an 'average' short term memory, as measured by such indicators as Digit Span etc., but well above average skills in other areas, does he or she qualify for the label? If this is the case it could be reasoned that it is easier for a very bright pupil to get the label if the discrepancy (between observed attainment and that predicted by IQ) deficit (relatively weak short term memory) definition of dyslexia is accepted.

  'He's certainly got difficulties with short term memory. Phonics are a nightmare to teach. He is underachieving in literacy but because

he is not of above average ability we can't really refer him for a
dyslexia assessment.' (Teacher)

- How justifiable is it to 'diagnose' a condition on the basis of
  severity and chronicity? Given the traditional description of
  dyslexia based on discrepancy, it logically follows that a pupil
  cannot be allocated the label 'dyslexic' until the delay in attainment of written language skills is significant.

'We've known that she was dyslexic since her first term at school.
We had a word tin home (to use) every evening and they kept
reducing Nikki's down from five words to one. Even that one she
couldn't remember. She could do other things at school and the
teachers said she would probably catch up and not to worry. She
got more and more behind but we had to wait until she was nine
before the school could get an assessment on the grounds that she
was two or more years behind in her reading age. She's now miles
behind and will have to go into a special unit or something.'
(Parent)

- Does the medical diagnostic label dyslexia carry with it a 'treatment' and a 'prognosis'?

'We've got him assessed at the Dyslexia Institute. They say that he
has dyslexia and that specialist teaching is necessary by a teacher
trained in specialist multi-sensory methods for dyslexic pupils.
Our LEA said that our son would learn to read best by learning to
read and that they would provide for him in the mainstream by
giving some extra classroom assistant support. One of our friends
told us that there is no treatment for dyslexia and that you have it
for life. She says we should get a computer and teach him strategies to compensate for his difficulties. My other friend's son went
to a special school and he loved it. We waited so long for someone
to tell us what is the matter with our son, and I was relieved about
it when they said he was dyslexic, but now we don't know what to
do for the best, and what's more who is going to pay?' (Parent)

- Can underlying 'neurological' causes give rise to more than one
  diagnosis?

'He had some developmental difficulties but is overall a child of
normal ability. He has problems with his short term memory and is
very disorganised. He has difficulties putting his ideas on paper
and when he does it looks very untidy, as if he hasn't tried very
hard. He is always in trouble for not listening and not getting on

with his work. He doesn't try because he knows he is going to fail, so he just messes around in class. We're not sure whether he has got ADD (Attention Deficit Disorder), or whether he is just EBD (emotionally and behaviourally disturbed). I think he has got some dyslexic features but if he gets labelled EBD he can't really be dyslexic as well, can he?' (Teacher)

Thus in discovering the disadvantaged dyslexia embryo, nurturing it with a placenta of research and academic debate, and protecting it in a womb of voluntary bodies, the medical fraternity offered the education-.alists the challenge of providing an environment which would allow their offspring to reach full academic potential. Whilst clinicians tend to be concerned with assessment and treatment of individual patients, educationalists are charged with making policy for groups of conscripts. Characteristically, dyslexics do not need individual provision from medical agencies although some individuals benefit from provision of occupational therapy for dyspraxia, or perhaps coloured lenses for visual anomalies. Dyslexics do, however, need special educational provision, and thus they are dependent upon the educational legislation which controls provision in the State sector.

How well then did dyslexia survive educational legislation?

Surviving educational legislation

Pumphrey and Reason (1992) produced a 'Cook's tour' of reports and key documents pertinent to provision for dyslexia. Selections from this are summarised in Table 11.1 below.

As can be seen from the table, in the 1970s references to dyslexia were couched in medical terminology '..who suffer from acute dyslexia'. In seeking to address the obvious problems inherent in identifying pupils with 'acute' symptoms in an educational setting, the Department for Education and Science (DES) accepted the recommendations of the Tizard report (1972) and used the discrepancy definition to inform an educational translation of 'acute dyslexia' into 'specific reading difficulties'. This served as an impetus for the development of psychometric assessment techniques undertaken by educational psychologists to replace the clinical diagnostic procedure normally undertaken by neurologists and/or paediatricians. Predictably this transfer of professional responsibility for the identification of dyslexia and the use of educational terminology were not fully accepted by medical practitioners and voluntary dyslexia organisations who argued that developmental dyslexia is a complex syndrome which could not simply be conveyed by the term 'specific reading retardation'. Discussions concerning the feasibility of translating medical deficits into educational descriptors were curtailed in 1978 by the publication of the Warnock

Table 11.1: Educational legislation and reports pertinent to dyslexia

Date and name	Reference to dyslexia	Outcome
1970: Chronically Sick and Disabled Act.	Required that every LEA provide information to the Secretary of State on 'special educational facilities for children who suffer from acute dyslexia'. Authorities also had to provide 'special educational treatment for children suffering from acute dyslexia'.	Confusion re: terminology 'acute dyslexia' confusing. Acute is a medical term inappropriate for reading difficulties. Criteria for acute/severe not clear. Problem referred by Secretary of State to Advisory Committee on Handicapped Children chaired by Prof. J Tizard. Subsequent report 'Children with Specific Reading Difficulties' considered the utility of the terms 'dyslexia', 'acute dyslexia', 'developmental dyslexia' and 'specific developmental dyslexia'. The report recommended the adoption of 'specific reading difficulties' as the most appropriate term for describing pupils whose literacy skills were 'significantly below the standards which their abilities in other spheres would lead one to expect' (GB.DES, 1972). The pattern of abilities characterising children with specific reading difficulties remained obscure. Reference to 'discrepancy' between ability and literacy attainment focused attention on the development of psychometric and psychological assessment.
1975 Language for Life (GB.DES,1975b) Sir A Bullock	As part of an investigation commissioned by the Secretary of State for Education to investigate all aspects of the teaching of English including reading, writing, spelling and speech, the Committee recognised that the term dyslexic was used to describe a particular group of children but criticised it because of the 'lack of agreed operational definition or indication of means of alleviating the difficulty.' A more helpful term to describe the	1) Educationalists: Specific reading retardation remained a controversial term in that, from the findings of Rutter and Yule, it was claimed that pupils with specific reading retardation could be discriminated from pupils with general reading retardation and that in fact specific reading retardation was the extreme end of the continuum of under-achievement. 2) Medical practitioners and voluntary organisations:

situation of these children would be 'specific reading retardation' – a term previously used by Rutter and Yule 1973. Stressed *no implications concerning aetiology* and does not imply any unitary causal factors.

term specific reading retardation not broad enough to encompass developmental dyslexia.

Dyslexia is difficulty not just in reading but in the use of words, how they are identified, what they signify etc. The term specific reading retardation is, therefore, not appropriate as it indicates an isolated symptom whereas developmental dyslexia is a complex syndrome.

1978: Special Educational Needs (GB. DES,1978) Warnock

Reoriented conceptual framework within which special educational provision is made from one based on discrete categories of handicap to the specification of a continuum of special educational needs. Warnock led to Education Act 1981 and an important survey (Tansley and Pankhurst, 1981). The term 'acute dyslexia' appears in the report which states that 'although no agreed criteria for distinguishing those children with severe and long term difficulties in reading, writing, and spelling from others who may require remedial teaching in these areas, there are nevertheless children whose difficulties are marked but whose general ability is at least average and for whom distinctive arrangements are necessary'. (para.11.48)

Problem in defining 'need' in relation to what do children need to read fluently, better etc. It was suggested in the report that 'children with specific reading difficulties' might be described as having 'specific learning difficulties' (GB.DES,1978, para.3.26). In line with the notion of describing children with ESN plus remedial under the umbrella term 'learning difficulties' the DES considers that the term includes pupils with specific learning difficulties and dyslexia. Tansley and Pankhurst (1981) disagreed with the plea by Warnock for distinctive arrangements for SpLD pupils and the term 'specific learning difficulties' as used by Tansley becomes included in the generic term 'learning difficulties' (against advice of Warnock and British Dyslexia Association (BDA)). The Education Act 1981 is seen by the BDA as making it a duty of the LEAs to provide resources to identify and alleviate specific learning difficulties as defined in the Warnock report.

Table 11.1: (cont)

Date and name	Reference to dyslexia	Outcome
1981: Education Act. Followed by guidance from Circular 1/83.	LEAs charged with responsibility to make an assessment of those children in their area who require, or who may require, special educational provision. Children under five are covered by the provision. Such identification might lead to a formal Statement of Educational Need and LEAs are expected to afford the protection of a Statement by researching either extra or specialist provision: 2% of school population and 20% at any one time.	Implication is that with appropriate teaching most pupils' educational needs could be met within the mainstream classroom. Concept of learning difficulty: The Act states that a child has a learning difficulty if : – he or she has a significantly greater difficulty in learning than the majority of his or her age; – he or she has a disability which either prevents or hinders him or her from making use of educational facilities of a kind generally provided in school, within the area of the local authority concerned, for children of his or her age.
1988: Education Reform Act. 1989: Circular 22/89: (GB.DES,1989f).	Schools required to have a National Curriculum from which modification and disapplication must be justified. Local Management of Schools brought into operation, with LEAs having discretion over whether or not to delegate provision for Statemented pupils in ordinary schools. Maximum time taken for completion of Statement should not exceed six months.	Pupils with a Statement who attend mainstream schools have the specified additional resources funded by the LEA. Pupils cannot permanently be exempted from parts of the National Curriculum without a Statement. Harder for LEAs to defend segregation of pupils with SEN in general and dyslexia in particular. Statement must not be limited to those needs that an LEA can meet.

report. This report reoriented the conceptual framework within which special educational provision was made from one based on discrete handicap to one based on a continuum of special educational needs. Although the Warnock philosophy questioned the use of discrete categories of handicap the report still deemed children 'whose difficulties (with literacy) are marked but whose general ability is at least average' to be in need of 'distinctive arrangements' (para.11.48). The decision by the DES that the terms 'specific learning difficulties and dyslexia' could be logically included in the umbrella term 'learning difficulties' was made contrary to the advice given by Warnock and supported by the British Dyslexia Association (BDA). The BDA, in seeking to ensure provision for dyslexic pupils, selected Warnock's definition of specific learning difficulties, and combined that with the specification from the 1981 Act that Local Education Authorities (LEAs) had a statutory duty to provide resources to identify and alleviate specific learning difficulties. By using this selected combination from the Report and the Act, parents of dyslexic pupils succeeded in submitting a disproportionate number of appeals to the Secretary of State in response to the 1981 Education Act. The observable discrepancy between the pupil's intellectual ability and their attainment in written language now had two labels – a medical – 'dyslexia' and an educational – 'specific learning difficulties'. Pupils with 'specific learning difficulties' had 'educational needs' which must be resourced. Pupils with dyslexia did not fit the definition of learning difficulties given in the 1981 Act, ie. 'a significantly greater difficulty in learning than the majority of his or her age'.

The discrepancy definition central to dyslexia and specific learning difficulties was not referenced by the peer group but by the individuals themselves.

The 1981 Education Act brought with it an emphasis on integration and access to the curriculum. Many parents of special educational needs (SEN) pupils welcomed the move away from the 'deficit' model and the specialist withdrawal techniques which had resulted in their children being segregated from their mainstream peers. Parents of some dyslexic pupils, represented by their voluntary bodies, were not fully accepting of this agenda and sought to use the interpretation inherent in the wording of Warnock and the 1981 Act in order to fight for 'distinctive arrangements' for dyslexic pupils.

Overview: Section 1

When parents and teachers ask 'Is he (or she) dyslexic?' they do so in the knowledge that dyslexia has an inheritance from its medical origins which sanctions the use of 'aetiology' and 'treatment'. Thus they can attribute any causal explanations for the child's literacy difficulties to factors beyond their control. The comfort of a 'cause' is often a relief to all concerned – 'he is having difficulties with literacy because he is dyslexic'. The causal explanation becomes the condition itself. The emphasis on the discrepancy definition of dyslexia has resulted in dyslexia being associated with 'above average intelligence' and also with individuals who have achieved fame in spite of having dyslexia. Dyslexia, unlike some educational category labels (eg. Emotionally and Behaviourally Disordered – EBD), is socially acceptable. The emphasis on the discrepancy definition of dyslexia favoured the identification of individuals who were placed at the lower end of the continuum for literacy attainment and the upper end of the continuum for verbal ability for inclusion into research cohorts, and as exemplars of the need for special educational provision. 'Classic ' dyslexics, by this definition, are likely to have parents who exhibit average to above average ability and are also likely to have experienced considerable difficulties at school. The dyslexia voluntary bodies tend to be made up of active, vociferous, articulate and determined parents who have been motivated to fight for better provision as a consequence of personal experiences of their child's schooling difficulties. Thus for parents and their children the label 'dyslexia' carries with it the support of powerful voluntary bodies. These voluntary groups will offer the child's parents support and encouragement to fight for the funded specialist provision which has arisen from interpretation of Warnock and the 1981 Act. It is also the case, however, that the label 'dyslexia' may carry with it connotations of 'pushy parents' and teachers may be reluctant to positively identify a 'dyslexic' child for additional provision if they perceive that other pupils in their class have a similar or greater need.

However, for dyslexics, labelling can be linked to provision via the protection of a Statement and also allows the option of special examination arrangements. Given the ratio of advantages:disadvantages for having the label 'dyslexic' it is little wonder that the question 'Is he dyslexic?' has survived the potentially damaging effects of post-Warnock educational legislation.

SECTION 2: CAUGHT IN THE ACT : SEEKING SOME EXCLUSION FROM THE INTEGRATION MOVEMENT

'Shouldn't he learn to read before he reads to learn?'

In the wake of the 1988 Education Act: 'Mainstreaming Dyslexia' : a research study.

The 1988 Education Act brought with it a National Curriculum and the philosophy of 'access and entitlement'. Differentiated delivery, modified assessment, whole school policies and in-class support increasingly became the jargon of the post 1981 era and LEAs and schools were challenged to develop systems and strategies to support a population of SEN pupils who had not been specifically considered by the 1988 Act. The National Curriculum provided a framework against which 'educational need' could be assessed. The utility of medical or psychometric definitions of dyslexia which sought to describe or quantify deficits and discrepancies needed to be examined in the light of legislation. In addition to the 1988 Education Act there was a recognition that technology would play an increasing role in the education of all pupils, not least pupils with written language difficulties, and the Government supported the creation of City Technology Colleges (CTCs).

During 1990–1993 the then Department for Education and Science funded a research project to be undertaken at the new, urban Harris City Technology College. The aim of the project was to examine the use of technology in facilitating access and response to the National Curriculum for pupils with specific learning difficulties/dyslexia.

The timing of the project was such that it was important to note the joint implications of the 1981 and 1988 Education Acts. Prior to this time dyslexics had been formally identified within a norm-referenced psychometric framework and taught primarily through a remedial system in which pupils were withdrawn from their regular classrooms and provided with specialist teaching for a defined amount of time, for example 'three hours per week'. Academic debate and practitioner activity tended to be focused around the development and evaluation of specialist techniques for boosting the literacy attainment of dyslexic pupils. The 1981 Act emphasised the notion of educational need and integration, and this was followed by the 1988 Act which stressed the need for all pupils to have 'access and entitlement' to a broad, balanced, relevant, and differentiated National curriculum. It was thus important that post-1988 research acknowledged this emphasis and appropriately directed the research focus towards 'mainstreaming'. Table 11.2 below describes the change in focus resulting from the 1978 Warnock report and the subsequent 1981 and 1988 Education Acts.

One of the aims of the project was to relocate the assessment of dyslexia within the framework of mainstream provision and access to a National Curriculum. The traditional psychometric assessment of dyslexia is suited more to quantifying deficit and attainment delay than to identifying 'educational need'. Children are assessed out of the context of their classroom and thus it is difficult to identify 'need' in relation to the demands imposed by the curriculum. For example, a child may score appropriately on a spelling test given in a one-to-one situation, but exhibit considerable difficulty when having to generate ideas

Table 11.2: The change in focus resulting from the Warnock report and the subsequent Education Acts

Pre-1981 Education Act	Post-1981 and 1988 Education Acts
Deficit model: assessment carried out by 'specialists' (Educational Psychologists).	Needs model: assessment carried out in context with the involvement of classroom teachers.
Specialist teaching to address deficits via remediation programmes. Teaching often delivered in separatist /withdrawal setting.	*Access* to mainstream curriculum is an *entitlement* – pupils' needs addressed via differentiation strategies delivered by classroom teacher with additional in-class support.
Pupils resourced via extra time (3-5hrs per week) with specialist provision. Parental and peer involvement minimal.	Needs addressed via targeted funding of extra resources such as additional IT (laptops), classroom assistant time etc. Whole school policies, parental and peer involvement encouraged in order to increase 'exposure time'.

for written work and spell at the same time. In addition, although the psychometric model can identify dyslexia in many pupils, it tends to be more appropriate at certain ages and stages. A model which seeks to identify whether a child is underachieving in written language cannot identify a pre-school child who is not yet expected to be able to read. Children thus have to wait until they exhibit a significant delay in the development of written language before they can be 'diagnosed' as dyslexic. Their condition thus becomes chronic as they progress through school life with their inheritance from late identification of their specific learning difficulties. The search for a quantifiable delay in literacy, rather than qualitative differences in performance, may lead to the child who can read, but reads slowly, or who can either read or comprehend but not both at the same time, being denied identification. Lower ability children and pupils whose literacy difficulties are wrongly attributed to behavioural problems are also disadvantaged by an assessment model which uses IQ to predict expected levels of attainment. As children proceed to secondary phase schooling they have less chance of scoring at an 'above average' level on traditional IQ tests if the development of their vocabulary has been adversely affected by their delay in developing literacy skills. They are thus less likely to meet the criteria for dyslexia identification as they get older and may simply be seen as exhibiting an overall attainment delay. It is apparent then, that the difficulty for many children who exhibit dyslexic difficulties is not in getting the label but in getting referred for assessment in the first place.

The project findings have been reported in detail to the DfE (Tod & Bramley, 1993), but findings pertinent to the 1988 Education Act are described below.

Methodology

- *Overview*
  The aim of the study was to establish whether the traditional psychometric definition of dyslexia would translate into an educational definition within the context of dyslexia.
- *Sample*
  Of the 180 pupils who formed the first intake to the CTC, nineteen had been selected on the basis that the College positively discriminated towards those individuals who exhibited significant delay in relation to written language, so that advantage could be taken of the purpose-built dyslexia unit. Due to staffing difficulties, National Curriculum assessment data of two tutor groups was not completed, reducing the sample size to 139.
- *Procedure*
  This comprised three distinct components:
1 Classification of cohort members by BDA (British Dyslexia Association) trained teachers.
2 Administration of the BAS (British Ability Scales) to cohort members.
3 Collection and analysis of English National Curriculum data.

Teacher classification

Given that the cohort admitted as 'dyslexic' represented a heterogeneous group of pupils who exhibited delayed attainment in written language, it was necessary to classify them into 'true' dyslexics and 'possible' dyslexics for the purposes of the research study. (All students admitted with significant delayed attainment in written language were eligible for admission to the dyslexia centre.) It was considered appropriate to employ an eclectic approach to assessment as the two comparison measures were psychometric assessment and National Curriculum assessment. The range of procedures employed by the two experienced BDA trained teachers were:

- timed piece of written work.
- standardised reading test.
- analysis of spelling errors.
- pupil records and parent interview data.
- teacher-based screening tests – Aston Index and Bangor.

After data collection was complete the two teachers independently judged the pupils as 'dyslexic and 'non-dyslexic'. Inter-judge agreement was calculated to be 84.2%. Of the sixteen pupils who were consistently grouped, eight were classified as 'dyslexic', eight as 'possible dyslexics'. The remaining three were referred to as 'unknowns'.

Administration of the British Ability Scales (BAS)

This procedure was carried out independently of and simultaneously with the BDA Teacher Classification procedure. The BAS was administered by a chartered educational psychologist who was blind to how members of the cohort had been classified. To enable an unbiased interpretation of the test data the educational psychologist did not have access to either pupil files or teacher assessment data.

Collection of National Curriculum data

English subject teachers were simply asked to submit assessment data of all pupils at the end of their first year at the CTC, ie. end of year 7, based on pupils' observed attainment in relation to statements of attainment. The limitations of using National Curriculum assessment as an instrument for measuring attainment is well documented. Validity and reliability have yet to be demonstrated. Of particular concern at the time of the research was the high inference level inherent in the Statements of Attainment: For example:

AT1   (Speaking and Listening) Level 4d: 'participates in presentation'.
AT2   (Reading) Level 3d 'has begun to use inference, deduction, and previous reading to appreciate meaning beyond the literal'.
AT3   (Writing) Level 4c 'organises non-chronological writing for different purposes'.

However, the justification for using National Curriculum assessment data is the fact that it is the method by which pupil attainment is judged nationally in between Key Stage Statement of Amendments.

Results

The characteristics of pupils admitted to the CTC under the positive discrimination for dyslexics are described in Table 11.3 below. This illustrates that the cohort could be described as of average intelligence with reading and spelling attainment significantly below the pupils' chronological age.

Table 11.3: Mean IQ and attainment test scores: $n = 19$ (Year 7)

Ability/Attainment measures	Mean score	Standard deviation
Short form IQ	90	14.6
General IQ	95	14.08
Verbal 1Q	90	14.6
Visual IQ	100	16.86
Aston reading test	99.58 mths	14.58 mths
Macmillan reading test	98.31 mths	14.84 mths
Macmillan comprehension	99.68 mths	19.05 mths
Suffolk reading test	82.89 mths	12.85 mths
Aston spelling test	90.00 mths	13.22 mths

The psychometric data obtained from the British Ability Scales (BAS) for 'dyslexic' and 'possible dyslexics' is described in Table 11.4 below.

This table reflects that the 'true dyslexic' cohort identified by BDA trained teacher classification score higher on all subtests than those identified as 'possible dyslexics'.

The difference is statistically significant on all IQ measures and reflects that dyslexics can be discriminated from possible dyslexics by their higher test scores on Similarities (verbal reasoning), Digit span (short term auditory memory) and Word definitions.

According to the BAS scores the dyslexic group can be described as exhibiting a discrepancy between verbal ability (as measured by Similarities and Word definitions), and attainment (as measured by Word reading and Basic number). In addition, there is a significant difference between the verbal reasoning scores (Similarities) and short term memory as measured by Digit span ($t = 2.06$, $p=0.04$). The BAS scores for dyslexic pupils thus conform to the discrepancy (between observed and predicted attainment) deficit (short term working memory) model which has traditionally characterised dyslexia.

The 'possible dyslexics', in contrast, are of lower average verbal ability as measured by verbal reasoning (Similarities) and vocabulary (Word definitions). In addition, although 'possible dyslexics' score significantly lower on Digit span than dyslexics, the discrepancy between this score and their verbal reasoning score (Similarities) was not statistically significant ($t=2.16$, $p=0.07$). Thus according to their BAS profile the attainment delay of 'possible dyslexics' cannot be attributed to 'specific' learning difficulty.

An examination of National Curriculum English assessment data (see the chart in Figure 11.1) reveals that dyslexics can be discriminated from their mainstream peers on the basis of significantly lower performance on AT2 (Reading), AT3 (Writing) and AT4 (Presentation/Spelling), ie. all

Table 11.4: Comparison of BAS scores for dyslexics and possible dyslexics

BAS subtest	Mean Score for 'dyslexic' group (standard deviation in brackets)	Mean Score for 'possible dyslexics' (standard deviation in brackets)	t value	p (two tailed)
General IQ	107.71 (9.21)	89.50 (11.54)	3.34	0.005**
Verbal IQ	102.42 (9.43)	80.75 (14.84)	3.32	0.006**
Visual IQ	112.28 (14.75)	96.37 (13.00)	2.22	0.045*
Speed of information processing	53.71 (13.52)	46.37 (13.94)	1.03	0.321
Similarities	57.28 (8.86)	42.12 (10.29)	3.03	0.01**
Digit Span	44.29 (5.44)	35.75 (7.87)	2.47	0.029*
Word Definitions	51.71 (5.25)	41.25 (5.85)	3.62	0.0003**
Matrices	50.71 (6.05)	44.87 (6.88)	1.73	0.107
Block Design (L)	60.00 (10.79)	56.37 (12.60)	0.59	0.5663
Block Design (P)	61.57 (9.69)	53.00 (9.26)	1.75	0.104
Recall of Designs	50.14 (6.26)	45.13 (7.16)	1.43	0.175
Basic Number	45.28 (11.32)	35.50 (6.68)	2.07	0.059
Word Reading	40.57 (7.23)	33.75 (5.78)	2.03	0.06

**Significant at 1% level, *Significant at 5% level

those attainment targets concerned with *written* language. A significance level of < 0.01 was adopted to allow for the small sample size. The largest difference was on AT4, $p < 0.003$.

Dyslexics evidence that they are weaker than their mainstream peers in Speaking and Listening but this is only significant at the 0.05 level which is rather lenient for the small sample size. There is only 0.5 of a National Curriculum Level difference between dyslexics (Level 4) and the mainstream (Level 4.5) in this area of *oral* language. The discrepancy between the dyslexics and mainstream is particularly evident in the two ATs concerned with the *generation* of written language, ie. AT3 Writing and AT4 Spelling. The dyslexics attain, on average, two National Curriculum Levels below their mainstream peers.

This is an interesting finding which lends support to the observation that dyslexics' residual difficulty is in the *generation* of written language. Pupils who have conquered the decoding of print (but may nonetheless read more slowly or experience difficulty whilst reading aloud or trying to comprehend and read at the same time) may not be identified at primary school because they are able to *read* commensurate with their chronological age. However, they may experience increasing specific difficulty with writing and spelling as they progress through to the secondary phase of their schooling. Girls, who tend to work hard to acquire reading skills at primary school, may be particularly vulnerable to remaining undiagnosed until they experience difficulty at secondary age when the demand to produce accurate and speedy written evidence of attainment increases.

The observation that National Curriculum assessment carried out as an integral part of the English subject teacher's job produced a significantly different profile for dyslexic students and the rest of the year group was replicated on the two following year intakes. These findings suggest that it is feasible to translate a psychometric definition of dyslexia into an educational definition within the context of the National Curriculum. Indeed, the SEN criterion 'significantly greater difficulty than their peers' might reasonably be expressed for dyslexics as 'a greater-than-one National Curriculum Level difference' in areas of written language.

A discriminate function analysis performed on the first year's intake data suggests that the best *single* discriminator for dyslexia was AT4 (presentation/spelling).

A small scale study was carried out in a nearby secondary school to see if teacher assessment data could be used to screen pupils for specific learning difficulties/dyslexia based on the profile 'a significant discrepancy between AT1 Speaking and Listening and the ATs concerned with written language'. Of the profiles screened as 'fitting' the dyslexic profile, 66% of the pupils were subsequently identified as dyslexic based on their psychometric profile.

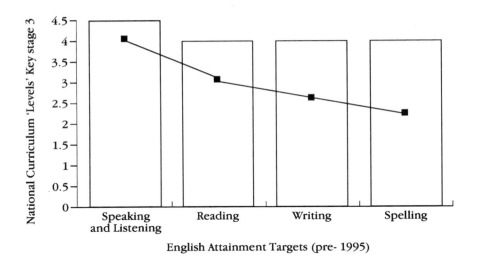

Figure 11.1: Comparison of attainment in National Curriculum English between dyslexic and non-dyslexic pupils end of year 7. Key: □ Mainstream —■— Dyslexic.

An examination of Maths and Science National Curriculum teacher assessment data revealed some interesting preliminary findings. Dyslexic pupils performed significantly less well than their mainstream peers on Maths AT2 (Number) which would be expected given their documented difficulties with short term memory. Analysis of the Science data for dyslexics and mainstream revealed no statistically significant differences. This is an interesting finding given that the delivery of Science tends to be characterised by the following features:

- it tends to be multi-sensory, ie. practical, hands-on.
- in writing up Science work pupils tend to follow a given structure.
- Science tests (see, for example, Key Stage Standard Assessment Tasks (SATs) tend to require recognition rather than recall responses.

It would thus be interesting to examine Key Stage SATs profiles to see if the performance of dyslexic pupils is comparable with their non-dyslexic peers for Science but significantly lower for English. If dyslexic pupils can achieve better in a subject which involves experiential learning, and which reduces emphasis on the generation of written language by the use of enabling strategies such as having a given format and multi-choice responses, then it should be possible to transfer some of these strategies into the teaching of less practical subjects. Obviously, students do have to generate their own written responses eventually, but the difficulties dyslexic students experience with generation justify the use of 'bridging' strategies such as those inherent in the delivery and assessment of Science.

Overall, the findings from the research study suggest cautious optimism for the use of teacher-based National Curriculum assessment in identifying pupils who experience specific difficulty with written language. It is acknowledged that the study used relatively small sample sizes of dyslexic pupils and only examined pupils at Key Stage 3. The National Curriculum profile scores were based on the Old National Curriculum Orders and the findings have not been replicated using the New 1995 Orders. The Statements of Attainment were the basis of the assessment and these do not feature in the New Orders. However, if National Curriculum English continues to have both oral and written language components it seems reasonable to continue to consider using an examination of pupil profiles as a way of identifying pupils with dyslexia. In looking at the difference between a pupil's oral and written language attainment it is important to have a reliable assessment of 'Speaking and Listening'. This attainment target has proved difficult to assess (Stables, 1992) and teachers tend to give more weight to pupils' written work. Oral language is not formally assessed by SATs and the teachers observed during the CTC research study used a variety of ways to assess this attainment target. Some used group work, others asked pupils to deliver a short prepared talk on a topic, and some said they based assessment on pupils' oral response in class.

The assessment of pupil attainment by reference to National Curriculum assessment is a statutory task for all teachers. Looking at individual pupils' profiles and comparing them with the class group would seem to be a useful and relevant activity particularly in the light of the Code of Practice. National Curriculum assessment does allow for assessment in context which is consistent with an 'educational needs' model of identification and provision. Teachers have been marginalised from contributing to the identification of dyslexic pupils and, as a consequence, feel that they need very specialist training before they can provide appropriate in-class support. Dyslexics may share a label but they do not necessarily share needs.

Class/subject teachers and parents are in a unique position to observe qualitative differences in a child's performance and to know under which conditions he or she learns best, and which conditions create barriers to learning. Pupils themselves gradually develop insights into their own learning strengths and weaknesses and can contribute to the planning of provision. Research, personal accounts, and the media tend to cite case studies which are 'typical' of the dyslexia condition, that is those individuals who lie at the extreme end of the continuum of written language difficulties. Obviously there are a few individuals who exhibit 'classic' features of named conditions and these individuals are not usually difficult to identify.

However, in mainstream settings the pupils who cause problems are those who show some but not all of the difficulties, ie. those pupils who lie in the middle of a particular continuum on need.

During the late 1980s and early 1990s considerable efforts were made by schools and LEAs to develop systems and strategies which supported integrated provision for SEN pupils and which assured 'access and entitlement' to a National Curriculum. The findings from the above research study were consistent with these approaches and could usefully be developed to support the assessment required at Stage 1 of the Code of Practice.

Overview: Section 2

During the post-1981 period of intense mainstreaming activity, the parents of dyslexic pupils did not tend to prioritise the need for integration or 'access and entitlement'. Appeals and requests to LEAs suggest that their priority need was for specialist provision (in mainstream units or special schools) that would enable their child to develop the literacy skills needed to 'access' the curriculum. Parents were concerned that, in enabling their child to access and respond to the curriculum via the then current jargon of 'differentiated delivery and modified assessment', there would be insufficient directed teaching of literacy skills. In essence, the parents of some dyslexic pupils requested that their child went against the 'in-class support model' and opted for the 'specialist provision' model characteristic of pre-Warnock thinking. LEAs argued that the in-class support model enabled dyslexic pupils to improve their literacy skills through exposure to a broad, balanced, relevant and differentiated curriculum. Parents were not easily convinced and tended to ignore the notions of 'broad and balanced' in order to fight for the 'relevant' (literacy) and 'differentiated' (multi-sensory/specialist). Formal assessment remained rooted in the psychometric model. In the wake of the 1988 Act parents of dyslexic pupils and voluntary dyslexia bodies were not fully convinced by the rhetoric or the reality of 'mainstreaming' and 'access and entitlement'. Parents continued to fight for the 'different and/or extra' identified by reference to their own child even if such provision did not fit with the current educational philosophy which informed policy for the generic population of SEN pupils. Dyslexia survived and was strengthened by the educational legislation of the 1980s and early 1990s. It may well be that the dissenting voice of the dyslexia voluntary bodies, and the number of dyslexia-related appeals against LEA decisions, contributed to the design of the Code of Practice which aimed to incorporate the 'specialist provision' requested for dyslexic pupils via Individual Education Plans (IEPs) within a framework of integrated mainstream provision.

The next section describes the principles behind the Code of Practice and examines whether it will meet the needs of dyslexic pupils and their parents.

SECTION 3: CASHING IN ON THE CODE

'Will the Individual Education Plan result in better educational provision for my child?'

In 1994 schools were instructed to 'have regard to' the Code of Practice for the Identification and Assessment of Special Educational Needs (DfE, 1994). This model, conscious of the limitations of having either an individual deficit model or a curricular needs model, has combined the two. As pupils move through the stages of the Code, curriculum differentiation gives way to individual targeted, and then specialist provision via an Individual Education Plan (IEP). Whilst movement through the stages prescribes an increasing degree of individualisation and specialism, the preferred locational setting – the mainstream school – remains stable.

The fundamental principles of the Code (Code of Practice, p.2, 1:2) are that : (emphasis is the author's, not DfE)

- the needs of all pupils who may have special educational needs either throughout, or at any time during, their school careers must be addressed; the Code recognises that there is a *continuum of needs and a continuum of provision*, which may be made in a variety of forms.
- children with special educational needs require the *greatest possible access to a broad and balanced education*, including the National Curriculum.
- the needs of most pupils will be *met in the mainstream*, and *without a statutory assessment* or statement of special educational needs. Children with special educational needs, including children with statements of special educational needs, should, where appropriate and *taking in the wishes of their parents*, be educated alongside their peers in mainstream schools.
- even before he or she reaches compulsory school age a *child may have special educational needs* requiring the intervention of the LEA as well as the health services.
- the knowledge, views, and experience of parents is vital. Effective assessment and provision will be secured if there is the *greatest possible degree of partnership* between parents and their children and schools, LEAs and other agencies.

The practices and procedures essential in pursuit of these aims are that:

- all children with special educational needs should be *identified and assessed as early as possible* and as quickly as is consistent with thoroughness.

- *provision* for all children with SEN should be made by the most appropriate agency. In most cases this will be the *child's mainstream school*, working in partnership with the child's parents: no statutory assessment will be necessary.
- where needed, LEAs must make assessments and statements in accordance with prescribed time limits; must write clear and thorough statements, setting out the child's educational and non-educational needs, *the objectives to be secured*, the provision to be made and the arrangements for monitoring and review; and ensure the annual review of the special educational provision arranged for the child and the updating and monitoring of educational targets.
- special educational provision will be most effective when those responsible take into account the *ascertainable wishes of the child concerned*, considered in the light of his or her age and understanding.
- there must be *close co-operation* between all agencies concerned and a *multi-disciplinary approach* to the resolution of these issues.

The principles of the Code are effected by the use of a 5-Staged Model and schools are judged by their ability to evidence that they have developed procedures and strategies which support this model. The Stages given by the Code (DfE,1994, p. 3) are:

Stage 1: *Class or subject* teachers *identify* or register child's special educational needs and, consulting the school's SEN coordinator, take initial action.

Stage 2: *The school's SEN coordinator* takes lead responsibility for managing the child's special educational provision, working with child's teachers.

Stage 3: *Teachers and the SEN coordinator* are supported by *specialists* from outside the school.

Stage 4: the *LEA* considers the need for a statutory assessment and, if appropriate , makes a multi-disciplinary assessment.

Stage 5: the *LEA* considers the need for a statement of special educational needs and, if appropriate, makes a statement and arranges, monitors, and reviews provision.

Whilst the notions of continuum of provision and mainstreaming have been carried over from the 1981 and 1988 Education Acts there are some notable changes to provision. Of particular interest is the prescription for a Staged model which includes class/and or subject teacher assessment of special educational need at Stage 1 and the implementation of Individual Education Plans (IEPs) at Stages 2 and 3. The need to involve parents has also been retained but is emphasised as crucial to effective provision. Parental involvement is sought in the design and delivery of IEPs. The 1993 Act also established a new SEN tribunal and extends parents' rights of appeal as originally set out in the 1981 Education Act.

The principles and procedures as described in the Code have not addressed issues of concern to the parents of dyslexic pupils.

Of primary importance is the problem with definition of 'special educational need'. This has been retained unchanged in the Code:

'a child has a special educational need if he or she has a learning difficulty which calls for special educational provision to be made for him or her'. A child has learning difficulty if he or she:

a) has a significantly greater difficulty in learning than the majority of children of the same age.

b) has a disability which either prevents or hinders the child from making use of the educational facilities of a kind provided for the child of the same age in schools within the area of the LEA.

c) is under five and falls within the definition a) or b) above or would do if special educational provision was not made for the child.

It can be seen that the definition is a *relative* one made by reference either to the norm for the peer group or the norm in relation to local educational provision. The dyslexic pupil, by definition, exhibits discrepant attainment in relation to *himself* or *herself*. For example, a parent may have a child aged 10 years who reads at a level expected from the average 8 year old. If this child is placed in a class with same-aged peers in which the average reading age is at the 9 year level, then the school would not identify him or her as having a *significant* difficulty. By using a definition of need which is *relative* to 'where', and 'with whom', the child is schooled, parents have difficulty in convincing LEAs that their child does have a need in that he or she has a 'significantly greater difficulty with written language than he or she does with other aspects of *his or her own* attainment and cognition'. Dyslexic pupils who achieve at a level above their peer group, but who still exhibit specific difficulties, are disadvantaged by a definition of learning difficulty which is normatively referenced. In essence the State uses a definition which focuses upon 'between' child differences in attainment whereas parents of dyslexic pupils are concerned with 'within' child discrepancies. The identification of dyslexic pupils is thus likely to remain a contentious issue. Parents seeking a grammar school placement for their child may be told that their child would have a special educational need if placed in a selected setting but would not have one if placed in a mixed ability unselected setting where pupils were 'set' in subject groups or streamed into ability groupings.

Another contentious issue retained in the Code relates to mainstream provision and access to the National Curriculum '...should be educated where appropriate and taking in the wishes of their parents in mainstream schools with their peers'. The problem here is in the interpretation of 'appropriate' (need or resource led?), and also the weighting given to parental wishes should these conflict with LEA opinion. It seems that another problem, that of 'where' dyslexic pupils should be schooled, will join 'identification and assessment' as a continued area of debate and confusion.

The continued mention in the Code, that special educational need can *normally* be met in the mainstream and 'without a statutory assessment or statement', has led to the concern by parents of dyslexic pupils that this will result in a significant reduction in the number of children who are allocated statements (and LEA funding) of educational need. They fear that provision for their child will vary depending on the ethos and specialist help available in their child's local school.

It has to be noted that the Code of Practice was issued at a time when there was an increasing emphasis on raising attainment, published 'league' tables, local management of schools and open enrolment. Schools and their staff have thus been asked both to raise attainment and improve GCSE (General Certificate of Secondary Education) grades whilst simultaneously developing whole school strategies for implementing the Code of Practice. The New National Curriculum Orders were made statutory in 1995, and 1996 has seen schools under pressure to continue to raise attainment via notions of selection of pupils, whole class teaching, and grouping by ability. Such demands can hardly be compatible with the demands for increased differentiation at Stage 1 and Individual Education Plans for SEN pupils at Stages 2 and 3 of the Code. Schools have been placed further under pressure by the fact that there has been no additional funding to schools to implement the Code of Practice apart from that allocated through the GEST programme. There is unlikely to be additional funding for SEN, and schools will need to evidence that they can offer effective provision from within existing resources.

In spite of reported difficulties with the Code of Practice, the House of Commons Select Committee report *Special Educational Needs: The Working of the Code of Practice* and the *Tribunal*, published in March 1996 by HMSO, acknowledged the positive influence that the Code has had in raising the profile of special educational needs in mainstream schools. Schools, LEAs and Special Educational Needs Coordinators (SENCos) and teachers have worked hard to try and meet the administrative requirements laid down by the Code. In this report the British Dyslexia Association submitted evidence based on consultation with 97 local dyslexia associations, collation of comments from parents of dyslexic children and 170 British Dyslexia Association (BDA) Befrienders. This evidence (Appendix 10, pp. 28–33) fully supports the introduction of the Code but notes that serious consideration needs to be given to resource implications, appropriate training for teachers involved in delivering the Code, and for managers in ensuring effective use of resources. Parents report confusion about what Stage their child is at and how long it will take to get to the next Stage. There is expressed concern about increasing class sizes, and stringent cuts in school budgets. 'LEAs and schools seem to have redefined special educational need, ie. a child has to be more severe before he or she is regarded as having learning difficulties.' The BDA is also worried that the effect of such Local Management of Schools (LMS) formula will militate against early identification of special educational needs. There is concern that statementing is resource led rather than needs led, and will result in a decrease in the number of statements issued. In discussing the Statement of Special Educational Need the BDA notes that 'it is established in Case Law that part 2 of the statement should be a 'diagnosis'. The medical analogy is a helpful one and should lead to an effective 'prescription' or provision. The BDA welcomes the setting of objectives but notes that those normally written cannot be accurately assessed eg. 'needs to improve reading'. The BDA feels that specialist teaching should always be specified in a statement made for a dyslexic child.

Of all appeals heard by the Special Educational Needs tribunal, 40% concern dyslexic children. Given that the reported benefits from the implementation of the Code concerning increased emphasis on SEN provision in mainstream have not yet been fully translated into effective educational provision for individual dyslexic pupils, it is useful to consider particular issues pertinent to this group.

Early identification and 'non-specialist' support: Stage 1

The discrepancy model of dyslexia negates against early identification of dyslexia. If the condition is described as a specific difficulty with literacy then obviously one must wait until those difficulties become apparent. Dyslexia has been plagued by the fact that children have had to wait until they exhibit 'a significant discrepancy' between expected and observed attainment in literacy before they can be referred for assessment or receive additional resourced help. During recent years there have been notable advances in definitions, assessment and remediation for dyslexia and the theory that appears to be gaining more support is that dyslexia can be attributed to a weakness at the level of phonological processing (Frederickson & Reason, 1995). The importance of the role of phonological processing ability as a requisite for reading success is supported by many authorities. For many children phonological processing becomes an 'automatic' process but Miles (1995, p. 28) reports that:

–   dyslexics are likely to have extra difficulty in segmenting words

into their constituent phonemes or synthesising phonemes to form whole words.
- dyslexics are likely to have more difficulty than non-dyslexics in recognising that words rhyme.
- dyslexics tend to need more time than non-dyslexics 'retrieving' from memory the names of familiar objects , colours etc.
- given that the amount of information that can be held in working memory is, in part, a function of time, it follows that over a given period of time fewer items will be recalled.

This longer 'retrieval time' thus makes sense of the fact that many dyslexics are poor at the recall of auditory or visually presented digits or items which follow one another.

Given this emphasis on defining what specific learning difficulties are, rather than what they are not, provides a sound basis for developing strategies and screening instruments for the early identification of specific learning difficulties. Bradley and Bryant (1985) were proactive in suggesting that the ability to syllabify and rhyme words was an important predictor of reading ability. Government initiatives in relation to the education of nursery-age children and the Schools Curriculum and Assessment Authority (SCAA) guidelines issued to nursery schools also provide an impetus to develop curriculum based assessment procedures for nursery-age pupils who exhibit discrepant patterns of functioning linked to dyslexia. Two relatively new instruments have been developed for the early identification of dyslexia/specific learning difficulty (SpLD): the Phonological Assessment Battery (PhAB) published by NFER in April 1996 and CoPS computer screening test (1996) developed at Hull University available from Chameleon Educational Systems Ltd in Nottinghamshire, England. Although CoPS is costly for individual schools and PhAB may prove time consuming for individual teachers to administer, both instruments serve to focus attention on the feasibility and utility of early identification of specific learning difficulties. CoPS is fun for children to do and tests a range of cognitive abilities. It falls short on assessing children's ability to generate appropriate responses as the set tasks rely on recognition responses. Both screening devices could be used as a focus for the development of curriculum-linked in-class assessment materials.

Stage 1 of the Code gives class and subject teachers the responsibility for early identification and assessment of SEN. The adaptation of screening devices, training in observation of behaviours linked to phonological processing difficulty, and emphasis on early phonological awareness training (Wilson, 1993) are all areas which could be usefully targeted for teacher training and school based INSET for class teachers. Whole school strategies, designed to focus attention upon written language, need to be delivered by all teachers, not just those who teach English. For example, the development of spelling skills can be facilitated by subject or class teachers focusing attention on the meaning and structure of key curriculum vocabulary. A geography teacher could, when introducing the word 'erosion', briefly discuss its meaning, syllabification, and visual image (erosion, in contrast to its meaning, has an even shape). This affords pupils the opportunity to focus attention on the word, actively process and share strategies for developing correct usage and spelling with their peers.

The inclusion of class and subject teachers in the assessment, identification and provision for SEN pupils at Stage 1 of the Code should enable them to increase their skills in teaching SEN pupils. At this stage of development of the Code, class and subject teachers have not been targeted for GEST-funded SEN training. It is essential that, as well as learning through experience of the Code, they are offered appropriate training to enable them to fulfil their role effectively as described by the Code. A model of assessment which may be useful for teachers to follow is described in Figure 11.2.

Stages 2 and 3: Individual Education Plans

At Stage 2 of the Code the SEN coordinator takes overall responsibility for the assessment of the child's learning difficulties. As part of this process it is necessary to prepare an Individual Education Plan (IEP). This plan is drawn up in consultation with the child's class teacher and any relevant curriculum specialists, and it is also recommended that the pupil's parents are involved. Recent reports (OFSTED, 1996) reflect that schools have developed IEP formats either individually or in collaboration with their LEA. The IEP has to meet certain administrative requirements which are described in the Code (2:93).

The IEP for a dyslexic pupil may be conceptualised as described in Figure 11.3 below. Central to the thinking behind IEPs is the principle of setting learning outcomes in advance as targets to be attained within a set time period. This emphasis on clearly defined targets and structured teaching is entirely consistent with specialist dyslexia teaching and the introduction of such strategies into mainstream practice is welcomed. However IEPs have not yet provided the answer to meeting individual needs simply because there are problems inherent in their delivery and evaluation. The paper work created by the IEP procedure has increased the workload for Special Educational Needs Coordinators (SENCos) and reduced the contact time they used to have for specialist support of SEN pupils. Many SENCos, and most teachers, have not had sufficient training to enable them to set targets for the range of SEN pupils for whom they are responsible. The delivery and monitoring of IEPs in secondary schools, and schools with a high ratio of SEN pupils, is proving very difficult. There are real concerns that pupils, such as dyslexics, may receive an inappropriate diet of narrow targets delivered

---

Strategies for assessment for SEN pupils in the mainstream setting

Stage of Code of Practice	Suggested mechanisms for class teachers

| Stage 1: identification and registration of pupil's SEN and taking of action within the normal classroom situation. Trigger: expression of concern that pupil is showing signs of having SEN. Class teacher/Form tutor | 1) Question: Does this pupil exhibit a discrepancy *between* his attainment and that of peers? (English plus others). If yes: **Inform parents*** –Resource implications: DIFFERENTIATION (informed from assessment) |

1 x TERM review: parents invited*

| Stage 2: SEN Coordinator takes overall responsibility for assessment and then planning. IEP has to be prepared. Outlining curricular needs, teaching arrangements, non-curricular needs. | 2) Question: Are there discrepancies *within* the individual pupil's profiles? Does he/she share difficulties/strengths with any other pupil? |

1 x TERM review with parents** (2)

INDIVIDUALISED Education Plans. (resources/grouping etc) **Inform parents***

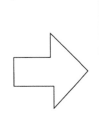

| Stage 3: Teachers and SEN coordinator supported by specialists from outside the school. Curricular priorities Specific learning objectives Criteria for evaluating success Arrangements for monitoring and review General Strategies (Specialist teaching etc) Equipment Frequency of support from outside | 1) Analysis of Tasks child required to do. 2) Assessment through teaching. INDIVIDUAL EDUCATION PLAN *Linked* to NC curriculum Plan, Implement, **Monitor, Evaluate** (note administrative versus educational purpose) |

REVIEW with PARENTs 1 x TERM (2)

Class teacher assessment needs only to be undertaken to a level which can inform avaliable/feasible action

Figure 11.2

Figure 11.3

outside the classroom setting mainly by classroom assistants. The increase in commercial material to support the Code may lead to 'dyslexic targets' being prescribed for pupils on the basis of labelled deficit rather than on individual educational need.

At Stage 3 of the Code specialist help is added to the IEP, but again there is concern that this specialist help refers to outside agencies such as health and social services whereas parents feel that their dyslexic children require specialist 'teaching' which is additional to that offered by the class teacher or classroom assistant. Extra help at higher stages of the Code is increasingly being interpreted as 'additional classroom assistant' time. Whilst LEAs are encouraging the training of specialist classroom assistants, the help a particular child receives under the Code at Stage 3 cannot be assured to be 'specialist'. IEPs represent a way of prescribing the 'different and extra' that a child needs in order to address individual educational needs. The delivery of IEPs within the mainstream setting allows for pupil access and entitlement and also increases the time allocated to special provision by the coordinated targeted efforts of mainstream teachers, pupils and parents. However, as schools try to mange the demands created by the collective effect of their IEPs, there is concern that the procedure as it stands is unmanageable and weighted towards accountability rather than educational effectiveness. There are real strengths in the Code's SEN procedures and it is imperative that training and resources are allocated to allow teachers to continue to develop their skills in assessment, delivery and evaluation of this extra provision for SEN pupils.

Parental partnership

'The relationship between parents of children with special educational needs and the school which their child is attending has a crucial bearing on the child's educational progress and the effectiveness of any school based action'(Code of Practice, 2:28). Many schools are working towards increasing effective parental partnership and the IEP procedure has provided a useful focus for this activity. However, callers to the BDA help line report (House of Commons Education Committee Second Report 1996, p. 28) voiced the following parental concerns:

-   Schools do not always inform parents what Stage their child is at or when review dates are due.
-   Parents are not allowed to be a 'trigger' for Stage 1.
-   Individual Education Plans do not always comply with the advice in the Code.
-   Schools are reluctant to let parents have access to documents and test results.

- Some parents feel that their child's problems are belittled and look elsewhere for advice.
- Independent evidence is often ignored by the school and LEA.

Parents report finding it more difficult to argue with their child's teacher than the LEA. Many fear that questioning school provision will lead to their child being victimised.

This feedback from calls to the British Dyslexia Association (BDA) help line suggest that the antagonism between schools and parents of dyslexic pupils has not been alleviated by the introduction of the Code. If anything, parents perceive that partnership cannot be developed until both school and home are working on agreed aims.

There is still a perception from schools that parents of dyslexic pupils are particularly demanding, and from parents that schools are not providing sufficient specialist help for their children. Schools need to develop strategies for parental involvement which enable parents to receive information via effective communication systems such that they can liaise with schools and actively participate in contributing to their child's special educational provision. Parents obviously do not represent a homogeneous group and it is important that schools develop flexible strategies for working with them. Dyslexia carries with it an inheritance of perceptions concerning the characteristics of parents of dyslexic pupils. It is important that parents are treated as individuals and not pre-judged by reference to their child's label. There is consensus of opinion that working with parents is effective and dyslexic pupils are vulnerable to the damaging effects of discordant parent–school relationships. Two areas for development would seem to be targeted: training for teachers in working effectively with parents (Hornby, 1995) and channelling the time and energy which parents use in fighting with schools and LEAs into working in partnership to improve existing provision for their dyslexic child.

Overview: Section 3

The principles of the Code of Practice were warmly welcomed by many SEN professionals and optimism that the Code would result in better provision for SEN pupils has resulted in significantly increased SEN activity within LEAs, schools and voluntary bodies. It is too early to state whether the Code, as prescribed, will result in more effective provision for individual SEN pupils or whether it will just prove to be the account-ability-led, paper-work dominated 'Emperor's New Clothes' of SEN provision. Early identification, the involvement of class and subject teachers in identification and provision, particularly at Stage 1, the emphasis on parental partnership and pupil involvement, the identification of learning outcomes expressed as targets, the regular monitoring of the effectiveness of provision, are recognised as important elements of good practice for SEN pupils. It would seem important that continued effort is directed towards identifying and achieving the *educational principles* that inform the Code of Practice. Schools have individual differences (size, phase, number of SEN pupils, staff expertise in SEN issues, ethos, etc.) which affect the extent to which they can evidence their 'regard to' the Code.

Summary

In looking at the history of dyslexia within an educational context it can be seen that the construct sat comfortably within a pre-Warnock model. Assessment was based on the description or quantification of 'deficit' and 'discrepancy' and was carried out by specialists outside the context of the classroom. The inheritance of specialist assessment and the consensus view from the voluntary dyslexia bodies that specialist teaching was needed for dyslexic children did not sit comfortably with the 1981 Education Act. This Act, in the wake of Warnock's 'needs' model, brought with it increased emphasis that curriculum differentiation was the answer to individual learning needs. Parents of dyslexic pupils did not prioritise the integrationist aspects of the Act, neither did they see the relevance of a peer-referenced definition of learning needs. For them *their* child was, and is, the reference point against which to judge significant specific attainment delay. They were not prepared to settle for anything less than specialist help, even if that meant segregated provision. The 1988 Act prescribed a National Curriculum and provided a medium in which to develop some curriculum-based assessment procedures for dyslexic pupils which were included in the subsequent 1994 Code of Practice. The Code provided a compromise between the specialist provision developed from medically influenced deficit models, and the curriculum differentiation strategies which characterised the post-1981 and 1988 era. The principle of 'access and entitlement' has been met by the directive in the Code 'that pupils' educational needs should be met within the mainstream' and 'that they should have the greatest possible access to a broad and balanced curriculum'. Their individual learning needs, based on an informed assessment of their strengths and weaknesses, are addressed by Individual Education Plans. Whilst the principles of the Code have been welcomed, there is an increasing awareness that the linking of integrationist and specialist philosophies by the use of a Staged Response Strategy is unlikely to result, in the short term, in significantly improved educational provision for SEN pupils. Dyslexia has characteristically been constructed as a *specific deficit*, or a *specific learning difficulty*. History reflects that the construct has been nurtured and strengthened by contentious debate which has succeeded in getting dyslexia recognised as a specific and not generic learning difficulty. Changes in educational policy for SEN pupils legislated by the 1981, 1988 and 1993 Education Acts have failed to persuade the parents of dyslexic pupils to accept a model of provision prescribed for the generic SEN population. Response from voluntary dyslexia bodies reflects that the Code of Practice offers necessary, but not sufficient, provision for dyslexic pupils. Initial responses to the Code suggest that the efficacy of Stage 1 of the Code is dependent on class and subject teacher expertise in SEN which has yet to be achieved through targeted training; Stages 2 and 3 of the Code house the rhetoric of individual education planning but carry the reality of unmanageable administrative requirements; Stages 4 and 5 are seen as unattainable for the majority of dyslexic pupils and are resourced via increased classroom assistant support which does not assure parity of provision. The summary statement from the British Dyslexia Association contained in the response to the Education Committee's second report on the Working of the Code of Practice and the Tribunal (1996) reads: 'Until the Code is seen to be effective in ensuring good quality provision for pupils with special educational needs there will continue to be pressure on the Special Educational Needs Tribunal'.

It appears that educational 'legislation' has once again provided a medium for nurturing and strengthening the construct of dyslexia.

Survival of the Fittest ?

Dyslexia inherited the advantage of the 'cause' and 'cure' afforded by its medical origins. However, reared in a 'deficit' model of educational provision the construct ensured that its strengths, namely level of intellectual ability, were intrinsic to its character. Dyslexia could then justifiably seek specialist provision for its deficits, and equal opportunity for its strengths. Dyslexia has benefited from the collective, directed power of informed parents, in the form of voluntary bodies, who offer support to individuals and are a force to be reckoned with by those who legislate and deliver educational policy. These voluntary bodies, such as the British Dyslexia Association, fully use the interpretative elements afforded by the wording of educational legislation and seek to become selective beneficiaries, not passive victims, of generic SEN policy decisions.

Obviously there are useful lessons to be learned from dyslexia's survival in an ever changing educational climate.

References

Bradley L, Bryant PE (1985) Rhyme and Reason in Reading and Spelling. Ann Arbor MI: University of Michigan Press.

Bullock A (1975) A Language for Life (GB. DES. 1978b).

Chronically Sick and Disabled Persons Act (1970).

Circular 22/89: Assessments and Statements of Special Educational Needs: Procedures within the Education, Health, and Social Services. GB. DES,1989f.

Critchley M (1970) The Dyslexic Child. London: Heinemann.

DfE (1994) Code of Practice on the Identification and Assessment of Special Educational Needs. HMSO: EDUC JO22465NJ 5/94.

Education Act (1981) Circular 8/81 (GB. DES,1981a).

Education Reform Act (1988) (GB. DES 1988).

Frederickson N, Reason R (1995) Phonological assessment of specific learning difficulty. Educational and Child Psychology Vol. 1.

GB.DES 1975b A language for life (Chairman, Sir A Bullock).

Hornby G (1995) Working with the Parents of Children with Special Needs. London: Cassell.

Kerr J (1986) In Pumphrey PD, Reason RS (1992) Specific Learning Difficulties (Dyslexia): Challenges and responses. London: Routledge. p.9.

Miles TR (1995) Dyslexia: The current status of the term. Child Language Teaching and Therapy Vol. 11, No. 1.

OFSTED (1996) The Implementation of the Code of Practice: For pupils with special education needs. London: HMSO.

Pringle-Morgan W (1986) 'A case of congenital word blindness'. British Medical Journal 2: 1378.

Pumphrey PD, Reason RS (1992) Specific Learning Difficulties (Dyslexia): Challenges and responses. London: Routledge.

Rutter M, Yule W (1973) Specific reading retardation In: Mann L, Sabatino D (Eds) The First Review of Special Education. Bullonwood Farms: JSE Press.

Rutter M, Yule W (1975) The concept of specific reading retardation. Journal of Child Psychiatry and Psychology 16: 181–97.

Special Educational Needs: The Working of the Code of Practice and the Tribunal (1996). London: HMSO.

Stables A (1992) Speaking out and listening at Key Stage 3 – some problems of teacher assessment. Educational Research 34(2): 107–15.

Tansley P, Pankhurst J (1981) Children with Specific Learning Difficulties. Windsor: NFER-Nelson.

The Implementation of the Code of Practice for Pupils with Special Educational Needs (1996) Report from the Office of Her Majesty's Chief Inspector for Schools. London: HMSO.

Tizard J (1972) Children with Specific Reading Difficulties (GB.DES).

Tod J, Bramley G (1993) Assessment and Identification of Pupils with Specific Learning Difficulties (Dyslexia). Report of findings from Harris CTC Dyslexia research project submitted to DfE (Department for Education).

Tod J, Bramley G (1994) Identification and Monitoring of Special Educational Needs: Pupils within a Mainstream Setting Using National Curriculum Assessment. Paper presented to British Psychological Society Education Section Conference 19th November 1994.

Warnock HM (1978) Special Educational Needs (GB. DES, 1978).

Wilson J (1993) PAT Phonological Awareness Training: A new approach to phonics. London: Educational Psychology Publishing, University College.

Chapter 12

'I don't want to be independent.' Does human life need to be viewed in terms of potential autonomy?

Issues in the education of children and young people with severe and profound and multiple learning difficulties

CHRISTOPHER ROBERTSON

Introduction

This chapter critically examines the concept of autonomy and its application to the field of special education in the UK. Particular attention is given to the problems of education premised on autonomy, for children and young people with severe learning difficulties (SLD), especially those with profound and multiple learning difficulties (PMLD). The discussion of these problems raises wider concerns about paternalism and offers a positive perspective on the fostering of flourishing educational lives.

> They would not entertain the thought that some pupils were down there, in darkness. They did not want to know anything about the darkness, everything in the universe had to be light. With the knife of light they would scrape the darkness clean........
>
> ....*It is as though that thought were almost insane.*
>
> (Peter Hoeg, *Borderliners*,1995)

The concept of autonomy

The concept of autonomy has long been held in some kind of esteem in the education system of the UK. The reasons for this are not entirely clear, but certainly it has something to do with the fact that philosophers of education interested in the idea and ideal of autonomy have been notable influences on the growth of educational theory and practice. Having said this, it is not apparent that a philosophical framework for education, including special education, has ever been comprehensively developed and applied in the UK (or more particularly, England and Wales). Instead, philosophical ideas tend to have been plucked from some partial framework or other, and then applied in crude and incomplete form to suit a political purpose, whim, or some consequent educational policy initiative. Eminent special educators (Mittler, 1995; Wedell, 1995) have pleaded for more rational and comprehensive educational planning. Whether one can ever hope for such an approach to educational change is much more debatable than was once thought to be the case (Fullan, 1991, 1993).

It is in this context that the concept of autonomy has been applied, as an aim or ideal for children, if not a fully understood one, for the past thirty years or so. Its application to special education has uncritically developed in the furrow of Warnock-influenced legislation and practice, most notably the 1981 Education Act, which expounded among other things the orthodoxy that educational aims were the same for *all* children. These aims, through discursive practice, have been assimilated, not always critically (Norwich, 1993), by many educators and are frequently characterised by the amorphous but valued overarching aim of autonomy.

Dearden (1972) had earlier attempted to define the concept and apply it to education whilst recognising its elusiveness. He noted its etymology and difficulty of interpretation with reference to modern thought:

> But what precisely is autonomy? Piaget writes that 'autonomy follows upon heteronomy: the rule of the game appears to the child no longer as external law, sacred so far as it has been laid down by adults; but as the outcome of a free decision and worthy of respect in the measure that it has listed common consent . Is it then, that, as a debatable occurrence, I must myself (*autos*) have consented to be bound by a rule (*nomos*)? Or must I myself have originated the rule? Commonly at this point writers are content to say that a rule must have been 'internalized' (Dearden, 1972).

Two obvious points are raised here. The first is that autonomy is concerned at least with the individual as a decision maker. The second is that perhaps autonomy also involves reflectiveness in decision making, or the development of a critical faculty that is more complex than simply decision making. For Dearden this centres around an individual's activity of mind and he says:

> A person is autonomous then, to the degree that what he thinks and does in important areas of his life cannot be explained without reference to his own activity of mind. That is to say, the explanation of why he thinks and acts as he does in these areas must include a reference to his own choices, deliberations, decisions, reflections, judgments, plannings or reasonings (Dearden, 1972).

Clearly, there are difficulties in trying to define just how reflective one has to be to function autonomously at the level described by Dearden. Other philosophers have continued to look closely at the nature of autonomy and have intellectualised it as a concept and acted as 'moral imperialists' on its behalf, as Norman (1994) has noted. Benn (1988), Raz (1986) and White (1990) have all suggested that some stronger sense of autonomy is a central ideal for people living in a modern (liberal democratic) society with its many vicissitudes and rapidity of change. Both White and Benn also distinguish between the concept of autarchy and that of autonomy. The autarchic person for White 'enjoys negative freedom from force and coercion, and is also rationally self-determining, in that he (or she) has engaged in rational deliberation on the alternatives open to him (or her).' (White, 1991). But the autonomous person claims more than this; he argues that an autonomous person has the features of the autarchic person but 'must also have distanced himself in some measure from the conventions of his social environment and from the influence of people surrounding him. His actions express principles and policies which he himself has ratified by a process of critical reflection' (Gray, 1983, p.74).

The author believes that the continuing debate around the conception autonomy is a very valuable one that has a particular relevance in the context of living in a liberal democracy, as Lindley (1986) has argued, and one that should inevitably impinge on the defining of educational aims. However, the intellectual nature of the debate that surrounds the idea of 'stronger autonomy' can lead to misconceptions about the valid application of the loose or wider concept of autonomy in the realm of special education. In the author's view, it is realistic to see a 'weaker' sense of autonomy, or autarchy as some would call it, as having relevance to the interests of children and young people with special educational needs. One has to go further in thinking about this relevance in relation to profound and multiple learning difficulties and to ask if the concept of autonomy is in any real sense valuable?

Here, there is an important difficulty regarding the language and the nature of 'discourse' (Foucault, 1974) that is worth considering briefly.

The philosophical use of a term like autonomy represents possible problems for many educators of children and young people with profound and multiple learning disabilities who may not be familiar with its specific usage within a particular discipline of study. So autonomy is often taken by them to mean a working towards some kind of independence, however minimal this might be for their pupils. To be told by a philosopher such as White (1991) that autonomy is not a realistic aim for children with profound and multiple learning difficulties is obviously a wounding experience that can be felt to be professionally undermining and morally offensive. This is especially the case when one considers teachers are likely to be working to ideas that see education as a right for all and educational aims (including autonomy) as being the same for all. White is at least partly right in his usage of the term autonomy and that it is not a very realistic aim for some children, but the author would argue that a different sense of autonomy or a positive alternative to it could help to provide a framework for understanding and developing complex lives.

Norman (1994), talking about a weaker sense of autonomy (placing less emphasis on intellect) as 'living one's life generally', has suggested that to do this one has to be one's self and reflect a little, to have a biography and to be going somewhere – through – the obvious stages of life. It seems that the child or young person with profound and multiple learning difficulties can readily be viewed in these terms and be seen as moving towards some realisable sense of autonomy. However, autonomy may not be the right, or best way of describing this kind of personal development. The term already carries a meaning that conveys a moral imperative which suggests that autonomy is the ideal for which we should strive to educate a child. Such an ideal would appear to be linked to a view of children's learning, predominant in our culture, that is highly focused on facilitating linear progress. As Ware (1994) has noted, the idea that progress can be easily measured in linear terms is highly questionable.

We turn now to the relationship between autonomy and the concept of what it is to be a person, to try and provide a more helpful and perhaps optimistic understanding of children and young people with profound and multiple learning difficulties. In doing this, one must be aware of the danger of indulging in drawing boundaries based on certain attributes *around* some human beings. Burleigh (1994) has strongly cautioned against this philosophical activity and cogently criticised the purposive pragmatism evident in the influential writing of Singer (1979, 1993) in *Practical Ethics*.

Autonomy and the concept of a person

The idea of a 'concept' of a person as discussed by certain philosophers is again a problematic one for many teachers of children and young people with profound and multiple learning difficulties – and perhaps for other people not engaged in the discourse of philosophy. For most of us it seems common sense to regard all living humans as persons. In reality of course we may think that some persons are more developed than others, and occasionally we may think that a profoundly disabled infant, or the victim of a road accident kept alive on a life support machine, leads an intolerable life. We then test our common sense view of what it is to be a person and perhaps feel that being a particular person involves too much pain or suffering. By doing this we then put ourselves in a more philosophical, questioning position or frame of mind, in that we are beginning to question what we might mean by the idea of a person. Of course, this questioning does not have to lead one to reject some humans as persons. In debates around issues of abortion, 'life support' and euthanasia however, significant and worrying discussion has focused on just this matter of rejection. But these important ethical issues will not be addressed here. Instead, we shall try and get a more positive grasp of what being a person and human being is. The author suggests that there is a conception of it that ought to be helpful to both educators and philosophers, as well as to other people less professionally engaged in thinking about such matters.

Frankfurt (1971) in his paper *'Freedom of the Will and the Concept of a Person'* identified a concept of a person that can be linked to that of autonomy. Indeed as Lindley (1986) has suggested, Frankfurt's 'person' acting with a free will is the only kind of person who has the conditions necessary for becoming autonomous. The full complexity of Frankfurt's argument cannot be analysed here but it is summarised well by Lindley:

> As creatures with a will we are able to act in the light of deliberation about our beliefs and desires. Whereas a non-rational animal will act on whatever inclination is strongest at a particular time, human beings are able, at least sometimes, to defer immediate gratification, to choose that option which is best overall. This entails that we have desires and therefore preferences, of different levels. Not only do we have desires, but we have desires about desires (Lindley, 1986).

This conception of being a person has a value in the context of discussion about senses of autonomy, but it is cited here simply to indicate how it can also lead to a conflation of concepts (autonomy and personhood) in an unhelpful way. This is particularly the case when considering the lives of people with profound and complex learning disabilities.

Harris (1982) also looks at what it is to be a person in trying to assess and define a political status for children, and though he too is demanding of the concept, his criteria for recognising human beings as persons is a little more helpful than Frankfurt's. He is not quite so concerned to link it to any strong sense of autonomy. As a result, his person is nearer to a realistic understanding of a person with profound and multiple learning difficulties. He writes:

> How do we recognise beings as people? What is it about people which persuades us that they are worthy of the same concern and respect that we show to one another? I think the features to which we are responsive and make our concern and respect appropriate are those which allow us to think of other beings as creatures who value their own lives. It is difficult to know quite what this involves but I suppose at the very least it would involve such a person as having a conception of their life as their own – that they had a life to lead and valued leading it. To get even this far a creature would have to be self-conscious, it would have to be aware of itself as an independent being existent over time and be aware and able to make sense of that awareness (Harris, 1982).

He also feels that a being has to have a language to be a person, a language that is their 'vehicle of thought'. He allows that closely defining such a language is difficult and he does not say that it must be a spoken language. Perhaps this view of the concept of a person can be of use when related to the empirical work of educators and researchers such as Goldbart (1994) and Goode (1979, 1994), working in the field of profound disability. It may also resonate with the understanding that parents, teachers and carers of people with profound and multiple learning difficulties have – and positively so.

To build a slightly larger picture of what being a person can be seen as, in the light of this relatively positive view that Harris expresses, we must turn to other writers on the subject.

Aspin (1982) refers to the idea of potentiality and has argued that this is a recognisable feature of all newborn human beings who have an interest in coming to language and rationality. Fromm (1942), too, comments on this potentiality, linking the very potential to become a person to the frailty and vulnerability of the newborn infant, which does not carry the imprinted instincts of a newly born animal. He writes 'this very helplessness of man is the basis from which human development springs; man's biological weakness is the condition of human culture (Fromm, 1942). One could argue that the potentiality described here is not achievable by some children, but some would argue that this is not the case and that an awareness of some kind is part of almost every human. Here, the author would differ completely from the philosopher Peter Singer (1993) and the theologian Joseph Fletcher (1972) who adopt negative stances regarding potentiality. Benn (1988) uses the term 'natural person' to describe some kind of personal growth concept and this is surely recognisable in children and young people with profound and multiple learning disabilities. Benn says of the newborn infant:

> It has to learn, to begin with, to differentiate what is its own – its body and limbs – from the rest of the world which is other than itself, a level of self-differentiation which some autistic children do not in fact achieve. Without this differentiation it would be conceptually impossible for it to move to the next stage, of discovering that the world can be changed, and that one changes it by behaving in one way rather than another – by screaming, for instance. Only when one learns to scream *in order* to change the world is one equipped to recognize the difference between 'world changing entities' – personal agents and other things. Only at this stage could the child recognise himself as a world changing entity and become a fully natural person (Benn, 1988).

The author would not concur with Benn seeing the autistic child as 'not qualifying' for natural personage here. It might be that Benn lacks empirical experience in such matters. The important point though, is that children and young people with profound and multiple learning difficulties can scream at the world (not always literally), to change it for themselves, or they have the recognisable potential to do so.

Freire (1972) has also provided a helpful and different approach to understanding the concept of a person. As a liberative pedagogue he has not sought to locate the idea of a person so centrally in the notion of individuality. He does not appear to have written about children and young people with learning disabilities, but his work lends itself to consideration in this context as both Dumbleton (1990) and Brennan (1991) have shown. Freire sees people as having histories of their own, and personal views, however incipiently formed they may be. He believes that their lives can cease to be depersonalised through an educational relationship that is symbiotic. His *person* is one who can be part of a relationship with others who are sympathetic. There is no individual locus for a person in Freire's thinking. This way of viewing things is liberating when thought of in the context of children and young people with profound and multiple learning difficulties. Perhaps the continual striving for a close definition of autonomy, or the concept of a person, is too spliced to a particular way of thinking. Brennan (1991) makes this point well:

> What is odd about the liberal conception of the person is the narrow depiction of the self lying at its centre. There is little recognition that persons come in many different forms, with a multiplicity of abilities and that development of our rational capacities is only one of several routes to growth (Brennan, 1991).

The positive conceptions of personhood expressed by Aspin (1982),

Benn (1988), and perhaps Harris (1982) too, do not have to be seen as incompatible with Freire's person of relationships. For children and young people with profound and multiple learning difficulties the conception of a person of potential, growing and developing in various ways through relationships seems to be a helpful one – recently emergent teaching approaches make extensive use of interaction and place great emphasis on the development of relationships (Smith 1989, Nind & Hewett 1994). The concept of autonomy seems less appropriate and too exclusive. As Brennan (1991) notes, 'There are many ways in which persons can develop and many forms of engagement with culture open to them.'; one does not have to be autonomous to be a participant in life.

Paternalism and the problem of educational intervention

It is clear from the foregoing argument that there is a difficulty in intervening in the lives of children and young people with profound and multiple learning difficulties in a way that recognises their lack of autonomy and their right to respect as both human beings and learners. Clearly, paternal intervention is necessary and not wrong, but as Norwich (1990) has noted there must be some 'consultation', lest we deny individuals respect. This may be difficult to do in overt or orthodox ways, but it must be done. What is important, is that our intervention is in the best interests of an individual. This is where the Kantian (Kant, 1948) view of means and ends is applicable. Reflecting on the non-autonomous, non-autarchic person and the need for intervention, Benn makes the same point:

> What remains unchanged, however, is the condition that the person shall not be used merely as the means to another person's ends. Where paternal interference is justifiable on grounds of defective autarchy it must be exercised as a trust in the best interest of the beneficial subject, not of the trustee, or for the sake of whatever projects the latter might deem valuable. Defective autarchy is not a justification, for instance, *for treating a person as an available experimental object, as one might a fruit fly* (Benn, 1988). (Author's italics.)

It may be argued that it is not in the best interests of some children and young people to be educated (experimented on?), given that they are so profoundly disabled, and that intervention should be focused entirely on providing good quality care. But if we do care about well being, we are going to learn, through that relationship, about many needs and potentials. Dworkin (1977) has spoken of the natural right of all men and women 'simply as human beings' to both equality of respect and concern. It is the principle of concern that underpins how we might try to direct and guide a profound and multiply disabled person's life, and education is a prime constituent (not the only one) of this concern.

Another way of thinking about this concern is to be found in Benn's (1988) notion of 'shadow respect' for a child. He writes of the respect for a child that can be reflected upon by 'that person to be' in later years: 'if it is neglected and grows up stunted in consequence, the adult has genuine grounds for complaint that the treatment earlier accorded to him had ignored his nature as a person-to-be'.

One must not take Benn's use of the phrase person-to-be here as hinting at excluding some humans from being viewed as persons. Rather, it should be seen as positive acknowledgement of the need to see respect and concern as imperatives in thinking about educational development and potential.

Flourishing and education

White (1991) has raised some important issues concerning the aims and purposes of education for children and young people with profound and multiple learning difficulties. A cursory glance through his paper *The Goals are the Same ... are they?'* could lead the reader to believe that White is suggesting that some children who cannot ever become autonomous are ineducable. In fact he only notes that a tiny minority of children might theoretically be ineducable and he recognises that his knowledge of such children is very limited. He argues that we still need to respect the least able of children and that we should be concerned for their well being and try to help them to flourish.

> Such children, if they exist, will have to be labelled ineducable. We can, and should, provide for their well being – by keeping them warm, fed, clothed, occupied and so on – but it makes no sense to talk of educating them (White, 1991).

Can such care really be called flourishing? Possibly not, but the rationale behind such a perspective could be underpinned by a narrow view of what constitutes learning, which is in turn premised on a commitment to a strong form of autonomy as an educational aim.

A different kind of education to that which White values is required for some children and young people. This kind of education should have overlaps with caring for physical well being, by paying particular attention to experiential learning, relationships and to qualitative as well as quantitative activities. White's ineducable child cannot flourish as well as she or he might, because attention is being paid primarily to only one aspect of that person's needs – physical well being. Fostering well being should include the widest consideration of needs, interests and potentials. It should be concerned with developing as well as maintaining quality of life. Quality here is important (though one must be very wary of seeing it as reducible to the crude level of measurement indicators utilised in a range of health related contexts) because it is a key feature of education as well as care. The danger of neglecting quality is highlighted by Pirsig (1974):

> If quality were dropped, only rationality would remain unchanged ... by subtracting Quality from a picture of the world as we know it, he'd revealed a magnitude of importance to this term he hadn't known was there. The world *can* function without it, but life would be so dull as to be hardly worth living. The term *worth* is a Quality term. Life would be just living without any values or purpose at all (Pirsig, 1974).

There is clearly a further danger here in taking White's position on educability. It exposes the possibility of reducing quality of life debates to matters of occupation, comfort and health, to the neglect of the culturally valued enterprise of education. This neglect may lead to a limited consideration of life's worth and the dangers of this are self-evident. More positively, it is only through providing education, embedded in ideals of personal dignity and self-knowledge, that some children and young people will have the opportunity to mature and make progress. Without education this possibility is likely to be to be closed.

Two final points on helping children and young people with profound and multiple learning difficulties to lead flourishing lives are worth making. Firstly, our knowledge of such children and young people is incomplete and though we have learnt much in recent years we still know little. As Clements (1987) notes, a recognition is required of the 'complexity of the phenomena with which one is faced'. This recognition is a humbling one, for it is an acknowledgement of our limited understanding, and of our bewilderment at times. At the same time it is a spur to innovation.

Secondly, much of the discussion in this paper has been imprecise and elliptical in its attempt to make sense of what the concept of a person is. Brennan (1991) has made the point, with reference to Dennett (1979), that our recognition of a person depends on the 'stance' we adopt towards someone and the 'attitude' we take to them. We need to understand, therefore, that there is a strong element of subjectivity in our viewing others. Dennett, who sees the idea of a person as a normative conception, even ponders whether we can recognise persons (at all), or see ourselves as persons, when we are continually confronted with the 'apparent irrationality' of human behaviour. A recognition of the subjective understanding of children and young people with profound and multiple learning disabilities is to be valued and made sense of.

Education and quality of life

We have argued in this paper that there are difficulties in attaching too much importance to the concept of autonomy when thinking about educational aims for children and young people with profound and multiple learning disabilities. It has also been suggested that a positive appraisal of the concept of personhood is helpful in trying to identify a rationale for specialist education.

Such a rationale needs to be viewed in relation to the curriculum, and whatever form that takes. In England and Wales curriculum guidance and development for children and young people with profound and multiple learning disabilities has gone through a period of turmoil over the past eight years. At the same time, in a climate of constant change, much innovation has taken place and tensions that have become apparent have served as a catalyst for some creative thinking about the underlying aims and approaches of special education.

In this context, Dumbleton (1990) has usefully reflected on the value of Dewey's thinking on education, and has argued that it has a particular relevance to aspects of special education. The concept of 'growth' is central to Dewey's work and it would appear to have a special value to those working in the field of profound and multiple disability because it is not attached purely to a strongly intellectual view of development. Rather, it is aligned with the broader idea of experience. Dewey (1938) brings together the concepts of growth and experience and writes: 'the principle of continuity of experience means that every experience takes up something from those which have gone before and modifies in some way the quality of those which come after'.

This view of educational development would seem to be particularly applicable to children and young people with profound and multiple learning difficulties. But Dewey does not only outline an ideal of growth based on continuity of experience. He discusses in detail the direction that experiences should lead into, and talks of criteria to ensure educational growth is taking place. Growth must, if it is to be educational, have a direction that promotes further growth, not only of a specific kind but of a general kind too. It must therefore have a complex continuity.

Dewey also believes that quality of educational experience serves as a positive criterion for growth. So, 'if an experience arouses curiosity, strengthens initiative, and sets up desires and purposes that are sufficiently intense to carry a person over dead places in the future' then it is a 'moving force', leading to real personal growth.

Dewey is also careful to point out that growth cannot take place in a vacuum, and that a child both influences and is influenced by the environment. This too has important educational implications – for it would be easy to see growth in terms of the individual and her or his very specialist needs. Dewey's perspective is continually outward looking though, and concerned to place learning in an ever-widening context with a view to enhancing personal growth.

The concept of growth could valuably be 'revisited' to inform thinking about quality, highly specialist education. Such thinking, debate and practical consideration of curriculum implications for children and young people with profound and multiple learning difficulties needs to be outlined. That positive task lies beyond the scope of this chapter but it should include a consideration of important issues to do with pedagogy, relationships and the potentially complex tasks of schooling and caring.

Some brief pointers to these key issues are:

- In a period of volatile educational change, teachers and teacher educators working under many constraints have, quite remarkably, continued to develop innovative curriculum content for children and young people with profound and multiple learning difficulties (eg. Byers and Rose, 1995; *EQUALS* research project, 1996) – content that is firmly placed within a National Curriculum framework accessible to all children. More needs to be done however, to address complex issues of needs that are not going to be readily incorporated within a National Curriculum framework – needs related to physical development and well being, and needs related to the care of children and young people who may be physically frail and medically dependent on specialist support. Individual Education Plans (IEPs), that have assumed such importance following the implementation of the Code of Practice (DfE 1994), will have to incorporate a wide range of needs, and not only educational ones, to be valuable to children and young people with the greatest needs.

- For this to be done well, then significant concepts and practices will need to be challenged. For example, simplistic notions of inclusive education based solely on ideologically derived egalitarian perspectives will need to be critically examined (White, 1994). Further study of the concepts of both differentiation and difference will also be imperative (Burbules, 1996; Norwich, 1990).

- The boundaries of education will also have to be further explored, not with a view to defining anyone as ineducable, but rather to further understanding of profound complexities of need. Such exploration may also lead to a reconsideration of educational perspectives such as those espoused by the Camphill Communities (Baron & Haldane, 1991) which are premised on *alternative views* of what it is to be a person. This kind of re-evaluation of ideas could also lead to a radical review of what specialist school settings and related adult communities are for. Christie (1989) has already 'signposted' how specialist communities can be viewed positively. Interestingly, this kind of radical review of specialist education has parallels with Wedell's (1995) writing about the need for all education to be based on the recognition of the diversity of pupils' learning needs.

To conclude, here is a cautionary comment regarding the possibility of becoming fixated with the view that a positive conception of growth, and a positive grappling with the issues outlined above, can solve all problems and difficulties. Benn (1988) takes note of Marcuse who in his book *Eros and Civilization* argued that we live in a repressive world which puts false ceilings on the potential development of people; *but* he cautions against the idea of unfeasible postulating about potential – something which becomes pointless. The challenge for educators and other people working with children and young people who have profound and multiple learning disabilities is to find a balance between developing potential, and being concerned with other aspects of life such as comfort and care and qualities associated with these. Young (1990) has written eloquently as a parent on this matter, cautioning against therapeutic optimism that can pervade professional educational thinking, and arguing that education of children and young people with profound and multiple learning difficulties should be directed 'towards a realistic hope'. The importance and 'value' of care in education, particularly special education, has been neglected. The influential work of both Gilligan (1982) and Noddings (1992) is concerned with a clear assertion of the value of both caring and relationships. Their work could fruitfully be applied to the field of education for children and young people with profound and multiple learning difficulties.

References

Aspin D (1982) Towards a concept of human being as a basis for a philosophy of special education. Educational Review 34: (2): 113–23.
Baron S, Haldane D (1991) Approaching Camphill: From the boundary. British Journal of Special Education 18(2): 75–8.
Benn S (1988) A Theory of Freedom. Cambridge: Cambridge University Press.
Brennan A (1991) A contradiction in terms? British Journal of Special Education 18(4): 163–6.
Burbules N (1996) Deconstructing 'Difference' and the Difference this Makes to Education. In: Papers of the Philosophy of Education Society of Great Britain. Annual conference.
Burleigh M (1994) Death and Deliverance: Euthanasia in Germany 1900–1945. Cambridge: Cambridge University Press.
Byers R, Rose R (1995) Planning the Curriculum for Pupils with Special Educational Needs: A practical guide. London: David Fulton.

Christie N (1989) Beyond Loneliness and Institutions. Norway: Norwegian University Press.

Clement J (1987) Severe Learning Disability and Psychological Handicap. London: Wiley

Dearden R (1972) Autonomy and education. In Dearden R, Hirst P, Peters R (Eds) Education and the Development of Reason (part 3). International Library of Philosophy of Education. London: Routledge & Kegan Paul. Ch.4 pp.58–75.

Dennett D (1979) Brainstorms. Brighton: Harvester Press.

Department for Education (1994) The Code of Practice on the Identification and Assessment of Special Educational Needs. London: Department for Education.

Dewey J (1938) Experience and Education. New York: Macmillan.

Dumbleton P (1990) A philosophy of education for all? British Journal of Special Education 17(1): 16–18.

Dworkin R (1977) Taking Rights Seriously. London: Duckworth.

EQUALS (1996) Curriculum Research Project. Work in progress. Newcastle: EQUALS, University of Northumbria.

Fletcher J (1972) Indicators of Humanhood: A tentative profile of man. The Hastings Center Report Vol. 2, No.5.

Foucault M (1974) The Archaeology of Knowledge. London: Tavistock.

Frankfurt H (1971) Freedom of the will and the concept of a person. Journal of Philosophy. Vol. LXVIII, No.1, 5–20.

Freire P (1972) Pedagogy of the Oppressed. London: Penguin.

Fromm E (1942) The Fear of Freedom. London: Kegan Paul.

Fullan M (1991) The New Meaning of Educational Change. London: Cassell.

Fullan M (1993) Change Forces: Probing the depths of educational reform. London: Falmer Press.

Gilligan C (1982) In a Different Voice: Psychological theory and women's development. Cambridge: Harvard University Press.

Goldbart J (1994) Opening the communication curriculum to students with PMLDs. In Ware J (Ed) Educating Children with Profound and Multiple Learning Difficulties. London: David Fulton.

Goode D (1979) The world of the congenitally deaf-blind: towards the grounds for achieving human understanding. In Schwarz H, Jacobs J (Eds) Qualitative Sociology: A method to madness. New York: The Free Press.

Goode D (1994) A World Without Words: The social construction of children born deaf and blind. Philadelphia: Temple University Press.

Gray J (1983) Mill on Liberty: A defence. London: Routledge & Kegan Paul.

Harris J (1982) The political status of children. In Graham K (Ed) Contemporary Political Philosophy: Radical studies. Cambridge: Cambridge University Press.

Hoeg P (1995) Borderliners. London: Harvill Press.

Kant I (1948) The Moral Law (translated by Paton H). London: Hutchinson.

Lindley R (1986) Autonomy. London: Macmillan.

Mittler P (1995) Special needs education: An international perspective. British Journal of Special Education 22(3):105–8.

Nind M, Hewett D (1994) Access to Communication: Developing the basics of communication with people with severe learning difficulties through interaction. London: David Fulton.

Noddings N (1992) The Challenge to Care in Schools: An alternative approach to education. New York: Teachers College Press.

Norman R (1994) I did it my way: Some thoughts on autonomy. The Journal of the Philosophy of Education Society of Great Britain 28(2): 25–34.

Norwich B (1990) Reappraising Special Needs Education. London: Cassell.

Norwich B (1993) The National Curriculum and special educational needs. In O' Hear P, White J (Eds) Assessing the National Curriculum. London: Paul Chapman.

Norwich B (1994) Differentiation: From the Perspective of Resolving Tensions Between Basic Social Values and Assumptions about Individual Differences. Curriculum Studies 2 (3): 289–308.

Pirsig R (1974) Zen and the Art of Motorcycle Maintenance. London: Bodley Head.

Raz J (1986) The Morality of Freedom. Oxford: Clarendon Press.

Singer P (1979) Practical Ethics. Cambridge: Cambridge University Press.

Singer P (1993) Practical Ethics. Revised Second Edition. Cambridge: Cambridge University Press.

Smith B (1989) (Ed) Interactive Approaches to the Education of Children with Severe Learning Difficulties. Birmingham: Westhill College.

Ware J (1994) Educating Children with Profound and Multiple Learning Difficulties. London: David Fulton.

Warnock Report (1978) Special Educational Needs. London: HMSO.

Wedell K (1995) Making inclusive education ordinary. British Journal of Special Education 22(3): 100–4.

White J (1990) Education and the Good life: Beyond the National Curriculum. London: Kogan Page.

White J (1991) The goals are the same … are they? British Journal of Special Education. 18(4): 167–8.

Young F (1990) Face to Face: A narrative essay in suffering? Edinburgh: T & T Clark.

Index